Social Intelligence

ALSO BY DANIEL GOLEMAN

THE MEDITATIVE MIND
VITAL LIES, SIMPLE TRUTHS
EMOTIONAL INTELLIGENCE
WORKING WITH EMOTIONAL INTELLIGENCE
PRIMAL LEADERSHIP (co-author)
DESTRUCTIVE EMOTIONS

SOCIAL
intelligence

*The New Science
of Human Relationships*

• • •

DANIEL GOLEMAN

HUTCHINSON
LONDON

Published by Hutchinson in 2006

1 3 5 7 9 10 8 6 4 2

Published by arrangement with Bantam Dell, a division of Random House Inc., New York, USA

Hutchinson
The Random House Group Limited
20 Vauxhall Bridge Road, London SW1V 2SA

Random House Australia (Pty) Limited
20 Alfred Street, Milsons Point, Sydney,
New South Wales 2061, Australia

Random House New Zealand Limited
18 Poland Road, Glenfield, Auckland 10, New Zealand

Random House (Pty) Limited
Isle of Houghton, Corner of Boundary Road & Carse O'Gowrie,
Houghton 2198, South Africa

Random House Publishers India Private Limited
301 World Trade Tower, Hotel Intercontinental Grand Complex,
Barakhamba Lane, New Delhi 110 001, India

The Random House Group Limited Reg. No. 954009
www.randomhouse.co.uk

A CIP catalogue record for this book is available from the British Library

Papers used by Random House are natural, recyclable products made from wood
grown in sustainable forests. The manufacturing processes conform to
the environmental regulations of the country of origin

Printed and bound in Great Britain by
William Clowes Ltd, Beccles, Suffolk

ISBN 9780091799731 (trade paperback – from Jan 2007)
ISBN 0 09 179973 2 (trade paperback)
ISBN 9780091799434 (hardback – from Jan 2007)
ISBN 0 09 179943 0 (hardback)

For the grandchildren

CONTENTS

PART ONE

WIRED TO CONNECT

Unveiling a New Science

During the early days of the second American invasion of Iraq, a group of soldiers set out for a local mosque to contact the town's chief cleric. Their goal was to ask his help in organizing the distribution of relief supplies. But a mob gathered, fearing the soldiers were coming to arrest their spiritual leader or destroy the mosque, a holy shrine.

Hundreds of devout Muslims surrounded the soldiers, waving their hands in the air and shouting, as they pressed in toward the heavily armed platoon. The commanding officer, Lieutenant Colonel Christopher Hughes, thought fast.

Picking up a loudspeaker, he told his soldiers to "take a knee," meaning to kneel on one knee.

Next he ordered them to point their rifles toward the ground.

Then his order was: "Smile."

At that, the crowd's mood morphed. A few people were still yelling, but most were now smiling in return. A few patted the soldiers on the back, as Hughes ordered them to walk slowly away, backward—still smiling.[1]

That quick-witted move was the culmination of a dizzying array of split-second social calculations. Hughes had to read the level of hostility in that crowd and sense what would calm them. He had to bet on the discipline of his men and the strength of their trust in him. And he had to gamble on hitting just the right gesture that would pierce the barriers of language and culture—all culminating in those spur-of-the-moment decisions.

That well-calibrated forcefulness, combined with adeptness at reading people, distinguishes outstanding law enforcement officers—and certainly military officers dealing with agitated civilians.[2] Whatever one's feelings about the military campaign itself, that incident spotlights the brain's social brilliance even in a chaotic, tense encounter.

What carried Hughes through that tight spot were the same neural circuits that we rely on when we encounter a potentially sinister stranger and decide instantly whether to run or engage. This interpersonal radar has saved countless people over human history—and it remains crucial to our survival even today.

In a less urgent mode, our brain's social circuits navigate us through every encounter, whether in the classroom, the bedroom, or on the sales floor. These circuits are at play when lovers meet eyes and kiss for the first time, or when tears held back are sensed nonetheless. They account for the glow of a talk with a friend where we feel nourished.

This neural system operates in any interaction where tuning and timing are crucial. They give a lawyer the certainty that he wants that person on a jury, a negotiator the gut sense that this is the other party's final offer, a patient the feeling she can trust her physician. It accounts for that magic in a meeting where everyone stops shuffling papers, quiets down, and locks in on what someone is saying.

And now science can detail the neural mechanics at work in such moments.

THE SOCIABLE BRAIN

In this book I aim to lift the curtain on an emerging science, one that almost daily reveals startling insights into our interpersonal world.

The most fundamental revelation of this new discipline: we are wired to connect.

Neuroscience has discovered that our brain's very design makes it *sociable*, inexorably drawn into an intimate brain-to-brain linkup whenever we engage with another person. That neural bridge lets us affect the brain—and so the body—of everyone we interact with, just as they do us.

Even our most routine encounters act as regulators in the brain, priming our emotions, some desirable, others not. The more strongly connected we are with someone emotionally, the greater the mutual force. Our most potent exchanges occur with those people with whom we spend the greatest amount of time day in and day out, year after year—particularly those we care about the most.

During these neural linkups, our brains engage in an emotional tango, a dance of feelings. Our social interactions operate as modulators, something like interpersonal thermostats that continually reset key aspects of our brain function as they orchestrate our emotions.

The resulting feelings have far-reaching consequences that ripple throughout our body, sending out cascades of hormones that regulate biological systems from our heart to our immune cells. Perhaps most astonishing, science now tracks connections between the most stressful relationships and the operation of specific genes that regulate the immune system.

To a surprising extent, then, our relationships mold not just our experience but our biology. The brain-to-brain link allows our strongest relationships to shape us on matters as benign as whether we laugh at the same jokes or as profound as which genes are (or are not) activated in T-cells, the immune system's foot soldiers in the constant battle against invading bacteria and viruses.

That link is a double-edged sword: nourishing relationships have a beneficial impact on our health, while toxic ones can act like slow poison in our bodies.

Virtually all the major scientific discoveries I draw on in this volume have emerged since *Emotional Intelligence* appeared in 1995, and they continue to surface at a quickening pace. When I wrote *Emotional Intelligence,* my focus was on a crucial set of human capacities *within* us as individuals, our ability to manage our own emotions and our inner potential for positive relationships. Here the picture enlarges beyond a one-person psychology—those capacities an individual has within—to a two-person psychology: what transpires as we connect.[3]

I intend this book to be a companion volume to *Emotional Intelligence,* exploring the same terrain of human life from a different vantage point, one that allows a wider swath of understanding of our personal world.[4] The spotlight shifts to those ephemeral moments that emerge as we interact. These take on deep consequence as we realize how, through their sum total, we create one another.

Our inquiry speaks to questions like: What makes a psychopath dangerously manipulative? Can we do a better job of helping our children grow up to be happy? What makes a marriage a nourishing base? Can relationships buffer us from disease? How can a teacher or leader enable the brains of students or workers to do their best? What helps groups riven by hatred come to live together in peace? And what do these insights suggest for the kind of society we are able to build—and for what really matters in each of our lives?

SOCIAL CORROSION

Today, just as science reveals how crucially important nourishing relationships are, human connections seem increasingly under siege. Social corrosion has many faces.

• A kindergarten teacher in Texas asks a six-year-old girl to put her toys away, and she launches into full tantrum mode, screaming and knocking over her chair, then crawling under the teacher's desk and kicking so hard the drawers spill out. Her outburst marks an epidemic of such incidents of wildness among kindergartners, all documented in a single school district in Fort Worth, Texas.[5] The blow-ups occurred not just among the poorer students but among better-off ones as well. Some explain the spike in violence among the very young as due to economic stress that makes parents work longer, so that children spend hours after school in day care or alone and parents come home with a hair trigger for exasperation. Others point to data showing that even as toddlers, 40 percent of American two-year-olds watch TV for at least three hours a day—hours they are not interacting with people who can help them learn to get along better. The more TV they watch, the more unruly they are by school age.[6]

• In a German city a motorcyclist gets thrown onto the roadway in a collision. He lies on the pavement, unmoving. Pedestrians walk right by, and drivers gaze at him while they wait for the light to change. But no one stops to help. Finally, after fifteen long minutes, a passenger in a car that is stopped for the light rolls down a window and asks the motorcyclist if he's been hurt, offering to call for help on a cell phone. When the incident is telecast by the station that has staged the accident, there is a sense of scandal: in Germany, everyone who has a driver's license has been trained in emergency first aid, precisely for moments like this. As a German emergency room physician comments, "People just walk away when they see others in danger. They don't seem to care."

• In 2003 single-person households became the most common living arrangement in the United States. And while once families would gather together in the evening, now children, parents, and spouses find it increasingly difficult to spend time together. *Bowling Alone,* Robert Putnam's acclaimed analysis of the fraying American social fabric, pointed to a two-decade decline in "social capital." One way such capital can be gauged for a society is the number of public meetings held and club memberships maintained. While in the 1970s two-thirds of Americans belonged to organizations with regular meetings that they attended, that number had dropped to around one-third by the 1990s. These numbers, Putnam argued, reflected a loss of human connection in American society.[7] Since then, a new kind of organization has mushroomed from just 8,000 in the 1950s to more than 20,000 by the end of the 1990s.[8] But unlike the old clubs, with their face-to-face meetings and ongoing social web, these new organizations keep people at a distance. Membership comes via e-mail or mass mailings, and the main activity boils down to sending money, not getting together.

Then there are the unknowns in the ways humans around the world are connecting—and disconnecting—as technology offers more varieties of nominal communication in actual isolation. These trends all signal the slow vanishing of opportunities for people to connect. This inexorable technocreep is so insidious that no one has yet calculated its social and emotional costs.

CREEPING DISCONNECTION

Regard the plight of Rosie Garcia, who manages one of the busiest bakeries anywhere, the Hot & Crusty in New York City's Grand Central Station. The throngs of commuters passing through the station ensure that on any working day long lines of customers will be waiting to place their orders.

But Rosie finds that more and more of the customers she waits on seem utterly distracted, staring vacantly into space. She'll say, "Can I help you?" and they notice nothing.

She'll repeat, "Can I help you?" and they pay no attention.

Shouting, *"Can I help you?"* usually breaks through to them.[9]

It's not that Rosie's customers are deaf; it's that their ears are stuffed with two little headphones from an iPod. They're dazed, lost in any of scads of tunes on their personalized playlist, oblivious to what's going on around them—and more to the point, tuned out to everyone they go by.

Of course, long before the iPod, the Walkman, and the cell phone cauterized people walking down the street, blocking off raw contact with the bustle of life, the auto—a mode of passing through a public space utterly insulated by wraparound glass, a half-ton or more of steel, and the lulling sound of a radio—started the process. Before the auto became commonplace, typical modes of travel—from walking or being pulled along by a horse to riding a bullock cart—kept travelers in easy proximity to the human world around them.

The one-person shell created by headphones intensifies social insulation. Even when the wearer has a one-on-one, face-to-face encounter, the sealed ears offer a ready excuse to treat the other person as an object, something to navigate around rather than someone to acknowledge or, at the very least, notice. While life as a pedestrian offers the chance to greet someone approaching, or spend a few minutes chatting with a friend, the iPod wearer can readily ignore anyone, looking right through them in a universal snub.

To be sure, from the iPod wearer's perspective, he *is* relating to someone—the singer, the band, or the orchestra plugged into his ears. His heart beats as one with theirs. But these virtual others have nothing whatever to do with the people who are just a foot or two away—to whose existence the rapt listener has become largely indifferent. To the extent that technology absorbs people in a virtual reality, it deadens them to those who are actually nearby. The resulting social autism adds to the ongoing list of unintended human consequences of the continuing invasion of technology into our daily lives.

Constant digital connectivity means that even when we are on vacation, work stalks us. A survey of American workers found during their vacation time 34 percent check in with their office so much that they come back as stressed—or more so—than they were when they left.[10] E-mail and cell phones penetrate essential barriers around private time and family life. The cell phone can ring on a picnic with the kids, and even at home Mom or Dad can be absent from the family as they diligently go through their e-mail every evening.

Of course the kids don't really notice—they're fixated on their own e-mail, a Web game, or the TV screen in their bedroom. A French report of a worldwide survey of 2.5 billion viewers in seventy-two countries revealed that in 2004 people spent an average of 3 hours and 39 minutes each day watching television; Japan was highest, with 4 hours and 25 minutes, and the United States came in a close second.[11]

Television, as the poet T. S. Eliot warned in 1963, when the then-new medium was spreading into homes, "permits millions of people to listen to the same joke at the same time, and yet remain lonesome."

The Internet and e-mail have the same impact. A survey of 4,830 people in the United States found that for many the Internet has replaced television as the way free time gets used. The math: for every hour people spent using the Internet, their face-to-face contact with friends, coworkers, and family fell by 24 minutes. We stay in touch at arm's length. As the Internet survey leader Norman Nie, director of the Stanford Institute for the Quantitative Study of Society, put it, "You can't get a hug or a kiss over the Internet."[12]

SOCIAL NEUROSCIENCE

This book unveils eye-opening findings from the emerging field of social neuroscience. Yet when I started research for this book, I did not know that that field existed. Initially my eye was caught by a scholarly article here, a news clip there, all pointing to a sharper scientific understanding of the neural dynamics of human relationships:

• A newly discovered class of neuron, the spindle cell, acts the most rapidly of any, guiding snap social decisions for us—and has proven to be more plentiful in the human brain than in any other species.

• A different variety of brain cells, mirror neurons, sense both the move another person is about to make and their feelings, and instantaneously prepare us to imitate that movement and feel with them.

• When the eyes of a woman that a man finds attractive look directly at him, his brain secretes the pleasure-inducing chemical dopamine—but not when she looks elsewhere.

Each of these findings offered an isolated snapshot of the workings of the "social brain," the neural circuitry that operates as we interact. None in itself told the whole story. But as they accumulated, the outlines of a major new discipline became visible.

Only long after I started to track these isolated dots did I understand the hidden pattern that connects them all. I chanced upon the name for this field, "social neuroscience," when reading about a scientific conference that had been held on the topic in Sweden in 2003.

Searching for the origins of the term "social neuroscience," the earliest use I found was in the early 1990s, by psychologists John Cacioppo and Gary Berntson, who back then were lone prophets of this brave new science.[13] When I spoke with Cacioppo recently, he recalled, "There was a lot of skepticism among neuroscientists about studying anything outside the cranium. Twentieth-century neuroscience thought social behavior was just too complex to study."

"Today," Cacioppo adds, "we can start to make sense of how the brain drives social behavior and in turn how our social world influences our brain and biology." Now director of the Center for Cognitive and Social Neuroscience at the University of Chicago, Cacioppo has witnessed a sea change: this field has become a hot scientific topic for the twenty-first century.[14]

This new field has already begun solving some older scientific puzzles. For instance, some of Cacioppo's initial research uncovered links between involvement in a distressing relationship and hikes in stress hormones to levels that damage certain genes that control virus-fighting cells. A missing piece in that trajectory had been the neural pathways that could convert relationship troubles into such biological consequences—one focus of social neuroscience.

The emblematic research partnership in this new field is between psychologists and neuroscientists who are jointly using the functional MRI (or fMRI), a brain imaging machine that until now was usually devoted to making clinical diagnoses in hospitals. The MRI uses powerful magnets to render an astonishingly detailed depiction of the brain; insiders actually call MRIs "magnets" (as in "Our lab has three magnets"). The fMRI adds massive computing power that yields the equivalent of a video, showing what parts of the brain light up during a human moment like hearing the voice of an old friend. From such studies are flowing answers to questions like: what happens in the brain of a person who is gazing at her lover, or of someone gripped by bigotry, or of someone plotting how to win a competitive game?

The social brain is the sum of the neural mechanisms that orchestrate our interactions as well as our thoughts and feelings about people and our relationships. The most telling news here may be that the social brain represents the only biological system in our bodies that continually attunes us to, and in turn becomes influenced by, the internal state of people we're with.[15] All other biological systems, from our lymphatic glands to our spleen, mainly regulate their activity in response to signals emerging from within the body, not beyond our skin. The pathways of the social brain are unique in their sensitivity to the world at large. Whenever we connect face to face (or voice to voice, or skin to skin) with someone else, our social brains interlock.

Our social interactions even play a role in reshaping our brain, through "neuroplasticity," which means that repeated experiences sculpt the shape, size, and number of neurons and their synaptic connections. By repeatedly driving our brain into a given register, our key relationships can gradually mold certain neural circuitry. In effect, being chronically hurt and angered, or being emotionally nourished, by someone we spend time with daily over the course of years can refashion our brain.

These new discoveries reveal that our relationships have subtle, yet powerful, lifelong impacts on us. That news may be unwelcome for someone whose relationships tend toward the negative. But the same finding also points to reparative possibilities from our personal connections at any point in life.

Thus how we connect with others has unimagined significance.

That brings us to what it might mean, in view of these new insights, to be intelligent about our social world.

| ACTING WISELY |

Way back in 1920, just after the first burst of enthusiasm about then-new IQ tests, psychologist Edward Thorndike created the original formulation of "social intelligence." One way he defined it was as "the ability to understand and manage men and women," skills we all need to live well in the world.

But that definition by itself also allows pure manipulation to be considered a mark of interpersonal talent.[16] Even now some descriptions of social intelligence offer no distinctions between the callow aptitudes of a con man and the genuinely caring acts that enrich healthy relationships. In my view, simply being manipulative—valuing only what works for one person at the expense of the other—should not be seen as socially intelligent.

Instead, we might think of "social intelligence" as a shorthand term for being intelligent not just *about* our relationships but also *in* them.[17] This concept broadens the focus of social intelligence to a two-person perspective: what emerges as a person engages in a relationship. Expanding our focus in this way lets us look beyond the individual to understand what actually transpires as people interact—and to look beyond narrow self-interest to the best interests of others, too.

That more expanded view leads us to consider within the scope of social intelligence capacities that enrich personal relationships, like empathy and concern. So in this book I consider a second, wider principle that Thorndike also proposed for our social aptitude: "acting wisely in human relationships."[18]

The social responsiveness of the brain demands that we be wise, that we realize how not just our own moods but our very biology is being driven and molded by the other people in our lives—and in turn, it demands that we take stock of how we affect other people's emotions and biology. Indeed, we can take the measure of a relationship in terms of a person's impact on us, and ours on them.

The biological influence passing from person to person suggests a new dimension of a life well lived: conducting ourselves in ways that are beneficial even at this subtle level for those with whom we connect.

Relationships themselves take on new meaning, and so we need to think about them in a radically different way. The implications are of more than passing theoretical interest: they compel us to reevaluate how we live our lives.

But before we explore these grand implications, let's go back to the beginning of this story: the surprising ease with which our brains interlock, spreading our emotions like a virus.

The Emotional Economy

One day, late for a meeting in midtown Manhattan, I was looking for a shortcut. So I walked into an indoor atrium on the ground floor of a skyscraper, planning to use an exit door I had spotted on the other side that would give me a faster route through the block.

But as soon as I reached the building's lobby, with its banks of elevators, a uniformed guard stormed over to me, waving his arms and yelling, "You can't walk through here!"

"Why not?" I asked, puzzled.

"Private property! It's private property!" he shouted, visibly agitated.

I seemed to have inadvertently intruded into an unmarked security zone. "It would help," I suggested in a shaky attempt to infuse a bit of reasoning, "if there were a sign on the door saying 'Do Not Enter.'"

My remark made him even angrier. "Get out! Get out!" he screamed.

Unsettled, I hastily beat my retreat, his anger reverberating in my own gut for the next several blocks.

When someone dumps their toxic feelings on us—explodes in anger or threats, shows disgust or contempt—they activate in us circuitry for those very same distressing emotions. Their act has potent neurological consequences: emotions are contagious. We "catch" strong emotions much as we do a rhinovirus—and so can come down with the emotional equivalent of a cold.

Every interaction has an emotional subtext. Along with whatever else we are doing, we can make each other feel a little better, or even a lot better, or a little worse—or a lot worse, as happened to me. Beyond what transpires in the moment, we can retain a mood that stays with us long after the direct encounter ends—an emotional afterglow (or afterglower, in my case).

These tacit transactions drive what amounts to an emotional economy, the net inner gains and losses we experience with a given person, or in a given conversation, or on any given day. By evening the net balance of feelings we have exchanged largely determines what kind of day—"good" or "bad"—we feel we've had.

We participate in this interpersonal economy whenever a social interaction results in a transfer of feeling—which is virtually always. Such interpersonal judo has countless variations, but they all come down to our ability to change another person's mood, and they ours. When I make you frown, I evoke in you a touch of worry; when you make me smile, I feel happy. In this clandestine exchange, emotions pass from person to person, from outside to inside—hopefully for the best.

A downside of emotional contagion comes when we take on a toxic state simply by being around the wrong person at the wrong time. I was an unwitting victim of that security guard's fury. Like secondhand smoke, the leakage of emotions can make a bystander an innocent casualty of someone else's toxic state.

In moments like mine with that guard, as we confront someone's anger, our brain automatically scans to see if it signals some further danger. The resulting hypervigilance is driven largely by the amygdala, an almond-shaped area in the midbrain that triggers the fight, flight, or freeze response to danger.[1] Of the entire range of feeling, fear most powerfully arouses the amygdala.

When it is driven by alarm, the amygdala's extensive circuitry commandeers key points throughout the brain, shepherding our thoughts, attention, and perception toward whatever has made us afraid. We instinctively become more attentive to the faces of the people around us, searching for smiles or frowns that give us a better sense of how to interpret signs of danger or that might signal someone's intentions.[2]

This increased amygdala-driven vigilance heightens our alertness to emotional cues in other people. That intensified focus in turn more powerfully evokes their feelings in us, lubricating contagion. And so our moments of apprehension increase our susceptibility to another person's emotions.[3]

More generally, the amygdala acts as a radar for the brain, calling attention to whatever might be new, puzzling, or important to learn more about. The amygdala operates the brain's early warning system, scanning everything that happens, ever vigilant for emotionally salient events—especially for potential threats. While the amygdala's role as a sentinel and trigger for distress is old news to neuroscience, its social role, as part of the brain's system for emotional contagion, has been revealed only recently.[4]

THE LOW ROAD: CONTAGION CENTRAL

A man doctors call Patient X had suffered two strokes that destroyed the connections between his eyes and the rest of the brain's system for sight in the visual cortex. Though his eyes could take in signals, his brain could not decipher them, nor even register their arrival. Patient X was completely blind—or so it seemed.

On tests where Patient X was presented with various shapes like circles and squares, or photos of faces of men and women, he hadn't a clue what his eyes were gazing at. Yet when he was shown pictures of people with angry or happy faces, he suddenly was able to guess the emotions expressed, at a rate far better than chance. But how?

Brain scans taken while Patient X guessed the feelings revealed an alternative to the usual pathways for seeing that flow from the eyes to the thalamus, where all the senses first enter the brain, and then to the visual cortex. The second route sends information straight from the thalamus to the amygdala (the brain has a pair, right and left). The amygdala then extracts emotional meaning from the nonverbal message, whether it be a scowl, a sudden change of posture, or a shift in tone of voice—even microseconds before we yet know what we are looking at.

Though the amygdala has an exquisite sensitivity for such messages, its wiring provides no direct access to the centers for speech; in this sense the amygdala is, literally, speechless. When we register a feeling, signals from our brain circuits, instead of alerting the verbal areas, where words can express what we know, mimic that emotion in our own bodies.[5] So Patient X was not *seeing* the emotions on the faces so much as *feeling* them, a condition called "affective blindsight."[6]

In intact brains, the amygdala uses this same pathway to read the emotional aspect of whatever we perceive—elation in someone's tone of voice, a hint of anger around the eyes, a posture of glum defeat—and then processes that information subliminally, beneath the reach of conscious awareness. This reflexive, unconscious awareness signals that emotion by priming the same feeling (or a reaction to it, such as fear on seeing anger) in us—a key mechanism for "catching" a feeling from someone else.

The fact that we can trigger *any* emotion at all in someone else—or they in us—testifies to the powerful mechanism by which one person's feelings spread to another.[7] Such contagions are the central transaction in the emotional economy, the give-and-take of feeling that accompanies every human encounter we have, no matter what the ostensible business at hand may be.

Take, for example, the cashier at a local supermarket whose upbeat patter infects each of his customers in turn. He's always getting people to laugh—even the most doleful folks leave smiling. People like that cashier act as the emotional equivalent of *zeitgebers,* those forces in nature that entrain our biological rhythms to their own pace.

Such a contagion can occur with many people at one time, as visibly as when an audience mists up at a tragic movie scene, or as subtly as the tone of a meeting turning a bit testy. Though we may perceive the visible consequences of this contagion, we are largely oblivious to exactly how emotions spread.

Emotional contagion exemplifies what can be called the brain's "low road" at work. The low road is circuitry that operates beneath our awareness, automatically and effortlessly, with immense speed. Most of what we do seems to be piloted by massive neural networks operating via the low road—particularly in our emotional life. When we are captivated by an attractive face, or sense the sarcasm in a remark, we have the low road to thank.

The "high road," in contrast, runs through neural systems that work more methodically and step by step, with deliberate effort. We are aware of the high road, and it gives us at least some control over our inner life, which the low road denies us. As we ponder ways to approach that attractive person, or search for an artful riposte to sarcasm, we take the high road.

The low road can be seen as "wet," dripping with emotion, and the high road as relatively "dry," coolly rational.[8] The low road traffics in raw feelings, the high in a considered understanding of what's going on. The low road lets us immediately feel with someone else; the high road can think about what we feel. Ordinarily they mesh seamlessly. Our social lives are governed by the interplay of these two modes [see Appendix A for details].[9]

An emotion can pass from person to person silently, without anyone consciously noticing, because the circuitry for this contagion lies in the low road. To oversimplify, the low road uses neural circuitry that runs through the amygdala and similar automatic nodes, while the high road sends inputs to the prefrontal cortex, the brain's executive center, which contains our capacity for intentionality—we can think about what's happening to us.[10]

The two roads register information at very different speeds. The low road is faster than it is accurate; the high road, while slower, can help us arrive at a more accurate view of what's going on.[11] The low road is quick and dirty, the high slow but mindful. In the words of the twentieth-century philosopher John Dewey, one operates "slam-bang, act-first and think-afterwards," while the other is more "wary and observant."[12]

The speed differential between these two systems—the instant emotional one is several times faster in brain time than the more rational one—allows us to make snap decisions that we might later regret or need to justify. By the time the low road has reacted, sometimes all the high road can do is make the best of things. As the science fiction writer Robert Heinlein wryly noted, "Man is not a rational animal, but a rationalizing one."

| MOOD DRIVERS |

While visiting a certain region of the country, I remember being pleasantly surprised by the friendly tones of the taped voice on the telephone that informed me, "Your call cannot be completed as dialed."

The warmth in that bland recorded message, believe it or not, gave me a small trill of good feeling—due largely to my years of irritation with that same message as delivered by my own regional phone company's computerized voice back home. For some reason, the technicians who programmed that message had decided that a grating, hectoring tone hit the right note, perhaps as an immediate punishment for misdialing.

I had grown to resent the obnoxious tones of that taped message—it brought to my mind the image of a too-prissy, judgmental busybody. Without fail, it put me in a bad mood, if just for a moment.

The emotional power of such subtle cues can be surprising. Consider a clever experiment done with student volunteers at the University of Würzburg in Germany.[13] Students listened to a taped voice reading the driest of intellectual material, a German translation of the British philosopher David Hume's *Philosophical Essay Concerning Human Understanding*. The tape came in two versions, either happy or sad, but so subtly inflected that people were unaware of the difference unless they explicitly listened for it.

As muted as the feeling tones were, students came away from the tape either slightly happier or slightly more somber than they had been before listening to it. Yet the students had no idea that their mood had shifted, let alone why.

The mood shift occurred even when the students performed a distracting task—putting metal pins into holes in a wooden board—as they listened. The distraction, it seems, created static for the high road, hampering intellectual understanding of the philosophical passage. But it did not lessen a whit how contagious the moods were: the low road stayed wide open.

One way moods differ from the grosser feeling of emotions, psychologists tell us, has to do with the ineffability of their causes: while we typically know what has triggered an outright emotion, we often find ourselves in one or another mood without knowing its source. The Würzburg experiment suggests, though, that our world may be filled with mood triggers that we fail to notice—everything from the saccharine Muzak in an elevator to the sour tone in someone's voice.

For instance, take the expressions we see on other people's faces. As Swedish researchers found, merely seeing a picture of a happy face elicits fleeting activity in the muscles that pull the mouth into a smile.[14] Indeed, whenever we gaze at a photograph of someone whose face displays a strong emotion, like sadness, disgust, or joy, our facial muscles automatically start to mirror the other's facial expression.

This reflexive imitation opens us to subtle emotional influences from those around us, adding one lane in what amounts to a brain-to-brain bridge between people. Particularly sensitive people pick up this contagion more readily than most, though the impervious may sail through even the most toxic encounter. In either case, this transaction usually goes on undetected.

We mimic the happiness of a smiling face, pulling our own facial muscles into a subtle grin, even though we may be unaware that we have seen the smile. That mimicked slight smile might not be obvious to the naked eye, but scientists monitoring facial muscles track such emotional mirroring clearly.[15] It's as though our face were being preset, getting ready to display the full emotion.

This mimicry has a bit of biological consequence, since our facial expressions trigger within us the feelings we display. We can stir any emotion by intentionally setting our facial muscles for that feeling: just clench a pencil in your teeth, and you will force your face into a smile, which subtly evokes a positive feeling.

Edgar Allan Poe had an intuitive grasp of this principle. He wrote: "When I wish to find out how good or how wicked anyone is, or what are his thoughts at the moment, I fashion the expression of my face, as accurately as possible, in accordance with the expression of his, and then wait to see what thoughts or sentiments arise in my own mind or heart, as if to match or correspond with the expression."[16]

| CATCHING EMOTIONS |

The scene: Paris, 1895. A handful of adventurous souls have ventured into an exhibition by the Lumière brothers, pioneers in photography. For the first time in history, the brothers are presenting to the public a "moving picture," a short film depicting—in utter silence—a train chugging into a station, spewing steam and charging toward the camera.

The audience's reaction: they scream in terror and duck under their seats.

People had never before seen pictures move. This utterly naïve audience could not help but register as "real" the eerie specter on the screen. The most magical, powerful event in film history may well have been these very first moments in Paris, because the realization that what the eye saw was merely an illusion had not registered with any of the viewers. So far as they—and their brain's perceptual system—were concerned, the images on the screen *were* reality.

As one movie critic points out, "The dominating impression that *this is real* is a large part of the primitive power of the art form," even today.[17] That sense of reality continues to ensnare filmgoers because the brain responds to the illusion created by the film with the same circuitry as it does to life itself. Even onscreen emotions are contagious.

Some of the neural mechanisms involved in this screen-to-viewer contagion were identified by an Israeli research team, who showed clips from the 1970s spaghetti western *The Good, the Bad, and the Ugly* to volunteers in an fMRI. In what may be the only article in the annals of neuroscience to acknowledge the help of Clint Eastwood, the researchers came to the conclusion that the movie played the viewers' brains like a neural puppeteer.[18]

Just as with those panicked filmgoers in 1895 Paris, the brains of the viewers in this study were acting as though the imaginary story on the screen were *happening to them.* When the camera swooped in for a close-up of a face, the face-recognition areas in the viewers' brains lit up. When the screen showed a building or a vista, a different visual area that takes in our physical surroundings activated.

When the scene depicted some delicate hand movements, the brain region governing touch and movement engaged. And at scenes with maximal excitement—gunshots, explosions, surprising plot twists—the emotional centers roared into action. In short, the movies we watch commandeer our brain.

Members of an audience share this neural puppetry. Whatever happened in one viewer's brain occurred in lockstep in the others, moment by moment throughout the film. The action onscreen choreographed the identical inner dance in everyone watching.

As a maxim in social science holds, "A thing is real if it is real in its consequences." When the brain reacts to imagined scenarios the same way it reacts to real ones, the imaginary has biological consequences. The low road takes us along for the emotional ride.

The one major exception to this puppetry is the high-road prefrontal areas, which house the brain's executive centers and facilitate critical thinking (including the thought *This is just a movie*) and which did not join in this coordination. And so today we do not run in panic as an onscreen train roars toward us, despite the fear we feel welling up inside.

The more salient or striking an event, the more attention the brain deploys.[19] Two factors that amplify the brain's response to any virtual reality, such as a movie, are perceptual "loudness" and emotionally strong moments, like screaming or crying. Small wonder so many movies feature scenes of mayhem—they dazzle the brain. And the very immensity of the screen—creating monstrously huge people to watch—in itself registers as sensory loudness.[20]

Yet moods are so contagious that we can catch a whiff of emotion from something as fleeting as a glimpse of a smile or frown, or as dry as the reading of a passage of philosophy.

RADAR FOR INSINCERITY

Two women, complete strangers, had just watched a harrowing documentary, a film of the poignant human aftermath of the nuclear bombing of Hiroshima and Nagasaki during World War II. Both women felt deeply disturbed by what they had seen, a mix of disgust, anger, and sadness welling up inside.

But when they started talking about how they felt, something strange happened. One of the women was utterly frank about her feelings of upset, while the other suppressed her emotions, feigning indifference. Indeed, it seemed to the first woman that the second woman, strangely, had no emotional reaction at all; if anything, she seemed somewhat distracted and removed.

That was exactly how the conversation was meant to go: both women were volunteers in an experiment at Stanford University on the social consequences of emotional suppression; one woman had been instructed to hide her true feelings.[21] Understandably, the emotionally open one felt "off" with her partner as they talked—indeed, she had the sense that this was someone she would not want as a friend.

The one who suppressed her true feelings felt tense and ill at ease in the conversation, distracted and preoccupied. Tellingly, her blood pressure rose steadily as the conversation went on. Suppressing such disturbing feelings takes a physiological toll; her heightened blood pressure reflected this emotional effort.

But here's the big surprise: the woman who was open and honest exhibited the same steady rise in blood pressure as the one suppressing her feelings. The tension was not just palpable but contagious.

Forthrightness is the brain's default response: our neural wiring transmits our every minor mood onto the muscles of our face, making our feelings instantly visible. The display of emotion is automatic and unconscious, and so its suppression demands conscious effort. Being devious about what we feel—trying to hide our fear or anger—demands active effort and rarely succeeds perfectly.[22]

A friend told me, for instance, that she "just knew" the first time they talked that she should not have trusted a man who sublet her condominium. And sure enough, the week she was to move back in, he told her he refused to move out. Meanwhile, she had no place to go herself. She faced a thicket of regulations protecting renters' rights that meant she would be homeless while her lawyer fought to get her back into her own condo.

She had met the man just once, when he came to look at her

condo. "There was just something about him that told me he was going to be a problem," she later lamented.

The "something about him" reflects the workings of specific high-and-low-road circuitry that serves as our early warning system for insincerity. This circuitry, specialized for suspicion, differs from that for empathy and rapport. Its existence suggests the importance of detecting duplicity in human affairs. Evolutionary theory holds that our ability to sense when we should be suspicious has been every bit as essential for human survival as our capacity for trust and cooperation.

The specific neural radar involved was revealed in a study where volunteers' brain images were taken as they watched any of several actors tell a tragic story. A strong difference emerged in the particular neural regions activated, depending on the facial expression of the actor doing the telling. If the face of the actor showed an appropriate sadness, the listener's amygdala and related circuits for sadness activated.

But if the actor's face was smiling during the sad tale—an emotional mismatch—the listener's brain activated a site specializing in vigilance for social threats or conflicting information. In that case the listeners actively disliked the person telling the story.[23]

The amygdala automatically and compulsively scans everyone we encounter for whether they are to be trusted: *Is it safe to approach this guy? Is he dangerous? Can I count on him or not?* Neurological patients who have extensive amygdala damage are unable to make judgments of how trustworthy someone might be. When shown a photo of a man who ordinary people find highly suspicious, these patients rate him on a par with the man others rated most deserving of their trust.[24]

Our warning system for whether we can trust someone has two branches, high and low.[25] The high road operates when we intentionally make a judgment of whether someone might be trustworthy. But a continual amygdala-driven appraisal goes on outside our awareness, regardless of whether we consciously think about the issue. The low road labors to keep us safe.

| A   C A S A N O V A ' S   D O W N F A L L |

Giovanni Vigliotto was remarkably successful as a Don Juan; his charm brought him romantic conquests one after another. Well, not exactly one after another: actually, he was married to several women at the same time.

No one knows with certainty how many times Vigliotto wed. But he may have married one hundred women over the course of his romantic career—and it *did* seem to be a career. Vigliotto made a living by marrying wealthy women.

That career crash-landed when Patricia Gardner, one of his would-be conquests, took him to court for bigamy.

Just what made so many women swoon for Vigliotto was hinted at during his trial. Gardner admitted that one of the things that attracted her to the charming bigamist was what she called "that honest trait": he looked her directly in the eyes, smiling, even as he lied through his teeth.[26]

Like Gardner, experts on emotion read much into a person's gaze. Ordinarily, they tell us, we avert our eyes downward with sadness, away with disgust, and down or away while feeling guilt or shame. Most people sense this intuitively, and so folk wisdom advises us to check if someone "looks us in the eye" as a gauge of whether he might be lying.

Vigliotto, like many a con artist, apparently knew this all too well and was skillful enough to offer a seemingly sincere locking of eyes with his romantic victims.

He was on to something—but perhaps it was more about rapport-building than lying. That believe-what-I'm-saying eyelock actually reveals little about whether someone is telling us the truth, according to Paul Ekman, a world-class expert on detecting lies from a person's demeanor.

In his years of studying how we express emotions in our facial muscles, Ekman became fascinated by the ways we can detect lies. His keen eye for facial subtleties detected discrepancies between the mask of a person's faked emotions and leakage of what they actually felt.[27]

The act of lying demands conscious, intentional activity in the high road, which handles the executive control systems that keep our words and deeds smoothly on track. As Ekman points out, liars pay most attention to their choice of words, censoring what they say, and less to their choice of facial expression.

Such suppression of the truth takes both mental effort and time. When a person tells a lie in answering a question, he begins his response about two-tenths of a second later than does a person telling the truth. That gap signifies an effort to compose the lie well and to manage the emotional and physical channels through which truth might inadvertently leak.[28]

Successful lying takes concentration. The high road is the site for this mental effort, but attention is a limited capacity, and telling a lie demands an extra dose. This extra allocation of neural resources leaves the prefrontal area less wherewithal to perform another task: inhibiting involuntary displays of emotion that might betray that lie.

Words alone may betray a lie. But more often than not the clue that someone may be misleading us will be a discrepancy between their words and their facial expression, as when someone assures us they "feel great" yet a quaver in their voice reveals angst.

"There is no surefire lie detector," Ekman told me. "But you can detect hot spots"—points where a person's emotions don't fit the words. These signs of extra mental effort call out for examination: the reasons for the glitch can range from simple nervousness to bald-faced lying.

The facial muscles are controlled by the low road, the choice to lie by the high road; in an emotional lie, the face belies what's said. The high road conceals, the low road reveals.

Low-road circuits offer multiple lanes in the silent bridge that connects us, brain to brain. These circuits help us navigate the shoals of our relationships, detecting who to trust or avoid—or spreading good feeling infectiously.

LOVE, POWER, AND EMPATHY

In the interpersonal flow of emotion, power matters. It happens in couples. One partner will make a larger emotional shift to converge with the other: the partner who has less power.[29] Gauging relative power within a couple raises complex issues. But in a romantic relationship "power" can be roughly assessed in practical terms like which partner has more influence on how the other feels about him- or herself, or which has more say in making joint decisions on matters like finances, or in making choices about the details of everyday life, like whether to go to a party.

To be sure, couples tacitly negotiate which partner will have more power in what domain; one may be dominant in finances, and the other in social scheduling. In the realm of emotions, however, the less powerful partner all in all makes the greater internal adjustments in their emotional convergence.

Such adjustments can be better sensed if one partner in a duo intentionally takes a neutral emotional stance, as is the case in psychotherapy. Since Freud's time psychotherapists have noticed that their own body mirrors emotions their clients are feeling. If a client cries over a painful recollection, the therapist will feel tears well up; if she is terrified by a traumatic memory, feelings of fear will stir in the pit of the therapist's stomach.

Freud pointed out that attuning themselves to their own body gives psychoanalysts a window into their clients' emotional world. While most anyone can detect emotions that are openly expressed, great psychotherapists go a step further, picking up emotional undertones from patients who have not even allowed these feelings into their own consciousness.[30]

Not until almost a century after Freud first noted these subtle shared sensations did researchers develop a sound method for tracking such simultaneous changes in two people's physiology during an ordinary conversation.[31] The breakthrough came with new statistical methods and computing power that allowed scientists to analyze an immense number of data points, from heart rate and the like, during a live interaction.

These studies revealed, for instance, that when a married couple argues, each partner's body tends to mimic the disturbances in the other. As the conflict progresses, they drive each other into escalating states of anger, hurt, and sadness (a scientific finding that will surprise no one).

More interesting was what the marital researchers did next: they videotaped couples having arguments, then invited total strangers to watch these tapes and guess which emotions one of the partners was feeling as the argument went on.[32] As these volunteers made their guesses, their own physiology tracked those they were watching.

The more strongly a stranger's body *mimicked* that of the person she watched, the more accurate was her sense of what that person felt—an effect most marked for negative emotions like anger. Empathy—sensing another's emotions—seems to be as physiological as it is mental, built on sharing the inner state of the other person. This biological dance occurs when *anyone* empathizes with someone else—the empathizer subtly shares the physiological state of the person with whom she attunes.

People whose own faces showed the strongest expressions were the most accurate at judging the feelings of others. The general principle: the more similar the physiological state of two people at a given moment, the more easily they can sense each other's feelings.

When we attune ourselves to someone, we can't help but feel along with them, if only subtly. We resonate so similarly that their emotions enter us—even when we don't want them to.

In short, the emotions we catch have consequences. And that gives us a good reason to understand how to shift them for the better.

A Recipe for Rapport

A psychotherapy session is well under way. The psychiatrist sits in a wooden armchair, stiffly formal in manner. His patient slumps on a leather couch, her very air one of defeat. They are not on the same wavelength.

The psychiatrist has made a therapeutic gaffe, an off-kilter interpretation of what the patient has just said. He offers an apology: "I was concerned I was doing something disruptive to the treatment."

"No—" the patient begins.

The therapist cuts her off and makes another interpretation.

The patient starts to reply, and the therapist just talks over her.

Finally able to get a word in, the patient starts complaining about all she had to put up with over the years from her mother—a backhanded comment on what the therapist has just been doing.

And so the session wobbles on, off-key and out of synch.

Switch to a different patient and psychotherapist in the midst of a session, at a peak moment of rapport.

Patient Number Two has just told his therapist that he proposed to his longtime girlfriend—now fiancée—the day before. The therapist had spent months helping him explore and overcome his fears of intimacy, in order to work up the courage to commit to marriage. So they both share in this moment of triumph. Their mood is upbeat, therapist and patient both quietly exultant.

Their rapport is so thick that their posture and movements mirror each other as though intentionally choreographed: when the therapist shifts one foot and then the other, the patient immediately does the same.

There's something peculiar about these two therapy sessions, both of which were captured on videotape: two rectangular metal boxes, stacked like stereo components, sit between therapist and client, extruding wires that lead to a metal clip that each person wears on a fingertip. The wires to therapist and client feed a stream of readings revealing subtle shifts in their sweat response as they speak.

The sessions were part of a study of the hidden biological dance that glides along as the subterranean component of everyday interactions.[1] The videos of the psychotherapy sessions depict those continuous readings as a wiggling line that floats under each person, blue for the patient, green for the therapist. The lines undulate with rising and falling emotions.

During those anxious, jarring exchanges of the first session, the two lines move like jittery birds, their ups and downs on private trajectories. They etch a portrait of disconnection.

But during the rapport of that second session, the lines fly like birds in formation, a graceful ballet of coordinated movement. When two people feel rapport, the gliding lines reveal, their very physiology attunes.

These therapy sessions are at the cutting edge of methods for studying the otherwise invisible activity of the brain while people relate. Though the sweat response may seem remote from the brain, a bit of reverse engineering of the central nervous system allows us to make an educated guess as to which brain structures are doing what during these interpersonal tangos.

That neural calculus was performed by Carl Marci, a psychiatrist at Harvard Medical School, who conducted the study, lugging a suitcase filled with monitoring gear to the offices of willing therapists all over the Boston area. Marci has joined an elect group of pioneers who are finding inventive ways to cross what was once an impenetrable barrier for brain science: the skull. Until now neuroscience has studied just one brain at a time. But now two are being analyzed at once, unveiling a hitherto undreamed-of neural duet between brains as people interact.

Marci has extracted from his data what he calls a "logarithm for empathy," a specific interplay of the sweat response of two people as they enjoy rapport. That logarithm reduces to a mathematical equation the precise pattern of two people's physiology at that peak of rapport when one feels understood by the other.

| THE GLOW OF *SIMPATICO* |

I remember feeling such rapport years ago in the office of Robert Rosenthal, my statistical methods professor when I was a psychology graduate student at Harvard. Bob (as everyone called him) was by reputation just about the most likable professor in the entire department. Whenever any of us went to see Bob in his office, regardless of our reason and no matter what our anxiety was at the outset, we came out feeling heard, understood, and—almost magically—better.

Bob had a gift for emotional uplift. But small wonder that he was so adept at spreading a mellow mood: the nonverbal links that build connection were his scientific turf. Years later Bob and a colleague published a landmark article revealing the basic ingredients of relationship magic, the recipe for rapport.[2]

Rapport exists only between people; we recognize it whenever a connection feels pleasant, engaged, and smooth. But rapport matters far beyond those fleeting pleasant moments. When people are in rapport, they can be more creative together and more efficient in making decisions—whether it's a couple planning a vacation itinerary, or top management mapping a business strategy.[3]

Rapport feels good, generating the harmonious glow of being *simpatico,* a sense of friendliness where each person feels the other's warmth, understanding, and genuineness. These mutual feelings of liking strengthen the bonds between them, no matter how temporary.

That special connection, Rosenthal has found, always entails three elements: mutual attention, shared positive feeling, and a well-coordinated nonverbal duet. As these three arise in tandem, we catalyze rapport.[4]

Shared attention is the first essential ingredient. As two people attend to what the other says and does, they generate a sense of mutual interest, a joint focus that amounts to perceptual glue. Such two-way attention spurs shared feelings.

One indicator of rapport is mutual empathy: both partners experience being experienced. That was how we felt when talking with Bob—he was fully present to us, paying utter attention. This marks one difference between mere social ease and full rapport; in social ease we feel comfortable, but we do not have the sense of the other person tuning in to our feelings.

Rosenthal cites a study where people were put in pairs. One of the two, who was secretly working with the researchers, had what looked like a painful splintered and bandaged finger. At one point he seemingly reinjured himself. If the other person happened to be looking the supposed victim in the eye during the injury, that person winced, mimicking his pained expression. But people who were not looking at the victim were far less likely to wince, even though they were aware of his pain.[5] When our attention is split, we tune out a bit, missing crucial details—especially emotional ones. Seeing eye to eye opens a pathway for empathy.

Attention in itself is not enough for rapport. The next ingredient is good feeling, evoked largely through tone of voice and facial expression. In building a sense of positivity, the nonverbal messages we send can matter more than what we are saying. Remarkably, in an experiment where managers gave people unflattering feedback while still exhibiting warm feelings toward them through their voice and expression, those receiving the critiques nevertheless felt positively about the overall interaction.[6]

Coordination, or synchrony, is the third key ingredient for rapport in Rosenthal's formula. We coordinate most strongly via subtle nonverbal channels like the pace and timing of a conversation and our body movements. People in rapport are animated, freely expressing their emotions. Their spontaneous, immediate responsiveness has the look of a closely choreographed dance, as though the call-and-response of the interaction has been purposefully planned. Their eyes meet, and their bodies get close, pulling chairs near—even their noses get closer than is typical during conversation. They are comfortable with silences.

Lacking coordination, a conversation will feel uncomfortable, with mistimed responses or awkward pauses. People fidget or freeze. Such mismatches torpedo rapport.

| IN SYNCH |

At a local restaurant there's a waitress everyone loves to have serve them. She has an uncanny knack for matching the mood and pace of her customers, gliding into synch.

She's quiet and discreet with the morose man nursing a drink at that table over there in the dark corner. But then she's sociable and outgoing with a noisy batch of coworkers laughing it up on their lunch hour. And for that young mom with two hyperactive toddlers, she wades right into the frenzy, entrancing the kids with some funny faces and jokes. Understandably, this waitress gets by far the biggest tips of any.[7]

That wavelength-sensing waitress embodies the principle that getting in synch yields an interpersonal benefit. The more two people unconsciously synchronize their movements and mannerisms during their interaction, the more positively they will feel about their encounter—and about each other.

The subtle power of this dance was revealed in a clever set of experiments with students at New York University who volunteered for what they thought was an evaluation of a new psychological test. One at a time they sat with another student—actually a confederate of the researchers—and judged a series of photos for the supposed test.[8] The confederate was instructed to either smile or not, to shake his foot or rub his face while they went through the pictures.

Whatever the confederate did, the volunteers tended to mimic. Face-rubbing elicited face-rubbing, a smile primed a smile in return. But careful questioning later revealed that the volunteers had no idea they had been smiling or shaking their foot in imitation; nor had they noticed the choreographed mannerisms.

In another part of the same experiment, when the confederate intentionally mimicked the motions and gestures of the person he was talking with, he was not particularly liked. But when the confederate was spontaneous in his mimicry, he was found more appealing.[9] Contrary to the advice of popular books on the matter, *intentionally* matching someone—imitating the position of their arms, say, or taking on their posture—does not in itself heighten rapport. Such mechanical, faked synchrony feels off.

Social psychologists have found again and again that the more two people naturally make coupled moves—simultaneous, at a similar tempo, or otherwise coordinated—the greater their positive feelings.[10] If you watch two friends talking from a distance where you can't hear what they're saying, you can better observe this nonverbal flow: an elegant orchestration of their movements, smooth turn-taking, even coordination of gazes.[11] One acting coach assigns his students to watch entire movies with the sound off, to study this silent dance.

A scientific lens can reveal what the naked eye can't detect: the way that, as each friend speaks, the other's breath subtly falls into a complementary rhythm.[12] Studies where friends in conversation wore sensors that monitored breathing patterns found the listener's breathing roughly mirroring that of the speaker by inhaling as the partner exhaled, or matching by breathing together.

This respiratory synchrony heightens as the moment to switch speakers approaches. And during those frequent moments of levity when close friends talk, the matchup strengthens further: both begin laughing at virtually the same moment, and during the laughter the rhythm of their breathing aligns remarkably.

Coordination offers a social buffer during a face-to-face encounter: so long as synchrony continues via meshing of movements, an otherwise awkward conversational moment will still feel smooth. This reassuring harmonization tends to continue during rough patches like long pauses, interruptions, and simultaneous speaking. Even when a conversation frays or lapses into silence, physical synchrony maintains the sense that the interaction persists nonetheless. The synchrony telegraphs a tacit understanding or agreement between the speaker and listener.

A conversation that lacks this reassuring physical synchrony has to be even smoother in its verbal coordination to feel harmonious. For example, when people cannot see each other—as in a phone call or over an intercom—their pattern of speaking and taking turns tends to become more studiedly coordinated than when they are physically present.

Merely matching postures matters surprisingly in the ingredients of rapport. For instance, one study tracked postural shifts among students in a classroom. The more similar their postures were to their teacher's, the more strongly they felt rapport and the greater their overall level of involvement. In fact, posture matching may offer a quick reading of classroom atmosphere.[13]

Getting in synch can be a visceral pleasure, and the larger the group, the better. The aesthetic expression of group synch can be seen in the universal enjoyment of dancing or moving together to a beat. The same delight in mass synchronization propels arms that swing as one in a "wave" sweeping through a stadium.

The wiring for such resonance seems built into the human nervous system: even in the womb, infants synchronize their movements to the rhythms of human speech, though not to other sounds. One-year-olds match the timing and duration of their baby talk to the beat of their mother's speaking. Synchrony between a baby and her mother, or between two strangers meeting for the first time, sends the message "I'm with you"—an implicit "please continue."

That message maintains the involvement of the other person. As two people approach the end of their conversation, they fall out of synchrony, thereby sending the tacit signal that it's time to end their interaction. And if their interaction never gets into synch in the first place—when two people are talking over each other or otherwise fail to mesh—they create an uneasy feeling.

Any conversation operates on two levels, high road and low. The high road traffics in rationality, words, and meanings. But the low expresses a free-form vitality that runs beneath the words, holding the interaction together through an immediately felt connection. The sense of connection hinges less on what's said than on the more direct and intimate, unspoken emotional link.

This subterranean connection should be no mystery: we always display our feelings about things through spontaneous facial expressions, gestures, gaze, and the like. At that subtle level we carry on a constant silent chatter, a kind of thinking aloud that offers a between-the-lines narrative, letting the other person know how we feel from moment to moment and so adjust accordingly.

Whenever two people converse, we can see this emotional minuet being played out in the dance of flashing eyebrows, rapid hand gestures, fleeting facial expressions, swiftly adjusted word pacing, shifts of gaze, and the like. Such synchrony lets us mesh and connect and, if we do so well, feel a positive emotional resonance with the other person.

The more synchrony occurs, the more alike the emotions both partners will feel; getting in synch creates an emotional match. For instance, as a baby and mother move in tandem from a low level of energy and alertness to a higher one, their shared pleasure steadily heightens. The very ability to resonate in this way, even in babies, points to an underlying wiring in the brain that makes all this synchrony so natural.

THE INNER TIMEKEEPERS

"Ask me why I can't tell a good joke."

"Okay. Why can't y—"

"Poor timing."

The best comedians display an effortless sense of rhythm, a feel for timing that makes their jokes work. Like concert musicians examining a musical score, professionals in the world of comedy can analyze precisely how many beats to pause before delivering a punch line (or exactly when to interrupt, as in this joke about timing). Getting the beat just right ensures that a joke will be delivered artfully.

Nature loves good timing. The sciences find synchronies through-out the natural world, whenever one natural process entrains or os-cillates in rhythm with another. When waves are out of synch, they cancel each other; when they synchronize, they amplify.

In the natural world, pacing occurs with everything from ocean waves to heartbeats; in the interpersonal realm, our emotional rhythms entrain. When a human *zeitgeber* draws us into an upbeat range, they do us a favor. And when we do the same for someone else, we pass that favor on.

To witness such entrainment, watch any virtuoso display of musi-cal prowess. The musicians themselves seem enraptured, swaying as one, in rhythm with the music. But beneath this visible syn-chrony, the musicians are joined in a way an audience can never know: in their brains.

If any two of those musicians were to have their neural activity measured during their rapture, it would show a remarkable syn-chronicity. For instance, when two cellists play the same bit of mu-sic, the rhythms of neuronal firing in their right hemispheres are extraordinarily close. The synchrony of these zones for musical abil-ities is far greater *across* brains of the two than is the case for the left and right hemispheres within each brain.[14]

Whenever we find ourselves in such harmony with someone else, we can thank what neuroscientists call "oscillators," neural systems that act like clocks, resetting over and over their rate of firing to co-ordinate with the periodicity of an incoming signal.[15] That signal may be as simple as the rate at which a friend hands you the dishes she's washed so you can dry them, or as complex as the movements in a well-choreographed pas de deux.

While we take such everyday coordination for granted, elegant mathematical models have been developed describing the loga-rithms that allow for this micromeshing.[16] That neural math applies whenever we time our movements to the outer world, not just with other people, but also, say, when intercepting a soccer ball at top speed, or hitting a ninety-five-mile-per-hour pitch.

The rhythmic undertones and fluid synchrony of even the barest interactions can be as remarkably complex as the improvised coor-dination of jazz. If such meshing were true only, say, for nodding, there would be little surprise—but the entrainment goes further.

Consider the many ways we mesh movements.[17] As two people are engrossed in conversation, their bodies' motion seems to track the very pace and structure of their speech. Frame-by-frame analyses of pairs talking reveal how each person's movements punctuate their conversation's rhythm, head and hand actions coinciding with stress points and hesitations in speech.[18]

Remarkably, such body-to-speech synchronies occur within a fraction of a second. As these synchronies interlock while we speak with someone, our own thoughts can't possibly track the complexity of the dance. The body is like the brain's puppet, and the brain's clock ticks in milliseconds, or even tinier microseconds—while our conscious information processing, and our thoughts about it, lope along seconds at a time.

Yet outside our awareness our body synchronizes with the subtle patterns of whomever we happen to be interacting with. Even a bit of peripheral vision offers enough information about a body-to-body linkage to set up a coupled oscillation, a tacit interpersonal synchrony.[19] You might notice this as you walk with someone: within minutes both of you will be moving your hands and legs in perfect harmony, just as two pendulums swinging freely come into synch.

Oscillators echo the neural equivalent of the ditty from *Alice's Adventures in Wonderland*, "Will you, won't you, will you, won't you, will you join the dance?" When we are with another person, these timekeepers put us in synch unconsciously, like the flowing ease with which lovers approach for an embrace, or take each other's hands at just the right instant as they walk down the street. (On the other hand, a friend tells me that when she was dating, if she kept falling out of step with the guy she was walking with, she was alerted that there might be trouble ahead.)

Any conversation demands that the brain make extraordinarily complex calculations, with oscillators guiding the continuous cascade of adjustments that keep us in synch. From this microsynchrony flows an affinity, as we participate in a slice of our conversational partner's very experience. We so readily slide into a brain-to-brain link in part because we've been practicing this silent rhumba all our life, since we first learned the basic moves.

THE PROTOCONVERSATION

Picture a mother holding her baby. The mother makes an affectionate "kissy-face," pursing her lips. At that her baby draws his lips inward, in a somewhat sober-looking expression.

The mother widens her mouth into a slight smile, and her baby relaxes his lips, hinting at widening his mouth into a grin, and mother and baby join in a slight smile.

Then the baby breaks into a full-blown beam, moving his head to the side and up, almost flirtatiously.

The entire interaction takes less than three seconds. Not much happened, yet there was a definite communication. Such rudimentary engagements are called "protoconversation," the prototype of all human interaction, communication at its most basic.

Oscillators are at work in the protoconversation. Microanalysis reveals that babies and mothers precisely time the start, end, and pauses in their baby talk, creating a coupling of rhythm. Each captures and coordinates what they do with the timing of the other.[20]

These "conversations" are nonverbal, resorting to words only as sound effects.[21] We engage in protoconversation with a baby through our gaze, touch, and tone of voice. Messages go via smiles and coos and most especially "Motherese"—the adult complement to baby talk.

More like a song than a sentence, Motherese deploys prosody, melodic overtones of speech that transcend culture, and that are much the same whether the mother speaks Mandarin Chinese, Urdu, or English. Motherese always sounds friendly and playful, with a high pitch (around 300 hertz, to be technical) and short, spiked, undulating or gliding pitch contours.

Often a mother will synchronize Motherese with patting or stroking her baby in a repeated, periodic rhythm. Her face and head movements are in synch with her hands and voice, and the baby in turn responds with smiles, cooing, and movements of jaws, lips, and tongue in synch with his hand motions. Such mother-baby pirouettes are short, a matter of just seconds or even milliseconds—and they end when both partners match states, typically happy ones. Mother and infant fall into what seems much like a duet of synchronized or alternating parts, paced by a steady adagio pulse at about 90 beats per minute.

Such scientific observations are made painstakingly, through the tedious examination of endless hours of videotaped mother-infant interactions, by developmental psychologists like Colwyn Trevarthen at the University of Edinburgh. Trevarthen's studies have made him the world expert on protoconversation, a duet where both performers, as he describes it, "seek harmony and counterpoint on one beat to create a melody."[22]

But more than marking out a kind of melody, the two are having a discussion of sorts that centers on one central theme: emotions. The frequency of the mother's touch and the sound of her voice give the baby the reassuring message of her love—resulting, as Trevarthen puts it, in an "immediate, unverbalized, conceptless, rapport."

The exchange of these signals forges a link with a baby through which we can make her happy and excited, calm and quiet—or upset and in tears. During a happy protoconversation, mother and baby feel upbeat and attuned to each other. But when either the mother or the infant fails to hold up their part of the conversation, the outcomes are quite different. If the mother, for instance, pays too little attention or responds without enthusiasm, the baby reacts by withdrawing. If the mother's responses are poorly timed, the baby will look puzzled, then distressed. And if it's the baby who fails to respond, the mother in turn will get upset.

These sessions are a kind of tutorial: the protoconversation marks a baby's first lesson in how to interact. We learn how to synchronize emotionally long before we have words for those feelings. Protoconversations remain our most basic template for interacting, a tacit awareness that quietly gets us in step as we link with someone else. The ability to get into synch as we did when we were babies serves us through life, guiding us in every social interaction.

And just as feelings were the main topic of protoconversation for us as infants, they remain the bedrock of communication in adulthood. This silent dialogue on feelings is the substrate on which all other encounters build and the hidden agenda in every interaction.

3

Neural WiFi

As I settled into a seat on a New York City subway, one of those ambiguous, possibly ominous moments of urban life occurred: I heard a shriek far behind me, from the opposite end of the car.

My back was to the source of the scream. But I faced a gentleman whose face suddenly took on a slightly anxious look.

My mind raced to comprehend what was going on and what—if anything—I should do. Was it a fight? Was someone running amok on the subway? Was danger headed my way?

Or was it merely a shriek of delight, maybe a group of teenagers having a whooping good time?

My answer came swiftly, from the face of the man who could see what was happening: his worried features settled into calm, and he went back to reading his newspaper. Whatever was going on back there, I knew all was well.

My initial apprehension was calmed by seeing his face relax. In moments like my sudden wariness on the subway, we instinctively become more attentive to the faces of the people around us, searching for smiles or frowns that give us a better sense of how to interpret signs of danger or that might signal someone's intentions.[1]

In human prehistory a primal band with its numerous eyes and ears could be ever more vigilant for danger than could an isolated individual. And in the tooth-and-claw world of early humans, that ability to multiply sentinels—and a brain mechanism attuned to pick up signs of danger automatically and mobilize fear—no doubt had great survival value.

Although at the extremes of anxiety we may become too swallowed up in our own fear to attune at all, in most of its range anxiety heightens emotional transactions, so that people who feel threatened and anxious are especially prone to catching other people's emotions. In one of those early human groups, no doubt the terrorized face of someone who had sighted a prowling tiger was enough to set off the same panic in whoever saw that expression—and set them running to safety.

Gaze for a moment at this face:

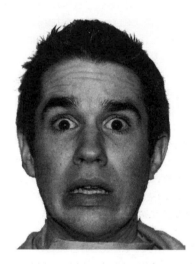

The amygdala instantly reacts to such a photograph, and the stronger the emotion displayed, the more intense the amygdala's reaction.[2] When people looked at such pictures while undergoing an fMRI, their own brain looked like *they* were the frightened ones, though in a more muted range.[3]

When two people interact face to face, contagion spreads via multiple neural circuits operating in parallel within each person's brain. These systems for emotional contagion traffic in the entire range of feeling, from sadness and anxiety to joy.

Moments of contagion represent a remarkable neural event: the formation between two brains of a functional link, a feedback loop that crosses the skin-and-skull barrier between bodies. In systems terms, during this linkup brains "couple," with the output of one becoming input to drive the workings of the other, for the time being forming what amounts to an interbrain circuit. When two entities are connected in a feedback loop, as the first changes, so does the second.

As people loop together, their brains send and receive an ongoing stream of signals that allow them to create a tacit harmony—and, if the flow goes the right way, amplify their resonance. Looping lets feelings, thoughts, and actions synchronize. We send and receive internal states for better or for worse—whether laughter and tenderness, or tension and rancor.

In physics, the defining property of resonance is sympathetic vibration, the tendency of one part to amplify its vibratory rate by matching the pace at which another part vibrates. Such resonance produces the largest and most prolonged possible response between the two interacting parts—an afterglow.

Brains loop outside our awareness, with no special attention or intention demanded. While we can intentionally try to mimic someone in order to foster closeness, such attempts tend to come off as awkward. Synchrony works best when it is spontaneous, not constructed from ulterior motives such as ingratiation or any other conscious intention.[4]

The low road's automaticity allows its rapidity. For instance, the amygdala spots signs of fear in someone's face with remarkable speed, picking it up in a glimpse as quick as 33 milliseconds, and in some people even in a mere 17 milliseconds (less than two-hundredths of a second).[5] This quick read attests to the hyperspeed of the low road, so fast that the conscious mind remains oblivious to that perception (though we might sense the resulting vague stirring of uneasiness).

We may not consciously realize how we are synchronizing, yet we mesh with remarkable ease. This spontaneous social duet is the work of a special class of neurons.

| N E U R A L   M I R R O R S |

I must have been just two or three years old, but the memory remains vivid in my mind. As I wandered down the aisle of the local grocery store at my mother's side, a lady spotted me—a cute little toddler—and gave me a warm smile.

My own mouth, I still recall, startled me by involuntarily moving into a smile in return. It felt as though somehow my face had become puppetlike, drawn by mysterious strings that widened the muscles around my mouth and puffed out my cheeks.

I distinctly felt that my smile had come unbidden—directed not from within but from outside myself.

That unbidden reaction no doubt signaled the activity of what are called "mirror neurons" in my young brain. "Mirror" neurons do just that: they reflect back an action we observe in someone else, making us mimic that action or have the impulse to do so. These do-as-she-does neurons offer a brain mechanism that explains the old lyric, "When you're smiling, the whole world smiles with you."

Major lanes of the low road surely run through this kind of neuron. We have multiple systems of mirror neurons, with more being discovered as time goes on. There seems to be a multitude of such neural systems that remain as yet unmapped. And they explain a huge swath of life, from emotional contagion and social synchrony to how infants learn.

Neuroscientists stumbled on this neural WiFi by accident in 1992. They were mapping the sensorimotor area of monkeys' brains by using electrodes so laser-thin they could be implanted in single brain cells, and seeing which cell lit up during a specific movement.[6] The neurons in this area were proving to be remarkably precise; for instance, some neurons lit up only when the monkey was grasping something in its hand, others only when it was tearing it apart.

But the truly unexpected discovery came one hot afternoon when a research assistant came back from a break eating an ice-cream cone. The scientists were astonished to see a sensorimotor cell activate as one monkey watched the assistant lift the cone to his lips. They were dumbfounded to find that a distinct set of neurons seemed to activate when the monkey merely *observed* another monkey—or one of the experimenters—making a given movement.

Since that first sighting of mirror neurons in monkeys, the same systems have been discovered in the human brain. In a remarkable study where a laser-thin electrode monitored a single neuron in an awake person, the neuron fired both when the person anticipated pain—a pinprick—and when merely *seeing* someone else receive a pinprick—a neural snapshot of primal empathy in action.[7]

Many mirror neurons operate in the premotor cortex, which governs activities ranging from speaking and movement to simply intending to act. Because they are adjacent to motor neurons, their location means that the areas of the brain that initiate a movement can readily begin to activate even as we watch someone else make that same movement.[8] When we mentally rehearse an action—making a dry run of a talk we have to give, or envisioning the fine points of our golf swing—the same neurons activate in the premotor cortex as if we had uttered those words or made that swing. Simulating an act is, in the brain, the same as performing it, except that the actual execution is somehow blocked.[9]

Our mirror neurons fire as we watch someone else, for example, scratch their head or wipe away a tear, so that a portion of the pattern of neuronal firing in our brain mimics theirs. This maps the identical information from what we are seeing onto our own motor neurons, letting us participate in the other person's actions as if *we* were executing that action.

The human brain harbors multiple mirror neuron systems, not just for mimicking actions but also for reading intentions, for extracting the social implications from what someone does, and for reading emotions.[10] For instance, when volunteers lay in an fMRI watching a video showing someone smile or scowl, most brain areas that activated in the observers were the same as those active in the person displaying the emotion, though not as extreme.[11]

Mirror neurons make emotions contagious, letting the feelings we witness flow through us, helping us get in synch and follow what's going on. We "feel" the other in the broadest sense of the word: sensing their sentiments, their movements, their sensations, their emotions as they act inside us.

Social skill depends on mirror neurons. For one thing, echoing what we observe in another person prepares us to make a speedy and fitting response. For another, the neurons respond to the mere hint of an *intention* to move, and they help us track what motivation may be in play.[12] Sensing what other people intend—and why—offers invaluable social information, letting us keep a step ahead of whatever will happen next, like social chameleons.

Mirror neurons appear to be essential to the way children learn. Imitative learning has long been recognized as a major avenue of childhood development. But findings about mirror neurons explain how children can gain mastery simply from watching. As they watch, they are etching in their own brains a repertoire for emotion, for behavior, and for how the world works.

Human mirror neurons are far more flexible and diverse than those in monkeys, reflecting our sophisticated social abilities. By mimicking what another person does or feels, mirror neurons create a shared sensibility, bringing the outside inside us: to understand another, we become like the other—at least a bit.[13] That virtual sense of what someone else experiences fits with an emerging notion in the philosophy of mind: that we understand others by translating their actions into the neural language that prepares us for the same actions and lets us experience alike.[14]

I understand your action by creating a template for it in my own brain. As Giacomo Rizzolatti, the Italian neuroscientist who discovered mirror neurons, explains, these systems "allow us to grasp the minds of others not through conceptual reasoning but through direct simulation; by feeling, not by thinking."[15]

This triggering of parallel circuitry in two brains lets us instantly achieve a shared sense of what counts in a given moment. This creates an immediacy, a sense of sharing the moment. Neuroscientists call that mutually reverberating state "empathic resonance," a brain-to-brain linkage that forms a two-person circuitry via the low road.

The external signs of such inner links have been detailed by an American psychiatrist working at the University of Geneva, Daniel Stern, who has for decades made systematic observations of mothers and infants. A developmental scientist in the tradition of Jean Piaget, Stern also explores adult interactions, such as between psychotherapists and their clients, or between lovers.

Stern concludes that our nervous systems "are constructed to be captured by the nervous systems of others, so that we can experience others as if from within their skin."[16] At such moments we resonate with their experience, and they with ours.

We can no longer, Stern adds, "see our minds as so independent, separate and isolated," but instead we must view them as "permeable," continually interacting as though joined by an invisible link. At an unconscious level, we are in constant dialogue with anyone we interact with, our every feeling and very way of moving attuned to theirs. At least for the moment our mental life is cocreated, in an interconnected two-person matrix.

Mirror neurons ensure that the moment someone sees an emotion expressed on your face, they will at once sense that same feeling within themselves. And so our emotions are experienced not merely by ourselves in isolation but also by those around us—both covertly and openly.

Stern suggests that the neurons for mimicry are at play whenever we sense another person's state of mind and resonate with their feelings. This interbrain linkage makes bodies move in tandem, thoughts go down the same roads, and emotions run along the same lines. As mirror neurons bridge brains, they create a tacit duet that opens the way for subtle but powerful transactions.

| THE HAPPY FACE ADVANTAGE |

When I first met Paul Ekman, in the 1980s, he had just spent a year gazing into a mirror while learning to voluntarily control each one of the close to two hundred muscles of the face. This entailed some heroic scientific research: he had to apply a mild electrical shock to locate some hard-to-detect facial muscles. Once he had mastered his feat of self-control, he was able to map precisely how different sets of these muscles move to exhibit each of the major emotions and their variations.

Ekman has identified eighteen kinds of smiles, all various permutations of the fifteen facial muscles involved. To name but a few: A miserable smile pastes over an unhappy expression, like a grin-and-bear-it comment on feeling dismal. A cruel smile shows that the person relishes being angry and mean. And then there's the supercilious smile that was Charlie Chaplin's hallmark, which draws on a muscle most people can't move deliberately—a smile, as Ekman puts it, that "smiles at smiling."[17]

Of course there are also genuine smiles of spontaneous pleasure or amusement. These are the smiles that are most likely to evoke one in return. That action signals the work of mirror neurons dedicated to detecting smiles and triggering our own.[18] As a Tibetan saying has it, "When you smile at life, half the smile is for your face, the other half for somebody else's."

Smiles have an edge over all other emotional expressions: the human brain prefers happy faces, recognizing them more readily and quickly than those with negative expressions—an effect known as the "happy face advantage."[19] Some neuroscientists suggest that the brain has a system for positive feelings that stays primed for activity, causing people to be in upbeat moods more often than negative, and to have a more positive outlook on life.

That implies that Nature tends to foster positive relationships. Despite the all-too-prominent place of aggression in human affairs, we are not innately primed to dislike people from the start.

Even among complete strangers, a moment of playfulness, even outright silliness, forms an instant resonance. In what may be yet another instance of psychology trying to prove the obvious, pairs of strangers were assigned to play a series of silly games together. During the games one person had to talk through a straw while directing the other, wearing a blindfold, to toss a Nerf ball back and forth. The strangers invariably fell into guffaws at their haplessness.

When strangers played the same silly games without the blindfold and straw, however, they never cracked a smile. Yet the laughing pairs felt a strong, immediate sense of closeness, even after spending just a few minutes together.[20]

Indeed, laughter may be the shortest distance between two brains, an unstoppable infectious spread that builds an instant social bond.[21] Take two teenage girls giggling together. The more giddily playful the two teen best friends become, the more synchronous, animated, and happy they feel together—in other words, they resonate.[22] What to a parent may seem an ungodly racket will be, for the teenagers making it, one of their most bonding moments.

MEME WARS

Since the 1970s rap songs have glorified the thug's life, with its guns and drugs, gang violence and misogyny, and the pimp's and hustler's lust for bling. But that seems to be changing, as have the lives of some of those who write such lyrics.

"It seems like hip-hop has mostly been about parties and guns and women," Darryl McDaniels, the DMC in the rap group Run-DMC, has acknowledged. But McDaniels, who himself prefers listening to classical rock rather than rap, adds, "That's fine if you're in a club, but from 9 a.m. till I went to bed at night, the music had nothing to say to me."[23]

His complaint heralds the emergence of a new breed of rap music, one that embraces a more wholesome, if still grittily frank, view of life. As one of these reformed rappers, John Stevens (known as Legend), admits, "I wouldn't feel comfortable making music that glorifies violence or such things."[24]

Instead Legend, like his fellow rap reformer Kanye West, has turned to lyrics in a positive key that mix confessional self-criticism with wry social commentary. That nuanced sensibility reflects their life experience, which has followed paths markedly different from those of most gangsta rap stars of the past. Stevens has a degree from the University of Pennsylvania, and Kanye is the son of a college professor. As Kanye observes, "My mom's a teacher, and I'm kind of a teacher too."

He's on to something. Rap lyrics, like any poem, essay, or news story, can be seen as delivery systems for "memes," ideas that spread from mind to mind, much as emotions do. The notion of a meme was modeled on that of a gene: an entity that replicates itself by getting passed on from person to person.

Memes with particular power, like "democracy" or "cleanliness," lead us to act in a specific way; they are ideas with impact.[25] Some memes naturally oppose others, and when they do, those memes are at war, a battle of ideas.

Memes seem to gather power from the low road, through their association with strong emotions. An idea matters to us to the extent that it moves us—and that is precisely what emotions do. The low-road force of rap lyrics (or any song), made all the stronger by oscillator-riveting beats, may gather special force—certainly more than they would if read on a page.

Memes may one day be understood as mirror neurons at work. Their unconscious scripting steers much of what we do, particularly when we are on "automatic." But the subtle power of memes to make us act often eludes detection.

Consider their surprising power to prime social interactions.[26] In an experiment one group of volunteers heard a list of cue words that referred to impoliteness, such as "rude" and "obnoxious," while another group heard cue words like "considerate" and "polite." They then were put in a situation where they had to deliver a message to someone who was talking with another person. Two out of three of those primed for rudeness butted in to interrupt, while eight of ten primed for politeness waited the full ten minutes for the conversation to end before speaking up.[27]

In another form of priming, an unnoticed cue can lead to surprising synchronicities. How else to explain what happened when my wife and I visited a tropical island. One morning we spotted a marvel far out on the horizon: a strikingly graceful, four-masted ship sailing by. My wife suggested I take a photo, so I dug out my camera and snapped one. It was the first time I'd taken a photo in the ten days we'd been there.

A few hours later, as we left for lunch, I decided to take the camera along and slipped it into a backpack. As we walked toward a lunch shack on a beach nearby, it occurred to me to mention that I had the camera along with me. But out of the blue, before I could say a word, my wife asked, "Did you bring the camera?"

It was as though she had read my mind.

Such synchronicities seem to stem from the verbal equivalent of emotional contagion. Our trains of association run on set tracks, circuits of learning and memory. Once any of these trains has been primed, even by a simple mention, that track stirs in the unconscious, beyond the reach of our active attention.[28] As the Russian playwright Anton Chekhov famously put it, never put a gun on a wall in the second act of a play without using it by the end of the third—for the audience will be expecting gunshots.

Because simply thinking of an action prepares the mind to perform it, priming guides us through our daily routines without our having to exert mental effort in thinking what we should do next—something like a mental to-do list. Seeing our toothbrush on the bathroom sink in the morning cues us to automatically reach for it and start brushing.

This urge to enact guides us everywhere. When someone whispers to us, we whisper back. Talk about a Grand Prix race to someone driving on a highway, and he will speed up. It's as though one brain implants similar feelings, thoughts, and impulses in the other.

In similar fashion, parallel trains of thought can lead two people to think, do, or say virtually the same thing at the same moment. When my wife and I suddenly attuned to the identical thought, presumably some shared momentary perception had triggered an identical train of association, bringing to mind the camera.

Such mental intimacy bespeaks an emotional closeness; the more satisfied and communicative a couple, the more accurate their mutual mindreading.[29] When we know someone well or experience strong rapport, conditions are near optimal for a confluence of our internal thoughts, feelings, perceptions, and memories.[30] We are in what amounts to a mind-meld where we tend to perceive, think, and feel in the same way as the other person.

Such convergence goes on even when strangers become friends. Take two college students assigned to the same dorm room. Researchers at Berkeley recruited new roommates and tracked their emotional responses as they separately watched some short films. One featured Robin Williams in a hilarious comedy; another, a tearjerker, depicted a boy crying at the death of his father. On first viewing the films, the new roommates reacted as differently from each other as any pair of random strangers would. But seven months later, when the researchers invited the roommates back to see similar short films, their reactions had converged strikingly.[31]

THE MADNESS OF CROWDS

They call them "superhooligans," the gangs of soccer fans who spark riots and mass fights at European matches. The formula for a soccer riot is the same, no matter the country. A small, tight-knit gang of fans arrives for the match hours early and goes out on a drinking binge, singing their club's songs and having a rollicking time.

Then as the crowds are gathering for the match, the gangs get caught up in waving team flags, singing boisterous songs, and chanting against the other team, all of which spreads to the gathering mass. The superhooligans gravitate to points where their team's fans mix with those of their rivals, and the chants change to outright threats. Then comes the flashpoint, when a gang leader attacks a rival fan, triggering others to join in. And the fights spread.

That formula for violent mass hysteria has been repeated over and over since the early 1980s, with tragic consequences.[32] In a drunken belligerent mob, conditions are ideal for sparking violence: the alcohol disinhibits neural controls over impulses, and so the moment a leader models the first carnage, contagion primes the rest to follow.

Elias Canetti, in his study *Crowds and Power,* observes that what coalesces a mass of individuals into a crowd is their domination by a "single passion" everyone shares—a common emotion that leads to united action: collective contagion.[33] A mood can sweep through a group with great rapidity, a remarkable display of the parallel alignment of biological subsystems that puts everyone there in physiological synchrony.[34]

The swiftness of shifts in the activity of crowds looks suspiciously like mirror neuron coordination writ large. Crowd decision-making goes on within seconds—presumably the time it takes for a person-to-person transmission of mirror neuron synchrony to sweep through (though for now that remains a matter of speculation).

Group contagion in its more sedate forms can be witnessed at any great performance, where actors or musicians create a field effect, playing the audience's emotions like instruments. Plays, concerts, and movies all let us enter a shared field of emotions with large numbers of strangers. Looping together in an upbeat register is, as psychologists like to say, "inherently reinforcing"—that is, it makes everyone feel good.

Crowd contagion goes on even in the most minimal of groups, three people sitting face to face with each other in silence for a few minutes. In the absence of a power hierarchy, the person with the most emotionally expressive face will set the shared tone.[35]

Contagion will seep through almost any coordinated collection of people. Take an experiment in high-stakes decision-making, where a group met to decide how much of a bonus to give each employee from an end-of-year pool of money. Each person in the meeting was trying to get as large a bonus as possible for one or another employee, while still making the best overall distribution for the group as a whole.

The conflicting agendas led to tension, and by the end of the meeting everyone was feeling distressed. But in a meeting of another group with an identical goal, everyone ended up feeling good about the outcome.

The two meetings were business simulations done in a now-classic study at Yale University, where volunteers were put in groups to make the bonus decisions.[36] No one knew that one of the participants in each meeting was actually a seasoned actor whose secret assignment was to be confrontational and downbeat with some of the groups, and helpful and upbeat with the others.

In whichever direction his emotions went, his lead was followed; the group members showed a distinct shift in their own mood, becoming upset or feeling pleasant accordingly. But none of the group members seemed to know why their mood had changed. Unwittingly, they had been looped into a mood shift.

The feelings that pass through a group can bias how all the group members process information and hence the decisions they make.[37] This suggests that in coming to a decision together, any group would do well to attend not just to what's being said, but to the shared emotions in the room as well.

This convergence bespeaks a subtle, inexorable magnetism, a gravitylike pull toward thinking and feeling alike about things in general among people who are in close relationships of any kind—family members, workmates, and friends.

$$\dashv \boxed{4} \vdash$$

An Instinct for Altruism

One afternoon at the Princeton Theological Seminary, forty students waited to give a short practice sermon on which they would be rated. Half the students had been assigned random biblical topics. The other half had been assigned the parable of the Good Samaritan, who stopped to help a stranger by the roadside, an injured man ignored by people supposedly more "pious."

The seminarians worked together in a room, and every fifteen minutes one of them left to go to another building to deliver his sermon. None knew they were taking part in an experiment on altruism.

Their route passed directly by a doorway in which a man was slumped, groaning in evident pain. Of the forty students, twenty-four passed right by, ignoring the plaintive moans. And those who were mulling over the lessons of the Good Samaritan's tale were no more likely to stop and help than were any of the others.[1]

For the seminarians, time mattered. Among ten who thought they were late to give their sermon, only one stopped; among another ten who thought they had plenty of time, six offered help.

Of the many factors that are at play in altruism, a critical one seems to be simply taking the time to pay attention; our empathy is strongest to the degree we fully focus on someone and so loop emotionally. People differ, of course, in their ability, willingness, and interest in paying attention—a sullen teen can tune out her mother's nagging, then a minute later have undivided concentration while on a phone call to her girlfriend. The seminarians rushing to give their sermon were apparently unwilling or unable to give their attention to the moaning man, presumably because they were caught up in their thoughts and the press of hurrying, and so never attuned to him, let alone helped him.[2]

People on busy city streets worldwide are less likely to notice, greet, or offer help to someone else because of what has been called the "urban trance." Sociologists have proposed that we tend to fall into this self-absorbed state on crowded streets, if only to gird against stimulus overload from the swirl around us. Inevitably, the strategy requires a trade-off: we shut out the compelling needs of those around us along with the mere distractions. As a poet put it, we confront "the noise of the street dazed and deafened."

In addition, social divides shutter our eyes. A homeless person sitting dejectedly on the street of an American city asking for money may receive no attention from passersby, who a few steps away will gladly listen and respond to a well-dressed, outgoing woman asking for signatures on a political petition. (Of course, depending on our sympathies, the attention we give may be just the reverse: sympathy for the homeless person, but none for the political appeal.) In short, our priorities, socialization, and myriad other social-psychological factors can lead us to direct or inhibit our attention or the emotions we feel—and thus our empathy.

Simply paying attention allows us to build an emotional connection. Lacking attention, empathy hasn't a chance.

WHEN ATTENTION MUST BE PAID

Contrast those events at the Princeton seminary with what happened one rush hour in New York City as I headed for the Times Square subway station after work one day. As usual, a steady torrent of humanity was sweeping down the concrete stairs, rushing to get on the next subway train.

But then I saw something troubling: sprawled across the steps midway down was a shabby, shirtless man, lying motionless, eyes closed.

No one seemed to notice. People simply stepped over his body in their rush to get home.

But, shocked by the sight, I stopped to see what was wrong. And the moment I stopped, something remarkable happened: other people stopped, too.

Almost instantly there was a small circle of concern around the man. Just as spontaneously, messengers of mercy fanned out—one man went over to a hot dog stand to get him some food; a woman scurried to get him a bottle of water; another summoned a subway patrol officer, who in turn radioed for help.

Within minutes the man was revived, eating happily, and waiting for an ambulance. We learned he spoke only Spanish, had no money, and had been wandering the streets of Manhattan, starving. He had fainted from hunger there on the subway steps.

What made the difference? Just noticing for one. By simply stopping to take in the man's plight, I seemed to snap passersby out of their urban trance and called him to their attention. As we tuned in to his predicament, we were moved to help.

No doubt all of us upright citizens on our way home from work were susceptible to silent assumptions about that man on the stairs, stereotypes built from walking by the hundreds of homeless who, sad to say, inhabit the streets of New York and so many other modern urban centers. Urbanites learn to manage the anxiety of seeing someone in such dire straits by reflexively shifting attention away.

I think my own shift-away reflex had been altered by an article I had recently written for *The New York Times* on how closing mental hospitals had converted the city's streets into psychiatric wards. To do research for the article, I spent several days in a van with workers for a social agency that administered to the homeless, bringing them food, offering them shelter, and coaxing the mentally ill among them—a shockingly high proportion—to come to clinics to receive their medications. For quite a while afterward I saw homeless people through fresh eyes.

In other studies using the Good Samaritan situation, researchers find that those who do stop to help typically report that on seeing the other's distress, they felt upset too—and an empathic sense of tenderness.[3] Once one person noticed the other enough to feel empathy, the odds were very high that he would offer some help.

Just hearing about someone lending a helping hand can have a unique impact, inducing a warm sense of uplift. Psychologists use the term "elevation" for the glow stirred by witnessing someone else's kindness. Elevation is the state reported repeatedly when people tell how they felt on seeing a spontaneous act of courage, tolerance, or compassion. Most people find themselves moved, even thrilled.

The acts most commonly named as stirring elevation are helping the poor or sick, or aiding someone in a difficult predicament. But these good deeds need not be as demanding as taking in an entire family, nor as selfless as Mother Teresa working among the poor in Calcutta. Simple thoughtfulness can elicit a bit of elevation. In a study in Japan, for instance, people readily came up with accounts of *kandou,* times when the heart is so moved—for example, by seeing a tough-looking gang member give up his seat on a train to an elderly man.[4]

Elevation, the research suggests, may be catching. When someone sees an act of kindness, it typically stirs in them the impulse to perform one, too. These social benefits may be one reason mythic tales worldwide are rife with figures who save others through their courageous deeds. Psychologists speculate that hearing a story about such kindness—when it is told vividly—has the same emotional impact as seeing the act itself.[5] That elevation can be contagious suggests that it travels the low road.

FINE-TUNING

On a five-day visit to Brazil with my son, we noticed that the people we met seemed to get friendlier day by day. The change was striking.

At first we largely sensed aloofness or reserve from the Brazilians we met. But by the third day we encountered noticeably greater warmth.

On the fourth day it followed us wherever we went. And by our trip's end we were hugging people good-bye at the airport.

Was it the people of Brazil who had changed? Certainly not. What had melted away was our own uptightness as gringos in an unfamiliar culture. Our defensive reserve had initially closed us off to the Brazilians' open, friendly manner—and it may well have signaled them to keep their distance.

At the beginning of our trip—like a radio set to a slightly off-channel signal—we were too preoccupied to take in the friendliness of the people we encountered. As we relaxed and tuned in to those around us, it was as though we had zeroed in on the right station, the warmth that was there all along. While we are anxious or preoccupied, we fail to register the sparkle in someone's eye, the hint of a smile, or the warm tones of voice—all prime channels for sending messages of friendliness.

A technical explanation for this dynamic spotlights the limits on attention itself. Working memory, or the amount of memory that we can hold in our attention at any one moment, resides in the prefrontal cortex, the citadel of the high road. This circuitry plays a major role in allocating our attention, by managing the backstage business of an interaction. For instance, it searches our memory for what to say and do, even while it attends to incoming signals and shifts our responses accordingly.

As the challenges thicken, those multiple demands increasingly tax our capacity for paying attention. Signals of worry from the amygdala flood key regions of the prefrontal cortex, manifesting as preoccupations that steal attention away from whatever else we are dealing with. Distress overtaxes attention: merely being an uptight gringo will do it.

Nature puts a premium on smooth communication among members of a given species, sculpting the brain for a better fit—sometimes on the spot. In certain fish, for instance, during courtship a female's brain secretes hormones that temporarily reshape her auditory circuits to improve their attunement to the frequencies of the male's call.[6]

Something similar can be seen in a two-month-old baby who detects his mother approaching: he will instinctively become still, quiet his breathing a bit, turn toward her and look at her face, focus on her eyes or mouth, and orient his ears toward any sounds coming from her, all while making an expression researchers call "knit-brow with jaw-drop." Each of these moves enhances the perceptual ability of the baby to attune to what the mother says or does.[7]

The more sharply attentive we are, the more keenly we will sense another person's inner state: we will do so more quickly and from subtler cues, in more ambiguous circumstances. Conversely, the greater our distress, the less accurately we will be able to empathize.

In short, self-absorption in all its forms kills empathy, let alone compassion. When we focus on ourselves, our world contracts as our problems and preoccupations loom large. But when we focus on others, our world expands. Our own problems drift to the periphery of the mind and so seem smaller, and we increase our capacity for connection—or compassionate action.

INSTINCTIVE COMPASSION

• A laboratory rat, suspended in the air by a harness, screeches and struggles. Catching sight of the imperiled rat, one of its cagemates becomes upset too and manages to come to the rescue by pressing a bar that lowers the victim safely to the ground.

• Six rhesus monkeys have been trained to pull chains to get food. At one point a seventh monkey, in full view of the others, gets a painful shock whenever one of them pulls for food. On seeing the pain of that shocked monkey, four of the original rhesus monkeys start pulling a different chain, one that delivers less food to them but that inflicts no shock on the other monkey. The fifth monkey stops pulling any chain at all for five days, and the sixth for twelve days—that is, both starve themselves to prevent shocking the seventh monkey.

• Virtually from birth, when babies see or hear another baby crying in distress, they start crying as though they too are distressed. But they rarely cry when they hear a recording of their own cries. After about fourteen months of age, babies not only cry when they hear another, but they also try to relieve the other baby's suffering somehow. The older toddlers get, the less they cry and the more they try to help.

Lab rats, monkeys, and babies share an automatic impulse, one that rivets their attention on another's suffering, triggers similar distressed feelings in themselves, and leads them to try to help. Why should the same response be found in very different species? Simple: Nature conserves, preserving whatever works to use again and again.

In the design of the brain, winning features are shared among various species. Human brains have vast tracts of well-proven neural architecture in common with other mammals, especially primates. The similarity across species in sympathetic distress, coupled with the impulse to help, strongly suggests a like set of underlying circuitry in the brain. In contrast to mammals, reptiles show not the least sign of empathy, even eating their own young.

Although people can also ignore someone in need, that cold-heartedness seems to suppress a more primal, automatic impulse to aid another in distress. Scientific observations point to a response system that is hardwired in the human brain—no doubt involving mirror neurons—that acts when we see someone else suffering, making us instantly feel with them. The more we feel with them, the more we want to help them.

This instinct for compassion arguably offers benefits in evolutionary fitness—properly defined in terms of "reproductive success," or how many of one's offspring live to parent their own offspring. Over a century ago Charles Darwin proposed that empathy, the prelude to compassionate action, has been a powerful aid to survival in Nature's toolkit.[8] Empathy lubricates sociability, and we humans are the social animal par excellence. New thinking holds that our sociability has been the primary survival strategy of primate species, including our own.

The utility of friendliness can be seen today in the lives of primates in the wild, who inhabit a tooth-and-claw world akin to that of human prehistory, when relatively few infants survived to childbearing age. Take the thousand or so monkeys that inhabit Cayo Santiago, a remote island in the Caribbean; all descend from a single band transplanted from their native India in the 1950s. These rhesus macaques live in small groups. When they reach adolescence, the females stay, and the males leave to find their place in another group.

That transition holds real dangers: as the young males try to enter an unfamiliar troupe, up to 20 percent of them die in fights. Scientists have taken spinal fluid samples of one hundred teen macaques. They find that the most outgoing monkeys have the lowest levels of stress hormones and stronger immune function, and—most important—that they are best able to approach, befriend, or challenge monkeys in the new troupe. These more sociable young monkeys are the ones most likely to survive.[9]

Another primate data point comes from wild baboons living near Mount Kilimanjaro in Tanzania. For these baboons, infancy holds great perils: in a good year about 10 percent of infants die; in bad times up to 35 percent die. But when biologists observed the baboon mothers, they found that those who were most companionable—who spent the most time grooming or otherwise socializing with other female baboons—had the infants most likely to survive.

The biologists cite two reasons that a mother's friendliness may help her infants survive. For one, they are members of a clubby group who can help one another defend their babies from harassment, or find better food and shelter. For another, the more grooming the mothers give and get, the more relaxed and healthy they tend to be. Sociable baboons make better mothers.[10]

Our natural pull toward others may trace back to the conditions of scarcity that shaped the human brain. We can readily surmise how membership in a group would make survival in dire times more likely—and how being a lone individual competing for scarce resources with a group could be a deadly disadvantage.

A trait with such powerful survival value can gradually fashion the very circuitry of the brain, since whatever proves most effective in spreading genes to future generations becomes increasingly pervasive in the genetic pool.

If sociability offered humans a winning strategy throughout prehistory, so have the brain systems through which social life operates.[11] Small wonder our inclination toward empathy, the essential connector, has such potency.

| AN ANGEL ON EARTH |

A head-on collision had left her car crumpled like a piece of paper. With two bones broken in her right leg, pinned in the wreckage, she lay there in pain and shock, helpless and confused.

Then a passerby—she never found out his name—came over to her and knelt by her side. He held her hand, reassuring her while emergency workers tried to free her. Despite her pain and anxiety, he helped her stay calm.

"He was," as she put it later, "my angel on earth."[12]

We'll never know exactly what feelings moved that "angel" to kneel at that woman's side to reassure her. But such compassion depends on that crucial first step, empathy.

Empathy entails some degree of emotional sharing—a prerequisite to truly understanding anyone else's inner world.[13] Mirror neurons, as one neuroscientist puts it, are "what give you the richness of empathy, the fundamental mechanism that makes seeing someone hurt really hurt you."[14]

Constantin Stanislavski, the Russian developer of the famed Method for stage training, saw that an actor "living" a part could call up his emotional memories from the past to evoke a powerful feeling in the present. But those memories, Stanislavski taught, need not be limited to our own experiences. An actor can as well draw on the emotions of others through a bit of empathy. As the legendary acting coach advised, "We must study other people and get as close to them emotionally as we can, until sympathy for them is transformed into feelings of our own."[15]

Stanislavski's advice was prescient. As it turns out, brain imaging studies reveal that when we answer the question, "How are you feeling?" we activate much of the same neural circuitry that lights up when we ask, "How is *she* feeling?" The brain acts almost identically when we sense our own feelings and those of another.[16]

When people are asked to imitate someone's facial expression of happiness, fear, or disgust, this activates the same circuits involved when they simply observe the person (or when they spontaneously feel that emotion themselves). As Stanislavski understood, these circuits come even more alive when empathy becomes intentional.[17] As we notice an emotion in another person, then, we literally feel together. The greater our effort or the more intense the feelings expressed, the stronger we feel them in ourselves.

Tellingly, the German word *Einfühlung,* which was first rendered into English in 1909 as the newly coined word "empathy," more literally translates as "feeling into," suggesting an inner imitation of the other person's feelings.[18] As Theodore Lipps, who imported the word "empathy" into English, put it, "When I observe a circus performer on a high wire, I feel I am inside him." It's as though we experience the other person's emotions in our own body. And we do: neuroscientists say that the more active a person's mirror neuron systems, the stronger her empathy.

In today's psychology, the word "empathy" is used in three distinct senses: *knowing* another person's feelings; *feeling* what that person feels; and *responding compassionately* to another's distress. These three varieties of empathy seem to describe a 1-2-3 sequence: I notice you, I feel with you, and so I act to help you.

All three fit well with what neuroscience has learned about how the brain operates when we attune to another person, as Stephanie Preston and Frans de Waal observe in a major theory linking interpersonal perception and action.[19] These two scientists are uniquely suited to make the argument: Preston has pioneered using the methods of social neuroscience to study empathy in humans, and de Waal, director of Living Links at the Yerkes Primate Center, has for decades drawn lessons for human behavior from systematic observations of primates.

Preston and de Waal argue that in a moment of empathy, both our emotions and our thoughts are primed along the same lines as those of the other person. Hearing a frightened cry from someone else, we spontaneously think of what might be causing their fear. From a cognitive perspective, we share a mental "representation," a set of images, associations, and thoughts about their predicament.

The movement from empathy to act traverses mirror neurons; empathy seems to have evolved from emotional contagion and so shares its neural mechanisms. Primal empathy relies on no specialized brain area but rather involves many, depending on what we are empathizing with. We slip into the other's shoes to share what they experience.

Preston has found that if someone brings to mind one of the happiest moments of her life, then imagines a similar moment from the life of one of her closest friends, the brain activates virtually the identical circuitry for these two mental acts.[20] In other words, to understand what someone else experiences—to empathize—we utilize the same brain wiring that is active during our own experience.[21]

All communication requires that what matters for the sender also matters for the receiver. By sharing thoughts as well as feelings, two brains deploy a shorthand that gets both people on the same page immediately, without having to waste time or words explaining more pointedly what matters are at hand.[22]

Mirroring occurs whenever our perception of someone automatically activates an image or a felt sense in our own brain for what they are doing and expressing.[23] What's on their mind occupies ours. We rely on these inner messages to sense what might be going on in the other person. After all, what does a smile or a wink, a stare or a frown, "mean," except as a clue to what's happening in the other person's mind?

| AN ANCIENT DEBATE |

Today most people remember the seventeenth-century philosopher Thomas Hobbes for his assertion that life in our natural state—absent any strong government—is "nasty, brutish and short," a war of all against all. Despite this tough, cynical view, however, Hobbes himself had a soft side.

One day as he walked through the streets of London, he came upon an old, sickly man who was begging for alms. Hobbes, his heart touched, immediately gave the man a generous offering.

When asked by a friend if he would have done the same had there been no religious dictum or philosophical principle about helping the needy, Hobbes replied that he would. His explanation: he felt some pain himself when he saw the man's misery, and so just as giving alms to the man would relieve some of the man's suffering, it "doth also ease me."[24]

This tale suggests that we have a bit of self-interest in relieving the misery of others. One school of modern economic theory, following Hobbes, argues that people give to charities in part because of the pleasure they get from imagining either the relief of those they benefit or their own relief from alleviating their sympathetic distress.

Latter-day versions of this theory have tried to reduce acts of altruism to disguised acts of self-interest.[25] In one version, compassion veils a "selfish gene" that tries to maximize its odds of being passed on by gathering obligations or by favoring the close relatives who carry it.[26] Such explanations may suffice in special cases.

But another viewpoint offers a more immediate—and universal—explanation: as the Chinese sage Mengzi (or Mencius) wrote in the third century B.C.E., long before Hobbes, "All men have a mind which cannot bear to see the suffering of others."[27]

Neuroscience now supports Mengzi's position, adding missing data to this centuries-old debate. When we see someone else in distress, similar circuits reverberate in our brain, a kind of hardwired empathic resonance that becomes the prelude to compassion. If an infant cries, her parents' brains reverberate in much the same way, which in turn automatically moves them to do something to soothe their baby's distress.

Our brain has been preset for kindness. We automatically go to the aid of a child who is screaming in terror; we automatically want to hug a smiling baby. Such emotional impulses are "prepotent": they elicit reactions in us that are unpremeditated and instantaneous. That this flow from empathy to action occurs with such rapid automaticity hints at circuitry dedicated to this very sequence. To feel distress stirs an urge to help.

When we hear an anguished scream, it activates the same parts of our brain that experience such anguish, as well as the premotor cortex, a sign we are preparing to act. Similarly, hearing someone tell an unhappy story in doleful tones activates the listener's motor cortex—which guides movements—as well as the amygdala and related circuits for sadness.[28] This shared state then signals the motor area of the brain, where we prepare our response, for the relevant action. Our initial perception prepares us for action: to see readies us to do.[29]

The neural networks for perception and action share a common code in the language of the brain. This shared code allows whatever we perceive to lead almost instantly to the appropriate reaction. Seeing an emotional expression, hearing a tone of voice, or having our attention directed to a given topic instantly fires the neurons that that message indicates.

This shared code was anticipated by Charles Darwin, who back in 1872 wrote a scholarly treatise on emotions that scientists still regard highly.[30] Although Darwin wrote about empathy as a survival factor, a popular misreading of his evolutionary theories emphasized "nature red in tooth and claw" (as Tennyson phrased the notion of a relentless culling of the weak), a notion favored by "social Darwinists," who twisted evolutionary thinking to rationalize greed.

Darwin saw every emotion as a predisposition to act in a unique way: fear, to freeze or flee; anger, to fight; joy, to embrace; and so on. Brain imaging studies now show that at the neural level he was right. To feel *any* emotion stirs the related urge to act.

The low road makes that feeling-action link interpersonal. For instance, when we see someone expressing fear—even if only in the way they move or hold their body—our own brain activates the circuitry for fear. Along with this instantaneous contagion, the brain areas that prepare for fearful actions also activate. And so with each emotion—anger, joy, sadness, and so on. Emotional contagion, then, does more than merely spread feelings—it automatically prepares the brain for appropriate action.[31]

Nature's rule of thumb holds that a biological system should use the minimal amount of energy. Here the brain achieves that efficiency by firing the same neurons while both perceiving and performing an action. That economizing repeats across brains. In the special case of someone in distress, the perception-action link makes coming to their aid the brain's natural tendency. To feel *with* stirs us to act *for.*

To be sure, some data suggest in many situations that people tend to favor helping their loved ones over helping a stranger. Even so, emotional attunement with a stranger in distress moves us to help that person just as we would our loved ones. For instance, in one study the more saddened people were by the plight of a displaced orphan, the more likely they were to donate money or even offer the child a temporary place to live—regardless of how much social distance they felt.

The preference for helping those similar to ourselves washes away when we are face-to-face with someone in agony or dire straits. In a direct encounter with such a person the primal brain-to-brain link makes us experience their suffering as our own—and to immediately prepare to help.[32] And that direct confrontation with suffering was once the rule in human affairs, in the vast period when encounters were always within feet or yards, rather than at the artificial removes of modern life.

Back to that quandary of why—if the human brain contains a system designed to attune us to someone else's distress and prepare us to act to help—we don't always help. The possible answers are manifold, enumerated by countless experiments in social psychology. But the simplest answer may be that modern life militates against it: we largely relate to those in need at a distance. That separation means we experience "cognitive" empathy rather than the immediacy of direct emotional contagion. Or worse, we have mere sympathy, where we feel sorry for the person but do not taste their distress in the least.[33] This more removed relationship weakens the innate impulse to help.

As Preston and de Waal note, "In today's era of e-mail, commuting, frequent moves, and bedroom communities, the scales are increasingly tipped against the automatic and accurate perception of others' emotional state, without which empathy is impossible." Modern-day social and virtual distances have created an anomaly in human living, though one we now take to be the norm. This separation mutes empathy, absent which altruism falters.

The argument has long been made that we humans are by nature compassionate and empathic despite the occasional streak of meanness, but torrents of bad news through history have contradicted that claim, and little sound science has backed it. But try this thought experiment. Imagine the number of opportunities people around the world today *might* have to commit an antisocial act, from rape or murder to simple rudeness and dishonesty. Make that number the bottom of a fraction. Now for the top value, put the number of such antisocial acts that will *actually* occur today.

That ratio of potential to enacted meanness holds at close to zero any day of the year. And if for the top value you put the number of benevolent acts performed in a given day, the ratio of kindness to cruelty will be always be positive. (The news, however, comes to us as though that ratio was reversed.)

Harvard's Jerome Kagan proposes this mental exercise to make a simple point about human nature: the sum total of goodness vastly outweighs that of meanness. "Although humans inherit a biological bias that permits them to feel anger, jealousy, selfishness and envy, and to be rude, aggressive or violent," Kagan notes, "they inherit an even stronger biological bias for kindness, compassion, cooperation, love and nurture—especially toward those in need." This inbuilt ethical sense, he adds, "is a biological feature of our species."[34]

With the discovery that our neural wiring tips toward putting empathy in the service of compassion, neuroscience hands philosophy a mechanism for explaining the ubiquity of the altruistic impulse. Instead of trying to explain away selfless acts, philosophers might contemplate the conundrum of the innumerable times that cruel acts are absent.[35]

The Neuroanatomy of a Kiss

The couple vividly remembers the moment of their first kiss, a legendary landmark in their relationship.

Friends for many years, they had met one afternoon for tea. During their conversation they both acknowledged how hard it was to find just the right partner. That conversational moment was punctuated by a pointed pause as their eyes locked and they gazed thoughtfully at each other for a second or two.

Afterward, as they were standing outside saying good-bye, they again looked into each other's eyes. Out of the blue, each of them felt as though some mysterious force were bringing their lips together in a kiss.

Neither felt they had initiated it, but even years later they both distinctly remember having had the sensation of being propelled into that romantic act.

Those long gazes may have been a necessary neural prelude to their kiss. Neuroscience now tells us something akin to the poetic idea that the eyes are windows on the soul: the eyes offer glimpses into a person's most private feelings. More specifically, the eyes contain nerve projections that lead directly to a key brain structure for empathy and matching emotions, the orbitofrontal (or OFC) area of the prefrontal cortex.

Locking eyes loops us. To reduce a romantic moment to an aspect of its neurology, when two people's eyes meet, they have interlinked their orbitofrontal areas, which are especially sensitive to face-to-face cues like eye contact. These social pathways play a crucial role in recognizing another's emotional state.

As in real estate, location means much in the topography of the brain. The OFC, positioned just behind and above the orbits of the eyes (hence the "orbito-"), occupies a strategic site: the junction of the uppermost part of the emotional centers and the lowest part of the thinking brain. If the brain were like a fist, the wrinkly cortex would be roughly where the fingers are, the subcortical centers would be in the lower palm—and the OFC just where the two meet.

The OFC connects directly, neuron to neuron, three major regions of the brain: the cortex (or "thinking brain"), the amygdala (the trigger point for many emotional reactions), and the brain stem (the "reptilian" zones for automatic response). This tight connection suggests a rapid and powerful linkage, one that facilitates instantaneous coordination of thought, feeling, and action. This neural autobahn swirls together low-road inputs from the emotional centers, the body, and the senses, and high-road lanes that find meaning in that data, creating the intentional plans that guide our actions.[1]

This linkage of top-of-the-brain cortical and lower subcortical regions makes the OFC a pivotal meeting point of high and low, an epicenter for making sense of the social world around us. By putting together our inner and outer experience, the OFC performs an instant social calculus, one that tells us how we feel about the person we are with, how she feels about us, and what to do next in accord with how she responds.

Finesse, rapport, and smooth interactions depend to a great degree on this neural circuitry.[2] For instance, the OFC contains neurons that are keyed to detect the emotions on someone's face or to tease them from their tone of voice, and connect those social messages with the visceral experience: the two people sense they like each other.[3]

These circuits track affective significance—what something, or someone, means to us emotionally. When mothers of newborn infants viewed pictures of their own or of unfamiliar infants, fMRI readings revealed that the OFC lit up in response to the pictures of their infants but not to the others. The greater their OFC activity, the stronger their feelings of love and warmth.[4]

In technical terms, the OFC circuitry assigns "hedonic value" to our social world, letting us know we enjoy her, loathe them, adore him. And so it answers questions essential in the buildup to a kiss.

The OFC also assesses social aesthetics, such as how we feel about a person's aroma, a primal signal that evokes remarkably strong liking or disliking (a biological reaction underlying the success of every *parfumerie*). I recall a friend once saying that for him to love a woman, he had to like the way she tasted when they kissed.

Even before such out-of-awareness perceptions have reached consciousness, before we are fully cognizant of the subterranean feelings already stirring in us, we will have already begun acting on those feelings. Thus the self-propelled quality of that kiss.

Of course, other neural circuits are involved as well. The oscillators adapt and coordinate the rate of our neural firing and motor movements as we encounter a moving object. Here, presumably, they were hard at work guiding the two mouths together at just the right velocity and trajectory so that rather than teeth gnashing in collision, there was a soft meeting of lips. Even on a first kiss.

| LOW-ROAD VELOCITY |

Here's how a professor I know chose his assistant, the single person he spends most time with in his working day:

"I walked into the waiting room where she was sitting, and I immediately felt my physiology settle down. Instantly, I knew she would be easy to be with. Of course I looked at her resume and so on. But from the first moment I felt confident she was the one I should hire. And I haven't regretted it for a minute."

Intuiting whether we like a person we've just met amounts to guessing whether we will find a rapport, or at least get along, as a relationship unfolds. But of all the people we might potentially gravitate toward for friendship, business partnership, or marriage, how do we sort out those who draw us from those who leave us cold?

Much of that decision-making, it seems, goes on within moments of meeting someone for the first time. In one revealing study, students in a university course spent just three to ten minutes on the first day of class getting to know another student, a stranger. Immediately afterward they rated the likelihood of whether they and the other person would remain mere nodding acquaintances or become close friends. Nine weeks later it was found that those first impressions predicted the actual course of their relationship with remarkable accuracy.[5]

When we make such an instantaneous judgment, we depend to a large extent on the operation of an unusual set of neurons: brain cells shaped like a spindle, with a large bulb at one end and a long, thick extension. Spindle cells, neuroscientists now suspect, are the secret of the speed of social intuition. They put the "snap" in snap judgments.

The spindle shape holds the key: the body is about four times larger than other brain cells; from a very wide, long branch stem the dendrites and axons that act as cell-to-cell wiring. The velocity of a neuron's transmission to other cells increases with the size of the long arms that project to other neurons. The spindle's gargantuan dimensions ensure extremely high-velocity transmission.

Spindle cells form particularly thick connections between the OFC and the highest part of the limbic system, the anterior cingulate cortex (ACC). The ACC directs our attention and coordinates our thoughts, our emotions, and the body's response to our feelings.[6] This linkage creates a neural command center of sorts. From this critical junction, the spindle cells extend to widely diverse parts of the brain.[7]

The particular brain chemicals those axons transmit suggest their central role in social connection. Spindle cells are rich in receptors for serotonin, dopamine, and vasopressin. These brain chemicals play key roles in bonding with others, in love, in our moods good and bad, and in pleasure.

Some neuroanatomists suspect that spindle cells are crucial to what makes our species unique. We humans have about a thousand times more of them than do our closest primate cousins, the apes, who have but a few hundred. No other mammalian brain seems to contain spindle cells.[8] Some speculate that spindle cells may account for why some people (or primate species) are more socially aware or sensitive than others.[9] Brain imaging studies find enhanced functioning of the ACC in people who are more interpersonally aware—who can not only assess a social situation accurately but also sense how others in the situation would perceive it.[10]

Spindle cells concentrate in an area of the OFC which activates during our emotional reactions to others—particularly instant empathy.[11] For instance, when a mother hears her infant cry, or when we sense the suffering of a loved one, brain scans show that zone lights up. It also activates in emotionally loaded moments like when we look at a picture of someone we love, find someone attractive, or judge whether we are being treated fairly or being deceived.

The other place spindle cells can be found in abundance is an area of the ACC that plays equally key roles in social life. It guides our display and recognition of facial expressions and activates when we feel intense emotion. This area in turn has strong connections to the amygdala, the trigger point for many of these feelings, and the site where our first emotional judgments begin.[12]

These breakneck neurons seem to account for some of the high speed of the low road. For instance, even before we have a word for what we are perceiving, we already know whether we like it.[13] Spindle cells might help explain how the low road can offer up a snap judgment of "like" or "dislike" milliseconds before we realize exactly what "that" is.[14]

Such in-an-eyeblink judgments may matter most when it comes to people. Those spindly cells interweave what amounts to our social guidance system.

WHAT HE SAW HER SEE

Shortly after her own wedding, Maggie Verver, the heroine of Henry James's novel *The Golden Bowl*, visits her long-widowed father at a country estate, where other guests are staying. Among them are available ladies who seem interested in her father.

In a passing glance at her father, Maggie suddenly comprehends that he, who lived as a strict bachelor with her all the while she was growing up, was now feeling free to remarry.

And at that moment, her father realizes from the look in his daughter's eyes that she has fully understood what he feels but has not said. Without a word being spoken, as Maggie stands there, Adam, her father, has a sense "of what he saw her see."

In that silent dialogue, "Her face couldn't keep it from him; she had seen, on top of everything, in her quick way, what they both were seeing."

The unpacking of this brief moment of mutual recognition across a room takes up several pages toward the start of the novel. And the rest of that long tale plays out the aftershock of this single moment of shared understanding, as Adam eventually does remarry.[15]

What Henry James captured so well was the richness of the insights into another's mind that we can get from the merest of perceptions: in a flash, a single expression can tell us volumes. Such social judgments can come so spontaneously in part because the neural circuits that make them seem to always be "on," ever ready to act. Even while the rest of the brain is quiescent, four neural areas remain active, like idling neural motors, poised for quick response. Tellingly, three of these four ready-to-roll areas are involved in making judgments about people.[16] These idling neural zones increase their activity when we think about or see people interact.

A UCLA group led by Marco Iacoboni, a discoverer of mirror neurons, and Matthew Lieberman, a founder of social neuroscience, investigated these zones in an fMRI study.[17] They concluded that the brain's default activity—what happens automatically when nothing much else goes on—seems to be mulling over our relationships.[18]

The higher metabolic rate of these "person-sensitive" networks reveals the special import placed on the social world in the brain's design. Rehashing our social lives may rate as the brain's favorite downtime activity, something like its top-rated TV show. In fact, only when the brain turns to an impersonal task, like balancing a checkbook, do these "people" circuits quiet down.

By contrast, corresponding areas that judge objects have to rev up in order to operate. This may explain why we make judgments about people around a tenth of a second more quickly than we do about things—these parts of the brain have a continual head start. In any social encounter this same circuitry springs into action, making judgments of like or dislike that predict the course of their relationship, or whether there will be one at all.

The progression of brain activity begins with a quick decision involving the cingulate that spreads via spindle cells to heavily linked areas, especially the OFC. These low-road networks extend widely to reverberating circuits throughout the emotional areas. This network stirs a general sense that, with help from the high road, can develop into a more conscious reaction—whether it is an outright action or simply a silent understanding, as it was with Maggie Verver.

The OFC-cingulate circuitry springs into action whenever we choose the best response from many possibilities. This circuitry appraises all we experience, assigning value—liking or disliking—and so it shapes our very sense of meaning, of what matters. This emotional calculus, some now argue, represents the fundamental value system that the brain uses to organize our functioning, if only by deciding our priorities in any given moment. That makes this neural node crucial in our social decision-making—the guesses we continually make that determine our success or failure in relationships.[19]

Consider the staggering brain speed of such realizations in social life. In the first moment of an encounter with someone, these neural areas make their initial judgment pro or con in just one-twentieth of a second.[20]

Then there's the question of how we will react to the person concerned. Once the like-dislike decision registers firmly in the OFC, it guides neural activity there for another fifth of a second. Nearby prefrontal areas, operating in parallel, offer up information about social context, using a more refined sensibility such as what reactions are appropriate to the moment.

The OFC, drawing on data such as context, strikes a balance between a primal impulse (*get out of here*) and what works best (*make an acceptable excuse for leaving*). We experience what the OFC decides not as a conscious understanding of the rules guiding the decision but as a feeling of "rightness."

In short, the OFC helps guide what we do once we know how we feel about someone. By inhibiting raw impulse, the OFC orchestrates actions that serve us well—at the very least, by keeping us from doing or saying something we would regret.

This sequence happens not just once but continually, during any social interaction. Our primary social guiding mechanisms, then, rely on a stream of rough emotional inclinations: if we like her, one repertoire springs into action; if we loathe him, quite another. And should our feelings shift as the interaction goes on, the social brain quietly adjusts what we say and do accordingly.

What goes on during these eyeblinks is crucial for a satisfying social life.

HIGH-ROAD CHOICES

A woman I know tells me how troubling she finds her sister, who because of a mental disorder has become prone to attacks of anger. While at times the two are warm and close, without warning the sister will become sharply adversarial, paranoid in her accusations.

As my friend put it, "Every time I get close to her, she hurts me."

And so my friend has begun to insulate herself against what she experiences as an "emotional assault," by not returning every phone call right away and by not scheduling as much time together with her sister as they used to. And if she hears her sister's voice in an angry tone on her answering machine, she'll wait a day or two before returning her call, to give her time to cool down.

Still, she cares about her sister and wants to stay close. So when they do talk and her sister lashes out, she reminds herself of the mental disorder, which helps her not take the anger so personally. Her inner mental judo shields her from a toxic contagion.

While the automatic nature of emotional contagion makes us vulnerable to coming down with distressing emotions, that is just the beginning of the story. We also have the capacity for making strategic moves to counter contagion as needed. If a relationship itself has become destructive, these mental tactics can create a protective emotional distance.

The low road operates at hyperspeed, in the snap of a finger. But we are not at the mercy of all that comes at us so fast. When the low road's instant linkage pains us, the high road can protect us.

The high road gives us choices largely via wiring in the circuits linked to the OFC. One stream of messages shuttles back and forth to low-road centers that spawn our initial emotional reactions, including simple contagions. Meanwhile the OFC shunts a parallel flow upward to trigger our thoughts about that reaction. That upward branch allows us to make a more nuanced response, one that takes into account a refined understanding of what's going on. These parallel roads manage every encounter, and the OFC is the switching station between them.

The low road, with its ultrarapid mirror neuron links, operates as a sort of sixth sense, prompting us to feel with another person even though we may be only vaguely aware of our attunement. The low road triggers a sympathetic emotional state without an intervening thought: instant primal empathy.

The high road, by contrast, opens up as we monitor such a mood shift and intentionally attend to the person we're talking with, to understand better what has happened. This brings our thinking brain, especially the prefrontal centers, into play. The high road adds enormous flexibility to the far more fixed and limited repertoire of the low road. As the milliseconds tick away and the high road activates its vast array of neural branches, the possibilities for response increase exponentially.

So while the lower route gives us instantaneous emotional affinity, the higher route generates a more sophisticated social sense, which in turn guides an appropriate response. That flexibility draws on the resources of the prefrontal cortex, the brain's executive center.

Prefrontal lobotomies, a psychiatric fad in the 1940s and 1950s, surgically disconnected the OFC from other areas of the brain. (The "surgery" was often primitive, the medical equivalent of inserting a screwdriver alongside the eyeball, slicing into the buttery brain.) At the time neurologists had little idea of the specific functions of the zones of the brain, let alone the OFC. But they found that previously agitated mental patients became placid after a lobotomy, a major plus from the viewpoint of those running the bedlam of vast mental asylums that warehoused psychiatric patients of the day.

While a lobotomized patient's cognitive abilities remained intact, two then-mysterious "side effects" were observed: the patients' emotions were flattened or absent altogether, and they became disoriented in social situations new to them. Today neuroscience knows that that was because the OFC orchestrates the interplay between the social world and how we feel, telling us how to act. Lacking that interpersonal math, the lobotomized patients were utterly confused in any novel social situation.

ECONOMIC ROAD RAGE

Say you and a stranger are given ten dollars to split any way you can agree. The stranger offers you two dollars, take it or leave it. The decision to take it seems perfectly reasonable, as any economist can tell you.

But if you take the two dollars, the person making you the offer gets to keep eight. So reasonable or no, most people become indignant—and, if offered just one dollar, outraged.

That occurs over and over when people play what behavioral economists call the Ultimatum Game, where one partner makes proposals that the other can only accept or reject. If all offers are rejected, both end up with nothing.

A very low offer here can trigger the economic equivalent of road rage.[21] Long used in simulations of economic decision-making, the Ultimatum Game has been merged with social neuroscience through the work of Jonathan Cohen, director of the Center for the Study of Brain, Mind, and Behavior at Princeton University. His group studies partners who are playing the Ultimatum Game while their brains are scanned.

Cohen has pioneered in "neuro-economics," the analysis of the hidden neural forces that drive both rational and irrational decision-making in our economic lives—an arena where the high and low roads both play powerful roles. Much of this research centers on the brain areas that are active during interpersonal situations that have ready implications for understanding the irrational forces that move economic markets.

"If the first guy offers just one dollar," says Cohen, "the other's response might well be 'Go to hell.' But according to standard economic theory, that's irrational, because a dollar is better than nothing. This result drives economists crazy, because their theories assume people will always try to maximize their rewards. In fact, people will sometimes be willing to sacrifice up to a month's salary just to punish an unfair offer."

When the Ultimatum Game is played with only one round, lowball offers often result in anger. But if the players are allowed multiple rounds, then the two are more likely to reach a satisfactory bargain.

The Ultimatum Game does not just pit one person against another; within each of them it creates a tug-of-war at the junction of the high and low roads in their cognitive and emotional systems. The high road relies heavily on the prefrontal cortex, critical for rational thought. The orbitofrontal area, as we have seen, lies at the bottom of the prefrontal area, policing its border with the low road's emotionally impulsive centers like the amygdala, down in the midbrain.

By observing which neural circuits are at work during this microeconomic transaction when high and low roads are at odds, Cohen has been able to separate the influence of the rational prefrontal cortex from the "go to hell" rashness of the low road—in this case, the insula, which can react during certain emotions as strongly as the amygdala. The more powerful the low road's reactivity, Cohen's brain scans show, the less rational will be the players' reactions from the economic perspective. But the more active the prefrontal area, the more balanced will be the outcome.[22]

In an essay called "The Vulcanization of the Brain" (a reference to *Star Trek*'s Mr. Spock, the hyperrational character from planet Vulcan), Cohen focuses on the interaction between high-road abstract neural processing, where information that is valenced pro or con is considered in a careful and deliberative way, and low-road operations, where emotions and predispositions to act rashly run strong. Which prevails, he argues, depends on the forcefulness of the prefrontal area, that mediator of rationality.

Over the course of human brain development, the size of the prefrontal cortex has largely been what set us apart from other primates, which have much smaller prefrontal areas. Unlike other parts of the brain that are specialized for a particular job, this executive center takes a bit more time to do its jobs. But like some all-purpose brainbooster, the prefrontal area is spectacularly flexible, able to engage in a greater range of tasks than any other neural structure.

"The prefrontal cortex," Cohen told me, "has changed the human world so that nothing is the same anymore physically, economically, or socially."

Even as human genius spews a dizzying array of ever-evolving realities—gas guzzlers and oil wars, industrialized farming and overly abundant calories, e-mail and identity theft—our inventive prefrontal circuitry aids us in navigating through the very dangers it has helped create. Many of those perils and temptations stem from the more primal cravings of the low road as it confronts the explosion of opportunities for indulgence and abuse created by the high road. Surviving them depends equally heavily on the high road.

As Cohen put it, "We have more easy access to whatever we desire, like sugar and fat. But we have to balance our short- and long-term interests."

That balance comes via the prefrontal cortex, which wields the power to say no to impulse—squelching that reach for a second round of molten chocolate mousse—or that violent retaliation to a slight.[23] In such moments the high road masters the low.

| N O T O I M P U L S E |

A man in Liverpool, England, diligently played the same numbers in the National Lottery week after week: 14, 17, 22, 24, 42, and 47.

One day while watching television he saw that very sequence of numbers come up as the winner for the two-million-pound prize.

But this week, for once, he had forgotten to renew his ticket on time. It had expired just days before.

Overwhelmed by disappointment, he killed himself.

A news item on that tragedy was cited in a scientific article on the experience of regret over making a poor decision.[24] Such feelings stir in the OFC, driving pangs of remorse and, most likely, the self-recrimination that so unhinged that poor lottery player. But patients with lesions in key circuits of the OFC lack all such feelings of regret; no matter how bad their choice, they are utterly unfazed by missed opportunities.

The OFC exerts a "top-down" modulation of the amygdala, the source of unruly emotional surges and impulses.[25] Like small children, patients who have lesions in these inhibitory circuits typically lose the ability to suppress emotional impulses, unable for example to keep themselves from mimicking someone's scowling face. Lacking this emotional safety device, their rambunctious amygdala has free rein.

These patients are also unfazed by what other people would find mortifying social gaffes. They may greet a total stranger with a hug and a kiss, or make the kind of tasteless bathroom jokes that a three-year-old might find delightful. They blithely reveal the most embarrassing details about themselves to anyone within earshot, unaware of having done anything the least untoward.[26] Even though they can explain rationally the proper social norms for propriety, they are oblivious to those norms as they break them. With the OFC handicapped, the high road seems powerless to guide the low.[27]

The OFC also goes awry this way in those war veterans who, on seeing a battle scene on the evening news or hearing a truck backfire, are flooded with traumatic memories from their own wartime nightmares. The culprit is an overactive amygdala, one that sends surges of panic in mistaken reaction to cues vaguely reminiscent of the original trauma. Ordinarily the OFC would evaluate such primal feelings of fear and clarify that it's just a television show or a truck we're hearing rather than enemy guns.

While it is kept in line by high-road systems, the amygdala cannot play the brain's bad boy. The OFC contains one of the array of neurons that can inhibit those amygdala-driven surges, that can just say no to limbic impulses. As low-road circuitry sends up primitive emotional impulses (*I feel like yelling,* or *She's making me so nervous I want to get out of here*), the OFC evaluates them in terms of a more sophisticated understanding of the moment (*This is a library,* or *It's only our first date*) and modulates them accordingly, acting as an emotional brake.

When those brakes falter, we act inappropriately. Consider the results from a study where college students who did not know each other came to a lab and were "virtually" put together in pairs in an online chat room to get acquainted.[28] About one in five of these Internet conversations quickly became startlingly sexual, with explicit terms, graphic discussions of sex acts, and outright solicitation of sex.

But when the experimenter who conducted these sessions later read the transcripts, he was astounded. As far as he had seen while escorting the students in and out of the cubicles, they all had been low key, unassuming, and invariably polite—completely out of keeping with their uninhibited licentiousness online.

Presumably none would have dared plunge into such blatantly sexual talk had they instead been having a live, face-to-face conversation with someone they had met only minutes before. That is just the point: during in-person interactions we loop, getting an ongoing flow of feedback, mainly from the person's facial expressions and tone of voice, which instantly tell us when we are on track and off.

Something like the out-of-place sex talk in the lab has been documented ever since the earliest years of the Internet: "flaming," in which adults make childishly offensive comments online.[29] Ordinarily the high road keeps us within bounds. But the Internet lacks the sort of feedback the OFC needs to help us stay on track socially.

| **O N   S E C O N D   T H O U G H T** |

How sad. That poor woman standing there all alone, in front of that church, sobbing. The funeral must be going on inside. She must miss horribly whomever she's lost. . . .

On second thought, that's not a funeral. There's a white limo decorated with pretty flowers in front of the church—it's a wedding! How sweet . . .

Such were the thoughts of a woman as she studied the photo of a woman weeping by a church. Her first glimpse suggested to her the scene of a funeral, and she felt herself fill with sadness, her eyes welling up with tears in sympathy.

But her second thought changed the photo's impact entirely. Seeing the woman as attending a wedding and imagining that happy scene morphed her own sadness into delight. As we alter our perceptions, we can change our emotions.

That small fact of everyday life has been deconstructed into brain mechanics via a brain imaging study done by Kevin Ochsner.[30] Just thirty-something, Ochsner has already become a leading figure in this fledgling discipline. When I visited him in his neatly arranged office, an oasis of order in Schermerhorn Hall, the musty rabbit warren that houses Columbia's psychology department, he explained his methods.

In Ochsner's research a volunteer at Columbia's fMRI Research Center lies perfectly still on a gurney in the long, dark tube of an MRI machine. That willing soul wears what looks like a birdcage placed over his head; it detects radio waves emitted by atoms in the brain. A semblance of human contact comes via a mirror artfully placed at a forty-five-degree angle over the cage that reflects an image projected from the far end of the gurney, where the subject's feet stick out of the massive device.[31]

It's hardly a natural setting, but the setup renders meticulous maps of how the brain reacts to specific stimulus, be it a photo of someone in abject terror or, via earphones, a baby's laugh. Imaging studies using these methods have allowed neuroscientists to chart with unprecedented precision the zones of the brain that intertwine in orchestrated action during the vast variety of person-to-person encounters.

In Ochsner's study women saw a photo, letting their first thoughts and feelings wash through them. Then they were instructed to purposely rethink what might be happening, reconceiving the scene in a way that would be less distressing.

And so came the shift of scene from a funeral to a wedding. With that second thought, the woman's neural mechanisms damped down the emotional centers that had made her feel sadness. More specifically, the neural sequence went something like this: the right amygdala, a trigger point for distressing emotions, made an automatic, ultraquick emotional appraisal of what was happening in the photo—a funeral—and activated the circuitry for sadness.

That first emotional response happens so quickly and spontaneously that as the amygdala triggers its reactions and activates other brain areas, the cortical centers for thinking have not yet even finished analyzing the situation. Along with the amygdala's hair-trigger feelings, systems bridging emotional and cognitive centers verify and refine that reaction, further adding emotional flavor to what we perceive. And so we form our first impression (How sad— she's crying at a funeral).

The intentional reappraisal of the photo (It's a wedding, not a funeral) replaced the initial thought with a new one and the first flood of negative feeling with a happier dose, initiating a cascade of mechanisms that quieted the amygdala and related circuits. The more involved the ACC, Ochsner's study suggests, the more successful the rethinking is in altering moods for the better. In addition, the greater the activity in certain prefrontal areas, the more muted the amygdala became during the reappraisal.[32] When the high road speaks up, it takes away the low road's microphone.

When we intentionally relate to a disturbing situation, the high road can manage the amygdala through any of several prefrontal circuits. The specific mental strategy we deploy during reappraisal determines which of these circuits activates. One prefrontal circuit stirs when we view another person's distress—like the suffering of a severely ill patient—in an objective, clinically detached way, as though we had no personal connection (the strategy typical of those in the health professions).

A different circuit activates when we reappraise the patient's situation, for example by hoping for the best and reflecting that the patient is not mortally ill, has a strong constitution, and will most likely recover.[33] By changing the meaning of what we perceive, we also alter its emotional impact. As Marcus Aurelius said millennia ago, pain "is not due to the thing itself, but to your estimate of it, and this you have the power to revoke at any moment."

The emerging data on reappraisal offer a corrective to a widespread misimpression: that we have virtually no choice in our mental life because so much of what we think, feel, and do rushes by automatically, in a "blink."[34]

"The idea that it's all done 'on automatic' is depressing," Ochsner observes. "Reappraisal alters our emotional response. When we do it intentionally, we gain conscious control of our emotions."

Even just naming for ourselves the emotions we feel can calm the amygdala.[35] Such reappraisal has a host of implications for our relationships. For one thing, it affirms our capacity to reconsider knee-jerk negative reactions to someone, to more thoughtfully appraise the situation, and to replace an ill-considered attitude with one that better serves us—and the other person.

The high road to choice also means we are free to respond as we like, even to unwanted contagion.[36] Rather than, say, being flooded by someone who is hysterical with fear, we can stay cool and come to their rescue. If someone simmers with agitation that we would rather not share, we can buffer ourselves against contagion, resolutely remaining in our preferred mood.

The full panoply of life engages us with endless permutations. In reacting to any of them, the low road offers a first choice, but the high can decide where we end up.

REENGINEERING THE LOW ROAD

David Guy was sixteen when he suffered his first bout of stage fright. It happened in English class, when David's teacher asked him to read his weekly composition aloud.

What flooded David's mind at the very thought were images of his classmates. Though David already wanted to become a writer and was experimenting with new techniques, his classmates cared nothing for writing. They had the typical adolescent scorn for pretense, and their sarcasm was merciless.

David was desperate to avoid what he imagined would be their inevitable criticism and mockery. And so he found himself unable to speak a word. His stage fright was paralyzing: his face flushed, his palms were sweating, and his heart beat so rapidly he couldn't catch his breath. The harder he tried, the tighter the grip of panic.

The stage fright stayed with him. Though he was nominated for class president his senior year, he declined when he realized that acceptance would mean he'd have to give a speech. Even years later, after he published his first novel while in his thirties, David still found himself avoiding public speaking, declining offers to do readings from his novel.[37]

David Guy has ample company in his dread of public speaking. Surveys show it to be the most common of all phobias, claimed by one in five Americans. But the fear of getting up in front of an audience is only one of many forms taken by "social phobia," as the psychiatric diagnostic manual dubs these anxieties in public situations. Other forms range from meeting new people or talking with a stranger to eating in public or using a shared restroom.

And as it did with David, the first episode often occurs in adolescence, though the fear remains lifelong. People go to great ends to avoid the dreaded situation, as the very prospect of the feared setting provokes a flood of anxiety.

Stage fright like David's can have remarkable biological power. The mind's eye need only picture the scorn of an audience, and the amygdala activates, making the body respond with an overwhelming blitz of stress hormones. David's merely imagining his classmates' scorn was enough to activate this physiological storm.

Such learned fears are acquired in part in circuitry centering on the amygdala, which Joseph LeDoux likes to call the brain's "Fear Central."[38] LeDoux knows the neural terrain of the amygdala intimately; he's been studying this clump of neurons for decades at the Center for Neural Science at New York University. The cells in the amygdala where sensory information registers, and the adjacent areas that acquire fear, LeDoux has discovered, actually fire in new patterns at the moment a fear has been learned.[39]

Our memories are in part reconstructions. Whenever we retrieve a memory, the brain rewrites it a bit, updating the past according to our present concerns and understanding. At the cellular level, LeDoux explains, retrieving a memory means it will be "reconsolidated," slightly altered chemically by a new protein synthesis that will help store it anew after being updated.[40]

Thus each time we bring a memory to mind, we adjust its very chemistry: the next time we retrieve it, that memory will come up as we last modified it. The specifics of the new consolidation depend on what we learn as we recall it. If we merely have a flare-up of the same fear, we deepen our fearfulness.

But the high road can bring reason to the low. If at the time of the fear we tell ourselves something that eases its grip, then the same memory becomes reencoded with less power over us. Gradually, we can bring the once-feared memory to mind without feeling the rush of distress all over again. In such a case, says LeDoux, the cells in our amygdala reprogram so that we lose the original fear conditioning.[41] One goal of therapy, then, can be seen as gradually altering the neurons for learned fear.[42]

Treatments sometimes actually expose the person to whatever primes their fear. Exposure sessions begin with getting the person relaxed, often through a few minutes of slow abdominal breathing. Then the person confronts the threatening situation, in a careful gradation culminating in the very worst version.

One New York City traffic officer confided that she had flown into a rage at a motorist who called her a "low-life bitch." So in her exposure therapy that phrase was repeated to her, first in a flat tone, then with increasing emotional intensity, and finally with added obscene gestures. The exposure succeeds when, no matter how obnoxious the repeated phrase, she can stay relaxed—and presumably when back on the street she can calmly write a traffic ticket despite insults.[43]

Sometimes therapists go to great lengths to re-create the scene that triggers a social anxiety, albeit in the safety of therapy. One cognitive therapist known for his expertise in treating anxiety uses therapy groups as a trial audience for patients overcoming their fear of speaking in public.[44] The patient rehearses both relaxation methods and counterthoughts to challenge anxiety-provoking ones. Meanwhile the therapist coaches the group to act in ways that will be particularly difficult for the patient, from making snide comments to looking bored or disapproving.

To be sure, the intensity of the exposure must be kept within the limits of what the patient can handle. One woman about to face such a hostile audience excused herself to go to the ladies' room— where she locked the door and refused to come out. She was eventually coaxed to continue her treatment.

Simply reviewing something painful from the past with someone who helps us see a different perspective, LeDoux suggests, can gradually loosen some of the distress by reencoding disturbing memories. This may be one reason for the relief that can come when client and therapist rehash troubles: the talk itself may alter the way the brain registers what's wrong.

Says LeDoux, "It's something like what happens naturally when we churn a worry over in our mind, and come to a new perspective." We use the high road to reengineer the low.[45]

---| THE SOCIAL BRAIN |---

As any neuroscientist will tell you, the phrase "the social brain" does not refer to a phrenology bump or some specific brain nodule. Rather, it refers to the particular set of circuitry that is orchestrated as people relate to each other.[46] Though some brain structures play an especially large role in handling relationships, no major zone appears to be exclusively devoted to social life.[47]

This wide dispersion of neural responsibility for our social life, some speculate, may be due to the fact that only with the arrival of primates, toward the end of Nature's sculpting of the brain in ancient prehistory, did social groups become a vital part of our repertoire for survival. In creating a system to manage this late-blooming opportunity, Nature seems to have made do with the brain structures that were available at the time, melding together from preexisting parts a cohesive set of pathways to handle the challenges of these complex relationships.

The brain draws on any given piece of anatomy for countless tasks. But thinking about brain activity in terms of a specific function, like social interaction, offers neuroscientists a rough way to sort out the otherwise daunting complexity of the 100 billion neurons with their roughly 100 trillion interconnections—the thickest density of connectivity known to science. Those neurons are organized into modules that behave something like an intricate swinging mobile, where activity in any one part can reverberate through the whole system.

A further complication: Nature economizes. For instance, serotonin is a neurotransmitter that generates feelings of well-being in the brain. The SSRI (for selective serotonin reuptake inhibitor) antidepressants are known to raise the level of serotonin available, so lifting mood. But the very same substance, serotonin, also regulates the gut. About 95 percent of the body's serotonin occurs in the digestive tract, where seven different kinds of serotonin receptors manage activities ranging from starting the flow of digestive enzymes to moving things through the bowels.[48]

Just as the identical molecule can regulate both digestion and happiness, virtually all the neural tracts that combine in the social brain handle a range of activities. But when they work together, say, to execute a face-to-face interaction, the far-flung networks of the social brain create a common neural conduit.[49]

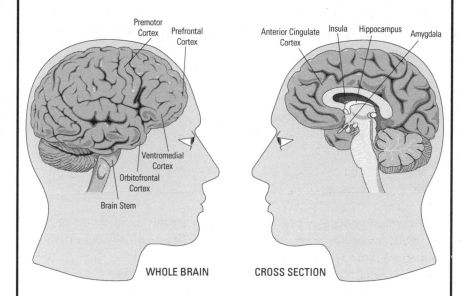

Premotor Cortex   Prefrontal Cortex   Anterior Cingulate Cortex   Insula   Hippocampus   Amygdala

Ventromedial Cortex   Orbitofrontal Cortex   Brain Stem

WHOLE BRAIN   CROSS SECTION

Some principal areas in the neural circuitry of the social brain.

Most of the mapping of the social brain has been through imaging. But like a tourist in Paris for only a few days, brain imaging of necessity concentrates on areas of immediate interest rather than visiting every landmark. That means a sacrifice in fine details. So while, for instance, fMRI images highlight a social superhighway connecting the orbitofrontal cortex and the amygdala, they miss the specifics of the fourteen or so separate nuclei in the amygdala, each of which has different functions. Much remains to be learned in this new science [see Appendix B for more details].

What Is Social Intelligence?

Three twelve-year-olds are heading to a soccer field for gym class. Two athletic-looking boys are walking behind—and snickering at—the third, a somewhat chubby classmate.

"So you're going to *try* to play soccer," one of the two says sarcastically to the third, his voice dripping with contempt.

It's a moment that, given the social code of these middle-school boys, can easily escalate into a fight.

The chubby boy closes his eyes for a moment and takes a deep breath, as though steeling himself for the confrontation that lies ahead.

Then he turns to the other two and replies, in a calm, matter-of-fact voice, "Yeah, I'm going to try—but I'm not very good at it."

After a pause, he adds, "But I'm great at art—show me anything, and I can draw it real good. . . ."

Then, pointing to his antagonist, he says, "Now you—*you're* great at soccer, really fantastic! I'd like to be that good someday, but I'm just not. Maybe I can get a little better at it if I keep trying."

At that, the first boy, his disdain now utterly disarmed, says in a friendly tone, "Well, you're not really *that* bad. Maybe I can show you a few things about how to play."

That short interaction offers a masterly display of social intelligence in action.[1] What could easily have led to a fight might now flower into a friendship. The chubby artist held his own—not just in the turbulent social currents of middle school but in a far more subtle struggle: in an invisible tug-of-war between the brains of the two boys.

By keeping cool, the aspiring artist resisted the pull to anger from the other's sarcastic taunt and instead brought the other boy into his own more friendly emotional range. It's a display of the highest order of neural jujitsu, transforming the boys' shared emotional chemistry from a hostile range to a positive one—sheer relationship brilliance.

"Social intelligence shows itself abundantly in the nursery, on the playground, in barracks and factories and salesrooms, but it eludes the formal standardized conditions of the testing laboratory." So observed Edward Thorndike, the Columbia University psychologist who first proposed the concept, in a 1920 article in *Harper's Monthly Magazine*.[2] Thorndike noted that such interpersonal effectiveness was of vital importance for success in many fields, particularly leadership. "The best mechanic in a factory," he wrote, "may fail as a foreman for lack of social intelligence."[3]

But by the late 1950s David Wechsler, the influential psychologist who created what still remains one of the most widely used measures of IQ, had dismissed social intelligence, seeing it merely as "general intelligence applied to social situations."[4]

Now, a half-century later, "social intelligence" has become ripe for rethinking as neuroscience begins to map the brain areas that regulate interpersonal dynamics [see Appendix C for details].

A fuller understanding of social intelligence requires us to include "noncognitive" aptitudes—the talent, for instance, that lets a sensitive nurse calm a crying toddler with just the right reassuring touch, without having to think for a moment about what to do.

Psychologists argue about which human abilities are social and which are emotional. Small wonder: the two domains intermingle, just as the brain's social real estate overlaps with its emotional centers.[5] "All emotions are social," as Richard Davidson, director of the Laboratory for Affective Neuroscience at the University of Wisconsin, observes. "You can't separate the cause of an emotion from the world of relationships—our social interactions are what drive our emotions."

My own model of emotional intelligence folded in social intelligence without making much of that fact, as do other theorists in the field.[6] But as I've come to see, simply lumping social intelligence within the emotional sort stunts fresh thinking about the human aptitude for relationship, ignoring what transpires as we interact.[7] This myopia leaves the "social" part out of intelligence.

The ingredients of social intelligence I propose here can be organized into two broad categories: social awareness, what we sense about others—and social facility, what we then do with that awareness.

SOCIAL INTELLIGENCE

Social Awareness

Social awareness refers to a spectrum that runs from instantaneously sensing another's inner state, to understanding her feelings and thoughts, to "getting" complicated social situations. It includes:

- *Primal empathy:* Feeling with others; sensing nonverbal emotional signals.
- *Attunement:* Listening with full receptivity; attuning to a person.
- *Empathic accuracy:* Understanding another person's thoughts, feelings, and intentions.
- *Social cognition:* Knowing how the social world works.

Social Facility

Simply sensing how another feels, or knowing what they think or intend, does not guarantee fruitful interactions. Social facility builds on social awareness to allow smooth, effective interactions. The spectrum of social facility includes:

- *Synchrony:* Interacting smoothly at the nonverbal level.
- *Self-presentation:* Presenting ourselves effectively.
- *Influence:* Shaping the outcome of social interactions.
- *Concern:* Caring about others' needs and acting accordingly.

Both the social awareness and social facility domains range from basic, low-road capacities, to more complex high-road articulations. For instance, synchrony and primal empathy are purely low-road capacities, while empathic accuracy and influence mingle high and low. And as "soft" as some of these skills may seem, there are already a surprising number of tests and scales to assess them.

| P R I M A L E M P A T H Y |

The man had come to an embassy for a visa. As they talked, the interviewer noticed something strange: when asked why he wanted the visa, a momentary look of disgust flitted across the man's face.

Alerted, the interviewer asked the applicant to wait a few minutes and went to another room to consult an Interpol data bank. The man's name popped up as a fugitive, wanted by police in several countries.

The interviewer's detection of that fleeting expression shows a gift for primal empathy, the ready ability to sense the emotions of another. A low-road capacity, this variety of empathy occurs—or fails to—rapidly and automatically. Neuroscientists see this intuitive, gut-level empathy as largely activated by mirror neurons.[8]

Even though we can stop talking, we cannot stop sending signals (our tone of voice, our fleeting expressions) about what we feel. Even when people try to suppress all signs of their emotions, feelings have a way of leaking anyway. In this sense, when it comes to emotions, we cannot *not* communicate.

An apt test of primal empathy would assess the low road's rapid, spontaneous reading of these nonverbal clues. To do that well, such a test must have us react to a depiction of another person.

I first encountered one such test while struggling with my dissertation research. Two other graduate students just down the hall from my travails, I recall, seemed to be having far more fun. One was Judith Hall, who is now a professor at Northeastern University; the other was Dane Archer, now at the University of California at Santa Cruz. Back then they were students of Robert Rosenthal in social psychology. The two were in the midst of making a set of videotapes, starring Hall, that are now among the most widely used measures of interpersonal sensitivity.

Archer videotaped, while Hall re-created situations ranging from returning a faulty item to a store to talking about the death of a friend. The test, dubbed the Profile of Nonverbal Sensitivity (PONS), asks people to guess what's going on emotionally from seeing a two-second snippet of a given scene.[9] For example, they might see a snippet showing only Hall's face or only her body, or they might hear just her voice.

Those workers who do well on the PONS tend to be rated as more interpersonally sensitive by their peers or supervisors. Such clinicians and teachers get higher job performance ratings. If they are physicians, their patients are more satisfied with their medical care;

if they are teachers, they are seen as more effective. Across the board, such people are liked more.

Women tend to do a bit better on this dimension of empathy than men, scoring about three percent higher on average. No matter what our ability may be now, empathy seems to improve with time, honed by the circumstances of life. For example, women with toddlers are better at nonverbal decoding than their agemates who are childless. But nearly everyone improves from early adolescence into their mid-twenties.

Another measure of primal empathy, the Reading the Mind in the Eyes test, was designed by Simon Baron-Cohen, an expert on autism, and his research group at Cambridge University.[10] (Three images from the thirty-six in the complete test are on the facing page.)

Those who score at the high end in reading messages from the eyes will be gifted at empathy—and in any role that demands it, from diplomacy and police work to nursing and psychotherapy. Those who do poorly in the extreme are likely to have autism.

| ATTUNEMENT |

Attunement is attention that goes beyond momentary empathy to a full, sustained presence that facilitates rapport. We offer a person our total attention and listen fully. We seek to understand the other person rather than just making our own point.

Such deep listening seems to be a natural aptitude. Still, as with all social intelligence dimensions, people can improve their attunement skills.[11] And we all can facilitate attunement simply by intentionally paying more attention.

A person's style of speaking offers clues to their underlying ability to listen deeply. During moments of genuine connection, what we say will be responsive to what the other feels, says, and does. When we are poorly connected, however, our communications become verbal bullets: our message does not change to fit the other person's state but simply reflects our own. Listening makes the difference. Talking *at* a person rather than listening *to* him reduces a conversation to a monologue.

When I hijack a conversation by talking at you, I'm fulfilling my needs without considering yours. Real listening, in contrast, requires me to attune to your feelings, let you have your say, and allow the conversation to follow a course we mutually determine. Two-way listening makes a dialogue reciprocal, with each person adjusting what they say in keeping with how the other responds and feels.

Guess which of the four adjectives surrounding each pair of eyes most accurately describes what the eyes are communicating:

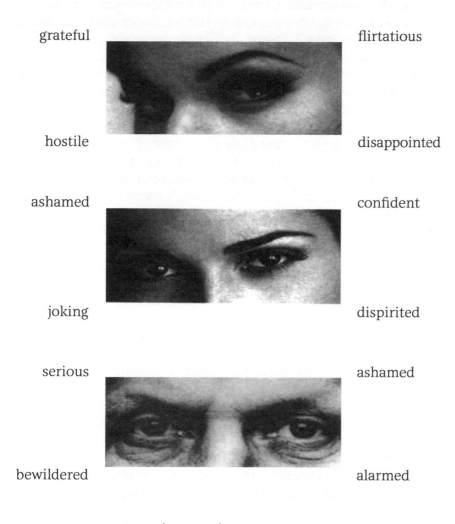

grateful   flirtatious

hostile   disappointed

ashamed   confident

joking   dispirited

serious   ashamed

bewildered   alarmed

Answers: flirtatious, confident, serious

This agendaless presence can be seen, surprisingly, in many top-performing sales people and client managers. Stars in these fields do not approach a customer or client with the determination to make a sale; rather they see themselves as consultants of sorts, whose task is first to listen and understand the client's needs—and only then match what they have to those needs. Should they not have what's best, they'll say so—or even take a client's side in making a justified complaint about their own company. They would rather cultivate a relationship where their advice is trusted than torpedo their reliability just to make a sale.[12]

Listening well has been found to distinguish the best managers, teachers, and leaders.[13] Among those who are in the helping professions, like physicians or social workers, such deep listening numbers among the top three abilities of those whose work has been rated as outstanding by their organizations.[14] Not only do they take the time to listen and so attune to the other person's feelings; they also ask questions to better understand the person's background situation—not just the immediate problem or diagnosis at hand.

Full attention, so endangered in this age of multitasking, is blunted whenever we split our focus. Self-absorption and preoccupations shrink our focus, so that we are less able to notice other people's feelings and needs, let alone respond with empathy. Our capacity for attunement suffers, snuffing out rapport.

But full presence does not demand that much from us. "A five-minute conversation can be a perfectly meaningful human moment," an article in the *Harvard Business Review* notes. "To make it work, you have to set aside what you are doing, put down the memo you were reading, disengage from your laptop, abandon your daydream, and focus on the person you're with."[15]

Full listening maximizes physiological synchrony, so that emotions align.[16] Such synchrony was discovered during psychotherapy at moments when clients felt most understood by their therapists (as described in Chapter 2). Intentionally paying more attention to someone may be the best way to encourage the emergence of rapport. Listening carefully, with undivided attention, orients our neural circuits for connectivity, putting us on the same wavelength. That maximizes the likelihood that the other essential ingredients for rapport—synchrony and positive feelings—might bloom.

EMPATHIC ACCURACY

Empathic accuracy represents, some argue, *the* essential expertise in social intelligence. As William Ickes, the University of Texas psychologist who has pioneered this line of research, contends, this ability distinguishes "the most tactful advisors, the most diplomatic officials, the most effective negotiators, the most electable politicians, the most productive salespersons, the most successful teachers, and the most insightful therapists."[17]

Empathic accuracy builds on primal empathy but adds an explicit understanding of what someone else feels and thinks. These cognitive steps engage additional activity in the neocortex, particularly the prefrontal area—so bringing high-road circuitry to the primal empathy of the low.[18]

We can measure empathic accuracy through psychology's equivalent of hidden-camera television. Two volunteers for an experiment come into a waiting room and are seated together on a couch. A research assistant asks them to wait a few minutes while he tries to find some missing bit of equipment.

To pass the time, the two chat a bit. After approximately six minutes the assistant comes back, and they expect to start. But the experiment has *already* begun: while they thought they were merely waiting, the two were secretly being videotaped from a camera concealed in a closet.

Then each participant is sent to a separate room, where they watch the six-minute video. There they write down a record of their thoughts and feelings at key points in the tape—and what they suspect the other person was thinking and feeling at those points. That sneaky form of research has been repeated in university psychology departments across the United States and around the world, to test one's ability to infer another person's unspoken thoughts and feelings.[19]

For example, one participant reported that she had felt silly while conversing because she couldn't remember the name of one of her teachers; her partner accurately guessed that "she was maybe feeling sort of odd" at the lapse. On the other hand, in a classic college-years gaffe, one woman was idly recalling a stage play, but her male partner guessed, "She was wondering if I would ask her out."

Empathic accuracy seems to be one key to a successful marriage, especially in the early years. Couples who during the first year or two of their marriage are more accurate in their readings of each other have higher levels of satisfaction, and their marriage is more likely to last.[20] A deficit in such accuracy bodes poorly: one sign of a rockier relationship can be read when a partner realizes the other feels bad but has no clue as to what exactly might be on their mind.[21]

As the discovery of mirror neurons revealed, our brain attunes us to what someone intends to do, but it does so at a subliminal level. Conscious awareness of someone's intentions allows for more accurate empathy, so we can better predict what that person will do. A more explicit understanding of underlying motives can mean the difference between life and death if, for example, we are face to face with a mugger—or with an angry crowd, as was the case with those soldiers approaching the mosque described in the tale that begins this book.

| SOCIAL COGNITION |

Social cognition, the fourth aspect of interpersonal awareness, is knowledge about how the social world actually works.[22] People adept at this variety of cognition know what's expected in most any social situation, such as the manners appropriate in a five-star restaurant. And they are adept at semiotics, decoding the social signals that reveal, for example, who might be the most powerful person in a group.

Such social savvy can be seen in those who accurately read the political currents of an organization, as well as in the five-year-old who can list the best friends of every child in her kindergarten class. The social lessons we learned about playground politics in school—like how to make friends and form alliances—are on a continuum with the unspoken rules we follow in building a winning work team or playing office politics.

One way social cognition can manifest is in the ability to find solutions to social dilemmas such as how to seat rivals at a dinner party or how to make friends after moving to a new city. The best social solutions come most readily to those who can gather the relevant information and think through solutions most clearly. The chronic inability to solve social problems not only confounds relationships, but is a complicating factor in psychological difficulties ranging from depression to schizophrenia.[23]

We mobilize social cognition to navigate the interpersonal world's subtle and shifting currents and to make sense of social events. It can make the difference in understanding why a remark that one person sees as witty banter may seem insulting sarcasm to another. With poor social cognition, we may fail to recognize why someone seems embarrassed or that someone's offhand comment will be taken as a slight by a third party. Understanding the unspoken norms that govern interaction is crucial for smooth interactions with someone from a different culture, where norms can differ markedly from those we learned in our own group.

This knack for interpersonal knowledge has been understood as a bedrock dimension of social intelligence for decades. Some theorists have even argued that social cognition, in the sense of general intelligence applied to the social world, is the only true component of social intelligence. But this view focusing solely in terms of what we know *about* the interpersonal world ignores what we actually *do* while interacting with people. The result has been measures of social intelligence that test our knowledge of social situations but ignore how we fare in them—a rather blatant failing.[24] Someone bright at social cognition, but who lacks the basics of social facility, will still be painfully awkward with people.

The social awareness abilities interact: empathic accuracy builds on listening and primal empathy; all three enhance social cognition. And interpersonal awareness in all its guises provides the foundation for social facility, the second part of social intelligence.[25]

| S Y N C H R O N Y |

Synchrony lets us glide gracefully through a nonverbal dance with another person. The foundation of social facility, it is the bedrock on which other aspects build. A failure in synchrony sabotages social competence, throwing interactions off-kilter.

The neural capacity for synchrony resides in low-road systems like oscillators and mirror neurons. Getting in synch demands that we both read nonverbal cues instantaneously and act on them smoothly—without having to think about it. The nonverbal signs of synchrony include the range of harmoniously orchestrated interactions, from smiling or nodding at just the right moment to simply orienting our body toward the other person.[26] Those who fail to get in synch may, instead, fidget nervously, freeze, or simply be oblivious to their failure to keep step in the nonverbal duet.

When one person botches synchrony, the other feels uneasy—never mind getting anywhere near rapport. People who fare poorly at this social ability typically suffer from "dyssemia," a deficit in reading—and so acting on—the nonverbal signs that guide smooth interactions.[27] The outward indicators of this subtle social disability are all too obvious: dyssemic people are "off," oblivious to cues that, for example, a conversation is ending. They unsettle those they interact with because they fail to observe the unspoken signs that keep two-way traffic unsnarled.

Dyssemia has been studied most intensively in children, largely because it plagues so many who end up as social rejects in school.[28] A child who has this problem may, for instance, fail to look at people who are speaking to them, stand too close while talking with someone, have facial expressions inappropriate for their emotional state, or seem tactless and insensitive to how others feel. While all these may seem simply signs of "being a kid," most other children of the same age will not have these difficulties.[29]

In adults, dyssemia shows up in similarly out-of-synch behavior.[30] The social blind spots that plague dyssemic children make for troubled relations in the adult world, from the inability to follow nonverbal cues to difficulty in starting new relationships. Moreover, dyssemia can torpedo navigating the social expectations placed on an adult hired for a job. Dyssemic adults often end up socially isolated.

These social deficits are usually not caused by neurological conditions like Asperger's syndrome or autism (which I discuss in Chapter 9). An estimated 85 percent of those with dyssemia have the deficit because they failed to learn how to read nonverbal signals or how to respond to them, either because they did not interact enough with their peers or because their family did not display a given range of emotion or followed eccentric social norms. Another 10 percent or so have the deficit because an emotional trauma short-circuited the necessary learning. Only an estimated 5 percent have a diagnosable neurological disorder.[31]

Because dyssemia stems from a failure to learn, remedial programs have been developed—both for children and for adults—that are geared to teach these skills.[32] The tutorials begin by making the person aware of the nonverbal ingredients of synchrony that usually flit by out of their awareness, like gestures and posture, the use of touch, eye contact, tone of voice, and pacing. Once the person learns the more effective ways to use these ingredients, they practice them until, say, they can maintain eye contact while talking to someone without having to make any special effort.

Getting into synch naturally gives rise to emotional resonance.[33] But, since the low-road brain systems that create synchrony operate out of our awareness and spontaneously, self-conscious attempts to control them can impede their smooth operation. Thus people in remedial programs need to "overlearn" by practicing to the point where the new, more harmonious response comes spontaneously.

| S E L F - P R E S E N T A T I O N |

Professional actors are especially clever at self-presentation, or the ability to present oneself in ways that make a desired impression. In 1980, when Ronald Reagan was running for the Republican presidential nomination, he participated in a televised debate among the candidates. At one point the time-keeping moderator cut off Reagan's microphone before he had finished making a point. Reagan reacted by leaping to his feet, grabbing another microphone, and declaring in angry tones, "I paid for this show. I'm paying for this microphone."

The crowd cheered this display of raw assertiveness—especially in a man better known for his geniality—and the moment has been cited as a turning point in his campaign. Later, a campaign adviser confessed that the seemingly spontaneous outburst had actually been planned, should a likely moment arise.[34]

Charisma is one aspect of self-presentation. The charisma of a powerful public speaker, or a great teacher or leader, comprises their ability to spark in us the emotions they exude, entraining us to that emotional spectrum. We witness such emotional contagion writ large while watching a charismatic figure entrance a crowd.[35] Charismatic people have a flair for expressivity that engages others to come into synchrony with their rhythm and catch their feelings.[36]

Charisma appears at peak form in a speaker who can "play" an audience, making a conceptual point with just the right emotional mix for maximum impact. Entertainers use timing and rhythmic cadence—heightening and lowering the amplitude of their voice on just the right beat—to entrain their audience. They become senders of emotion, while their audience is the recipient of this contagion. But that takes skill.

A certain college student was well liked by her peers for her animated energy. She was remarkably open with her own feelings, and her expressivity let her make friends easily. But her professor had a different impression. In his large lecture class, she was noticeable for her outbursts: she would gasp with delight or make sounds of disgust, offering an ongoing commentary of pleasure or antipathy at the various points he made. A few times she was so overcome by her emotions that she had to leave the classroom.

Her professor's assessment was that she had exuberant expressivity, but also gaps in self-control. Her animated energy served her well in many social settings but not where some degree of reserve was needed.

The ability to "control and mask" the expression of emotions is sometimes considered key to self-presentation. People adept in such control are self-confident in just about any social situation, possessed of savoir faire. Those for whom poised performances come easily will be naturals at any situation where a nuanced response is crucial, from sales and service to diplomacy and politics.

Women by and large are more expressive emotionally than men, but in some situations women may need to balance expressiveness with the constraints of self-presentation. To the extent that social norms devalue expressiveness, as is the case in most workplaces, women need to contain the urge in order to fit in. Our society has subtle norms for who "should" express what emotions, implicitly constraining both men and women. In private life, women are generally perceived as more appropriately expressing fear and sadness, and men anger—a norm that tacitly approves of a woman crying openly but frowns on men shedding tears when upset.[37]

In professional situations, however, the taboo against crying extends to women. And when a woman holds a position of power, the prohibition on showing anger evaporates. On the contrary, a powerful leader is expected to display anger when a group's goal has been frustrated. Alpha women, it seems, meet the entrance requirement. Regardless of whether anger is the most effective response in a given moment, it does not seem *socially* out of place when it comes from the boss.

Some people are all self-presentation, with no substance to back it up. The varieties of social intelligence are no substitute for the other kinds of expertise that a given role may call for. As I overheard one businessman say to another over lunch while we shared seats at a Manhattan sushi bar, "He's got that ability to make people like him. But you couldn't pick a worse person—he's got no follow-up tech skills."

| I N F L U E N C E |

The Cadillac was double-parked on a narrow, tree-lined street in one of Manhattan's better neighborhoods, blocking cars from exiting their parking spaces. A parking enforcement officer was in the midst of writing a ticket for the Caddy.

Suddenly came an anguished and angry yell: "Hey! What the hell do you think you're doing?" The Cadillac's driver, a well-groomed middle-aged man in a business suit, was shouting as he emerged from a laundry with his dry cleaning.

"I'm just doing my job. You're double-parked," the ticket-writer responded, with measured calmness.

"You can't do this to me! I know the mayor! I'm going to get you fired!" the Caddy driver threatened, furious.

"Why don't you just take the ticket and get out of here before I call the tow truck?" the officer replied evenly.

The driver grabbed the ticket, got in his car, and drove away, still muttering.

The very best police officers are adept at exercising influence, in the sense of constructively shaping the outcome of an interaction, using tact and self-control. Paragons of law enforcement use the least force necessary, though they may make a strong show of force to back it up. They approach volatile people with a professional demeanor, calmly and attentively.

And as a result they have more success at getting people to comply. For example, certain New York traffic cops who use the least-force approach report the fewest incidents with angry motorists that escalate into violence. Such officers can simply note how their body reacts to a motorist's disrespect—an ominous sign of a shift in power between the two—and calmly but firmly assert their authority with a professional demeanor. The alternative, letting those gut reactions dictate their response, would lead to meltdown.[38]

Strong force, if wisely applied, can be an efficient tactic for resolving—or better, avoiding—conflict. But the skillful use of an implicit threat of physical aggression lies not in the application of force itself but in neural mechanisms that fine-tune a response to best fit the circumstances. It combines self-control (modulating an aggressive impulse) with empathy (reading the other person to gauge what the least force necessary might be) and with social cognition (recognizing the operative norms in a situation). Educating the underlying neural circuitry has been an unrecognized task of those who train people in the artful use of force, whether civilian or military. As someone becomes increasingly adept in applying the means of violence, a parallel inhibition of aggressive urges becomes essential.

In everyday social encounters, we draw on much the same circuitry to mitigate aggression, but to more subtle effect. Achieving constructive influence involves expressing ourselves in a way that produces a desired social result, like putting someone at ease. Artfully expressive people are viewed by others as confident and likable and in general make favorable impressions.[39]

Those adept at deploying influence rely on social awareness to guide their actions; for example, they recognize situations where turning a blind eye may benefit a relationship.[40] It can be counter-productive to signal your empathic accuracy by saying "I don't turn you on" or "You don't love me!" In such moments simply absorbing such an insight and acting on it tacitly is more prudent.

Deciding on the optimal dose of expressivity depends, among other factors, on social cognition, knowing the governing cultural norms for what's appropriate in a given social context (another example of how social intelligence abilities work synergistically). The muted tones that are best for Beijing will seem too understated in Guadalajara.[41] Tact balances expressivity. Social discretion lets us fit in wherever we are, leaving the fewest untoward emotional ripples in our wake.

| C O N C E R N |

Let's go back to those seminary students who were rushing to a building to give a practice sermon on the parable of the Good Samaritan. There was a crucial moment for each one in turn, when they heard the moans of the man in the doorway they had to pass. Even those who rushed by him may have felt a bit of empathy. But empathy alone matters little if we fail to act.[42] Those students who *did* stop to help were exhibiting another sign of social intelligence: concern.

As we saw in Chapter 4, feeling another's needs can be a prod to activity, thanks to the brain's wiring. For example, when women watched videotapes of a baby crying, those who most strongly "caught" the baby's sadness showed the biggest frowns, an indicator of empathy. These women not only mirrored the baby's physiology but had the strongest desire to pick him up and hold him.[43]

The more we both empathize with someone in need and feel concern, the greater will be our urge to help them—a link seen wherever people are moved to remedy human suffering. A study of charitable giving done in the Netherlands found that a person's sense of social concern predicted the likelihood that they would donate to the needy.[44]

In the world of work, concern that propels us to take responsibility for what needs doing translates into good organizational citizenship. Concerned people are those most willing to take the time and make the effort to help out a colleague. Rather than just focusing on their own work, they understand the need for group cooperation to meet larger objectives.

Those who are most physiologically aroused by distress in others—that is, who are highly susceptible to emotional contagion in this range—are also those most moved to help. Conversely, those who are little moved by empathic concern most easily disregard someone else's distress. One longitudinal study found that those five-to-seven-year-olds who were least upset on seeing their own mother's distress were most likely to be "antisocial" as adults.[45] The researchers suggest that "fostering young children's attention to and concern for the needs of others" may be an effective strategy for preventing later misbehavior.

Simply feeling concern for others does not always suffice; we also need to act effectively. Too many leaders of organizations that have humanitarian goals flounder because they lack basic management skills; they need to be smarter about doing good. Concern takes on more potency when it draws on high-road abilities, harnessing expertise for its own ends. Bill and Melinda Gates exemplify such higher levels of concern: they have deployed the best practices of the business world to tackle the devastating health problems of the world's poor. And they also spend time meeting the people they are helping—mothers in Mozambique whose children are dying of malaria, victims of AIDS in India—which primes their empathy.

Concern is the impulse that lies at the root of the helping professions, such as medicine and social work. In a sense, these professions are the public embodiment of concern for those in need, be it the sick or the poor. Those who work in the helping professions thrive when this capacity waxes but burn out when it wanes.

Concern reflects a person's capacity for compassion. Manipulative people can be skilled in other abilities of social intelligence, but they fail here. Deficiencies in this aspect of social facility should most strongly identify antisocial types, who do not care about others' needs or suffering, let alone seek to help them.

EDUCATING THE LOW ROAD

Now that we've surveyed the terrain of social intelligence, the question arises: can we improve such essential human talents? Particularly when it comes to low-road capacities, this challenge may seem daunting. But Paul Ekman, the authority on reading emotions from facial expressions (last seen in Chapter 3), has devised a way to teach people how to improve primal empathy—despite its instantaneous, unconscious operation.

Ekman's training focuses on microexpressions, emotional signals that flit across the face in less than a third of a second, the snap of a finger. Because these emotional signals are spontaneous and made unconsciously, they offer a clue as to how a person actually feels at that moment—despite whatever impression she may be trying to project.

While a single discrepant microexpression does not inevitably indicate that the person is lying, outright falsehoods usually involve this sort of emotional deceptiveness. The better people are at spotting microexpressions, the more likely they will detect an attempt to suppress an emotional truth. The embassy interviewer who spotted the look of disgust flitting across the face of the criminal wanting a visa had been trained in Ekman's methods.

This skill has special value for diplomats, judges, and police because microexpressions reveal how a person truly feels at that moment. Then again, lovers, business people, teachers—just about anyone—can benefit from reading these affective signals.

These automatic and fleeting emotional expressions operate via low-road circuitry, which is distinguished by its automaticity and its quickness. And we need to use the low road to catch the low road. But that requires fine-tuning our capacity for primal empathy.

Ekman has devised a CD, called the MicroExpression Training Tool, that he claims can help most anyone vastly improve this microdetective work. By now tens of thousands of people have gone through his training procedure, which takes less than an hour to complete.[46]

I tried it this morning.

The first round presents a series of different people's faces, each at first frozen in a neutral look. Then for a startling wisp of a moment, they flash any of seven expressions: sadness, anger, fear, surprise, disgust, contempt, or happiness.

After each flash I had to guess which expression I had just witnessed, though as far as I could tell all I had seen was a blur of movement. The smiles and frowns flash by at high speed, in just a fifteenth of a second. This whiz-bang rate fits the speed window of the low road, leaving the high road befuddled.

Then I went through a series of three practice-and-review sessions that present sixty such tableaux in speeds up to a thirtieth of a second. After I made each guess, the format allowed me to study each expression in freeze-frame, the better to master the nuances that distinguish sadness from surprise, disgust from anger. Even better, it graded each guess I'd made right or wrong, providing the crucial feedback (which we virtually never get in life) that allows eager neural circuits to improve at this slippery task.

As I made my guesses, I could occasionally articulate to myself what expression I had seen and why: the flash of teeth indicating a smile, the half-smirk of contempt, the widened eyes of fear. But more often than not my rational mind was baffled, genuinely surprised when what seemed a desperate guess was vindicated as accurate intuition.

But when I tried to explain to myself why the blur I had just seen signaled one or another emotion—*surely that raised brow means surprise*—I usually was wrong. When I trusted my gut, I was more often right. As cognitive science tells us, we know more than we can say. To put it differently, this low-road job goes best when the high road just shuts up.

After twenty or thirty minutes of practice sessions, I took the post-test, scoring a respectable 86 percent, up from 50 percent on the pretest. Ekman finds that, like me, most people average around 40 to 50 percent right on the first try. But after just twenty minutes or so of training, virtually everyone gets 80 to 90 percent correct.

"The low road is eminently trainable. But why haven't we learned this already? Because we've never gotten the right feedback before," Ekman told me. The more people train, the better they get. "You want to overlearn this skill," Ekman advises, by practicing to perfection.

People who have been trained this way, Ekman has found, are more adept at detecting real-life microexpressions, like the look of abject sadness that flitted across the face of British spy Kim Philby in his last public interview before he fled to the Soviet Union, or the hint of disgust zipping by as Kato Kaelin testified at the O. J. Simpson murder trial.

Understandably, police interrogators, business negotiators, and a host of others whose professions demand that they detect the disingenuous have flocked to Ekman's training. More to the point here, this crash course for the low road reveals that these neural circuits are hungry to learn. They just need lessons in the language they understand—which has nothing to do with words.

For social intelligence, Ekman's program is a model for training people in low-road aptitudes like primal empathy and decoding nonverbal signals. While in the past most psychologists would have assumed that such rapid, automatic, and spontaneous behavior was largely beyond our ability to improve, Ekman shows it is not. A new model of learning, it bypasses the high road and connects directly to the low.

SOCIAL INTELLIGENCE RECONSIDERED

In the early years of the twentieth century a neurologist did an experiment with a woman who had amnesia. Her case was so severe that she had to be reintroduced to the doctor every time they met, which was almost daily.

One day the doctor hid a tack in his hand. As usual, he introduced himself to the patient and shook her hand. The tack pricked her skin. He then left, walked back in, and asked the woman if they'd ever met before.

She said they had not. But when he again introduced himself and stuck out his hand to shake hers, she held her hand back.

Joseph LeDoux (whom we met in Chapter 5) tells the tale to make a point about the high road and the low.[47] The woman's amnesia was caused by lesions in the temporal lobe, part of the high-road circuitry. Her amygdala, that central node for the low road, was intact. Though her temporal lobe could not remember what had just happened to her, the threat of the tack was imprinted in the circuitry of the amygdala. She did not recognize the doctor—but she knew not to trust him.

We can rethink social intelligence in light of neuroscience. The social architecture of the brain intertwines the high and low roads. In intact brains these two systems work in parallel, both necessary rudders in the social world.

Conventional ideas of social intelligence have too often focused on high-road talents like social knowledge, or the capacity for extracting the rules, protocols, and norms that guide appropriate behavior in a given social setting.[48] The "social cognition" school reduces interpersonal talent to this sort of general intellect applied to interactions.[49] Although this cognitive approach has served well in linguistics and in artificial intelligence, it meets its limits when applied to human relationships.

A focus on cognition *about* relationships neglects essential noncognitive abilities like primal empathy and synchrony, and it ignores capacities like concern. A purely cognitive perspective slights the essential brain-to-brain social glue that builds the foundation for any interaction.[50] The full spectrum of social intelligence abilities embraces both high- and low-road aptitudes. Presently both the concept and its measures omit too many lanes of the low road—and so exclude social talents that have been key to human survival.

Back in the 1920s, when Thorndike originally proposed measuring social intelligence, next to nothing was known about the neural basis of IQ, let alone about interpersonal skill. Now social neuroscience challenges intelligence theorists to find a definition for our interpersonal abilities that encompasses the talents of the low road—including capacities for getting in synch, for attuned listening, and for empathic concern.

These basic elements of nourishing relationships must be included in any full account of social intelligence. Without them the concept remains cold and dry, valuing a calculating intellect but ignoring the virtues of a warm heart.

On this point I stand with the late psychologist Lawrence Kohlberg, who argued that the attempt to eliminate human values from social intelligence impoverishes the concept.[51] Then such intelligence devolves into the pragmatics of influence and control. In these anonymous and isolated times we need to be ever vigilant against the spread of just that impersonal stance.

PART TWO

BROKEN BONDS

You and It

A woman whose sister had recently died got a sympathy call from a male friend who had lost his own sister a few years before. The friend expressed his condolences, and the woman, touched by his empathic words, told him poignant details of the long illness her sister had suffered, and she described how bereft she herself felt at the loss.

But as she talked, she could hear the clicking of computer keys at the other end of the line. A slow realization dawned: her friend was answering his e-mail, even as he was talking to her in her hour of pain. His comments became increasingly hollow, perfunctory, and off-point as the conversation continued.

After they hung up, she felt so dejected that she wished he had never called at all. She'd just had a gut punch of the interaction that the philosopher Martin Buber called "I-It."

In I-It interaction, Buber wrote, one person has no attunement to the other's subjective reality, feels no real empathy for the other person. The lack of connectedness may be all too obvious from the recipient's perspective. The friend may well have felt obligated to call and express his sympathy to the woman whose sister died, but his lack of a full emotional connection made the call a hollow gesture.

Buber coined the term "I-It" for the range of relations that runs from merely detached to utterly exploitative. In that spectrum others become objects: we treat someone more as a thing than as a person.

Psychologists use the term "agentic" for this cold approach to others, viewing people solely as instruments to be used toward our own goals.[1] I am agentic when I care not at all about your feelings but only about what I want from you.

That egocentric mode contrasts with "communion," a state of high mutual empathy where your feelings do more than matter to me—they change me. While we are in communion, we stay in synch, meshed in a mutual feedback loop. But during moments of agency, we disconnect.

When other tasks or preoccupations split our attention, the dwindling reserve left for the person we are talking with leaves us operating on automatic, paying just enough attention to keep the conversation on track. Should more presence be called for, the result will be an interaction that feels "off."

Multiple preoccupations take a toll on any conversation that goes beyond the routine, particularly when it enters emotionally troubling zones. To be charitable, the multitasking condolence caller may have meant no harm. But when we are multitasking—in that common addiction of modern life—and talking gets added to the mix of our activities, we readily slide into the It mode.

I - Y O U

From the next table in a restaurant I overhear the following tale:

"My brother has terrible luck with women. His first marriage was a disaster. He's thirty-nine and a nerd. He's got terrific technical skills, but zero social skills.

"Lately he's been trying speed dating. Single women sit at tables, and the men go from table to table, spending exactly five minutes talking with each woman. A bell rings at five minutes, and they rate each other to indicate if they might want to get together. If they do, then they exchange e-mail addresses to arrange a meeting another time.

"But my brother ruins his chances. I know just what he does: as soon as he sits down, he starts talking about himself nonstop. I'm sure he never asks the woman a single question. He's never had one say she wants to see him again."

For the same reason, when she was single, opera singer Allison Charney employed a "dating test": she counted the amount of time it took before her date asked her a question with the word "you" in it. On her first date with Adam Epstein, the man she married a year later, she didn't even have time to start the clock—he aced the test.[2]

That "test" looks for a person's capacity for attuning, for wanting to enter and understand another person's inner reality. Psycho-analysts use the somewhat cumbersome term "intersubjectivity" to refer to this meshing of two people's inner worlds.[3] The phrase "I-You" is a more lyrical way of describing the same sort of empathic connection.

As the Austrian-born Buber described it in his 1937 book on a philosophy of relationships, I-You (or "I and Thou," as the phrase entered American popular culture) is a special bond, an attuned closeness that is often—but of course not always—found between husbands and wives, family members, and good friends.[4] In German, the form of "you" that Buber used—*Du*—is the most inti-mate, the word friends and lovers use with each other.

For Buber, who was a mystic as well as a philosopher, "You" has a transcendental dimension. The human relationship with the divine is the one I-You connection that can be indefinitely sustained, the ultimate ideal for our imperfect humanity. But the everyday modes of I-You reach from simple respect and politeness, to affection and admiration, to any of the countless ways we show our love.

The emotional indifference and remoteness of an I-It relation-ship stands in direct contrast to the attuned I-You. When we are in the I-It mode, we treat other people as means to some other end. By contrast, in the I-You mode our relationship with them becomes an end in itself. The high road, with its facility in rationality and cogni-tion, may suffice for the It. But the You, where we attune, engages the low road.

The boundary between It and You is porous and fluid. Every You will sometimes become an It; every It has the potential for becom-ing a You. When we expect to be treated as a You, the It treatment feels terrible, as happened on that hollow phone call. In such mo-ments, You shrivels into It.

Empathy opens the door to I-You relations. We respond not just from the surface but with a wider swath; as Buber put it, I-You "can only be spoken with the whole being." A defining quality of I-You engagement is "feeling felt," the distinct sensation when someone has become the target of true empathy. At such moments we sense that the other person knows how we feel, and so we feel known.[5]

As one early psychoanalyst put it, client and therapist "oscillate in the same rhythm" as their emotional connection intensifies; this occurs physiologically too, as we saw in Chapter 2. Therapeutic em-pathy, as the humanistic theorist Carl Rogers proposed, is achieved when the therapist attunes to the client to a point where the client feels understood—feels known as a You.

| FEELING FELT |

Shortly after Takeo Doi, a Japanese psychiatrist, arrived on his first visit to America, he had an awkward moment. He was visiting the home of someone to whom he had just been introduced, and his host asked Doi if he was hungry, adding, "We have some ice cream if you'd like it."

Doi was in fact rather hungry. But being asked point-blank if he was hungry by someone he hardly knew was jarring. He would never have been asked such a thing in Japan.

Following the norms of Japanese culture, Doi could not bring himself to admit his hunger. So he passed up the offer of the ice cream.

At the same time Doi recalls cherishing a mild hope that his host would press him again. He was disappointed to hear his host say, "I see," and drop the offer.

In Japan, Doi notes, a host would simply have sensed his hunger and given him something to eat without having to ask if he wanted it.

That sensing of another person's needs and feelings, and the unsolicited response to them, bespeaks the high value placed on the I-You mode in Japanese culture (and in East Asian cultures generally). The Japanese word *amae* refers to this sensibility, empathy that is taken for granted, and acted upon, without calling attention to itself.

In the orbit of *amae* we feel felt. Takeo Doi sees the warm connectedness of the mother-infant relationship—in which the mother intuitively senses what the baby needs—as the prototype of this heightened attunement. It extends into every close social tie in Japanese daily life, creating an intimate atmosphere of connectedness.[6]

English has no word for *amae,* but it could certainly use one to refer to such a closely attuned relationship. *Amae* points to the empirical fact that we attune most readily with the people in our lives we know and love—our immediate family and relatives, lovers or spouses, old friends. The closer we are, the more *amae.*

Amae seems to take for granted a mutual priming of parallel feelings and thoughts in people who are attuned. The unvoiced attitude is something like: *if I feel it, so should you—and so I needn't tell you what I want, feel, or need. You should be closely enough attuned to me to sense it and so to act on it without a word needed.*

This concept makes not just emotional sense but cognitive sense as well. The stronger our relationship with someone, the more open and attentive to them we are likely to be. The more personal history we have shared, the more readily we will sense how they feel, and the more similarly we will think about and react to whatever may arise.

Buber is passé in philosophical circles these days, but the French philosopher Emmanuel Lévinas has largely filled his role as a commentator on relationships.[7] I-It, as Lévinas observes, implies the most superficial of relationships, thinking *about* the other person rather than attuning to her. I-It stays on the surface; I-You plunges into the depths. "It," Lévinas points out, describes You in the third person, just a mere idea, the greatest remove from intimate connection.

Philosophers see the implicit understandings of the world that guide how we think and act as invisible moorings in our constructed social reality. This knowledge can tacitly be shared culture-wide, within a family, or in any meeting of minds between people. As Lévinas notes, such a shared sensibility is "what emerges from two people interacting"; our private, subjective sense of the world has its roots in our relationships.

As Freud put it long ago, whatever establishes significant points in common between people arouses "fellow feelings"—a fact not lost on anyone who has successfully struck up a conversation with an attractive potential partner, made a sales call on a stranger, or simply passed the time with a seatmate on a long plane flight. But beneath this surface connection, Freud saw that intense looping could forge outright identification, a sense that the other and one-self are virtually one and the same.

At the neural level, my "getting to know you" means my acquiring a resonance with your emotional patterns and mental maps. And the more our maps overlap, the more identified we feel and the greater the shared reality we create. As we grow to identify with each other, the mind's categories undergo a merging of sorts, so that we unconsciously think about those most important to us in very much the same ways we think about ourselves. Husbands and wives, for instance, tend to find it easier to name ways they are similar to each other than the ways they differ—but only if they are happy with each other. If not, the differences loom larger.

Another, rather ironic indicator of similarity in mental maps occurs with self-serving biases: we tend to apply to those we value most the same distorted thinking we apply to ourselves. We commonly hold, for example, an overly optimistic "illusion of invulnerability," in which we see bad things as more likely to happen to other people than to ourselves or to those we care about most.[8] We typically estimate the odds that we or our loved ones will fall prey to cancer or an auto accident as much lower than the odds we estimate for other people.

Our experience of oneness—a sense of merging or sharing identities—increases whenever we take someone else's perspective, and it strengthens the more we see things from their point of view.[9] The moment when empathy becomes mutual has an especially rich resonance. Two tightly looped people mesh minds, even smoothly finishing sentences for each other—a sign of a vibrant relationship that marital researchers call "high-intensity validation."[10]

I-You is a unifying relationship, in which for the time being a special other is perceived as distinct from all others and is known in all her distinctive features. Such deep encounters are the moments we remember most vividly in our close relationships. Buber was referring to just this fully looped engagement when he wrote, "All real living is meeting."[11]

Short of sainthood, always to engage absolutely everyone we encounter as a You is to ask too much of ourselves. Ordinary life inevitably swings between the two modes, Buber saw: we have a sort of divided self, two "tidily circled-off provinces"—one It, the other You. You covers our connected moments. But we handle the details of life in the It mode, through utilitarian communications focused on getting things done.

THE UTILITY OF THE IT

New York Times columnist Nicholas Kristof has a distinguished record as a journalist and won a Pulitzer Prize for his investigative reporting. He has maintained his journalistic objectivity through wars, famines, and most of the major catastrophes of the last few decades.

But one day in Cambodia that detachment melted away. It happened while he was investigating the scandalous sale worldwide of thousands of children as slaves to sex traffickers.[12]

The decisive moment came when a Cambodian pimp presented to him a tiny, quivering teenage girl named Srey Neth. Kristof, as he tells it, did "something dreadfully unjournalistic": he bought her, for $150.

Kristof took Srey Neth and another girl back to their villages and set them free, helping them get a new start in their lives. A year later Srey

Neth finished at a beauty school in Phnom Penh and was looking forward to starting her own shop—though tragically, the other girl was drifting back to the easy money. Writing about the girls in his column, Kristof moved numbers of readers to send donations to a charity that has helped Srey Neth and others like her restart their lives.

Objectivity is one of the guiding principles of journalistic ethics. Ideally, the journalist remains a neutral observer, tracking events and reporting on them as they happen rather than interfering with them in any way. Kristof had stepped out of the tightly boundaried role of journalist, crossing that gap of detachment to enter the story himself.

The journalist's code is a mandate for an I-It relationship, much like the codes held by many other professionals, from doctors to police officers. A surgeon should not operate on someone with whom she has a strong personal relationship, lest her feelings interfere with her mental clarity; a police officer, in theory, should never let a personal connection influence impartial policing.

The principle of keeping a "professional distance" is intended to protect both parties from the wobbly, unpredictable influence of emotions in the execution of their expertise. Maintaining that distance means seeing a person in terms of their role—patient, criminal—without attuning to the person within the role. While the low road connects us instantly to the other person's distress, the prefrontal systems can increase our emotional separation enough so we can think more clearly.[13] This balance makes empathy effective.

The It mode has decided advantages for daily life, if only for getting routine business out of the way. Implicit social rules guide us in deciding which people we need not loop with. Daily life seems rife with them: anytime we are expected to interact with someone in terms of their social role alone—the waitress, the store clerk—we treat them as a one-dimensional It, ignoring the "rest" of them, their human identity.

Jean-Paul Sartre, the twentieth-century French philosopher, saw this one-dimensionality as a symptom of a broader alienation in modern life. He described public roles as a "ceremony" of sorts, a well-scripted way of acting in which we treat others as an It—and are treated as such in return: "There is the dance of the grocer, of the tailor, of the auctioneer, by which they endeavor to persuade their clientele that they are nothing but a grocer, a tailor, an auctioneer."[14]

But Sartre says nothing of the benefits we derive from avoiding an endless string of I-You encounters, thanks to this I-It masquerade. A waiter's dignified aloofness spares him intrusions into his private life and at the same time creates a sphere of privacy for the diners he serves. Staying in his role allows a waiter to get things done efficiently, while he retains the internal autonomy to turn his attention to his private interests and pursuits—even if they involve only daydreaming and fantasy. His role provides him with a bubble of privacy even in public life.

Making small talk poses no threat to this bubble, so long as it remains small. And the person in the It role always has an option to attend to someone as a You, temporarily stepping into full personhood. But generally the role itself operates as a sort of screen, partially blocking out the person who fills it. At least at first we see the It, not the person.

When we encounter casual acquaintances, our rapport heightens to the degree that we both engage in a nonverbal dance of mutual attention, smiling, coordinating posture and movement, and the like. But when we meet someone in a professional role, we tend to focus on a need or on some desired outcome. Studies of people interacting with those in a formal helping role—physician, nurse, counselor, psychotherapist—show that the standard ingredients of rapport there are notably weaker on both sides than between people in informal encounters.[15]

This goal-oriented focus presents a challenge to helping professionals. Rapport, after all, matters for the effectiveness of the professional encounter. In psychotherapy the interpersonal chemistry between therapist and client determines whether a working alliance will form. In medicine, a good rapport helps the patient trust the physician sufficiently to comply with his recommendations.

People in helping professions must work hard to ensure that the ingredients of rapport operate during their professional encounters. Their detachment needs to be balanced with sufficient empathy to allow at least a bit of I-You feeling to bloom.

THE PAIN OF REJECTION

The moment of truth for Mary Duffy—when she realized that she had ceased being known as a person and was now simply "the carcinoma in Room B-2"—came to her the morning after her surgery for breast cancer.

Duffy was still half-asleep when, without any warning, she was surrounded by white-coated strangers—a doctor and a group of medical students. The doctor, without a word, pulled off her blanket and stripped off her nightgown as though she were just a mannequin, leaving her naked.

Too weak to protest, Duffy managed a sarcastic "Well, good morning" to the doctor, who ignored her.

Instead he launched into a lecture on carcinoma for the gaggle of medical students who circled her bed. They duly stared at her naked body, detachedly indifferent to her.

Finally the doctor deigned to speak directly to Duffy, asking distractedly, "Have you passed gas yet?"

When she tried to assert a bit of humanity with a snappy comeback—"No, I don't do that until the third date"—the doctor looked offended, as though she had let him down.[16]

What Duffy so urgently wanted in that moment was for the doctor to affirm her personhood by even a small gesture that would allow her a bit of dignity. She needed an I-You moment. What she got was a cold dose of It.

As Duffy was, we are inevitably troubled when someone we expect to loop with for one reason or another fails to take up their half of the circuit. The result: we feel bereft—something like a baby whose mother refuses to pay attention to her.

That feeling of hurt has a neural basis. Our brain registers social rejections in the very area that activates when we are hurt physically: the anterior cingulate cortex (or ACC), which is known to generate, among other things, the distressing sensations of bodily pain.[17]

Matthew Lieberman and Naomi Eisenberger, who did the study at UCLA, suggest that the ACC operates as a neural alarm system for detecting the danger of rejection and for alerting other parts of the brain to react accordingly.[18] As such, they opine, it forms part of a "social attachment system" that piggybacks on the existing wiring for alerting the brain to physical harm.

Rejection resonates with a primal threat, one the brain seems designed to highlight. Lieberman and Eisenberger remind us that in human prehistory being part of a band was essential for survival; exclusion could be a death sentence, as is still true today for infant mammals in the wild. The pain center, they propose, may have evolved this sensitivity to social exclusion as an alarm signal to warn of potential banishment—and presumably to prompt us to repair the threatened relationship.

That idea makes sense of the very metaphors we use to indicate the sting of a rebuff: a "broken heart" and "hurt feelings" suggest the physical nature of the emotional ache. This equation of physical and social pain seems tacitly recognized in many different languages around the world: the words that describe social pain all borrow from the lexicon of physical hurts.

Tellingly, a monkey infant whose ACC is damaged will fail to cry in distress when separated from its mother; such a failure in nature could easily imperil its life. Likewise, a monkey mother whose ACC has lesions no longer responds to the cries of a distressed infant by gathering it close for protection. In humans, when a mother hears her baby cry, her ACC lights up with activity until she responds.

Our ancient need to maintain connection may explain why tears and laughter share proximity in the brain stem, the oldest part of the brain.[19] Laughing and crying come spontaneously in primal moments of social connection—births and deaths, weddings and long-deferred reunions. Distress at separation and joy at bonding both bespeak the primal power of connection.

When our need for closeness goes unmet, emotional disorders can result. Psychologists have coined the term "social depression" for the particular unhappiness caused by troubled, threatened relationships. Social rejection—or fearing it—is one of the most common causes of anxiety. Feelings of inclusion depend not so much on having frequent social contacts or numerous relationships as on how accepted we feel, even in just a few key relationships.[20]

Small wonder that we have a hardwired system that is alert to the threat of abandonment, separation, or rejection: these were once actual threats to life itself, though they are only symbolically so today. Still, when we hope to be a You, being treated like an It, as though we do not matter, carries a particularly harsh sting.

EMPATHY OR PROJECTION?

A psychoanalyst recounting his first meeting with a new patient recalled feeling subtly nervous: "I vaguely recognized it as one of the many versions of anxiety to which I am susceptible."

What exactly had made him so nervous? Scanning his patient while listening attentively, he realized that the most unsettling detail was that the patient was wearing pants that were crisply creased and wrinkle free.

His patient, as he wryly put it, looked like "the main Eddie Bauer catalog entry, and I was the addendum on the back page that stated that odd sizes and seconds were available on inquiry." The analyst felt so unnerved that he leaned forward in his chair, never breaking eye contact, to pull down the cuffs of his own totally wrinkled chinos.

Later, the patient mentioned a powerful memory of his mother's expression of stern and silent disapproval. That rang a bell with the analyst, who himself recalled repeated exhortations by his own mother to wear pressed slacks.

The psychoanalyst cited that moment to exemplify the crucial role in therapy of finely attuned empathy—those moments, as he put it, when the therapist feels "on target" with the patient, accurately sensing what feelings are roiling through the patient.[21] Unfortunately, part of what the analyst feels comes from his own emotional baggage, a projection of his own inner reality onto that of the patient. Projection ignores the other person's inner reality: when we are projecting, we assume the other feels and thinks as we do.

This tendency was noted long ago by the eighteenth-century philosopher David Hume, who observed a "remarkable inclination" in human nature to bestow on other people "the same emotions we observe in ourselves, and to find everywhere those ideas which are most present to us" in our own minds.[22] In full-fledged projection, though, we simply map our world onto someone else's, with no fit or attunement whatsoever. People who are self-absorbed, lost in their own inner world, have little choice but to project that sensibility onto whomever they perceive.

Some argue that every act of empathy entails a subtle sort of projection—that tuning in to someone else triggers in ourselves feelings and thoughts that we can readily, though mistakenly, attribute to them. The analyst's challenge is to distinguish her own projections—technically, the "countertransference"—from genuine empathy. To the degree that a therapist is aware of which of her inner feelings mirror the patient's and which come instead from her own history, she can sort out what the patient actually feels.

If projection makes the other an It, empathy sees the other as a You. Empathy creates a feedback loop, as we work toward a "fit" between our perception and the other person's reality. The therapist monitoring his own reactions might first note a feeling in his own body that did not originate there; the feeling arises from what he senses in the patient. Its meaning will emerge as it recurs, passed back and forth as the client-therapist relationship builds. By sharing that inner sense, he can reflect the other person's experience back to her, as empathy sharpens its attunement.

Our sense of well-being depends to some extent on others regarding us as a You; our yearning for connection is a primal human need, minimally for a cushion for survival. Today the neural echo of that need heightens our sensitivity to the difference between It and You—and makes us feel social rejection as deeply as physical pain.

If being treated as an It unnerves us so, then those who always regard others as such are particularly disturbing.

The Dark Triad

My brother-in-law, Leonard Wolf, is a gentle and caring man by nature, a Chaucer scholar by training—and also an expert in the terror and horror genres in film and literature. Those interests brought him, some years ago, to consider writing a book about a real-life serial killer.

The man had murdered ten people, including three of his own family members, before being caught. The murders were horrifyingly intimate: he strangled his victims.

Leonard visited the murderer in prison several times. Finally, he worked up the courage to ask the one question that most intrigued him: "How could you do such a terrible thing to people? Didn't you feel any pity for them?"

To which the killer replied very matter-of-factly, "Oh, no—I had to turn that part of me off. If I had felt any of their distress, I couldn't have done it."

Empathy is the prime inhibitor of human cruelty: withholding our natural inclination to feel with another allows us to treat the other as an It.

That strangler's chilling phrase—"I had to turn that part of me off"—alludes to the human capacity for intentionally capping off our empathy, for turning a cold eye and ear to another's plight. Suppressing our natural inclination to feel with another unleashes cruelty.

When being tuned out of caring is a person's defining trait, they typically belong to one of the types that psychologists dub "the Dark Triad": narcissists, Machiavellians, and psychopaths. All three types share to varying degrees an unappealing, though sometimes well-concealed, core: social malevolence and duplicity, self-centeredness and aggression, and emotional coldness.[1]

We would do well to familiarize ourselves with the hallmarks of this threesome, if only to better recognize them. Modern society, glorifying me-first motives and worshiping celebrity demigods of greed unleashed and vanity idealized, may be inadvertently inviting these types to flourish.

Most people who fall into the Dark Triad do not qualify for a psychiatric diagnosis, though at their extremes they shade into mental illness or become outlaws—particularly psychopaths. But the far more common "subclinical" variety live among us, populating offices, schools, bars, and the routine byways of daily life.

THE NARCISSIST: DREAMS OF GLORY

A football player whom we'll call Andre has a justified reputation as "flashy." He's adored for making tough, spectacular plays at crucial moments in important games. Andre does his best when the crowds roar loudest, when the spotlight shines, and when the stakes are highest.

"When the game is on the line," one teammate told a reporter, "we're happy to have Andre on the team."

But that same teammate also added, "Andre is a real pain in the neck. He's chronically late to practice and struts around like he's God's gift to football, and I don't think I've ever seen him throw a decent block for another player."

Moreover, Andre has a habit of blowing easy plays, especially in practice or in games with little significance. And on one infamous occasion he nearly got into a fight with a teammate who passed the ball to another player instead of to Andre—even though the other player scored.

Andre embodies garden-variety narcissism. Such people are driven by one motive: dreams of glory.[2] Narcissists, though bored by routine, flourish when they are facing a difficult challenge. This trait can be adaptive in domains where performance under stress counts, from litigation to leadership.

The healthy variety of narcissism originates in the well-loved infant's notion that she is the center of the world, that her needs are everyone else's priority. In adulthood this same attitude matures into a positive self-regard that gives her confidence appropriate to her level of talent—an essential ingredient for success. Lacking such self-confidence, people shrink from deploying whatever gifts or strengths they may have.

Whether a given narcissist is healthy or unhealthy can be gauged by their capacity for empathy. The more impaired the person's ability to consider others may be, the less healthy is their narcissism.

Many narcissists are drawn to pressured, high-profile jobs where they can use their talents well and the potential laurels are great—despite any risks. Like Andre, they make their best effort when a grand payoff beckons.

In the business world such narcissists can end up as larger-than-life leaders. Michael Maccoby, a psychoanalyst who has studied (and treated) narcissistic leaders, observes that the type has become increasingly common at the top echelons of business today as competitive tensions—as well as executive pay and glamour—have escalated.[3]

Such ambitious and self-confident leaders can be effective in the present cutthroat business world. The best are creative strategists who can grasp the big picture and navigate risky challenges to leave a positive legacy. Productive narcissists combine a justified self-confidence with openness to criticism—at least to criticism that comes from confidants.

Healthy narcissistic leaders have the ability for self-reflection and are open to reality checks. They develop a sense of perspective and can be playful even as they pursue their goals. If open to new information, they are more likely to make sound decisions and are less likely to be blindsided by events.

But unhealthy narcissists crave to be admired more than to be loved. Often innovators in business, they are driven to achieve—not because they have a high internal standard of excellence but because they want the perks and glory that achievement brings. Caring little about how their actions affect others, they feel free to pursue their goals aggressively, regardless of the human costs. In times of great turbulence, Maccoby proposes, such leaders can seem attractive, if only because they have the audacity to push through programs that bring radical changes.

But such narcissists empathize selectively, turning a blind eye to those who do not feed their striving for glory. They can close or sell a company, or lay off multitudes of employees, without feeling an ounce of sympathy for those for whom those decisions are personal disasters. In the absence of empathy, they have no regrets and are indifferent to the needs or feelings of their employees.

Unhealthy narcissists typically lack a feeling of self-worth; the result is an inner shakiness that in a leader, for example, means that even as he unfurls inspiring visions, he harbors a vulnerability that closes his ears to criticism. Such leaders avoid even constructive feedback, which they perceive as an attack. Their hypersensitivity to criticism in any form also means that narcissistic leaders don't seek out information widely; rather, they selectively seize on data that supports their views, ignoring disconfirming facts. They don't listen but prefer to preach and indoctrinate.

While some narcissistic leaders get spectacular results, others create disasters. When they harbor unrealistic dreams, lacking any restraint and ignoring wise counsel, they drag a company down the wrong track. Given the large number of narcissistic leaders at the helm of companies today, Maccoby warns, organizations must find ways to force leaders to listen and take others' views into account. Otherwise, such leaders will likely stay isolated behind a wall of sycophants who will be supportive no matter what.

One narcissistic CEO came to Maccoby for psychotherapy to learn why he so readily flew into rages at the people who worked for him. He would take even helpful suggestions as slights and turn on whoever had made them. The CEO traced his anger to childhood feelings of being unappreciated by his aloof father. No matter what he accomplished, his father was unimpressed. The CEO realized that now he sought emotional restitution in the form of unstinting praise from his employees, and that he needed to hear it in abundance. But when he felt underappreciated, he became enraged.

With that insight, the CEO began to change, even learning to laugh at his craving for applause. At one point he announced to his top team that he was in psychoanalysis and asked what they thought. There was a long pause; then one executive worked up the courage to say that he didn't seem as angry anymore, so whatever he was doing, he should keep it up.

The Dark Side of Loyalty

"My students," a business school professor confides, understand "organizational life as a kind of 'vanity fair,' in which those who want to get ahead can do so by playing to the vanity of their superiors."

One plays this game, his students know, by using outright flattery and adulation. Enough sycophancy, they believe, will lead to promotions. If in the process they have to withhold, downplay, or distort important information, so be it. Through guile and with a bit of luck, the hard consequences of that suppression will fall on someone else's watch.[4]

That cynical attitude goes to the heart of the danger of unhealthy narcissism in organizational life. An entire organization can be narcissistic. When a critical mass of employees share a narcissistic outlook, the outfit itself takes on those traits, which become standard operating procedures.

Organizational narcissism has clear perils. Pumping up grandiosity, whether it is the boss's or some false collective self-image held throughout the company, becomes the operating norm. Healthy dissent dies out. And any organization that is cheated of a full grasp of truth loses the ability to respond nimbly to harsh realities.

To be sure, every company wants its employees to be proud they work there and to feel that they share a meaningful mission—a bit of well-founded collective narcissism is healthy. Trouble creeps in when that pride builds on a desperate grasp for glory rather than on real accomplishment.

Trouble grows when narcissistic leaders expect to hear only messages that confirm their own sense of greatness. And when those leaders turn against bearers of bad news, subordinates naturally start to ignore data that do not fit the grandiose image. This skewed filter on reality need not be cynically motivated. Employees who themselves gain ego-inflation from belonging will bend the truth willingly, in exchange for the rosy feelings of group self-adulation.

A poignant casualty of such malignant group narcissism is not just truth but authentic connection among coworkers. Everyone tacitly colludes to maintain their shared illusions. Suppression and paranoia thrive. Work devolves to a charade.

In a prescient scene in the 1983 movie *Silkwood*, Karen Silkwood, a crusader against corporate corruption, watches a manager at a manufacturing plant retouch photos of welds on fuel rods that are headed for nuclear reactors. He's making dangerously faulty work seem safe.

The manager seems to harbor no second thoughts about his potentially lethal chore. He's just worried that the plant's late delivery of the fuel rods might hurt business and so endanger the people who work there. He thinks of himself as a good corporate citizen.

In the years since that movie was made, we have seen a series of actual meltdowns like those the scene implicitly warns against—not of nuclear reactors, but Chernobyls of entire corporations. Beneath the outright lies and elaborate fiscal cover-ups, those companies arguably shared a single root affliction: collective narcissism.

Narcissistic organizations implicitly encourage such duplicity, even while ostensibly asking for candor and hard data. Shared illusions flourish in direct proportion to the suppression of truth. When narcissism spreads within a company, then those who challenge the self-flattery—even with crucial information—threaten all those who count on the narcissistic high with a deflating feeling of failure or shame. In the psyche of the narcissist, the knee-jerk response to such a threat is rage. In a narcissistic company, those who imperil the group's grandiosity are typically demoted, upbraided, or fired.

The narcissistic organization becomes a moral universe of its own, a world where its goals, goodness, and means are not questioned but taken as holy writ. It's a world where doing whatever we need to, to get whatever we want, seems perfectly fine. The ongoing self-celebration fogs over how divorced from reality we've become. The rules don't apply to us, just to the others.

The Narcissist's Motto: Others Exist to Adore Me

She had promised to read him an erotic passage from a novel. But now he was furious.

At first everything seemed fine. She began reading to him in a low, seductive tone from a titillating scene about two lovers. He could feel himself getting a bit aroused.

But as the passage grew steamier, she grew nervous, alternately stuttering and hesitant, then plunging ahead in rapid chunks. She was clearly flustered.

Finally it was just more than she could handle. Pleading that the passage was just too pornographic after this point, she refused to read on.

To make matters worse, she added that "something" about him made her too uncomfortable to continue. Worse still, she admitted she had gone ahead and read the whole passage for other guys.

That scene was played out 120 times, each time with a different man, as part of an experiment at an unnamed university.[5] The woman reading the steamy prose was an assistant in a study of what provokes some men, but not most others, to force sex on women.

The scenario was set up deliberately to prod men first to feel aroused, then to feel frustrated and put down.

After that setup, each man had a chance for retribution. He was asked to rate the woman's performance, to set how much she should be paid or whether her pay should be withheld, and to decide if she should be asked back—or fired.

Most of the men forgave the woman, especially when they heard she needed the money to pay her tuition. But true to type, those with narcissistic tendencies were outraged by the slights and retaliated most. The narcissists, feeling they had been cheated of something to which they were entitled, were punitive on every count. And on a test of attitudes about sexual coercion, the more narcissistic the man, the more he approved of coercive tactics. Had this been a date where the couple made out and then the woman wanted to stop, the researchers concluded, such men were most likely to force sex on her despite her protests.

Even unhealthy narcissists can sometimes be charmers. The very name comes from the Greek myth of Narcissus, who was so entranced by his own beauty that he fell in love with his own image reflected in a lake. The nymph Echo also fell in love with him, but she ended up spurned and heartbroken, unable to compete with his self-adoration.

As the myth suggests, many narcissists attract people because the self-confidence they exude can lend them a charismatic aura. Though they are quick to put others down, unhealthy narcissists view themselves in absolutely positive terms. They are, understandably, happiest in a marriage with someone who will be unfailingly fawning.[6] The slogan of the narcissist might be "Others exist to adore me."

Among the Dark Triad, narcissists alone are blatant in their self-inflation and braggadocio—leavened with a necessary dose of self-deception.[7] Their bias is firmly self-serving: they take credit for successes but never blame for failure. They feel entitled to glory, even blithely claiming credit for others' work (but they see nothing wrong in this—nor in anything else they might do).

According to one standard test, a narcissist is someone who has a grandiose sense of self-importance, harbors obsessive fantasies of unbounded glory, feels rage or intense shame when criticized, expects special favors, and lacks empathy.[8] That deficiency in empathy means narcissists remain oblivious to the self-centered abrasiveness that others see in them so clearly.

Although they can selectively turn on the charm, narcissists can just as readily be disagreeable. Not in the least drawn to emotional intimacy, they are highly competitive, cynical and mistrustful of others, and readily exploit the people in their lives—glorifying themselves even at the expense of slighting someone close to them. Nonetheless, narcissists typically think of themselves as likable.[9]

Unrealistic self-inflation comes more readily in cultures that encourage individualistic striving rather than shared success. Collective cultures, prevalent in East Asia and Northern Europe, place a premium on harmonizing with the group and sharing both work and credit for success, while giving up expectations of being treated as special. But individualistic cultures, like the United States and Australia, tend to encourage striving for the glory of individual accomplishment and its rewards. Accordingly, American college students see themselves as "better" than two-thirds of their fellows in most endeavors, while Japanese students rate themselves exactly in the middle.[10]

THE MACHIAVELLIAN: MY ENDS JUSTIFY THE MEANS

The manager of a large division at a European industrial giant had an oddly split reputation: the people working for him feared and loathed him, while his boss found him utterly charming. Highly polished socially, the manager made considerable efforts to impress not just his boss but also clients outside the company. But once he was back in his own office suite, he became a petty tyrant, shouting at people whose performance displeased him, while uttering not a word of praise for those who excelled.

A consultant called in by the industrial company to evaluate its managers realized how demoralized the people in this autocrat's division had become. After only a few interviews of his coworkers, she saw that he was clearly self-centered, caring only about himself rather than about the organization or even the people whose hard work made him seem so praiseworthy to his own boss.

The consultant recommended that he be replaced, and the company CEO, rather reluctantly, asked him to leave. The manager, though, found another high-level job immediately—because he made such a good first impression on his new boss.

We instantly recognize this manipulative manager; we've seen him in countless movies, plays, and television dramas. The stereotype of the cad, the unfeeling but smooth villain who ruthlessly exploits, pervades popular culture.

The type stands as a perennial staple of popular entertainment—he's as old as the demon Ravana in the ancient Indian epic the *Ramayana,* as contemporary as the evil emperor in the *Star Wars* saga. In endless cinema incarnations he reappears as the mad scientist bent on world rule or the charming yet callous leader of a criminal gang. We instinctively loathe the type because of his unscrupulous cunning, his wile in the service of evil ends. He's the Machiavellian, the villain we love to hate.

When Niccolò Machiavelli wrote *The Prince,* the sixteenth-century manual for seizing and holding political power through cunning manipulation, he took for granted that the aspiring ruler had only his own interests at heart, caring not at all about the people he ruled nor those he crushed to gain power.[11] For the Machiavellian, the ends justify the means, no matter what human pain he may cause. That ethic prevailed among Machiavelli's fans in the hothouse of royal courts for centuries (and of course, it continues unabated in many contemporary political and business circles).

Machiavelli's assumption was that self-interest is the sole driving force in human nature; altruism nowhere enters the picture. To be sure, a political Machiavellian may in fact not consider his ends to be selfish or evil; he may come up with a convincing rationale, even one he believes. Every totalitarian ruler, for instance, justifies his own tyranny as needed to protect the state from some sinister enemy, even if only a concocted one.

The term "Machiavellian" (or the shorthand "Mach") is used by psychologists to apply to people whose outlook on life reflects just this cynical, anything-goes attitude. The first test for Machs was actually based on statements from Machiavelli's books, like "The biggest difference between most criminals and other people is that the criminals are stupid enough to get caught," and "Most people forget more easily the death of their parents than the loss of their property."

The psychological inventory makes no moral judgments, and in contexts ranging from sales to politics, the talents of the Mach—including a glib charm, cunning, and confidence—may be desirable assets. On the other hand, Machs tend to be cynically calculating and arrogant, readily behaving in ways that undermine trust and cooperation.

Though perhaps admirably coolheaded in their social interactions, they remain uninterested in establishing emotional connections. Machs, like narcissists, see others in strictly utilitarian terms—as an It to manipulate for their own ends. For instance, one confided to a counselor in matter-of-fact tones that he had just "fired" his girl-friend; he saw people in all realms of his life much as interchangeable parts, one as good as another.

The Mach shares many traits with the other two branches of the Dark Triad, such as a disagreeable nature and selfishness. But far more than the narcissist or psychopath, the Mach remains realistic about himself and others, neither making inflated claims nor striving to impress.[12] The Mach prefers to see things clearly, all the better to exploit them.

In human prehistory, some evolutionary theorists argue, human intelligence first emerged as such crafty operation in the service of one's own interests. In mankind's earliest eras, runs this argument, victory lay in displaying just enough deviousness to get a lion's share without getting booted out of the group.

Today Machiavellian types like the kiss-up-kick-down manager may well gain some personal success. But in the long run Machs run the risk that their poisoned relationships and resulting bad reputation may one day derail them. A Mach's personal history inevitably will be littered with resentful ex-friends, ex-lovers, and ex-business associates—all brimming with hurt or simmering resentment. Still, a highly mobile society may offer a receptive ecological niche for Machs, where they can readily move on to new conquests far enough afield from the last that their misdeeds never catch up with them.

Machs typically have tunnel-vision empathy: they can bring someone's emotions into focus mainly when they wish to use that person for their own ends. Otherwise, Machs are generally poorer at empathic attunement than others.[13] The coldness of the Mach seems to result from this core deficit in processing emotions—both in themselves and in others. They see the world in rational, probabilistic terms that are not only devoid of emotions but absent the ethical sense that flows from human concern. Hence their easy fall into villainy.

Lacking the full capacity to feel *with* others, Machs also cannot feel *for* them. Like that serial killer, a part of them has been turned off. Machs appear just as confused when it comes to their own emotions; at a moment of unease they may not know whether, as one expert put it, they are feeling "sad, tired, hungry or ill."[14] Machs appear to experience their emotionally dry inner world as rife with compelling primal needs for sex, money, or power. The Mach's predicament comes down to how to fulfill those drives with an interpersonal toolkit that lacks a crucial range of emotional radar.

Even so, their selective capacity for sensing what someone might be thinking can be quite incisive, and they seem to rely on this social cunning to make their way in the world. Machs become astute students of an interpersonal world they can penetrate only at the surface; their shrewd social cognition notes nuances and figures out how people might react to a given situation. These abilities allow their legendary social slickness.

As we've seen, some current definitions of social intelligence, based mainly on such social savvy, would give Machs high marks. But while their head knows what to do, their heart remains clueless. Some see this combination of strength and weakness as a disability Machs overcome through self-serving cunning.[15] Their manipulativeness, in this view, compensates for their blindness to the full range of emotion. That sorry adaptation poisons their relationships.

THE PSYCHOPATH: OTHER AS OBJECT

During a therapy group in a hospital, the discussion turned to the food in the cafeteria. Some mentioned how good the desserts were; others how fattening the food was. One just hoped there wouldn't be the same old thing again.

But Peter's thoughts went in another direction. He wondered how much money was in the cash register, how many staff might be between him and the exit, and how far he would have to get before he could find a chick and have a good time.[16]

Peter was in the hospital because of a court order that had been issued when he violated parole. Since his teen years Peter had abused drugs and alcohol, often becoming belligerent and physically threatening. His present conviction was for making harassing phone calls; before that he had been charged with damaging property and malicious injury. He freely admitted stealing from his family and friends.

Peter's diagnosis was that of psychopath, or "antisocial personality disorder" as the psychiatric diagnostic manual labels the problem these days. "Sociopath" has also had its vogue as the term of choice. No matter the name, its hallmarks are deceit and a reckless disregard for others. A psychopath's consistent irresponsibility begets no remorse—only indifference to the emotional pain others may suffer.

Peter, for example, found utterly foreign the idea that others could be hurt emotionally by what he did. In family conferences, when his mother talked about the anguish he had caused his family, Peter was surprised, becoming defensive, calling himself the "victim." He could not see how he had used his family and friends for his own ends, nor recognize the pain he had caused them.

For psychopaths, other people are always an It, a mark to be duped, used, and discarded. This may sound familiar: some argue that the Dark Triad actually describes different points along the same continuum, from healthy narcissism to psychopathy. Indeed, the Mach and the psychopath seem particularly similar, and some argue that the Mach represents the subclinical (or nonimprisoned) version of the psychopath.[17] The main test for psychopathy includes a measure of "Machiavellian egocentricity," such as agreeing with statements like "I always look out for my own interests before worrying about those of the other guy."[18]

But unlike Machs and narcissists, psychopaths feel virtually no anxiety. Fear seems unknown to them; in assessments they disagree with statements like "Making a parachute jump would really frighten me." They seem immune to stress, remaining calm in situations that would make many other people panic. The absence of apprehension in psychopaths has been found repeatedly in experiments where people wait to receive an electric shock.[19] Ordinarily, people waiting to be shocked show high levels of sweating and a quickened heart rate, autonomic indicators of anxiety. But psychopaths do not.[20]

This coolheadedness means that psychopaths can be dangerous in ways rarely seen in Machs or narcissists. Because psychopaths feel no anticipatory fears, staying utterly calm under even the most intense pressure, they are virtually oblivious to the threat of punishment. This indifference to consequences that keep others law-abiding makes psychopaths the most likely candidates for prison among the Dark Triad.[21]

When it comes to empathy, psychopaths have none; they have special difficulty recognizing fear or sadness on people's faces or in their voices. A brain imaging study with a group of criminal psychopaths suggests a deficit in circuitry centering on the amygdala, within a brain module essential for reading this particular range of emotions, and deficits in the prefrontal area that inhibits impulse.[22]

Looping ordinarily makes people feel within themselves the distress that another person expresses, but psychopaths fail to resonate in this way; their neural wiring deadens them to the range of emotions in the spectrum of suffering.[23] Psychopaths' cruelty appears truly "unfeeling" because they are literally numb in the face of distress, lacking the very radar for detecting human agony.[24]

Like Machs, psychopaths can be adept at social cognition, learning to get inside someone's head to surmise their thoughts and feelings so they can "push all the right buttons." They can be socially smooth, believing that "even when others are upset with me, I can usually win them over with my charm." Some criminal psychopaths make a point of reading self-help books to better learn how to manipulate their targets—something like a "paint-by-numbers" approach to getting what they want.

Some people now use the term "successful psychopaths" for those who have been involved in theft, drug dealing, violent crimes, and the like but have never been convicted or arrested for those acts. Their criminality, in combination with that classic pattern of glib superficial charm, pathological lying, and a history of impulsivity, earns them the status of psychopath. They are "successful," this theory holds, because although they have the same reckless tendencies as other psychopaths, they react more anxiously to anticipated threats. Their greater apprehension leads to a bit of caution, which makes them less likely to end up in prison.[25]

Even as children, many psychopaths displayed coldheartedness; at an early age the tender, caring emotional range seems to have been missing altogether from their inner world. For most children, seeing another child get angry, scared, or sad disturbs them too, so they try to help them feel better. But budding psychopaths fail to perceive others' emotional pain and so do not apply any inner brakes on their own meanness or cruelty. Torture of animals is a childhood precursor of psychopathy in adults. Other warning signs include bullying and intimidation, picking fights, forcing sex, setting fires, and other crimes against property and people.

If we regard someone as merely an object, then we can more easily mistreat them, abuse them, or worse. Such callousness finds an apex in criminal psychopaths like the serial killer, or habitual victimizers like child molesters. Their cold-bloodedness signals how morbidly confused they are when it comes to empathizing with their victim's distress. One jailed serial rapist even said of his victims' terror: "I don't really understand it. I've been frightened myself, and it wasn't unpleasant."[26]

MORAL PRODS

It was the final minutes of a close game that would decide which college's basketball team got to the playoffs. In the heat of the moment Temple University coach John Chaney resorted to desperate measures.

Chaney sent in a six-foot-three, 250-pound giant with orders to commit "hard fouls"—hurt players on the other team. One of those fouls sent an opposition player to the hospital with a broken arm, sidelining him for the rest of the season.

That's when Chaney himself committed a singular act: he suspended himself from coaching.

Then he called the injured player and his parents to apologize, offering to pay the hospital bills.[27] As Chaney told one reporter, "I feel very contrite," and another, "I'm very, very remorseful."

Remorse like Chaney's is the key distinction between the Dark Triad and others who commit reprehensible acts. Remorse and shame—and their close cousins embarrassment, guilt, and pride—are "social" or "moral" emotions. Members of the Dark Triad experience these prods to ethical action in only stunted ways if at all.

Social emotions presuppose the presence of empathy to sense how our behavior will be experienced by others. They act as inner police, keeping what we do and say in line with the interpersonal harmony of a given situation. Pride is a social emotion because it encourages us to do what others will laud, while shame and guilt keep us in line by serving as internal punishments for social misdemeanors.

Embarrassment, of course, is triggered when we violate some social convention, whether by being too intimate, by lacking poise, or by doing or saying the "wrong" thing. Thus the mortification of a gentleman who gave an unsparing critique of an actress's performance to a man he'd just met at a party, only to learn that the actress was the man's wife.

Social emotions can also serve to repair such missteps. When someone shows signs of embarrassment like blushing, others can perceive that she regrets her misstep; they may interpret her embarrassment as indicating a desire to make amends. One study found that when someone who knocks over a supermarket display seems mortified, the people nearby feel far more forgiving than when the culprit appears to be indifferent.[28]

The brain basis of social emotions has been studied in neurological patients prone to faux pas, inappropriate self-revelations, and other violations of interpersonal codes. These patients, who turn out to have lesions in the orbitofrontal area, are legendary for their social recklessness and gaffes.[29] Some neurologists theorize these patients are no longer able to detect expressions of disapproval or dismay and so miss how others are reacting to them. Others see their social lapses as due to the lack of inner emotional signals that would keep their behavior on track.

The basic emotions of anger, fear, and joy are all hardwired into the brain at birth or soon afterward, but social emotions require self-consciousness, a capacity that begins to emerge in the second year of life as a child's orbitofrontal region grows more mature. At around fourteen months babies start recognizing themselves in a mirror. This recognition of oneself as a unique entity brings the reciprocal understanding that other people are separate too—and the ability to feel mortified about what others may think of us.

Before age two, a toddler remains blessedly oblivious to how others might judge her and so feels no embarrassment about, say, dirtying her diapers. But as the realization dawns that she is a separate person, someone others can notice, she has all the ingredients for feeling embarrassed—typically a child's first social emotion. It requires her to be aware not only of how others feel about her, but of how she ought to feel in turn. This heightened social consciousness signals not just her emerging empathy but also her emerging abilities for comparisons, categorizing, and grasping social niceties.

Another kind of social emotion moves us to punish others who do wrong, even when there is a risk or cost to us. In "altruistic anger" one person punishes another's violation of a social norm, such as abusing trust, even when they are not the victim. This righteous anger seems to activate a reward center in the brain, so that enforcing norms by punishing violators (*How dare he cut in line!*) gives us a satisfying feeling.[30]

Social emotions operate as a de facto moral compass. We feel shame, for instance, when others become aware of a wrong we have done. When we feel guilt, on the other hand, it stays private, arising as the feeling of remorse when we realize we have done something amiss. Guilty feelings can sometimes spur people to rectify their wrongs, while shame more often leads to defensiveness. Shame anticipates social rejection, while guilt may lead to atonement. Shame and guilt together ordinarily operate to constrain immoral activities.

But with the Dark Triad these emotions lose their moral power. Narcissists are driven by pride and fear of shame, but they feel little guilt for their self-centered acts. Machs, too, fail to develop a sense of guilt. Guilt requires empathy, which the Mach's emotionally distant relationships lack. And shame stirs for Machs only in a stunted form.

The psychopath's backwardness in moral development stems from a slightly different set of lapses in social emotions. In the absence of both guilt and apprehension, potential punishments lose their power to deter—an explosively dangerous situation in combination with the psychopath's utter lack of empathy with another person's distress. Worse, even if their own actions are the cause of that distress, they feel neither remorse nor shame.

Even a psychopath may excel at social cognition: that purely intellectual grasp of people's reactions and social proprieties may guide a psychopath in setting up victims. A sound test for social intelligence should be able to identify and exclude members of the Dark Triad. We need a measure that cannot be aced by a well-prepped Mach. One solution is to include an evaluation for concern, empathy in action.

Mindblind

For Richard Borcherds, having friends over for a visit is just too confusing. As people get to chattering away, he has trouble following the back-and-forth, the interplay of glances and smiles, the subtleties of innuendo and double entendre, the sea of words—all moving at too high velocity.

He is oblivious to the bluffs and deft feints of the social world. Later, if someone takes the time to explain to him the punch line of a joke, or why one guest stalked out in a huff or another blushed with embarrassment, it can make sense to him. But in the moment all this social haze just goes over his head. So when guests come over, he often just reads a book or withdraws to his study.

Yet Borcherds is a genius, winner of the Fields Medal, the equivalent in mathematics of the Nobel Prize. His fellow mathematicians at Cambridge University hold him in awe, and most of them barely understand the specifics of his theories, so rarified is his field. Despite his social inabilities, Borcherds has found success.

When Borcherds commented in a newspaper interview that he suspected he might have Asperger's syndrome—the subclinical version of autism—Simon Baron-Cohen, head of the Autism Research Centre right there at Cambridge, contacted him. Baron-Cohen then described in great detail the hallmarks of the syndrome to Borcherds, whose matter-of-fact response was: "That's me." The math prodigy has offered himself up as Exhibit A in research on Asperger's.[1]

For Borcherds, communication is purely functional: find out what you need from someone and forget the small talk, let alone telling them what you're feeling or finding out how they're doing. Borcherds shuns the telephone—though he can explain the physics of how it works, the social bit confuses him. He restricts his e-mail to the bare basics of work-related information. When he goes from place to place, he runs, even when someone else has been walking along with him. Though he realizes other people sometimes think him rude, he sees nothing odd in his social habits.

All of this, for Baron-Cohen, bespeaks a classic case of Asperger's, and when Borcherds took standard tests for the syndrome, he fit the profile well. The medal-winning whiz had a low score on being able to read people's feelings from their eyes, on empathy, and on intimacy in friendships. But he scored in the very highest tiers on his understanding of physical causality and on being able to systematize complex information.

That picture—low on empathy, high on systematizing—is the underlying neural pattern in Asperger's, according to years of research by Baron-Cohen and many others. Despite his mathematical brilliance, Borcherds lacks empathic accuracy: he cannot sense what's going on in someone else's mind.

MEAN MONKEY

A cartoon shows a young boy and his father in a living room; a scary-looking creature from outer space crawls down the stairs out of sight of the father but visible to the son. In the caption, the father says, "I give up, Robert. What has two horns, one eye, and creeps?"

To get the joke we must be able to infer things that are unsaid. For one, we need to be familiar with the English language structure of a riddle, so we can deduce that the boy has asked his father, "What has two horns, one eye, and creeps?"

More to the point, we need to be able to read two minds, the boy's and the father's, to understand what the boy knows and contrast that with what the father does not yet realize, and so anticipate the shock he will soon feel. Freud proposed that all jokes juxtapose two different frames on reality: here, one frame is the alien on the stairs, and the other is the father's assumption his son is merely asking a riddle.

This ability to apprehend what seems to be going through someone else's mind is one of our most invaluable human skills. Neuroscientists call it "mindsight."

Mindsight amounts to peering into the mind of a person to sense their feelings and deduce their thoughts—the fundamental ability of empathic accuracy. While we can't actually read another person's mind, we do pick up enough clues from their face, voice, and eyes—reading between the lines of what they say and do—to make remarkably accurate inferences.

If we lack this simple sense, we are at a loss in loving, caring, co-operating—not to mention competing or negotiating—and awkward in even the least taxing social encounter. Without mindsight our relationships would be hollow; we would relate to other people as though they were objects, without feelings or thoughts of their own—the predicament of people with Asperger's syndrome or autism. We would be "mindblind."

Mindsight develops steadily over the first several years of a child's life. Each landmark in the development of empathy moves a child closer to understanding how other people are feeling or thinking or what their intentions might be. Mindsight dawns in stages as a child matures, starting with the simplest self-recognition and developing into sophisticated social awareness ("I know that you know that she likes him"). Consider the following well-established tests, used in experiments on mindsight to chart a child's progress:[2]

• At about eighteen months, place a large mark on a baby's forehead, then have her look in a mirror. Typically those younger than eighteen months will touch the mark on the image in the mirror; those older will touch their own forehead. The younger babies have not yet learned to recognize themselves. Social awareness requires we have a sense of self, distinguishing us from others.

• Offer a child around eighteen months old two different snacks, such as crackers or apple slices. Watch which one the child prefers. Let the child observe you taste each of the snacks, as you exhibit clear disgust at the child's choice and show a strong preference for the opposite choice. Then place the child's hand between the two snacks and ask, "Can you give me one?" Children younger than eighteen months will generally offer the snack *they* liked; older ones will offer the snack *you* preferred. The older toddlers have recognized that their own likes and dislikes can differ from other people's, and that others may think differently than they.

• For three- and four-year-olds, hide a treat somewhere in a room while this child and an older child watch. Have the older child leave the room. Then make sure the younger child sees you move the treat to a new hiding place. Ask the younger child where the older child will look for the treat when he comes back into the room. Four-year-olds will usually say he will look in the original hiding place; three-year-olds will guess the new place. Four-year-olds have realized that someone else's understanding can be different from their own, a lesson the younger ones have not yet grasped.

• The last experiment involves three- and four-year-olds and a hand puppet called Mean Monkey. You show children successively several pairs of stickers, and for each pair Mean Monkey asks which sticker the child wants. On every round Mean Monkey chooses for himself the child's preferred sticker, leaving the other for the child. (That's why he's called Mean Monkey.) By around age four, children "get" Mean Monkey's game and quickly learn to tell him the opposite of what they really want—and so end up with their desired sticker. Younger children typically don't understand the puppet's mean intention and so innocently continue telling the truth, never getting the sticker they want.[3]

Having mindsight demands these basic skills: distinguishing oneself from others, understanding that someone else can think differently from oneself and perceive situations from another perspective, and realizing that their aims may not be in one's own best interests.

As growing children master these social lessons—typically in their fourth year—their empathy approaches that of an adult. With this maturity, part of innocence ends: children become clear about the difference between what they merely imagine and what actually happens. Four-year-olds have attained the basics in empathy that they will draw on throughout life—albeit later on with higher levels of psychological and cognitive complexity.[4]

This maturation of intellect makes them far more adept at piloting themselves through the world they inhabit, from negotiating with siblings to thriving on the playground. These small worlds, in turn, are schools for life. The same lessons will become refined at new levels over the years as children expand their cognitive sophistication, their social networks, and their range of contacts.

Mindsight stands as a prerequisite for younger children's ability to joke, or to get a joke. Teasing, tricks, lying, and being mean all demand this same sense of the other's inner world. Deficiency in these capacities sets autistic children apart from those who develop a normal social repertoire.

Mirror neurons may be crucial for mindsight. Even among normal children, the ability to imagine another person's perspective and to empathize correlates with mirror neuron activity. And fMRI imaging of young teens reveals that, compared to normal children, an autistic group showed a deficiency in prefrontal cortex mirror neuron activity while reading and imitating facial expressions.[5]

Mindsight can go awry even in normal adults. Consider what some women students at Amherst College call "tray gazing." As they file into Valentine Dining Hall for a meal, their eyes gravitate to other women—not to see whom they are eating with or what they are wearing, but instead to study what foods they have on their trays. This helps them abstain from what they otherwise might want to eat but feel they should not.

Catherine Sanderson, the psychologist who discovered tray gazing, pinpointed the distortion in mindsight behind it: each woman saw the others as much thinner, as exercising more, and as more obsessed with how their body looked than they were themselves—when in fact there were no objective differences.

This distorted set of assumptions led the women who held them to diet and, for about a third of them, to engage in induced vomiting or purges—a habit that can evolve into a life-threatening eating disorder.[6] The more erroneous the women's assumptions were about the other women's attitudes, the more extreme their own dieting.

In part the deluded perceptions stem from fixating on the wrong bits of data: college-age women tend to focus on the most attractive or the thinnest women around, so they compare themselves to the most extreme standard rather than to the true average—they mistake the extreme for the norm.

College men are by no means impervious to making a parallel error, though in a different realm: drinking. Those prone to reckless binge drinking judge themselves by the standards of the most excessive drinkers. This misperception leads them to believe they have to overindulge to fit in.

In contrast, those who perform such everyday mindreading more accurately avoid the error of taking the extreme as the norm. Instead they first gauge how similar the other person is to them. If they sense similarity, they simply assume the other person thinks and feels much as they do. A seamless social life depends on a continual stream of such snap judgments—mindsight on the run. We are all mindreaders.

THE MALE BRAIN

Temple Grandin was diagnosed as autistic in childhood. As she tells it, the other kids in school called her Tape Recorder, because the young Temple used the same phrases over and over again in every conversation—and there were very few topics she found interesting.[7]

One of her favorites was to go up to another kid and announce, "I went to Nantasket Park, and I went on the rotor, and I really like the way it pushed me against the wall." Then she'd ask, "How did you like it?"

And once the other kids told her how they had liked the ride, Grandin would repeat herself word for word—over and over again, like a looping tape.

Adolescence announced itself to Temple as a "tidal wave of anxiety that never stopped," another symptom of autism. Here her unique insights into how animals perceive the world—which she likens to the hypersensitivities of people with autism—helped her immensely.

While visiting a dude ranch in Arizona owned by her aunt, Temple saw a herd of cattle on a nearby ranch being run through a "squeeze chute" made of metal bars in an open-V that get progressively narrower as the cow walks through. At one point an air compressor closes the V, squeezing the cow and holding it in place while a vet goes to work.

Instead of being scared by the squeeze, cows calm down while in its tight grasp. Deep pressure like that, Temple realized, is calming—like a baby in swaddling. She immediately saw that something like a squeeze chute would help her, too.

So with the help of a high school teacher, Temple patched together a human squeeze chute out of wood and an air compressor, sized to a person down on all fours. And it works. Whenever she feels the need to calm down, she uses it to this day.

Grandin is unusual in many ways, not the least of which is her diagnosis of autism. Boys are four times as likely as girls to develop autism and ten times more likely to be diagnosed with Asperger's. Simon Baron-Cohen makes the radical proposal that the neural profile of people with these disorders represents the utter extreme of the prototypical "male" brain.

The extreme male brain, he argues, has no clue when it comes to mindsight; its circuitry for empathy remains stunted. But that deficiency comes paired with intellectual strengths, like the mind-boggling laser-focused abilities of savants who can solve complex math problems at rates matched only by computers. Although mindblind, such hypermale brains can be gifted when it comes to understanding systems, such as the stock market, software, and quantum physics.

The most extreme "female" brain, in contrast, excels at empathy and understanding others' thoughts and feelings. Those with this pattern shine at callings like teaching and counseling; as psychotherapists, they are wonderfully empathic and attuned to the inner world of their clients. But those with the ultrafemale pattern have grave difficulties with systematizing, be it applying directions to that fork in the road up ahead or studying theoretical physics. They are, in his word, "systemblind."

Baron-Cohen devised a test to determine how easily someone senses what others feel. The test is called the EQ, for "empathy quotient" (not for "emotional intelligence," as EQ now signifies in several languages), and women on average outscore men. Women also outscore men on measures of social cognition like understanding what would be a faux pas in a given social situation, and on empathic accuracy, intuiting what another person would be feeling or thinking.[8] Finally, women tend to outscore men on Baron-Cohen's test of reading a person's feelings from their eyes alone (see Chapter 6).

But when it comes to systems thinking, the advantage tips to the male brain. As Baron-Cohen points out, men score higher than women, on average, on tests of an intuitive knack for mechanics; keeping track of complicated systems; "Where's Waldo?" fine attention, detecting figures hidden among complex designs; and visual search in general. And on these tests people with autism outscore most men, just as they score the poorest of any group on tests of empathy.

Talking about a so-called "male" or "female" brain gets us into dangerous terrain in social politics. As I write, the president of Harvard University has raised a ruckus with remarks implying that women are innately unsuited for careers in the hard sciences. But Baron-Cohen would abhor any attempts to use his theory to discourage women from becoming engineers—or men from entering the ranks of psychotherapists, for that matter.[9] For the vast majority of people, Baron-Cohen finds, men's and women's brains are in the same ability range for empathy and systems thinking; moreover, many women are brilliant in systematizing, while many men are superb at empathy.

Temple Grandin, perhaps has what Baron-Cohen would call a male brain. For one thing, she has published more than three hundred scholarly papers in animal science. A leading expert on animal behavior, Grandin has developed the designs used by half the cattle-handling systems in the United States. Those systems are based on her remarkable understanding of how to make conditions more humane for the thousands and thousands of cows who pass through them daily. Her expertise has made Grandin a leading reformer in the quality of life of the world's agricultural animals.

The optimal pattern, says Baron-Cohen, is to have a "balanced" brain, one that has strengths in both empathy and systematizing. A physician with these abilities, for instance, would be able to render precise diagnoses and elegant treatment plans, all the while making patients feel heard, understood, and cared about.

Even so, strengths can be found at each extreme. While those with the most "male" brain have a high likelihood of exhibiting symptoms of Asperger's or autism, they can excel in many fields if, like Professor Borcherds, they find a congenial setting to apply their talents. Yet the ordinary social world seems an alien planet to them, so that the most basic rudiments of interaction have to be learned by rote, if at all.

MAKING SENSE OF PEOPLE

"Oh! You're so old!" was the first thing Layne Habib's teenage daughter blurted out on seeing a middle-aged shopkeeper.

"Maybe she doesn't want to hear that," Habib whispered.

"Why not?" her daughter asked, adding matter-of-factly, "In Japan the elderly are honored."

This exchange typifies their ongoing mother-daughter dialogue. Habib spends a lot of time coaching her daughter about the implicit social rules that keep interactions smooth.[10] Like Richard Borcherds, her daughter has Asperger's syndrome and so has little grasp of such niceties.

But with her daughter's blunt frankness comes a refreshing clarity. When her mother told her she should wait for a pause to break off a conversation—rather than just saying "I feel like leaving now" and walking off—her daughter had an aha! moment.

"I get it now," her daughter replied. "You fake it. No one could be all that interested in everything a person says. You just have to wait for the pause to come so you can leave."

These disarmingly honest views have gotten Habib's daughter in trouble over and over. "I need to teach her social strategies for getting along with people," Habib told me. "She needs to learn the little white lies to use so as not to hurt a person's feelings."

Habib, who teaches social skills to groups of children with special needs like her daughter, says mastering these rudiments helps them "join the world, instead of staying isolated in their own." While members of the Dark Triad may scrutinize social rules in order to manipulate others, those with Asperger's study them just to get along.

In Habib's groups children with Asperger's and autism learn to recognize the right way to join a conversation gracefully. Instead of just butting in with their favorite topic, Habib coaches them to listen first to get the gist, then to join in on the same subject.

This difficulty with navigating the interpersonal world points to a more fundamental difficulty in Asperger's. Consider the following vignette:

> Marie dreaded her trips to meet her husband's relatives because they were so boring. Most of the time they all sat in awkward silence, and this occasion was no different.
>
> On the way home, Marie's husband asked her how she had found the visit. Marie said, "Oh, marvelous. I could hardly get a word in edge-wise."[11]

What prompted Marie to say that?

The obvious answer: Marie was being sarcastic, actually implying the opposite of what she said. But that seemingly self-evident deduction eludes people with autism or Asperger's syndrome. To "get" a sarcastic remark, we need to perform a subtle social math, premised on the realization that what the person says is not what the person means. But for people with autism, their deficiency in mindsight means that the simplest social algorithm, like why a snub makes someone feel badly, remains a mystery.[12]

Brain scans of people with autism have found inactivity in a region known as the "fusiform gyrus face area" while looking at a person's face. The facial fusiform area registers not just faces but whatever else we are most familiar with or fascinated by. In birdwatchers, this means the fusiform area lights up when a cardinal flies by; in auto enthusiasts, when a BMW drives up.

For autistic people, however, this area fails to activate when they look at a face—even the faces of their family—but it does activate while they are looking at whatever happens to fascinate them, such as the numbers in a phone directory. A simple rule of thumb has emerged in studies of those with autism: the less activation in the brain's face-reading area while they look at someone, the greater their interpersonal difficulties.

Signs of this social deficit emerge as early as infancy. Most infants show activity in the brain's facial fusiform area when they look at someone's eyes—but autistic children do not. Autistic children show the fusiform activation when they look at a cherished object or even just patterns, such as the way they have neatly arranged their favorite videotapes on a shelf.

Of the close to two hundred muscles of the face, those surrounding the eyes are particularly fine-tuned to express feelings. While normally people focus around the eyes when looking at someone's face, those with autism avoid looking there, so missing crucial emotional information. Avoidance of eye contact may be one of the earliest indicators that a baby will grow up to become autistic.

Largely indifferent to human interaction, people with autism make little or no eye contact with anyone, thereby missing out on the building blocks of human bonding as well as empathy. Though eye contact is a seemingly minor skill, it is crucial for learning the basics of relating to other people. In autistic people the resulting gap in social learning contributes to their massive failure to sense how another person feels and so what they are probably thinking.

Blind children, by contrast, make up for their inability to see faces by developing a keen sensitivity to the emotional cues in voices—made possible because their auditory cortex takes over their unused visual area (making some, like Ray Charles, superb musicians).[13] The resulting hyperawareness of feelings expressed vocally allows for the normal socialization of blind children, while those with autism remain tone deaf to emotion.

One reason autistic infants avoid eye contact seems to be that it makes them anxious—when they look at eyes, their amygdala reacts wildly, indicating intense fear.[14] So instead of looking at a person's eyes, the autistic child looks at the other person's mouth, which conveys little about someone's inner state. While this tactic lessens their anxiety, it means autistic kids miss out on the rudiments of face-to-face synchrony, let alone mindsight.

This deficit in reading emotions, Baron-Cohen reasoned, may help reveal the underlying brain circuitry that operates smoothly in ordinary people but malfunctions in those with autism. So his research team compared people with autism and ordinary people as each lay inside the fMRI while a small video monitor displayed a series of photos of people's eyes like those shown in Chapter 6. The subjects pushed a button to indicate their choice from two offered for what feelings the eyes were expressing, such as "sympathetic" or "unsympathetic."

The autistic subjects, as expected, were largely wrong. More telling, this simple task revealed which parts of the brain are involved in this small act of mindsight. In addition to the orbitofrontal cortex, the key regions included the superior temporal gyrus and the amygdala—areas that, along with a few others, have surfaced again and again in similar studies.

Paradoxically, examining the brains of those who lack finesse offers clues to the layout of the social brain. Comparing differences between normal and autistic brain activity, Baron-Cohen argues, highlights the circuitry that underlies a good part of social intelligence itself.[15]

As we shall see, such neural capacities matter immensely, not just for the richness of our interpersonal life but for the well-being of our children, for our ability to love well, and for our very health.

PART THREE

NURTURING NATURE

Genes Are Not Destiny

Take a four-month-old baby, put him in his baby seat, and show him a toy he's never seen before. Then after twenty seconds show him another one, followed twenty seconds later by another, then another.

Some babies love this onslaught of novelty. And others hate it, crying so hard they shake in protest.

Babies who hate it share a trait that Harvard psychologist Jerome Kagan has studied for close to three decades. As toddlers, such children are wary of strange people and places—"inhibited," Kagan calls them. Once they reach school, their inhibition shows up as shyness. Such children's shyness, Kagan speculates, appears to be due to an inherited neurotransmitter pattern that makes their amygdala more excitable. These kids are hyperaroused by startling things and novel events.

Kagan is among the most influential developmental psychologists to have emerged since Jean Piaget first keenly observed the shifts in cognitive abilities that his own children went through as they grew up. Kagan has the deserved reputation of a first-rate methodologist and thinker, combined with the rare gift of writing like a humanist. His books, with titles like *Galen's Prophecy*, suggest his fluency with philosophical as well as scientific issues.

So back in the late 1970s, when Kagan first pronounced that a trait of temperament like inhibition had biological causes, presumably genetic, many parents breathed a sigh of relief. The ethos of that time was that just about every problem a child showed could be traced back to some error in parenting. A shy child had been cowed by overbearing parents; a bully was hiding his shame, induced by belittling parents, behind a gruff exterior. Even schizophrenics were the product of "double-bind" messages that meant they could never please their parents.

Kagan was a professor in the Harvard psychology department when I was a graduate student. The suggestion by a scientist as eminent as he that biological currents rather than psychological ones were at work in shaping temperament came as a revelation—one quite controversial in some Cambridge circles, as I remember. I heard murmurs in the elevator of William James Hall, which houses Harvard's psychology department, that Kagan had gone over to the biological thinkers—who were at the same time eroding the hold of psychotherapists over the treatment of disorders like depression, which they had the audacity to suggest might have biological causes, too.[1]

Now, decades later, that debate seems a quaint relic of a naïve age. The march of genetic science daily adds to the list of temperamental and behavioral habits that are managed by one bunch of DNA or another. Neuroscience, likewise, continues to discover just which neural circuitry goes awry in a given mental disorder, and what neurotransmitters seem out of whack when a child displays one or another temperamental extreme, from the "overly sensitive" child to the budding psychopath.

And yet, as Kagan always delighted in pointing out, it's not that simple.

THE CASE OF THE ALCOHOLIC RODENTS

My best friend in third grade was John Crabbe, a wiry, brainy kid who wore horn-rimmed, Harry Potter–like glasses. I often rode my bike down the street to his place to spend lazy, pleasant hours playing marathon games of Monopoly. His family moved away the next summer, and I haven't seen him for half a century.

But I found myself calling him up after all these years when I realized that the very same John Crabbe was now a behavior geneticist at the Oregon Health and Science University and the Portland VA Medical Center—and of all things, renowned for his studies of alcoholic rodents. He has for years done research on mice from a strain called C57BL/6J, who are unique in their voracious appetite for alcohol. Studying them holds the promise of clues to the causes and, one hopes, cures for alcoholism in humans.

This strain of alcohol-loving mice is one of a hundred or so that are useful for medical research, such as a susceptibility to diabetes or heart disease. Each mouse in a given inbred strain is, in effect, a clone of every other such mouse; they share their genes like identical twins. One virtue of these strains for scientific researchers is their stability; a mouse of a given strain tested in various labs around the world should react like every other such mouse. But this very assumption of stability was questioned by Crabbe, in a now-famous, simple experiment.[2]

"We asked just how stable is 'stable,' " Crabbe told me when I called. "We did the identical tests in three different laboratories, trying to make every aspect of their environment identical, from the brand of mouse feed they ate—Purina—and their age, to their shipping history. We had them tested at the same hour on the same day with identical apparatus."

So at the identical point—April 20, 1998, between 8:30 and 9:00 A.M. local time—all the mice from eight different inbred strains, including C57BL/6J, were tested. One test simply offered them a choice of drinking regular water or an alcohol solution. True to form, the liquor-lovers chose the rodent martini far more often than did other mouse strains.

Next was a standard test for mouse anxiety. A mouse is placed at the crossroads of two runways, elevated three feet off the ground. Two arms of the crossroads have walls while the other two are open, which can be scary. Anxious mice cower next to the walls, while more adventurous ones explore the open runways.

To the great surprise of those who believe that genes alone determine behavior, however, within a given strain some decided differences on the anxiety test were found from lab to lab. For example, one strain, BALB/cByJ, was very anxious in Portland but quite adventurous in Albany.

As Crabbe noted, "If genes were all, you'd expect to find no differences whatever." What could have caused the differences? Certain variables were beyond control from lab to lab, like the humidity and the water the mice drank—and perhaps most important, the people who handled them. One research assistant, for example, was allergic to mice and wore a respirator while holding them.

"Some people are confident and skilled at handling mice, while others are anxious or too rough," Crabbe told me. "My bet is that mice can 'read' the emotional state of the person handling them, and that state in turn has an impact on the mouse's behavior."

His study, featured in the prestigious journal *Science,* aroused a storm of debate among neuroscientists. They had to grapple with the disturbing news that minor differences from one laboratory to another, such as how the mice were handled, created disparities in how the mice behaved—which implied a difference in how the identical genes acted.[3]

Crabbe's experiment, together with similar findings from other labs, suggests that genes are more dynamic than most people—and science for more than a century—have assumed. It's not just which genes we are born with, but their *expression,* that matters.

To understand how our genes operate, we must appreciate the difference between possessing a given gene and the degree to which that gene expresses its signature proteins. In gene expression, essentially, a bit of DNA makes RNA, which in turn creates a protein that makes something happen in our biology. Of the thirty thousand or so genes in the human body, some are expressed only during embryonic development, then shut off forever. Others turn on and off constantly. Some express themselves only in the liver, others only in the brain.

Crabbe's finding stands as a landmark in "epigenetics," the study of ways the experiences we undergo change how our genes operate—without altering our DNA sequence an iota. Only when a gene directs the synthesis of RNA does it actually make a practical difference in the body. Epigenetics shows how our environment, translated into the immediate chemical surround of a given cell, programs our genes in ways that determine just how active they will be.

Research in epigenetics has identified many of the biological mechanisms that control gene expression. One of them, involving the methyl molecule, not only turns genes on or off but also tones down or speeds up their activity.[4] Methyl activity likewise helps determine where in the brain the more than 100 billion neurons end up, and which other neurons their ten thousand connections will link to. The methyl molecule sculpts the body, including the brain.

Such insights put to rest the century-old debate on nature versus nurture: do our genes or our experiences determine who we become? That debate turns out to be pointless, based on the fallacy that our genes and our environment are independent of each other; it's like arguing over which contributes more to the area of a rectangle, the length or the width.[5]

Simply possessing a given gene does not tell the whole story about its biological value. For example, the food we eat contains hundreds of substances that regulate a host of genes, turning them on and off like flickering Christmas tree lights. If we eat the wrong foods over a period of years, we can activate a combination of genes that will result in the clogged arteries of heart disease. On the other hand, a bite of broccoli offers a dose of vitamin B6, which spurs the tryptophan hydroxalese gene to produce the amino acid L-tryptophan, which helps synthesize dopamine, a neurotransmitter that stabilizes mood, among other functions.

It is biologically impossible for a gene to operate independently of its environment: genes are *designed* to be regulated by signals from their immediate surround, including hormones from the endocrine system and neurotransmitters in the brain—some of which, in turn, are profoundly influenced by our social interactions.[6] Just as our diet regulates certain genes, our social experiences also determine a distinct batch of such genomic on-off switches.

Our genes, then, are not sufficient in themselves to produce an optimally operating nervous system.[7] Raising a secure child, or an empathic one, in this view, requires not just a necessary set of genes but also sufficient parenting or other apt social experiences. As we'll see, only this combination ensures that the right genes will operate in the best way. From this perspective, parenting exemplifies what we might call "social epigenetics."

"Social epigenetics is part of the next frontier in genomics," says Crabbe. "The new technical challenge involves factoring in the impact of environment on differences in gene expression. It's another blow against the naïve view of genetic determinism: that our experiences don't matter—that genes are all."

GENES NEED EXPRESSION

James Watson—who won the Nobel Prize for his seminal discovery, with Francis Crick, of the double-helix design of DNA—admits to having a hair-trigger temper. But, he adds, he also gets over his anger quickly. That rapid recovery, he observes, stands toward the better end of the spectrum of how genes associated with aggression can operate.

The gene in question helps *inhibit* anger and can operate in two ways. In one, the weaker, the gene expresses extra-small amounts of the enzyme that controls aggression, and so the person angers easily, stays much angrier than most, and will be more prone to violence. People at that extreme can readily end up in prison.

In the other form the gene expresses lots of its enzyme, so, like Watson, the person may get angry but will recover quickly. Having the second pattern of gene expression makes life a bit more pleasant, so that irritating moments don't linger too long. Some people with that pattern, apparently, can win the Nobel Prize.

If a gene never expresses the proteins that could direct the body's functioning in a given way, then we may as well not possess that gene at all. If it expresses them a small bit, then the gene will matter a little—and if the expression comes full force, then the gene matters maximally.

The human brain is designed to change itself in response to accumulated experience. Possessing the consistency of butter at room temperature and locked into its bony cage, the brain is as fragile as it is complex. Part of this fragility results from an exquisite attunement to its surroundings.

It had long been assumed that gene-controlling events were strictly biochemical—getting proper nutrition, or (in a worst case) exposure to industrial toxins. Now epigenetic studies are looking at how parents treat a growing child, finding ways child rearing shapes that child's brain.

A child's brain comes preprogrammed to grow, but it takes a bit more than the first two decades of life to finish this task, making it the last organ of the body to become anatomically mature. Over that period all the major figures in a child's life—parents, siblings, grandparents, teachers, and friends—can become active ingredients in brain growth, creating a social and emotional mix that drives neural development. Like a plant adapting to rich or to depleted soil, a child's brain shapes itself to fit its social ecology, particularly the emotional climate fostered by the main people in her life.

Some brain systems are more responsive to these social influences than are others. And each network of brain circuitry has its own peak period when social forces can shape it. Some of the most profound impacts seem to occur during the first two years of life, a period when the brain undergoes its biggest growth spurt—from a puny 400 grams at birth to a robust 1,000 grams at twenty-four months (on the way to an average of 1,400 grams in adulthood).

From this stage on, critical personal experiences in our lives seem to set biological rheostats that fix the level of activity for genes that regulate brain function, as well as other biological systems.

Social epigenetics expands the spectrum of what regulates certain genes to include relationships.

Adoption can be seen as a unique natural experiment, in which we may evaluate the impact of the adoptive parents' influences on a child's genes. One study of belligerence in adopted children compared the family atmosphere fostered by their biological parents with that of their adopted families. When children who were born into families with a history of aggressive, belligerent violence were adopted by peaceable families, just 13 percent of the adoptees displayed antisocial traits as they grew up. But when such children were adopted into "bad homes"—families where aggression had free rein—45 percent went on to become violent themselves.[8]

Family life seems to alter the activity of genes not just for aggression but for a vast number of other traits. One dominant influence seems to be how much nurturing love—or cold neglect—a youngster receives. Michael Meaney, a neuroscientist at McGill University in Montreal, is passionate about the implications of epigenetics for human connection. Meaney, slight of build and a charming speaker, shows scientific guts in his readiness to draw conclusions for the human case from his elaborate studies of lab mice.

Meaney has discovered, at least for mice, a vital way that parenting can change the very chemistry of a youngster's genes.[9] His research identifies a singular window in development—the first twelve hours after a rodent's birth—during which a crucial methyl process occurs. How much a mother rat licks and grooms her pups during this window actually determines how brain chemicals that respond to stress will be made in that pup's brain for the rest of its life.

The more nurturing the mother, the more quick-witted, confident, and fearless the pup will become; the less nurturing she is, the slower to learn and more overwhelmed by threats the pup will be. Just as telling, the mother's level of licking and grooming determines how much a female pup, in turn, will lick and groom her own pups one day.

The pups born to devoted mothers, who licked and groomed the most, grew up to have denser connections between their brain cells, particularly in the hippocampus, the seat of memory and learning. These pups were especially clever at a key rodent skill: finding their way around a physical layout. Moreover, they were less upset by life's stresses and were more able to recover from a stress reaction when they had one.

The offspring of less nurturing and inattentive mothers, on the other hand, ended up with less dense connections between neurons. They scored poorly on solving mazes—the "IQ test" equivalent for mice.

For rat pups, the greatest neural setback occurs if they are completely separated from their mothers while still quite young. This crisis flips off protective genes, leaving them vulnerable to a biochemical chain reaction that floods their brain with toxic stress-triggered molecules. Such young rodents grow up to be easily frightened and startled.

The human equivalents of licking and grooming seem to be empathy, attunement, and touch. If Meaney's work translates to humans, as he suspects it does, then how our parents treated us has left its genetic imprint over and above the set of DNA they passed down to us. And how we treat our children will, in turn, set levels of activity in *their* genes. This finding suggests that small, caring acts of parenthood can matter in lasting ways—and that relationships have a hand in guiding the brain's continuing redesign.

THE NATURE-NURTURE PUZZLE

It's all very easy to talk about epigenetics when you're dealing with genetically hybrid mice in meticulously controlled laboratories. But just try to sort it out in the messy human world.

That was the daunting challenge undertaken in the massive study led by David Reiss at George Washington University. Reiss, famed for his astute research on family dynamics, teamed up with Mavis Heatherington, an expert on stepfamilies, and Robert Plomin, a leader in behavior genetics.

The gold standard for studies of nature versus nurture has been to compare children who are adopted with those raised by their biological parents. This lets researchers assess how much a trait such as aggression seems due to influences from the family, and how much to biology alone.

In the 1980s Plomin had startled the scientific world with his data from studies of adopted twins showing what portion of a trait or ability was due to genes and what to the way a child was raised. A teenager's scholastic ability is about 60 percent due to genes, he asserted, while the sense of self-worth is only about 30 percent genetic, and morality but 25 percent.[10] But Plomin and others using his method came under scientific fire because they typically assessed impacts only in a limited range of families, mainly those where twins were raised by biological parents compared with those raised by stepparents.

So the Reiss group resolved to include many more variations on stepfamilies, working far greater specificity into the equation. Their rigorous design demanded that they find 720 pairs of teenagers representing the entire range of genetic closeness, from identical twins to several varieties of stepsiblings.[11]

The group combed the nation to recruit families with just two teenage children in any of six specific configurations. Finding families with identical and fraternal twins, the standard procedure in their field, was no problem. Harder to find, however, were families where each parent had been previously divorced and brought only one teenager to the new stepfamily. Harder still, the stepparents had to have been married for at least five years.

After the excruciating search to find and recruit just the right families, the researchers spent years analyzing the resulting vast mass of data. Then came more frustrations. Some were due to an unexpected finding: every child *experiences* the very same family in sharply idiosyncratic ways.[12] Studies of twins reared apart have taken for granted that every child in a given family experiences it alike. But the Reiss group research—like Crabbe's with lab mice genetics—blew that assumption to bits.

Consider an older sibling versus a younger one. From birth the older one has no rival for her parents' love and attention; then the younger one comes along. From day one the younger child needs to develop stratagems to compete for parental time and affection. Children vie to be unique, which results in their being treated differently. So much for the one-family-one-environment school of thought.

Even worse, these unique-to-one-child aspects of family life turned out to have great power in determining a child's temperament above and beyond any genetic influences. So the way a child defines her unique niche in the family can follow any of countless modes, making them epigenetic wild cards.

Moreover, although parents have some impact on a child's temperament, they are not the only ones. So do an array of other people in a child's life, particularly their siblings and friends.

To complicate the equation further, a surprise factor showed up as an independent, and powerful, shaper of a child's destiny: the ways a child comes to *think* about herself. To be sure, a teenager's sense of overall self-worth depends much on how that child has been treated and almost not at all on genetics. But then, once formed, the child's sense of self-worth shapes her behavior quite apart from the hapless ministrations of parents, the pressures of peers, or any genetic given.[13]

Now the equation for social impacts on genes takes another twist. A child's genetic givens in turn shape how everyone treats him. While parents naturally cuddle with babies who flirt and hug back, testy or indifferent babies get less cuddling. In the worst case, when a child's genetics lead him to be irritable, aggressive, and difficult, parents tend to respond in kind, with harsh discipline, tough talk, and their own criticism and anger. That route worsens the child's difficult side, which in turn evokes more of the parents' negativity, in a vicious spiral.[14]

The warmth of a child's parents, or how limits are set, or myriad other ways a family operates, the researchers concluded, help set the expression of many genes. But in addition a bossy sibling or screwy buddy both have their impact.

The old, once seemingly clear distinction between the aspects of a child's behavior that stem from genetics and those that derive from her social world blurs substantially. In the end, after all those millions of research dollars spent and the exhausting search for just the right families, the Reiss group yielded fewer specifics of the myriad complex interactions between family life and genes than they did puzzles yet to solve.

It appears too early in this science to track every epigenetic pathway in the chaotic fog of family life. Even so, from this mist a few crystal-clear bits of data are emerging. One suggests the power of life experiences to alter genetic "givens" in behavior.

FORGING NEURAL TRAILS

The late hypnotherapist Milton Erickson used to tell about growing up in a tiny town in Nevada early in the twentieth century. Winters there were quite severe, and one of his delights was to wake up and find that it had snowed during the night.

On such days young Milton would rush to get ready for school, to be sure that he was the first one to make a path through the snow to the schoolhouse. Then he would intentionally take a circuitous, zigzag route, his boots the first to plow a path through the new-fallen snow.

No matter how many twists and turns he made in the path, inevitably the next kid would follow this route of least resistance—and the next, and the next after that. By the end of the day, it would have become a fixed route, the invariable track everyone followed.

Erickson used the tale as a metaphor for how habits are formed. But his story of that first track through the snow, and the repeated traversing that followed, also offers an apt model for how neural pathways are laid down in the brain. The first connections made in a neural circuit become strengthened each time the same sequence gets followed, until the pathways become so strong that they are the automatic route—and a new circuit has been put in place.

Because the human brain packs so much circuitry in so little space, it creates continuous pressure to extinguish connections the brain no longer needs, to make space for those it must have. The adage "use it or lose it" refers to this ruthless neural Darwinism, where brain circuits vie with one another to survive. Those neurons we lose are "pruned," disappearing like twigs cut from a tree.

Like the mound of clay a sculptor starts with, the brain generates more material than it needs to take its final shape. Over the course of childhood and the teen years, the brain will selectively lose half those overabundant neurons, keeping the ones that are used and dropping those that are neglected, as the child's life experiences—including relationships—sculpt its brain.

In addition to determining what connections are preserved, our relationships help shape our brain by guiding the connections made by new neurons. Here too old assumptions in neuroscience crumble. Even today some students are taught that once we are born, the brain cannot manufacture new cells. This theory has now been soundly disproven.[15] In fact, we know that the brain and spinal cord contain stem cells that turn into new neurons at the rate of thousands a day. The pace of neuron creation peaks during childhood but continues into old age.

Once a new neuron has come into being, it migrates to its position in the brain and, over the course of a month, develops to the point where it makes about ten thousand connections to other neurons dispersed throughout the brain. Over the next four months or so, the neuron refines its connections; once these pathways are linked, they are locked in. As neuroscientists like to say, cells that fire together wire together.

During this five-or-six-month period, personal experience dictates which neurons the newborn cell will connect with.[16] The more often an experience repeats, the stronger the habit becomes, and the denser the resulting neural connectivity. Meaney has found that in mice repetitive learning speeds the rate at which new neurons integrate into circuits with other neurons. In this way the brain continues to be redesigned, as new neurons and their connections are put in place.

Well and good for mice—but what about for us humans? The same dynamics seem to apply, with profound implications for the shaping of the social brain.

Each brain system has an optimal period during which experience maximally shapes its circuitry. Sensory systems, for instance, are largely shaped during early childhood, and language systems mature next.[17] Some systems, like the hippocampus—in humans as in rats, the seat for learning and memory—continue to be strongly shaped by experience throughout life. Studies with monkeys reveal that specific cells in the hippocampus that take up their positions only during infancy may fail to migrate to their designated position if the infant undergoes extreme stress during that critical period.[18] Conversely, loving parental care can enhance their migration.

In humans, the longest window for shaping occurs with the prefrontal cortex, which continues to be molded anatomically into early adulthood. Thus the people in a child's life have a decades-long opportunity to leave an imprint on that child's executive neural circuitry.

The more a particular interaction occurs during childhood, the more deeply imprinted it becomes in the brain's circuitry—and the more "stickiness" it will have as that child moves through life as an adult. Those repeated moments from childhood will become automatic paths in the brain, like Milton Erickson's tracks in the snow.[19]

Take as an example spindle cells—those superrapid connectors of the social brain. Researchers find that in humans these cells migrate to their proper placement—largely in the orbitofrontal cortex and anterior cingulate cortex—at around four months, at which point they extend their connections to thousands of other cells. These neuroscientists propose that just where and how richly spindle cells connect depends on influences like family stress (for the worse) or a warm and loving atmosphere (for the better).[20]

Spindle cells, remember, bond the high and low roads, helping us orchestrate our emotions with our responses. That neural connectivity undergirds a crucial set of social intelligence skills. As Richard Davidson (the neuroscientist we met in Chapter 6) explained, "After our brain registers emotional information, the prefrontal cortex helps us manage our response to it skillfully. The shaping of these circuits by genes interacting with the experiences in our life determines our affective style: how quickly and strongly we respond to an emotional trigger, and how long it takes us to recover."

When it comes to learning the self-regulatory skills so vital for smooth social interactions, Davidson comments, "There is a lot more plasticity early in life than later. The animal evidence indicates that some of the effects of early experience can be irreversible so that once a circuit is shaped by the environment in childhood, it then becomes quite stable."[21]

Picture a mother and baby as they play an innocent game of peekaboo. As his mother repeatedly covers and uncovers her face, the baby grows increasingly excited; at the peak point of intensity, the baby abruptly turns away from her and sucks his thumb, dully staring into space.

That stare signals a time-out period the baby needs to calm himself down. The mother gives him the time he needs, waiting until he's ready to resume their game. A few seconds later he turns back to her and they beam at each other, smiling.

Contrast that game of peekaboo with this one: again the game reaches its crescendo of excitement, the point at which the baby needs to turn away, suck his thumb, and calm down before reengaging his mother. Except this time she doesn't wait for him to turn back to her. Instead she leans over into his line of vision, clicking her tongue to demand that his attention return to her.

Her baby just keeps looking away, ignoring his mother. Undaunted, she moves her head still closer, setting him off fussing and grimacing, pushing her face away. Finally, he turns even farther away from the mother, sucking feverishly on his thumb.

Does it matter that one mother attunes to the signal her baby sends, while the other ignores his message?

Nothing can be proven by a single game of peekaboo. But repeated, multiple failures by a caretaker to attune, much research suggests, can have lasting effects. When reprised throughout childhood, these patterns shape the social brain in ways that make one child grow up delighted with the world, affectionate, and comfortable with people, while others grow up sad and withdrawn, or angry and confrontational. Once such differences might have been attributed to the child's "temperament," a stand-in for genes. Now the scientific action centers on how a child's genes may be set by the thousands of routine interactions a child experiences growing up.

| HOPE FOR A CHANGE |

I can remember Jerome Kagan talking in the 1980s about the research he had under way in Boston and in faraway China that used a baby's reactions to novelty to identify children who would grow up to be timid and shy. Kagan, by now semiretired, still continues this line of investigation, following some of the "Kagan babies" into their early adult years.[22] I drop in on him every few years in his old office on the top floor of William James Hall, the tallest tower on the Harvard campus.

On my most recent visit he told me about his latest finding, from fMRI studies of Kagan kids. Kagan, always up to the minute in his research methods, had joined the fMRI crowd. As he told me, a study of twenty-two Kagan babies, who as children had been identified as inhibited and were now in their twenties, had just found that their amygdalas still overreacted to anything out of the ordinary just as they had done before.[23]

One neurological indicator of this timidity profile appears to be higher activity in the colliculus, a part of the sensory cortex that is activated when the amygdala detects something anomalous and possibly threatening. This neural circuitry triggers whenever we perceive a discrepancy, like a picture of a baby's head on a giraffe body. The images that elicit this activation need not be outright threats—anything strange-looking or "crazy" will do the trick.

Kids who have low reactivity in these circuits tend to be outgoing and sociable. But youngsters who have high reactivity shy away from anything unusual; the novel frightens them. Such predispositions in a young child tend to be self-reinforcing, as protective parents shield their timid toddlers from the very encounters that might help them learn an alternative reaction.

In earlier studies Kagan discovered that when parents encourage these timid kids to spend time with peers whom they might otherwise avoid (and sometimes parents have to be forceful), the children can often overcome the genetic predisposition to shyness. After decades of research Kagan has found that among children identified shortly after birth as "inhibited," only one-third still showed timid behavior as they entered early adulthood.

Now he realizes that what seems to change is not so much the underlying neural hyperreactivity—the amygdala and colliculus still overreact—but rather what the brain does with the impulse. Over time children who learn to resist the urge to withdraw become able to engage more fully, showing no outward signs of their inhibition.

Neuroscientists use the term "neural scaffolding" to describe how once a brain circuit has been laid out, its connections become strengthened with repeated use—like a scaffold being erected at a building site. Neural scaffolding explains why a behavioral pattern, once it is established, requires effort to change. But with new opportunities—or perhaps just with effort and awareness—we can lay down and strengthen a new track.

As Kagan told me about the inhibited children, "Seventy percent grow toward health. Temperament may constrain what can be, but it does not determine it. These kids are no longer frightened or hyperreactive."

Take as an example one boy, identified as inhibited in infancy, who had learned by his teen years to feel his fear and act anyway. Now no one, he said, realized that he still felt shy. But it took some help and effort—and a series of small victories, seemingly using the high road to tame the low.

One triumph he remembers was overcoming his fear of shots, which in childhood was so severe that he refused to go to the dentist—until he finally found a dentist who won his trust. Seeing his sister jump into a pool gave him the courage to overcome his own fear of getting water on his face, and so he learned to swim. While at first it took talking to his parents to get over a bad dream, eventually he learned to calm down on his own.

"I was able to get over my fears," the formerly worry-bound boy wrote in a school essay. "Because I now understand my predisposition towards anxiety, I can talk myself out of simple fears."[24]

And so with a bit of help, a positive change can occur naturally for many of these inhibited children. The right urging from family or others can help, as can understanding how to manage their own reticence. So does using naturally occurring "threats" to challenge their inhibited tendencies.

Kagan tells of his own granddaughter, who was very shy at six, saying to him: "Make believe I don't know you—I have to practice not being shy."

He adds, "Parents don't realize that though biology constrains certain outcomes, it does not determine what *can* happen."

Parenting cannot change every gene, nor modify every neural tic—and yet what children experience day after day sculpts their neural circuitry. Neuroscience has begun to pinpoint with surprising specificity how some of that sculpting operates.

A Secure Base

At twenty-three, he had just graduated from a well-known university—in those days in Britain, a ticket to a successful career. Yet here he was severely depressed, planning suicide.

As he revealed to his psychotherapist, his childhood had been one ongoing misery.

His parents' frequent quarrels often ended in violence. The eldest of a large family, he already had two younger siblings by the time he reached his third birthday. His father spent much time away from the family for work, and his mother—overwhelmed by the squabbles of her tribe of youngsters—would sometimes lock herself in her bedroom for hours, even days, at a time.

As a young child, he was left alone to cry for long periods—his parents believed that a child's crying was just an attempt "to be spoilt" by their attention. He felt that his most basic feelings and needs were ignored.

His signature memory from childhood was the night he developed appendicitis and lay awake until dawn, moaning and alone. He also remembers hearing his younger brothers and sisters as they cried themselves to exhaustion, his parents indifferent. And he remembers hating them for it.

His first day of school was the most miserable of his life. Being deposited there seemed like the final rejection by his mother. Desperate, he cried the whole day.

As his childhood went on, he came to hide all his yearning for love, refusing to ask his parents for anything. During therapy he was terrified that if he let his feelings into the open and cried, his therapist would see him as an attention-seeking nuisance and—he fantasized—lock himself away in another room until he left.[1]

That clinical account was offered up by the British psychoanalyst John Bowlby, whose writings on the emotional bonds between parent and child have made him the most influential thinker in child development to emerge from the followers of Freud. Bowlby tackled grand themes in human life like abandonment and loss—and the emotional attachments that make those so powerful.

Though trained in the classic patient-on-the-couch mode of psychoanalysis, Bowlby did something revolutionary for his time, roughly from the 1950s on: He observed mothers and infants directly rather than depending solely on the unverifiable memories of patients in psychoanalysis. And he followed up with those children to see how their early interactions shaped their interpersonal habits.

Bowlby identified a healthy attachment to parents as the crucial ingredient in a child's well-being. When parents act with empathy and are responsive to a child's needs, they build a basic sense of security. Such consistent empathy and sensitivity was precisely what that suicidal patient had lacked. And he continued to suffer because he saw his current relationships through the lens of his tragically troubled childhood.

Every child, Bowlby argues, needs a preponderance of I-You connections in childhood to thrive throughout life. Well-attuned parents offer a child a "secure base," people they can count on when they are upset and need attention, love, and comfort.

The notion of attachment and a secure base was elaborated by Bowlby's chief American disciple, the equally influential development theorist Mary Ainsworth.[2] Scores of researchers, following her lead, have by now accumulated mounds of data and have detected in the subtleties of early parent-infant interactions powerful impacts for whether a child will be secure for life.

Virtually from birth, babies are not mere passive lumps but active communicators seeking their own intensely urgent goals. The two-way emotional message system between a baby and her caretaker represents her lifeline, the route through which passes all the traffic to get her basic needs fulfilled. Babies need be tiny masters at managing their caretakers through an elaborate, built-in system of eyes contacted and avoided, smiles, and cries; lacking that social intercom, babies can remain miserable or even die from neglect.

Watch a protoconversation between any mother and her infant, and you will see a finely orchestrated emotional dance, one in which the partners switch taking the lead. As the baby smiles or cries, the mother reacts accordingly: in a very real sense, the emotions of the infant direct what the mother does as much as the mother directs the infant. Their exquisite responsiveness to each other indicates that their loop operates in both directions, a primal emotional highway.

This parent-child loop offers the central passageway for parents to help their children learn the ground rules for relationships—how to attend to another person, how to pace an interaction, how to engage in conversation, how to tune in to the other person's feelings, and how to manage your own feelings while you are engaged with someone else. These essential lessons lay the foundations for a competent social life.

Surprisingly, they also seem to shape intellectual development: the intuitive emotional lessons from the wordless protoconversation of the first year of life build the mental scaffolding for actual conversations at age two. And as a child masters the habit of talking, it primes that private inner conversation we call thinking.[3]

Research has also found that a secure base does more than provide an emotional cocoon: it seems to nudge the brain to secrete neurotransmitters that add a small bolt of pleasure to that feeling of being well loved—and it does the same for whomever provides that love. Decades after Bowlby and Ainsworth proposed their theories, neuroscientists identified two pleasure-inducing neurotransmitters, oxytocin and endorphins, that are activated by looping.[4]

Oxytocin generates a sense of satisfying relaxation; endorphins mimic the addictive pleasure of heroin in the brain (though not nearly so intensely). For a toddler, parents and family offer this savory security; playmates and, later in life, friendships and romantic intimacy activate the same circuits. The systems that secrete these chemicals of nurturing love include familiar parts of the social brain.

Injury to the areas with the most oxytocin receptors severely impairs maternal nurturing.[5] The wiring seems largely the same in infants as in their mothers—and also appears to provide some of the neural cement for the loving bond they form. Children who are well nurtured have the sense of a secure base in part because these very brain chemicals evoke the inner sense that "everything is all right" (possibly the biochemical basis for what Erik Erikson saw as an infant's basic sense of trust in the world).

Mothers whose children will grow up to be secure are more attentive and responsive to their baby's cries, more affectionate and tender, and more comfortable in close contact like cuddling. These attuned mothers repeatedly loop with their baby.[6] But those children whose mothers were often out of synch with them display insecurity, in either of two flavors. If a mother habitually intrudes, the infant copes by shutting down, actively trying to avoid interactions. When the mother seems uninvolved, the baby reacts with a helpless passivity at being unable to connect—the very pattern brought into his adult life by Bowlby's suicidal patient.

Less extreme than outright neglectful mothers are those who create emotional distance with their child, even keeping a physical gap between them, talking to or touching the child relatively little. Such children often display a "stiff-upper-lip" pretense of not caring, although in reality their bodies reveal signs of heightened anxiety. These children come to expect that others will be aloof and distant and so hold back emotionally. As adults they avoid emotional intimacy, tending to withdraw from people.

On the other hand, mothers who are anxious and self-preoccupied tend to be out of tune with their child's needs. When a mother fails to be dependably available and attentive, some infants react by feeling fearful and clingy. These children, in turn, can become absorbed in their own anxieties and so are less able to attune well. In adult relationships they tend toward anxious clinging.

Happy, attuned interactions are as much a basic need for an infant as is feeding or burping. Lacking such synchronous parenting, children are more at risk of growing up with disturbed attachment patterns. In short, well-empathized children tend to become secure; anxious parenting produces anxious children; and aloof parents produce avoidant children, who withdraw from emotion and from people. In adulthood, these patterns will manifest as secure, anxious, or avoidant styles of attachment in relationships.

The transmission of these patterns from parent to child appears to be largely through the relationship. For instance, twin studies find that if a secure child gets adopted by an anxious parent, the child will most likely end up sharing that anxious pattern.[7] The attachment style of a parent predicts the child's style with about 70 percent accuracy.[8]

But if an anxious child can find a secure "surrogate parent"—an older sibling, a teacher, or another relative who does much of the caregiving—her emotional pattern can shift toward the secure.

STILL FACE

A mother shares some pleasant moments with her baby, when suddenly a subtle change comes over her. The mother's face goes blank and unresponsive.

At that, her baby panics a bit, a look of anguish sweeping over his face.

The mother shows no emotion, makes no response to his distress. She has gone stone cold.

Her baby starts to whimper.

Psychologists call this scenario "still face," and they use it intentionally to explore the foundations of resilience, the ability to recover from distress. Even after the still-face mother returns to her well-connected manner, babies continue to show distress for a while. How quickly they recover indicates how well they have mastered the rudiments of emotional self-management. During the course of the first year or two of life, that basic skill builds, as babies practice over and over going from upset to calm, from out of synch to looping.

When a mother's face goes blank and she seems suddenly withdrawn, this invariably provokes the baby to make repair attempts to get his mother to respond. Babies signal their mother in every way they know, from flirting to crying; some eventually give up, looking away and sucking their thumb to try to soothe themselves.

In the view of Edward Tronick, the psychologist who invented the still-face method, the more successfully infants solicit "repairs" of that broken loop, the better at it they become. From this emerges another strength: such babies come to see human interactions as reparable—they believe that they have the capacity to set things right when something has gone out of synch with another person.

So they begin to build the scaffolding for a resilient lifelong sense of themselves and their relationships. Such children grow up seeing themselves as effective, as able to have positive interactions and to repair them if they go off track. They assume other people will be trustworthy and reliable partners.

Six-month-old babies have already started developing a typical style of interacting with other people and a habitual way of thinking about themselves and others. What makes this vital learning possible is that sense of safety and trust—in other words, rapport—developed with the person who is providing the guidance. This I-You relationship makes all the difference in a child's social growth.

Mother-infant synchrony operates from a child's first day of life; the more synchrony, the warmer and the happier are their overall interactions.[9] Being out of synch, however, makes newborns angry, frustrated, or bored. If a baby gets a constant diet of dis-synchrony and solitary misery, he will learn to rely on whatever strategy for calming down he has stumbled upon. Some, seemingly giving up hope of outside help, focus on finding ways to make themselves feel better. In the adult version of this attitude, countless people, when feeling down, turn to solitary consolations like overeating, drinking, or compulsive channel surfing.

As time goes on and the child grows up, he may deploy such strategies automatically and inflexibly, no matter what the situation may be—constructing a defense against anticipated bad experiences, whether that anticipation has a solid basis or not. So instead of approaching people with an open, positive attitude, the child may reflexively withdraw into a protective shell, seeming cold and distant.

THE DEPRESSED LOOP

An Italian mother sings a happy ditty to Fabiana, her baby: "Clap, clap, your little hands / Daddy will be here soon. / He'll bring you sweet candies / Fabiana, you'll eat them up."[10]

Her tone is joyful, the tune an upbeat allegro, and Fabiana delightedly joins in on the beat with coos.

But when another mother sings the same ditty to her baby—this time in a monotonous, low-pitched largo—her baby responds with signs of distress, not delight.

The difference? The second mother suffers from clinical depression; the first mother does not.

This simple discrepancy in how mothers sing to their babies bespeaks a vast difference in the emotional surround that their babies feel as they grow up—and in how they will feel in every other major relationship they have throughout life. Depressed mothers understandably find it difficult to engage their babies in happy protoconversation; they lack the energy for the lilting tones of Motherese.[11]

In their interactions with their babies, depressed mothers tend to be poorly timed and "off," or intrusive, angry, or sad. The failure to synchronize disables looping, while the negative emotions send the message that the baby has done something wrong and needs to change somehow. That message in turn upsets the baby, who can neither get his mother to help calm him down nor effectively do so himself. With this, the mother and her infant can all too easily fall into a downward spiral of miscoordination, negativity, and messages ignored.[12]

Depression, behavior geneticists tell us, can be inherited. Much research has tried to calculate the "heritability" of depression—the odds that such a child will herself become clinically depressed at some point in her life. But as Michael Meaney points out, children born with a parent prone to bouts of depression inherit not only that parent's genes but also the depressed parent—who may well act in ways that foster that gene's expression.[13]

For instance, studies of clinically depressed mothers and their infants reveal that depressed mothers tend to look away from their babies more than others, become angry more often, are more intrusive when their babies need a recovery time-out, and are less warm. Their babies typically make the only protest they know—crying—or seem to give up, becoming apathetic or withdrawn.

A given baby's typical response may vary: if the mother tends toward anger, the baby becomes angry too; if the mother tends to be passively withdrawn, so her baby becomes. Babies seem to learn these interaction styles from the ongoing series of out-of-synch moments with their depressed mother. Moreover, they are at risk for acquiring a faulty sense of themselves, having learned already that they cannot bring about a repair when they are unhappy and out of synch, or rely on others to help them feel better.

A mother's depression can become the transmission route by which all the personal and social ills bearing down on her affect her child. A mother's funk, for example, has negative hormonal effects on a child that show up as early as infancy: babies of depressed mothers have higher levels of stress hormones and lower levels of dopamine and serotonin, a chemical profile linked to depression.[14] A toddler may be unaware of the larger forces impinging on her family, but those forces will become embedded in her nervous system nonetheless.

Social epigenetics offers hope to such children. Parents who are somewhat depressed but can manage to show good cheer in the face of difficulty seem to minimize the social transmission of depression.[15] And having additional caretakers who are not depressed offers a reliably secure base.

Some children of depressed mothers learn another lesson, one that has adaptive qualities. Many of these children become exquisite readers of their mother's shifting emotions and as adults are artful at handling their interactions to keep them as pleasant (or minimally upsetting) as possible. Taken into the larger world, those skills can translate into a hard-earned social intelligence.[16]

THE WARPING OF EMPATHY

• *Johnny let his best friend use his new ball. But his friend wasn't careful and lost the ball. And he wouldn't give Johnny another one.*

• *Johnny's friend, who he really liked to play with, moved away. Johnny couldn't play with his friend anymore.*

Both of these small melodramas capture moments of high emotion in any young child's life. But just what emotion do they reflect?

Most children learn to distinguish one feeling from another and to grasp what has led to this feeling or that. But children who are severely neglected by their parents do not. When these vignettes were read to such preschoolers, the answers they gave were wrong half the time—a far poorer rate of recognition than for preschoolers who had been well nurtured.[17]

To the degree a child has been deprived of the very interactions that teach this lesson, his ability to read emotions in life's events will suffer. Children deprived of vital human contact fail to make crucial distinctions among emotions; their sense of what others feel remains fuzzy.[18]

When preschoolers who had been abused—whose caregivers had repeatedly injured or inflicted physical pain on them—were read the two vignettes about Johnny, they saw anger where none existed. Abused children perceive anger in faces that are neutral, ambiguous, or even sad. That overperception of anger suggests a hypersensitized amygdala. This heightened sensitivity seems selective for anger: when abused children look at faces that show anger, their brains react with stronger activation than do those of other children—though their brains respond normally to faces showing joy or fear.[19]

This warp in empathy means that the least sign that someone may be angry captures the attention of abused children. They scan for anger more than other kids do, "see" it when it is in fact not there, and keep looking at such signs longer.[20] Detecting anger where it does not exist may have crucial benefits for such children.

After all, at home they face real danger, so their hypersensitivity makes sense as protective radar.

Trouble brews when these children bring that heightened sensitivity with them into the world outside home. Schoolyard bullies (who typically have a history of physical abuse) overinterpret anger, reading antagonism into faces that are neutral. Their attacks on other children are often due to their misperceiving hostile intent where there is none.

Handling a child's angry outbursts poses any parent a great challenge—and an opportunity. Ideally the parent will not let herself become angry in return, nor simply be passive, abandoning the child to his pique. Instead, when a parent manages her own anger, neither pushing it away nor indulging in it, while staying looped, she offers the child a safe container for learning to handle his own irritations. This does not mean, of course, that the child's emotional surroundings must always be tranquil—just that there should be enough resilience in the family system to recover from upsets.

The family surround creates a young child's emotional reality. A cocoon of safety that stays intact can buffer a child even against the most terrible events. What kids are most concerned about in any major crisis comes down to: how does this affect my family? For example, children living in a war zone will skirt later trauma symptoms or heightened anxiety if their parents manage to create a stable, reassuring environment from day to day.

This does not mean that parents should suppress their distress to "protect the kids." Stanford University psychiatrist David Spiegel studied the emotional reactions in families after 9/11. Children, Spiegel notes, are hyperaware of the emotional currents within their family. As he explains, "The emotional cocoon works not when parents pretend nothing has happened but when they let children know we're dealing with how upset we are as a family, together."

THE REPARATIVE EXPERIENCE

His father was prone to violent rages, especially when drunk—which was just about every night. In those fits of anger, his father would grab one of his four sons and deliver a beating.

Years later he confided to his wife the fears he still carried. As he all too vividly recalled, "Whenever I saw my father's eyes narrow, we kids knew it was time to get out of the room."

His wife, telling me about that confession, added a more subtle lesson for her: "I realize my husband wasn't paid attention to as a child. So even when I'm hearing the same old story over and over, I remind myself, 'Stay here.'

"If he sees my attention flicker for a second, he gets hurt," she adds. "He's hypersensitive to the moments when I start to tune out. Even when I still *seem* to be listening, he knows the instant I go away inside."

Anyone who in childhood was treated by caretakers as an It rather than as a You is likely to bear such sensitivities and emotional wounds. Those tender spots emerge most often in close relationships—with a spouse, children, and good friends. But in adulthood close relationships can offer a healing scenario: the person, instead of being ignored or worse, is treated as a You—as was that hypersensitive husband and his assiduously attuned wife.

Like a nourishing parent or spouse, a good psychotherapist becomes a safe base for such neglected people. UCLA psychologist Allan Schore has become a heroic figure among many psychotherapists for his massive reviews of neuroscience that center on the patient-therapist relationship.

Schore's theory holds that the neural site for emotional malfunction is primarily in the orbitofrontal cortex (OFC), that keystone in the brain's relationship pathways.[21] The very growth of the OFC, he argues, depends on a child's experience. If parents offer attunement and a secure base, the OFC flourishes. If they are unresponsive or abusive, its development goes awry—resulting in a limited ability to regulate the length, intensity, or frequency of distressing emotions like anger, terror, or shame.

Schore's theory highlights how our interactions play a role in reshaping our brain, through neuroplasticity—the way repeated experiences sculpt the shape, size, and number of neurons and their synaptic connections. Some potent shaping occurs in our key relationships by repeatedly driving our brain into a given register. In effect, being chronically hurt and angered, or emotionally nourished, by someone we spend time with daily over the course of years, can refashion the circuitry of our brain.

Schore argues that nurturing relationships later in life can to some extent rewrite the neural scripts that were encrypted in the brain during childhood. In psychotherapy the active ingredients in this emotional repair work include rapport and trust, with patient and therapist looping well.

The therapist, Schore says, serves as a projection screen for reliving early relationships. But this time the patient can live those relationships more fully and openly, without judgment, blame, betrayal, or neglect. Where a father was distant, the therapist can be available; where a mother was hypercritical, the therapist can be accepting—so offering a reparative experience that may have been yearned for but never achieved.

One mark of effective psychotherapy is the opening up of a freer emotional flow between therapist and client, who learns to loop without dreading or blocking distressing feelings.[22] The best therapists create a secure emotional atmosphere, a safe container for whatever feelings the client may need to feel and express—from murderous rage to sullen sadness. The very act of looping with the therapist, then passing feelings back and forth, helps the client learn to handle those same emotions on her own.

Just as children learn how to manage their own feelings in the safety of a secure base, psychotherapists provide adults a chance to finish the job. Similar reparative effects can result with a romantic partner or a good friend who offers these nurturing human qualities. If effective, therapy—or other reparative relationships in life—can enrich the capacity for connection, which in itself has healing properties.

---------------------| **1 2** |---------------------

The Set Point for Happiness

A three-year-old in an ornery mood comes upon her visiting uncle, who is a handy target for her grumpiness.

"I hate you," she declares.

"Well, I love you." He smiles back, bemused.

"I hate you," she replies more loudly, adamant.

"I still love you," he says, more sweetly.

"I *hate* you!" she yells, with dramatic gusto.

"Well, I *still* love you," he reassures her, sweeping her up in his arms.

"I love you," she concedes softly, melting into his hug.

Developmental psychologists view such pithy interactions in terms of the underlying emotional communication. The I-hate-you/I-love-you disconnect is, in this view, an "interaction error," and getting back on the same emotional wavelength is "repair" of that error.

A successful repair, like the final rapport achieved between this three-year-old and her uncle, makes both partners feel good. Continued disrepair has the opposite effect. A child's ability to repair such a disconnection—to weather an interpersonal emotional storm and then reconnect again—is one key to lifelong happiness. The secret lies not in avoiding life's inevitable frustrations and upsets but in learning to recover from them. The faster the recovery, the greater the child's capacity for joyfulness.

That capacity, as with so many others in social life, begins in infancy. When a baby and his caregiver are in synch, each reciprocates the other's messages in a coordinated way. But during the first year of life, babies lack much of the neural wiring necessary to carry off such coordination. They stay well coordinated only about 30 percent of the time or less, with a natural cycle of going from in synch to out of synch.[1]

Being out of synch makes babies unhappy. They protest via signs of frustration—in effect, asking for help getting back in synch. This betokens their first attempts at interaction repair. Mastery of these essential human skills seems to begin in those small shifts from out-of-synch misery to in-synch calm.

Everyone in a child's day offers a model, for better or for worse, of how to handle distress. This learning goes on implicitly (no doubt via mirror neurons) as a child witnesses how an older sibling, a playmate, or a parent manages their own emotional storms. Through such passive learning, the OFC's regulatory circuits for calming the amygdala "rehearse" whatever strategy the child witnesses. A bit of this learning also goes on explicitly whenever someone reminds or helps a child to manage her own rocky feelings. With time and practice, the OFC circuitry for regulating emotional impulses gradually strengthens.

Children learn not only to calm down or resist emotional impulses but also to strengthen their repertoire of ways to affect others. This lays the foundation for becoming an adult who can react the way that three-year-old's uncle did when he lovingly melted away her grumpiness—rather than stiffening and warning, "Don't you dare speak to me that way!"

By age four or five, children are able to shift from simply trying to control their upsetting emotions to having a greater understanding of what causes their distress and what to do to relieve it—a sign of high-road maturation. Parental coaching in the first four years of life, some psychologists suspect, may be particularly potent in shaping a child's later abilities to manage her emotions well and to handle rocky encounters smoothly.

To be sure, adults do not always offer the best models. In one study parents of preschoolers were observed during a marital disagreement. Some couples were antagonistic and disjointed in their attempts to resolve their conflicts. Neither party listened to the other, they were angry and contemptuous, and they often withdrew from each other as their hostility grew. The children of these couples imitated this pattern with their playmates, being demanding and angry, bullying and hostile.[2]

In contrast, those couples who during their disagreements displayed more warmth, empathy, and mutual understanding also approached parenting together with greater harmony, even playfulness. And these parents had children who in turn got along better with playmates and could work disagreements out more productively. *How* couples work out their disagreements predicts their children's conduct, even years later.[3]

If all goes well, the result will be a child who is resilient in the face of stress and able to recover from distress and to attune effectively. It takes a socially intelligent family to help build what developmental psychologists call a "positive affective core"—in other words, a happy child.[4]

FOUR WAYS TO SAY NO

A fourteen-month-old boy, so typically for that mischievous age, gets into a dangerous fix as he tries to climb onto a table where a lamp perches precariously.

Consider several possible ways a parent could respond:

• Give a firm "No!" and then tell him climbing is for outdoors—and take him there to find a place to do so.

• Ignore the boy's climbing, only to hear the crash of the falling lamp, pick it up, and quietly tell him not to do that again—and then pay no attention to him.

• Shout an angry "No!" but feel guilty about reacting too harshly, give him a reassuring hug, then leave him alone because he has been such a disappointment.

These parental reactions—implausible as some may seem—all represent discipline styles that appear repeatedly in observations of parents and children. Daniel Siegel, the UCLA child psychiatrist who offers the scenarios, has emerged as one of the most influential contemporary thinkers in psychotherapy and child development as well as a pioneer in social neuroscience. Siegel argues that each of these types of parental reaction shapes centers in the social brain in unique ways.[5]

One moment for such shaping comes when a child confronts something upsetting or confusing, and she looks to her parents, reading not just what they say, but their entire demeanor, to learn how to feel and respond. The messages parents send at such "teachable moments" slowly build the child's sense of herself and how to relate to—and what to expect from—the people around her.

Take the parent who told the climbing boy no, then took him outside to redirect his energies. In the view of Siegel's colleague Allan Schore, that interaction optimally affects the boy's orbitofrontal cortex, strengthening the OFC's emotional "brake." Here that neuronal array tones down the youngster's initial excitement, helping him learn how to better manage his impulsivity.[6] Once the child applies these neural brakes, the parent teaches that a more appropriate excitement can continue—he can climb a jungle gym but not a table.

What the boy learns, in essence, comes down to: "My parents don't always like what I do, but if I stop and find something better, everything will be okay." This approach, in which the parent sets a boundary and then finds a better outlet for the child's energy, typifies the discipline style that results in secure attachment. Securely attached children experience attunement from their parents—even when they've been naughty.

The "terrible twos," when babies start to defy their parents by shouting "No!" when they are told to do something, signals a major milestone in brain development. The brain is beginning to be able to inhibit impulse—to say no to urges—a capacity that becomes refined throughout childhood and the teen years.[7] Apes and very young children alike have great trouble with this aspect of social life, for the same neural reason: the array of neurons in their OFC that can stop an impulse from being enacted is underdeveloped.

Over the course of childhood the OFC will gradually mature anatomically. A neural growth spurt starts at around age five, allowing more of this circuitry to come online just in time to send the child off to school. That spurt continues apace to around age seven, greatly boosting the child's self-control and making second-grade classrooms far less rambunctious than kindergarten. Each stage of intellectual, social, and emotional development in a growing child marks a similar step in the maturation of brain areas; this anatomical process continues into the mid-twenties.

What happens in a child's brain when parents consistently fail to attune well depends on the precise nature of that failure. Daniel Siegel describes ways parents can fall short and the resulting difficulties their children are likely to endure.[8]

Take the parent who responded to the table-climbing toddler by ignoring him. That response typifies a parent-child relationship where attunement of any kind occurs rarely, and the parents are emotionally uninvolved with the child. Such children encounter only frustration in trying to get empathic attention from their parents.

The absence of looping—and hence shared moments of pleasure or joy—increases the odds that a child will grow up with a diminished capacity for positive emotions and in later life will find it difficult to reach out to other people. Children of such avoidant parents grow up skittish; as adults, their expression of emotions is inhibited, particularly those emotions that would help them bond with a partner. In keeping with the model their parents displayed they avoid not just expressing their feelings but also emotionally intimate relationships.

The third parent reacted to the table-climbing first by becoming angry, then by feeling guilty, then by being disappointed with the boy. Siegel fittingly describes such parents as "ambivalent." They may on occasion be warm and caring, but more often they send signals to the child of disapproval or rejection—facial expressions of disgust or contempt, averting their gaze, body language signifying anger or disconnection. This emotional stance can leave the child repeatedly feeling hurt and humiliated.

Children often respond to such parenting with uncontrollable emotional swings, their impulses unchecked or running amok—like the classic "bad boy" who always gets into trouble. Siegel suggests that underlying such out-of-control behavior is a child's brain that has failed to master how to say no to impulse, a task of the OFC.

But sometimes the sense of not being cared about, or of "whatever I do it's wrong," leaves a child despairing—though still yearning for positive parental attention. Such children come to regard themselves as basically flawed. In adulthood, they tend to bring to their close relationships this same ambivalent combination of yearning for affection with an intense fear that they will not get it—and an even deeper fear of being abandoned altogether.[9]

THE WORK OF PLAY

Even now, in middle age, poet Emily Fox Gordon vividly remembers being "wildly, uncontrollably" happy as a young girl growing up with loving parents in a small New England village. The whole town seemed to embrace Emily and her brother as they zipped down the streets on their bikes: "The elms stood guard, the local dogs greeted us, and even the telephone operators knew us by name."

Traipsing freely through backyard gardens, racing around the local college campus, she felt as though she were wandering a gentle Eden.[10]

When a child feels well loved and cared for, worthy in the eyes of especially important figures in her life, the resulting well-being creates a reservoir of positivity. That in turn seems to fuel another basic impulse: the urge to explore the world at large.

Children need more than a secure base, a relationship where they can be soothed. Mary Ainsworth, Bowlby's chief American disciple, proposed they also need a "safe haven," an emotionally secure place, like their room or home, to return to after going out and exploring the wider world.[11] That exploration can be physical, as in riding a bike around the neighborhood; interpersonal, as in meeting new people and making friends—or even intellectual, as in pursuing a wide-ranging curiosity.

A simple sign that a child feels he has a safe haven is going out to play. Playful fun has serious benefits; through years of hard play, children acquire a range of social expertise. For one, they learn social savvy, like how to negotiate power struggles, how to cooperate and form alliances, and how to concede with grace.

All that practice can go on while playing with a relaxed sense of safety—even a mistake can trigger giggles, while in a schoolroom the same mistake might draw ridicule. Play offers children a secure space to try out something new in their repertoire with minimum anxiety.

Exactly why playing is so much fun has become clearer with the discovery that the brain circuitry that primes play also arouses joy. Identical circuitry for playfulness can be found in all mammals, including the ubiquitous laboratory mouse. This tract hides in the most ancient neural zones, down in the brain stem, a pocket near the spine that governs reflexes and our most primordial responses.[12]

The scientist who has studied the neural circuitry of play in greatest detail may be Jaak Panksepp, at Ohio's Bowling Green State University. In his masterwork, *Affective Neuroscience*, Panksepp explores the neural source of all the major human drives—including playfulness, which he sees as the brain's source of joy.[13] The primal subcortical circuitry that prompts the young of all mammals to romp in rough-and-tumble play, Panksepp says, seems to have a vital role in a child's neural growth. And the emotional fuel for all that developmental work seems to be delight itself.

In research with rodents in the lab, Panksepp's group has discovered that play offers another arena for social epigenetics, "fertilizing" the growth of circuitry in the amygdala and frontal cortex. His work has identified a specific compound generated during play that drives genetic transcription in these fast-developing areas of a youngster's social brain.[14] His findings, which likely extend to other mammals like humans that share that same neural landscape, add new significance to that young child's universal yearning, "I want to play."

Playing can go on most readily when a child feels she has a safe haven and can relax, sensing the comfort of a trusted caregiver's presence. Just knowing that Mommy or that nice babysitter is somewhere in the house gives a child enough security to lose herself in another world, one of her own invention.

A child's play both demands and creates its own safe space, one in which she can confront threats, fears, and dangers—but always come through whole. In this sense, play can be therapeutic. In play everything that goes on gets suspended in an "as if" reality. For example, play offers children a natural way to manage feared separations or abandonments, rendering them instead opportunities for mastery and self-discovery. Likewise, without fear or inhibition, they can face desires and impulses that are too dangerous to enact in reality.

A clue to why we want a play "mate"—why being two makes playing more joyful—lies in our wiring for being tickled. All mammals have "tickle skin," peppered with specialized receptors that transmit the brain messages for a playful mood. Tickling triggers the belly laugh, which has circuitry distinct from that for smiling. The human belly laugh, like play itself, has approximations in many mammals, which is always elicited by tickling.

In fact Panksepp discovered that like human toddlers, baby rats are drawn to adults who will tickle them. The tickled rat utters a chirp of delight that seems to be an evolutionary cousin of the rapturous laugh of a tickled three-year-old child. (In rats, it's a high-frequency chirping at about 50 kilohertz, out of range of the human ear.)

In humans the tickle zone runs from the back of the neck around the rib cage—the easiest patch of skin to launch a youngster into uncontrolled gales of laughter. But triggering that reflex demands another person. The reason we can't tickle ourselves seems to be that the neurons for tickling are tuned to react to unpredictability—which is why simply wiggling a finger at a youngster along with a threatening "coochi-coochi-coo" will set off wild laughter—the primal joke.[15]

The circuitry for playful joy has close ties to the neural networks that make a "ticklish" child laugh.[16] And so our brain comes hard-wired with an urge to play, one that hurls us into sociability.

Panksepp's research raises an intriguing question: what do you call a child who exhibits hyperactivity, impulsivity, and unfocused, rapid shifting from one activity to another? Some might see these shifts as indicators of attention-deficit/hyperactivity disorder (ADHD), which has reached epidemic proportions among schoolchildren, at least in the United States.

But Panksepp, extrapolating to humans from his work with rodents, sees the shifts instead as signs of an active neural system for play. He notes that the psychostimulant medications given to children for ADHD all reduce the activity of the brain's play modules when given to animals, just as they seem to snuff out playfulness in children. He makes a radical, though untested, proposal: let younger children "vent" their urge to play in an early-morning free-play, rough-and-tumble recess, then bring them into a classroom after their urge to play has been sated, when they can more easily pay attention.[17] (Come to think of it, that's just what used to happen in my grammar school, long before anyone ever heard of ADHD.)

At the brain level, time spent playing pays off in neuronal and synaptic growth; all that practice strengthens brain pathways. Beyond that, playfulness throws off a kind of charisma: adults, children, and even lab rats are drawn to spend more time with those who have had abundant practice playing.[18] Some primitive roots of social intelligence surely trace to this low-road circuitry.

In the interplay of the brain's myriad control systems, the play circuitry defers to bad feelings—anxiety, anger, and sadness—all of which suppress playfulness. Indeed, the urge to play does not emerge until a child feels protected: comfortable with newly encountered playmates, familiar with a strange playground. That same inhibition of playfulness by anxiety shows up in all mammals, reflecting a basic neural design that no doubt has survival value.

As a child matures, the circuitry for emotional control will slowly suppress the effervescent urge to giggle and romp. As the regulatory circuits of the prefrontal cortex develop in late childhood and the early teen years, children are more able to meet the social demands to "get serious." Slowly these energies are channeled into more "grown-up" modes of pleasure, as child's play becomes mere memory.

THE CAPACITY FOR JOY

When it comes to the capacity for joy, Richard Davidson nears the upper limits. Without question, he's just about the most upbeat person I know.

Davidson and I were graduate students together years ago, and he has had an outstanding research career. When I became a science journalist, I got in the habit of consulting him for explanations of new—and, for me, puzzling—findings in neuroscience. Just as I found his research pivotal when I was writing *Emotional Intelligence,* I drew on his work again in my exploration of social neuroscience. (For instance, his lab discovered that the more the orbitofrontal cortex activates as a mother gazes at a picture of her newborn, the stronger her feelings of love and warmth.)

As a founder of the field of affective neuroscience—the study of emotions and the brain—Davidson's research has mapped the neural centers that give each of us a unique emotional set point. This neural pivot point fixes the range that our emotions typically swing through during any given day.[19]

That set point—whether dour or upbeat—has remarkable stability. Research studies have found, for instance, that the elation people feel after winning a huge amount of money in a lottery settles back in about a year to the range of mood they felt before winning. The same holds true for people who become paralyzed in an accident; a year or so after the initial agony, most return to nearly the same daily moods they had before the accident.

When people are in the grip of distressing emotion, Davidson has found the two brain areas most active are the amygdala and the right prefrontal cortex. When we're feeling cheery, those areas are quiet, while part of the left prefrontal cortex lights up.

Activity in the prefrontal area alone tracks our moods: the right side activates when we are upset, the left when we are in good spirits.

But even when we are in a neutral mood, the ratio of background activity in our right and left prefrontal areas is a remarkably accurate gauge of the range of emotions we typically experience. People with more right-side activity are particularly prone to down or upsetting moments, while those with more activity on the left generally have happier days.

The good news here: our emotional thermostat does not seem to be fixed at birth. To be sure, each of us has an innate temperament that makes us more or less prone to happy or dour days. But even given that baseline, research links the kind of care we get as children to our brain's capacity for joy in adulthood. Happiness thrives with resilience, the ability to overcome upsets and return to a calmer, happier state. There seems to be a direct link between stress resilience and that capacity for happiness.

"A great deal of animal data," Davidson observes, "shows that nurturing parents—a rodent mother who grooms and licks, for example—promote happiness and resilience under stress in their young. In animals and humans alike, one index of positive affect is a youngster's capacity for exploration and sociability, especially under stress like that of an unfamiliar setting. Novelty can be appraised as a threat or as an opportunity. Animals who had more nurturing in their upbringing will view a strange place as an opportunity. They'll explore it more freely and be more outgoing."

That finding in animals fits a discovery Davidson made in studies of humans—specifically adults in their late fifties, who had been assessed every few years since their high school graduation. Those with most resilience and the best daily moods showed a revealing pattern of brain activity when Davidson's group measured their happiness set point. Intriguingly, those adults who recalled being most well nurtured as children tended to have the more joyous pattern.[20]

Were those warm memories of childhood just created by the rosy lens on life that good moods provide? Perhaps. But as Davidson told me, "The amount of joy in a toddler's relationships appears critical to setting the brain pathways for happiness."

RESILIENCE

A wealthy New York couple of my acquaintance had a daughter late in life. These middle-aged parents dote on her. They have hired a team of nannies to give her constant attention, and they have bought her what looks like an entire store's worth of toys.

But despite her castlelike dollhouse, jungle gym, and rooms packed with playthings, it all seems a bit forlorn: this four-year-old has never had a friend over to play. Why? Her parents are afraid that another child might do something that would upset her.

The couple subscribes to the misguided theory that if their child can avoid all stressful situations, she will develop into a happier person.

That notion misreads the data on resilience and happiness: such overprotection is in fact a form of deprivation. The idea that a child should avoid misery at all costs distorts both the reality of life and the ways children learn to find happiness.

More important for a child than seeking some elusive perpetual happiness, researchers find, is learning how to deescalate emotional storms. The goal for parenting should not be achieving a brittle "positive" psychology—clinging to a state of perpetual joy in one's children—but rather teaching a child how to return on her own to a state of contentment, whatever may happen.

For instance, parents who can "reframe" an upsetting moment (the wisdom in the old saying "No use crying over spilt milk") teach their children a universal method for undoing distressing emotions. Such small interventions instill in a child's repertoire for managing bad times the ability to look on the bright side. At the neural level these lessons become ingrained in the OFC circuitry for managing distress.[21]

If we fail to learn in childhood how to handle the full catastrophe of a rich life, we grow up emotionally ill prepared. Learning to build these inner resources for a happier life demands that we endure the hard knocks of the playground—boot camp for the inevitable upsets of everyday relationships. Given how the brain masters social resilience, children need to rehearse for the ups and downs of social life, not experience a steady monotone of delight.

When a child gets upset, the value lies in attaining some mastery over that reaction. A child's success or failure in this essential lesson will be reflected in his stress hormone levels. In the beginning weeks of the school year, for example, preschoolers who are most outgoing, socially competent, and well liked show high activity in the brain circuit that triggers stress hormones. This reflects their physiological effort to meet the challenge of entering a new social group, their playmates.

But for these more socially adept preschoolers, stress hormone levels decline as the year goes on, as they find a comfortable niche in this small community. In contrast, those preschoolers who remain unhappy and socially isolated as the year continues maintain high stress hormone levels or even increase them as the year wears on.[22]

The "first week jitters" rise in stress hormone activity is a helpful metabolic response, mobilizing the body to handle a dicey situation. The biological cycle of arousal and return to normal as a challenge becomes mastered etches the sine wave for resilience. By contrast, children who are slow to develop distress mastery show a very different pattern. Their biology seems inflexible, their arousal levels "stuck" in too high a gear.[23]

| J U S T   S C A R Y   E N O U G H |

When she was two, one of my granddaughters went through several months of being fascinated by the cartoon movie *Chicken Run,* a somewhat dark comedy about poultry trying to escape a farm where they are doomed to be slaughtered. Parts of the cartoon have the grim tone of a prison movie rather than the lightness of a children's cartoon. Some of the scary scenes arouse outright fear and terror in a two-year-old.

Yet for a long while my granddaughter insisted on seeing that movie over and over, week after week. She freely admitted she found *Chicken Run* "really scary." Yet in the next breath she would add that it was her favorite movie.

Why should a movie so scary exert such an inexorable pull on her? The answer may well lie in her neural learning as she repeatedly watched those frightening scenes, a delicious mix of still being a bit frightened yet knowing it would end up all right.

Some of the most convincing neuroscience data for the benefits of getting just scared enough comes from studies of squirrel monkeys.[24] When they were but seventeen weeks old (the monkey equivalent of young childhood), the monkeys were taken from their cozy cage once a week for ten weeks. They were put for an hour in another cage with adult monkeys they did not know—terrifying for squirrel monkey youngsters, as ample signs testified.

Then, when they had just been weaned (but were still emotionally dependent on their moms), the same monkeys were placed with their mothers in a strange cage. This cage had no other monkeys but offered abundant treats and many places to explore.

Those monkeys who had earlier been exposed to the stressful cages proved far braver and more curious than others their age who had never left their mothers' side. They explored the new cages freely and treated themselves to the snacks there; those who had never left the safe haven of their mothers just clung timidly to her.

Significantly, the independent youngsters showed no biological signs of fear arousal, although they had done so amply as youngsters while in the strange cage. The regular visits to a scary place acted as an inoculation against stress.

In humans as well as monkeys, neuroscientists conclude, if youngsters are exposed to stresses they learn to handle, this mastery becomes imprinted in their neural circuitry, leaving them more resilient when facing stress as adults. Repeating that sequence of fear-turning-into-calm apparently shapes the neural circuitry for resilience, building an essential emotional capacity.

As Richard Davidson explains, "We can learn to be resilient by being exposed to a threat or stress at a level that allows us to manage it." If we are exposed to too little stress, nothing will be learned; too much, and the wrong lesson might become embedded in the neural circuitry for fear. One sign that a scary movie is too overwhelming for a child can be seen in how quickly he recovers physiologically. If his brain (and body) stay stuck in the fear-arousal mode for a distressingly prolonged period, then what's being rehearsed is not resilience but the *failure* to recover.

But when the "threats" a child confronts are within an optimal range—where the brain temporarily mounts a full fear response but then returns to calm—we can assume that a different neural sequence has unfolded. This may well explain my two-year-old granddaughter's pleasure in that scary movie. And it may be why so many people (particularly preteens and teenagers) adore movies that scare them.

Depending on the age and the child, even mildly scary fare can be too much. The old Disney classic *Bambi,* in which a doe's mother dies, was in its day traumatic for many of the children who flocked to see it. A toddler, of course, should not watch a terror-stirring movie of the *Nightmare on Elm Street* variety, but the same movie might give a teenager's brain lessons in resiliency. While the toddler would be overwhelmed, the teen might enjoy a yeasty mix of peril and pleasure.

If a too-horrific movie haunts a child for months with nightmares and daytime fearfulness, then the brain has failed to master fear. Instead it merely primes, and perhaps subtly strengthens, the fear response itself. Researchers suspect that, for children who suffered repeatedly from overwhelming stress—not the on-screen variety, but the much scarier raw reality of disturbingly turbulent family life—this very neural path may lead in some cases to depression or anxiety disorders in later life.

The social brain learns well by imitating models—like a parent who calmly watches what otherwise seems so menacing. When my granddaughter would get to a particularly frightening moment in the movie and hear from her mommy the comforting words "It will be okay" (or get the same message tacitly by feeling the reassuring presence of her daddy as she sat in his lap), she felt secure and in control of her feelings, a sense that she can deploy in other trying times.

Such basic lessons in childhood will leave their mark through life, not just in a basic stance toward the social world but in one's ability to navigate the whirlpools of adult love. And love, in turn, fosters its own lasting biological imprints.

PART FOUR

LOVE'S VARIETIES

Webs of Attachment

In the terrain of the human heart, scientists tell us, at least three independent but interrelated brain systems are at play, all moving us in their own way. To untangle love's mysteries, neuroscience distinguishes between neural networks for attachment, for caregiving, and for sex. Each is fueled by a differing set of brain chemicals and hormones, and each runs through a disparate neuronal circuit. Each adds its own chemical spice to the many varieties of love.

Attachment determines who we turn to for succor; these are the people we miss the most when they are absent. Caregiving gives us the urge to nurture the people for whom we feel most concern. When we are attached, we cling; when we are caregiving we provide. And sex is, well, sex.

The three intermingle in an elegant balance, an interplay that, when all goes well, furthers Nature's design for continuing the species. After all, sex alone merely begins the job. Attachment provides the glue that keeps not just a couple but a family together, and caregiving adds the impulse to look after offspring, so our children can grow up to have their own. Each of these three strands of affection connects people in different ways.[1] When attachment entwines with caring and sexual attraction, we can savor full-blown romance. But when any of these three goes missing, romantic love stumbles.

This underlying neural wiring interacts in differing combinations in love's many varieties—romantic, familial, and parental—as well as in our capacities for connecting, whether in friendship, with compassion, or just doting on a cat. By extension, the same circuits may be at work to one extent or another in larger realms, like spiritual longing or an affinity for open skies and empty beaches.

Many pathways for love travel the low road; someone who fit the narrow definition of social intelligence as based on cognition alone would be clueless here. The forces of affection that bind us to each other preceded the rise of the rational brain. Love's reasons have always been subcortical, though love's execution may require careful plotting. And so loving well requires a full social intelligence, the low road married to the high. One or the other alone will not be enough to forge strong, satisfying bonds.

Untangling the complex neural web for affection may lay bare some of our own confusions and problems. The three major systems for loving—attachment, caregiving, and sexuality—all follow their own complex rules. At a given moment any of these three can be ascendant—say, as a couple feels a warm togetherness, or when they cuddle their baby, or while they make love. When all three of these love systems are operating, they feed romance at its richest: a relaxed, affectionate, and sensual connection where rapport blossoms.

The first step in forming such a union involves the attachment system, in its scouting mode. As we've seen, this system begins its operation in earliest infancy, guiding an infant to seek care and protection from others, most particularly from its mother or other caregivers.[2] And there are fascinating parallels between how we form our first attachments in life and how we form our initial connection to a romantic partner.

THE ART OF THE FLIRT

Friday night, and a horde of smartly dressed men and women are packed tightly into a bar on New York's Upper East Side. It's a singles event, and flirting is the order of the evening.

A woman parades past the bar heading for the powder room, tossing her hair and swaying her hips. As she promenades past a man who has caught her interest, she lets her eyes meet his for just a moment, and then, as she sees him start to return her gaze, she quickly looks away.

Her unstated message: *Notice me.*

That inviting look, followed by coyness, imitates an approach-withdrawal sequence found in most mammalian species where survival of newborns requires a father's help; the female needs to test a male's willingness to pursue and commit. Her flirtatious move is so universal in the art of flirting that ethologists have observed it even in rats: a female will repeatedly run toward and away from a male, or dart past him, wiggling her head, all the while emitting the same high-pitched squeal that rat pups make while playing.[3]

The flirtatious smile is catalogued among Paul Ekman's eighteen varieties: the flirter smiles while facing elsewhere, then gazes directly at the target of ardor just long enough to be noticed, before quickly looking away. That coy tactic takes advantage of an ingenious neural circuit that almost seems to have been planted in the male brain just for that moment. A team of neuroscientists in London discovered that when a man receives the direct gaze of a woman he finds attractive, his brain activates a dopamine circuit that delivers a dollop of pleasure.[4] Simply looking at beautiful women, or making eye contact with someone not perceived as attractive, fails to stir this circuitry.

But whether or not men find a given woman appealing, flirting itself pays off: men most frequently approach those women who flirt a lot, rather than more attractive women who don't flirt.

Flirting goes on among people in cultures around the world (as one researcher documented from Samoa to Paris with a camera that takes pictures from its side).[5] Flirting is the opening move in a continuing series of tacit negotiations at each step in courtship. The first strategic gambit involves casting a wide net, by reckless broadcasting of one's readiness to engage.

Very young infants do the same, promiscuously signaling their interest in interacting with just about any friendly person who happens by and lighting up to welcome whomever responds.[6] The parallel in adult flirting includes not just that flirtatious smile but making eye contact and talking animatedly in a high-pitched voice with exaggerated gestures—much like an infant on the prowl for friendly interaction.

Next comes the Talk. At least in American culture, this essential step in a budding courtship has an almost mythic quality: a conversation with the subtext of determining whether the prospective partner actually would be worth becoming attached to. This step gives the high road a central role in what has hitherto been largely a low-road process, something like a suspicious parent checking out a teenager's date.

While the low road propels us into each other's arms, the high road sizes up a prospective partner—hence the importance of having conversation over coffee after last night's tryst. A prolonged courtship lets partners take the full measure of each other on what counts most to both: that a romantic partner be considerate and understanding, responsive and competent—that is, worthy of a more intense attachment.

The stages of courtship are paced to give prospective partners a chance to guess whether the other person might be a good companion, a positive indicator that perhaps one day they would also be a good parent.[7] So during early conversations partners gauge each other's warmth, responsiveness, and reciprocity, and they make a tentative choice. Similarly, infants at around three months become more selective in whom they seek to engage, focusing on the people with whom they feel most secure.

Once a partner passes that test, synchrony marks the transition from attraction to feeling romantic longings. The increased ease of getting in synch, both for babies and for flirting adults, shows up in fond gazes, cuddling, and nuzzling—all reflecting an increase in intimacy. At this stage lovers regress to outright babyishness, using baby talk or cute private names, soothing whispers, and gentle caressing. This utter physical ease with each other marks the point where each has become a secure base for the other—still another echo of infancy.

To be sure, courtship can be as stormy as a toddler in a tantrum. Infants, after all, are self-centered, as lovers can be. And this general template morphs to contain all the ways risk and anxiety can bring couples together, from wartime romances and illicit affairs, to women who fall for "dangerous" men.

Neuroscientist Jaak Panksepp theorizes that as a couple fall in love, they literally become addicted to each other.[8] Panksepp finds a neural corollary between the dynamics of opiate addiction and our dependence on the people for whom we feel our strongest attachments. All positive interactions with people, he proposes, owe part of their pleasure to the opioid system, the very circuitry that links with heroin and other addictive substances.

That circuitry, it turns out, includes those two key structures of the social brain, the orbitofrontal cortex and anterior cingulate cortex. The OFC and the ACC activate in addicts while they are craving, intoxicated, and bingeing. When an addict goes through withdrawal from his addiction, these areas deactivate. This system accounts for the addict's overvaluing his favored drug as well as the utter failure of any inhibition in seeking it out.[9] All that may be true, too, with an object of ardor during the pangs of falling in love.

Panksepp theorizes that the gratification that addicts get from their drugs biologically mimics the natural pleasure we get from feeling connected to those we love; the neural circuitry for both are largely shared. Even animals, he finds, prefer to spend time with those in whose presence they have secreted oxytocin and natural opioids, which induce a relaxed serenity—suggesting that these brain chemicals cement our family ties and friendships as well as our love relationships.

THE THREE STYLES OF ATTACHMENT

It's been almost a year since Brenda and Bob's nine-month-old daughter tragically died in her sleep.

As Bob sits reading the newspaper, Brenda comes in, holding some photographs, her eyes red. She's been crying.

Brenda tells him she's found some photos from a day they took their baby to the beach.

Bob, not even looking up, mutters, "Yeah."

"She's wearing that hat your mother bought for her," Brenda begins.

"Hmmm," Bob mumbles, still not looking, clearly uninterested.

When Brenda asks if he wants to see the pictures, he just says no, brusquely turning the page of the newspaper, then scanning it aimlessly.

As Brenda watches him in silence, tears run down her face. She blurts out, "I don't understand you. She was our baby. Don't you miss her? Don't you care?"

"Of course I miss her! I just don't want to talk about it," Bob growls, as he storms out of the room.

That poignant exchange illustrates how differences in attachment styles can put a couple out of synch—in dealing not only with a shared trauma but with virtually everything else.[10] Brenda wants to talk about her feelings; Bob avoids them. She sees him as cold and uncaring; he sees her as intrusive and demanding. The more she tries to get him to talk about how he feels, the more he withdraws.

This "demand-withdraw" pattern has long been commented on by marital therapists, to whom such couples sometimes turn to help resolve their deadlock. But new findings suggest that this classic discrepancy has a brain basis. Neither way is "best." Rather, both tendencies reflect underlying neural patterns.

Our childhood leaves its stamp on our adult ardor nowhere more clearly than in our "attachment system," the neural networks that operate whenever we relate to the people who matter the most to us. As we have seen, children who are well nurtured and feel their caretakers empathize with them become secure in their attachments, neither overly clingy nor pushing away. But those whose parents neglect their feelings and who feel ignored become avoidant, as though they have given up hope of achieving a caring connection. And children whose parents are ambivalent, unpredictably flipping from rage to tenderness, become anxious and insecure.

Bob embodies the avoidant type; he finds intense emotions unpleasant and so tries to minimize them. Brenda is an anxious type, whose feelings bubble up irrepressibly and who needs to talk over her preoccupations.

Then there's the secure type, comfortable with emotions but not preoccupied by them. Had Bob been secure, presumably he could have been emotionally available to Brenda as she needed. If Brenda had been the secure one, she would not have been so desperate for Bob's attentive empathy.

Once it is formed in childhood, the *way* we attach ourselves stays remarkably constant. These distinct attachment styles emerge to some degree in every close relationship and nowhere so strongly as in our romantic ties. Each has marked consequences for a person's relationship life, according to a series of studies by Phillip Shaver, the psychologist at the University of California who has led much of the research on attachment and relationships.[11]

Shaver carries the mantle passed down from John Bowlby to his American disciple Mary Ainsworth, whose pioneering studies of how nine-month-olds reacted to a brief separation from their mothers first identified some infants as secure in their attachment and others as insecure in various ways. Shaver, taking Ainsworth's insight to the world of adult relationships, has identified those attachment styles as they show up in any close connection, whether it's a friendship, a marriage, or a parent-child relationship.[12]

Shaver's group finds that 55 percent of Americans (whether as infants, children, or adults) fall into the "secure" category, easily getting close to others and being comfortable depending on them. Secure people come to a romantic relationship expecting that a partner will be emotionally available and attuned—that their partner will be there for support in times of hardship or distress—just as they can be for their partner. They feel an ease in getting close to people. Securely attached people see themselves as worthy of concern, care, and affection, and others as accessible, reliable, and having good intentions toward them. As a result, their relationships tend to be intimate and trusting.

In contrast, about 20 percent of adults are "anxious" in their love relationships, prone to fret that their partner does not really love them or won't stay with them. Sometimes their apprehensive clinging and need for reassurance can inadvertently drive a partner away. These adults tend to see themselves as being unworthy of love and care—though they incline toward idealizing their romantic partners.

Once they form a relationship, anxious types can readily be beset by fears that they will be left or found wanting in some way. They are prone to all the signs of "love addiction": obsessive preoccupation, self-conscious anxiety, and emotional dependence. Often angst-ridden, they are beset by relationship worries of all kinds—such as about being abandoned by their partner—or they are hyper-vigilant and jealous about imagined dalliances. And they often bring the same set of overconcern to their friendships.

Around 25 percent of adults are "avoidant," uncomfortable being emotionally close, finding it hard to trust a partner or share feelings, and getting nervous when their partner seeks to get more emotionally intimate. They tend to suppress their own emotions, and especially to stifle their distressing feelings. Because avoidant people expect a partner to be emotionally untrustworthy, they find intimate relationships unpleasant.

The underlying difficulty with the anxious and avoidant types comes down to rigidity. Both represent strategies that actually make sense in a specific situation but are adhered to even where they fail. If there is a real danger, for example, anxiety arouses preparedness; but anxiety out of place creates relationship static.

When people are distressed, those of each type typically follow a different strategy for calming themselves. Anxious people, like Brenda, turn to other people, depending on the power of soothing interactions. Avoidant people, like her husband Bob, remain stridently independent, preferring to manage their upsets on their own.

Secure romantic partners seem able to buffer the perturbations of an anxious partner, so that the relationship does not rock too much. If one partner in a couple has the secure pattern, they have relatively few conflicts and crises. But when both partners in a couple are anxious, they are understandably prone to flare-ups and tiffs and demand constant high maintenance.[13] Apprehension, resentment, and distress, after all, are contagious.

| THE NEURAL BASIS |

Each of the three styles reflects a specific variation in the wiring of the brain's attachment system, as research by Shaver with neuroscientists at the University of California at Davis reveals.[14] These differences surface most boldly in disturbing moments, such as in an argument or when one is lost in fearful ruminations about such a tiff or, even worse, when one is obsessing about breaking up with a romantic partner.

During such distressing reveries, fMRI testing showed, a distinct brain pattern emerges with each of the three main attachment styles. (Though the study used only women, presumably the same conclusions apply to men—only future studies will tell.)[15]

The propensity of the anxious types to overworry, as when one fears losing a partner, lit up low-road zones including the anterior temporal pole (or ATP), which activates during sadness; the anterior cingulate, where emotions flare; and the hippocampus, a key site for memory.[16] Tellingly, the anxious women could not shut down this circuit for relationship disquiet even when they were specifically trying to; their obsessive worries overpowered their brain's ability to turn them off. This neural activity was specific to anxiety about relationships rather than fears in general. Their anxiety-calming circuits worked perfectly well for shutting off other kinds of worries.

In contrast, the secure women had no trouble shutting off fears about breaking up. Their sadness-generating ATP quieted down as soon as they turned their attention to other thoughts. The key difference: the secure women readily activated the OFC's neural switch for calming distress from the ATP.

By the same token, the anxious women could bring to mind some particular worry-provoking moment from their romantic relationship far more easily than could the other women.[17] Their readiness for preoccupation with relationship troubles, Shaver suggests, could well interfere with their ability to figure out what would be most constructive for them to do.

Avoidant women had a very different neural story; the crucial action hinged on an area in the cingulate that activates during suppression of upsetting thoughts.[18] In these women this neural brake on emotion seems jammed: just as the anxious women were unable to stop their worry, the avoidant women were unable to stop their *suppression* of worry, even when they were asked to. By contrast, the other women had no trouble flipping on and off the cingulate when they were asked to think about something sad and then to stop thinking about it.

This neural pattern for nonstop suppression explains why those with the avoidant style tend to be emotionally distant and uninvolved with life—when a relationship breaks up or someone dies, they do little grieving, and they feel emotionally unengaged during social interactions.[19] Some degree of anxiety seems to be a price we pay for true emotional intimacy, if only because it surfaces relationship problems that need to be resolved.[20] Shaver's avoidant types seem to have bartered away a fuller emotional connection with others for a protective disconnection from their own disturbing feelings. Tellingly, Shaver found it hardest to recruit avoidant women for this study, because one of the requirements was involvement in a serious, long-term romantic relationship—and so few were.

These styles, remember, are largely shaped in childhood, and so they do not seem genetic givens. If they were learned, then they should be modifiable to some extent by the right experience—whether in psychotherapy or in a reparative relationship. On the other hand, an understanding partner may simply be able to accommodate to these quirks, within limits.

We can think of the neural systems for attachment, sex, and caregiving as parts of one of those kinetic mobiles by Alexander Calder, where motion in any branch reverberates to the others. For example, attachment styles mold a person's sexuality. Avoidant types have more sexual partners and "one-night stands" than do anxious or secure people. True to their preference for emotional distance, avoidants are content with sex without caring or intimacy. Should they somehow end up in an ongoing relationship, they tend to oscillate between distance and coercion, and so they are understandably more likely to divorce or to break up—and then, oddly, to try to return to that same partner.[21]

The challenges to a love match posed by attachment styles merely begin the saga. Then there's sex.

Desire: His and Hers

One of my best friends during my freshman year in college was a brilliant, bearish rugby player we nicknamed "The Hulk." To this day I recall the advice he told me his German-born father had given him as he was preparing to leave home.

The maxim had a Brechtian, wryly cynical flavor. Roughly translated from the German, it went: "When the penis gets hard, the brain goes soft."

Put more technically, the neural wiring for sex inhabits low-road subcortical regions that are beyond the reach of the thinking brain. As these nether circuits drive us with ever more urgency, we care less and less about whatever advice the high-road rational regions might offer us.

In a more general sense, this wiring map accounts for the irrationality of so many romantic choices: our logical circuitry has nothing to do with the matter. The social brain both loves and cares, but lust travels some of the lowest branches of the low road.

Desire seems to come in two forms, his and hers. When couples in love gazed at photos of their partners, a brain imaging study revealed a telling difference: for men in love—but not for women—the centers for visual processing and sexual arousal lit up, showing how his lover's looks trigger a man's passion. Small wonder men worldwide seek out visual pornography, as anthropologist Helen Fisher notes, or that women tend to draw feelings of self-worth from their appearance and put so much energy into their looks, all the better to "advertise their assets visually," as she puts it.[1]

But for women in love, looking at their beloved activates very different centers in the brain's social circuitry: cognitive centers for memory and attention.[2] This difference suggests that women more thoughtfully weigh their feelings and assess a man as a prospective mate and provider. Women who are entering a romance notoriously tend to be more pragmatic than do men, and so of necessity they fall in love more slowly. "Casual sex" for women, Fisher comments, "is often not as casual as it is for men."[3]

After all, the brain's radar for attachment typically needs a series of meetings to make its decision about whether to commit. Men plunge down the low road while they are falling in love. To be sure, women cruise down the low—but they also circle back along the high.

A more cynical view has it, "Men look for sex objects, and women for success objects." But though women tend to find allure in signs of a man's power and wealth, and men in a woman's physical attractiveness, these are not the prime draws for either sex—just the ones they most differ on.[4] For men and women alike, kindness tops the list.

To further confuse our love life, circuits within the high road, whether through elevated sentiments or puritanical mores, resolutely strive to contain the red-hot subterranean currents of lust. Throughout history cultures have applied high-road brakes to low-road urges—in Freud's terms, civilization has always battled its discontents. For instance, for centuries marriages in European upper classes were simply a matter of landed families ensuring that their property would remain in a particular lineage; in essence, families married other families via arranged matches. Lust and love be damned—there was always adultery.

Social historians tell us that, at least in Europe, only during the Reformation did today's romantic notion of a lusty, loving, and committed emotional bond between husband and wife emerge—a departure from the medieval ideal of chastity, which viewed marriage as a necessary evil. Not until around the Industrial Revolution and the rise of the middle class did the notion of romantic love become a popular enough Western ideal that simply falling in love was a respectable reason for a couple to marry. And of course, in cultures like India that hang at the cusp between tradition and modernity, those couples who marry for love alone are still a small minority, frequently encountering strong objections from their families who would prefer an arranged marriage.

Then again, biology does not always cooperate with the modern ideal of marriage that combines lifetime companionship and caring with the more fickle delights of romantic heat. Years of familiarity famously weaken desire—and sometimes that can happen as soon as a partner becomes a "sure thing."

To thicken the plot, Nature has seen fit to endow men and women with different propensities even for the molecules of love. Men generally have higher levels of the chemicals that drive lust and lower levels of those that fuel attachment, than do women. These biological mismatches create many of the classic tensions between men and women in the arena of passion.

Culture and gender aside, perhaps the most fundamental dilemma for romantic love stems from the essential tension between the brain systems that underlie a secure sense of attachment and those that underlie caring and sex. Each of these neural networks fuels its own set of motives and needs—and these can either be in conflict or compatible. If they are at odds, then love will falter; if they are in harmony, love can flourish.

NATURE'S CUNNING LITTLE TRICK

A woman writer, though independent and enterprising, always traveled with a pillowcase her husband had slept on. She'd slip it onto the hotel pillow wherever she went. Her explanation: having his scent with her made it easier to fall asleep in a strange bed.

That makes biological sense and offers a clue about one of Nature's tricks in its drive to continue the species. The route taken in some of the very first stirrings of sexual attraction—or at least of interest—is low road: sensory rather than a formulated thought (or even an emotion). For women that initial subliminal intrigue can stem from an olfactory impression, for men a visual one.

Scientists have found that the scent of a man's perspiration can have remarkable effects on women's emotions, brightening their moods, relaxing them, and raising their levels of the luteinizing reproductive hormones that bring on ovulation.

The study that suggests this, however, was done under starkly clinical (and decidedly unromantic) circumstances, in a laboratory. Samples from the underarms of men who had not used deodorant for four weeks were blended into a concoction that was dabbed on the upper lip of young women who had volunteered for what they thought was a study of the scent of products like floor wax.[5] When the scent was from a man's sweat rather than from some other source, the women felt more relaxed and happy.

In a more romantic setting, researchers propose, these odors may also stir sexual feelings. So presumably, as couples dance, their hormonal hug quietly paves the way for sexual arousal, as their bodies subliminally orchestrate conditions conducive to reproduction. Indeed, the study was part of a search for new fertility therapies, to see if the active ingredient in the perspiration could be isolated; the research was published in the journal *Biology of Reproduction*.

The corollary for men may well be the impact of the sight of a woman's body on their brain's pleasure centers. The male brain contains seemingly hardwired signal detectors for key aspects of the female body, particularly the "hourglass" ratio of breast-to-waist-to-hips, a signal of youthful beauty that in itself can trigger sexual arousal in men.[6] When men around the world rated the attractiveness of line drawings of women with varying ratios, most chose women with a waist circumference about 70 percent of her hips.[7]

Just why men's brains are so imprinted has been the topic of vigorous debate for decades. Some see in this bit of neural circuitry a way to make biological signs of a woman's peak fertility singularly alluring to men, thereby economizing on the placement of their sperm.

Whatever the reason, these are elegant designs in human biology: the very sight of her delights him, and his scent readies her for love. That tactic no doubt worked well in early stages of human prehistory. But in modern life the neurobiology of love has undergone complications.

| LIBIDO'S BRAIN |

Being "truly, deeply and madly" in love was the one criterion for selecting men and women for a study at University College in London. The seventeen who volunteered underwent brain imaging while looking at a photo of their romantic partner, then while looking at photos of friends. The conclusion: they seemed addicted to love.

In men and women alike the object of ardor—unlike the friends—elicited fireworks in uniquely linked sectors of the brain, circuitry so specific it appears specialized for romantic love.[8] Much of that circuitry, as the neuroscientist Jaak Panksepp has proposed, lights up during another euphoric state: on cocaine or opiates. This finding suggests that the addictively ecstatic nature of intense romance has a neural rationale. Intriguingly, in men none of this love circuitry does much during sexual arousal per se, though areas adjacent to those for romance stir, suggesting an easy anatomical link when lust arises with love.[9]

Neuroscience, through such studies, has pierced the mystery of sexual passion, piecing together the mix of hormones and neurochemicals that give lust such spice. The recipe for desire varies a bit between the genders, to be sure. But the ingredients and their timing during the sexual act reveal an ingenious plan, one that adds the zing to propagating our species.

Lust's circuitry, where libido stirs, covers a broad swath of the limbic brain.[10] The sexes share much of this low-road wiring for sexual ardor, but with a few telling differences. These differences cause disparities in how each gender experiences lovemaking, as well as in how they value various aspects of a romantic encounter.

For men, both sexuality and aggressiveness are lifted by the sex hormone testosterone acting in connected areas of the brain.[11] When men become aroused sexually, their testosterone levels soar. The male hormone fuels a sexual itch in women as well, albeit not so strongly as in men.

Then there's that addictive quality. For men and women alike, dopamine—the chemical that injects intense pleasure in activities as diverse as gambling and drug addictions—rockets during sexual encounters. Pleasurable dopamine levels rise not just during sexual arousal but also with the frequency of intercourse and the intensity of a person's sex drive.[12]

Oxytocin, a chemical source of caregiving, permeates women's brains more than men's, and so it has more impact on women's sexual bonding. Vasopressin, a hormone closely related to oxytocin, can also play a role in bonding.[13] Intriguingly, receptors for vasopressin are abundant in spindle cells, those superfast connectors of the social brain. The spindle cells are involved, for instance, when we make very rapid, intuitive judgments about someone we are meeting for the first time. While no studies can yet tell us for sure, these cells seem apt candidates for part of the brain system that creates love—or at least desire—"at first sight."

In the run-up to lovemaking, oxytocin levels soar in a man's brain, as does the hormonal hunger driven by arginine and vasopressin (known together as AVP). The male brain has more AVP receptors than does the female, most of them concentrated in the sexual circuitry. AVP, which becomes abundant at puberty, seems to fuel a man's sexual hankering, builds up as ejaculation nears, and rapidly declines at the moment of orgasm.

In both men and women, oxytocin fuels many of the loving and delectable feelings of sexual contact. Ample doses release during orgasm, after which a flood of the chemical seems to stimulate the afterglow of warm affection—and put men and women on the same tenderly loving hormonal wavelength for the time being.[14] Oxytocin secretions remain strong after climax, particularly during "afterplay," the cuddling that follows intercourse.[15]

Oxytocin wells up in particular strength in men during this "refractory" period after orgasm, when they typically cannot get an erection. Intriguingly, at least in rodents (and possibly in humans), abundant sexual gratification in males spikes a threefold rise in oxytocin levels—a brain change that apparently brings male brain chemistry closer to that of females for the time being. In any case, that clever chemical endgame for lovemaking affords a relaxed time to build attachment, another function of oxytocin.

The lust circuitry also primes a couple for their next tryst. The hippocampus, the key structure in memory storage, holds neurons rich in receptors for AVP and oxytocin alike. AVP, particularly in a man, seems to imprint in memory with special strength the enticing image of his partner in passion, making his sexual mate singularly memorable. The oxytocin produced by orgasm also boosts memory, again imprinting in the mind's eye a lover's fond figure.

While this primal biochemistry stirs our sexual activity, highroad brain centers exert their own influences, not always compatibly. Brain systems that for aeons have worked well for human survival now seem vulnerable to conflicts and tensions that can make love's labor lost—not last.

| RUTHLESS DESIRE |

Consider a beautiful and independent young lawyer whose fiancé, a writer, worked at home. Whenever she came home, the fiancé would drop whatever he was doing and hover around her. One evening as she was coming to bed, he eagerly pulled her to him even before she had a chance to get under the sheets.[16]

"Just give me an ounce of space to love you from," she said to him—a comment that hurt his feelings. He threatened to go sleep on the couch.

Her comment bespeaks the underside of looping too tightly: it can be suffocating. The goal of attunement is not simply continual meshing, with an utter entrainment of every thought and feeling; it also includes giving each other space to be alone as needed. This cycle of connectedness strikes a balance between the individual's needs and the couple's. As one family therapist put it, "The more a couple can be apart, the more they can be together."

Each of love's major expressions—attachment, desire, and caring—has its unique biology, designed to loop partners together with its specific chemical glue. When they align, love grows robust. When they are at odds, love can flounder.

Consider the challenge to any liaison when the three biological love systems misalign, as commonly happens in the tension between attachment and sex. This mismatch occurs, for example, when one partner feels insecure or, even worse, nurses outright jealousy or harbors fears of abandonment. From the neural perspective, the system for attachment, when pitched in the direction of anxiety, inhibits the operation of the others. Such gnawing apprehension can easily wither the sexual urge and snuff out affectionate caring—at least for a time.

The fiancé's single-pointed fixation on the lawyer as a sexual object is akin to the ruthless desire of a nursing infant, who knows nothing of his mother's own feelings and needs. These archaic desires play out too during lovemaking, when two passionate adults delve into each other's bodies with the fervor of infants.

As we've noted, the childhood roots of intimacy resurface in the use of childlike, high-pitched voices or baby names between lovers. Ethologists argue that these cues trigger in lovers' brains parental responses of caregiving and tenderness. The difference between infant desire and adult, however, lies in the adult capacity for empathy, so that passion melds with compassion or at least caring.

So Mark Epstein, the lawyer's psychiatrist, suggested an alternative for the fiancé: slow down enough to attune emotionally and thereby create the psychological space that would let her stay in touch with her own desire. That mutuality of desire—and maintenance of the loop between them—offered a way to bring back the passion she was losing.

This harkens back to Freud's famous question, "What does woman want?" As Epstein answers, "She wants a partner who cares what she wants."

| **T H E   C O N S E N S U A L   " I T "** |

Anne Rice, author of a best-selling series of vampire novels—and of erotica under a nom de plume—remembers having vivid sado-masochistic fantasies as far back as childhood.

One of her earliest fantasies centered on elaborate scenarios of young men in ancient Greece being auctioned as sexual slaves; same-sex attraction between males fascinated her. In adulthood she found herself drawn to friendships with gay men and attracted to gay culture.[17]

Such is the stuff of which fiction is made; Rice's vampire novels, rife with homoerotic subthemes, set the tone for the romantic universe of the Goths. And in her steamy novels written under a pseudonym, she details sadomasochistic activities by both sexes. While those sexual fantasies are by no means everyone's favorites, nothing in them is beyond what researchers find typifies the erotic daydreams of ordinary people.

The flamboyant sexual scenes that Rice has elaborated in detail are not "deviant" in a normative sense; rather, they are among the fantasy themes commonly reported by men and women alike in study after study. For example, one survey found that the most frequent sex fantasies include: reliving an exciting sexual encounter, imagining having sex with one's partner or with someone else, having oral sex, making love in a romantic location, being irresistible—and being forced into sexual submission.[18]

A wide variety of sex fantasies can reflect a healthy sexuality, offering a font of stimulation that enhances arousal and pleasure.[19] When both parties consent, this goes even for more bizarre fantasies like Rice's, which would seem on their face to present cruel scenarios.

We've come a long way since Freud's proclamation, a century ago, that "a happy person never fantasizes, only an unsatisfied one."[20] But a fantasy is just that: vivid imagination. As Rice pointedly mentions, she has never acted on hers, despite being presented with opportunities. Sexual fantasies may not be enacted with another person, but they nevertheless find their uses. Alfred Kinsey's original studies (which in retrospect represented a skewed sample) showed that 89 percent of men and 64 percent of women admitted to having sex fantasies during masturbation—a shocking finding in that more sedate era, the 1950s, but rather ho-hum today. As the good Professor Kinsey first made glaringly clear, a surprising range of sexual behaviors in men and women are far more common than are publicly admitted.

The social taboos that reign even today—despite *The Jerry Springer Show* and the ubiquity of Web porn sites—mean that the actual incidence of various predilections is invariably higher than people are willing to admit. Indeed, sex researchers routinely assume that any statistics that are based on people's own reports of their sexual behavior underrepresent actual numbers. When college men and women duly recorded in a diary every sexual fantasy or sexy thought they had over the course of a day, men reported about seven daily, and women between four and five. But in other studies where college students answered a questionnaire asking them to *recall* the same information, the men estimated they had just one sexual fantasy per day, the women one per week.

Consider men and women who have sexual fantasies during intercourse. For virtually all forms of sexual behavior men tend to have higher numbers than women, but fantasizing during intercourse seems to level the playing field; up to 94 percent of women and 92 percent of men say that they have done so (though some reports range as low as 47 percent for men and 34 percent for women).

One study found that having sex with one's current lover is a popular daydream while one is *not* engaged in lovemaking, but imagining sex with someone else is a more popular fantasy *during* intercourse.[21] Such data have led one wag to observe that when romantic partners make love, there are in effect four people involved: the two actual ones, and the two that exist in their minds.

Most sex fantasies inherently depict the other as an object, a being created to fit the preferred ardor of the beholder, without regard to what the other himself or herself might want in that situation. But in the realm of fantasy, anything goes.

Consenting to enter, share, and act out a sex fantasy in vivo is an act of convergence; "playing" the script with a willing partner, rather than imposing the fantasy and so making the other an It, makes all the difference.[22] If partners both agree and so desire, even a seeming I-It scenario can create a closer sense of intimacy. Under the right circumstances, regarding a lover as an It—if mutually consensual—can be part of the play of sex.

"A good sexual relationship," one psychotherapist observes, "is like a good sexual fantasy"—exciting but safe. When partners have complementary emotional needs, he adds, the resulting chemistry—like fantasies that mesh—can breed an excitement that counters the usual downward drift in sexual interest among couples who have been together for many years.[23]

Empathy and understanding between partners make all the difference between a playful It fantasy and a hurtful one. If both see the loveplay as a game, their very ease with the fantasy creates a reassuring empathy. As they enter the fantasy reality, their looping within it enhances their mutual pleasure and bespeaks a radical acceptance—an implicit act of caring.

WHEN SEX OBJECTIFIES

Consider the love life of a pathological narcissist, from a case report by his psychotherapist:

Twenty-five and single, he easily becomes infatuated with women he meets and is obsessed by powerful fantasies about each one in turn. But after a series of sexual trysts with a lover, he always feels disappointed in her, suddenly finding her too dumb, or clinging, or physically repugnant.

For instance, when he felt lonely at Christmas, he tried to persuade his girlfriend of the moment—whom he'd only been seeing a few weeks—to stay in town with him instead of visiting her family. When she refused, he attacked her as self-centered and, enraged, decided never to see her again.

The narcissist's sense of entitlement endows him with the feeling that ordinary rules and boundaries do not apply to him. As we've seen, he feels entitled to sex if a woman encourages and arouses him—even if she clearly says she wants to stop. He will go ahead anyway, even if he has to use force.

A blunted empathy, remember, stands high on the list of traits of the narcissist, along with an exploitative attitude and vain self-centeredness. So it should come as no surprise that narcissistic men endorse attitudes that favor sexual coercion, such as the idea that victims of rape are "asking for it," or that when a woman says no to sex, she really means yes.[24] The narcissists among American college men tend to agree that "if a girl engages in necking or petting and she lets things get out of hand, it is her own fault if her partner forces sex on her." For some men, that belief explicitly rationalizes date rape, where the man coerces a woman who has been necking with him but wants to stop.

The prevalence of such attitudes among some men may in part explain why, in the United States, around 20 percent of women claim to have been forced into unwanted sexual activity despite their resistance—most often by a spouse or partner or someone with whom they were in love at the time.[25] Indeed, ten times as many women are forced into sex by someone they love as by a stranger. A study of self-confessed date rapists found that every instance of such coercion followed mutually consensual sex play; the rapist simply ignored the woman's protests about going further.[26]

Unlike the majority of men, narcissists actually enjoy and find sexually arousing films in which a couple are petting, the woman wants to stop—and the man then forces sex on her despite her evident pain and disgust.[27] While viewing such a scene, the narcissist tunes out of the woman's suffering and focuses only on the self-gratification of the aggressor. Intriguingly, narcissists in this study did not enjoy a sequence showing the rape alone, without the foreplay and refusal.

Their lack of empathy makes narcissists indifferent to the suffering they cause their "date." While she experiences the forced sex as a disgusting act of violence, he fails to understand, let alone have compassion for, her displeasure with the act. Indeed, the more empathic a man, the less likely he is to act as a sexual predator or even imagine doing so.[28]

An additional hormonal force may be at work in coercive sex. Extremely high levels of testosterone, studies find, make men more likely to treat another person as merely a sexual object. It also makes them troubling marital partners.

A study of testosterone levels among 4,462 American men found an alarming pattern among those with the very highest readings for the male hormone.[29] They were more aggressive overall, more likely to have been arrested and been in fights. They were also bad risks as husbands: they were prone to hitting or throwing things at their wives, to having extramarital sex, and—understandably—to have divorced. The higher the testosterone, the worse the picture.

On the other hand, the study notes, many high-testosterone men are happily married. What makes the difference, the authors propose, is the extent to which the men have learned to control their wilder testosterone-driven impulses. The prefrontal systems hold the keys to managing impulse of all kinds, sexual and aggressive alike. That gets us back to the need for the high road and its abilities to rein in the low, as a counterweight to raw libido.

Years ago as a science journalist for the *New York Times* I was talking to an FBI profiler who specialized in the psychological analysis of serial murderers. He told me that such murderers are almost invariably acting out perversely cruel sex fantasies, in which even the pleas of victims become fodder for arousal. Indeed, a (thankfully) tiny subset of men are sexually aroused by depictions of rape more than they are by erotic scenes of consensual sex.[30] Their weird appetite for suffering sets this group of outliers apart from the vast majority of men: not even the date-raping narcissists found outright rape a turn-on.

Such utter lack of empathy seems to explain why serial rapists are undeterred by the tears or screams of their victims. A significant number of convicted rapists later report that during the rape they felt nothing for their victim and simply did not know or care how she felt. Almost half convinced themselves she "enjoyed it" despite the fact that she was upset enough that the rapists were now in jail.[31]

One study of men imprisoned for rape found that they could be effective at understanding other people in most situations, with one notable exception: they were inept at perceiving negative expressions in women, though not positive ones.[32] So while they have the capacity for empathy in general, these rapists seem unable or unwilling to read the signals that will stop them. Such predators may well be selectively insensitive, misreading the signals they least want to see—a woman's refusal or distress.

Most troubling are the highly deviant men whose favored, compulsively acted-on fantasies center on I-It scenarios—a pattern typical of incarcerated sex offenders, particularly those convicted of serial rape, child molestation, and exhibitionism. These men typically are aroused by fantasies of these abusive acts far more than by more ordinary sexual scenes.[33] Of course merely having a fantasy by no means implies that someone will force sex on another to act it out. But those who, like sex offenders, actually inflict their fantasied acts on others have broken through the neural barrier between thought and action.

Once the low road has breached the high road's barrier to acting out an abusive impulse, fantasies become fuel for malevolence, stoking the unbridled libido (some say lust for power) that drives repeated sex crimes. In such cases, those fantasies become a danger signal—particularly when the man lacks empathy for his victims, believes that the victims "enjoy it," feels hostility toward his victims, and is emotionally lonely.[34] That explosive combination almost ensures trouble.

Contrast the cold dissociation of I-It sexuality with the connected warmth of an I-You tryst. Romantic love hinges on resonance; without this intimate connection, lust alone remains. With full two-way empathy, one's partner is a subject as well, attuned to as a You, and the erotic charge increases dramatically. When a couple mingles in emotional union along with physical intimacy, both lose their sense of separateness in what has been called an "ego orgasm"—a meeting not just of bodies but of their very beings.[35]

Still, even the most skyrocketing orgasm offers no guarantee that lovers will genuinely care for each other the next morning. Caring operates via its own neural logic.

The Biology of Compassion

In a classic Rolling Stones song Mick Jagger promises a lover, "I'll come to your emotional rescue"—thus expressing a feeling held by romantic partners everywhere. It's not just the attraction that keeps a couple together; their mutual caretaking plays a role as well. Such emotional caring can operate in any relationship.

A mother nursing her baby is the primal prototype for such nurturance. John Bowlby proposed that the same innate caregiving system springs into action whenever we have the urge to respond to a call for help—whether it is our lover, our child, our friend, or a stranger who is in distress.

Caregiving between romantic partners comes in two main forms: providing a secure base where a partner can feel protected and offering a safe haven from which that partner can take on the world. Ideally, both partners should be able to switch fluidly from one role to the other, providing solace or haven—or receiving it—as needed. Such reciprocity marks a healthy relationship.

We provide a secure base whenever we come to our partner's emotional rescue, by helping them solve a vexing problem, soothing them, or simply being present and listening. Once we feel a relationship offers us a secure base, our energies are freer to tackle challenges. As John Bowlby put it, "all of us, from the cradle to the grave, are happiest when life offers us a series of excursions, long or short, from a secure base."[1]

Those excursions can be as simple as spending a day at the office or as complex as making a world-class accomplishment. If you think of the acceptance speeches people give for major prizes, they typically include gratitude toward the person who provides them a safe base. This bespeaks the crucial importance of feeling secure and confident for our ability to achieve.

Our sense of security and our drive to explore are entwined. The more our partner provides us with a haven and security, Bowlby's theory proposes, the more exploration we can take on—and the more daunting the goal of our explorations, the more we may need to draw on the support of our base to boost our energy and focus, confidence, and courage. These propositions were tested with 116 couples who had been romantically involved for at least four years.[2] As predicted, the more a person felt his or her partner to be a dependable "home base," the more willing they were to pursue life's opportunities with confidence.

Videotapes of the couples discussing each other's goals in life revealed that *how* they talked also mattered. If one partner was sensitive, warm, and positive during the discussion of the other's goals, the recipient was understandably more confident by the end of the discussion, often raising the bar on their goals.

But if a partner was intrusive and controlling, the other partner became more downbeat and insecure about the goal, often ending up cutting back on their aspirations and feeling a lower self-worth. Partners who were controlling were perceived by the other as rude and critical—and their advice was generally rejected.[3] Attempts to take control violate the cardinal rule for providing a secure base: intervene only when asked to or when it is absolutely necessary. Letting a partner venture forth in his or her own way is a quiet vote of confidence; the more we try to control, the more we tacitly undermine that vote. Intruding hampers exploration.

Partners' support and attachment styles vary. People who are anxious in their attachments may have trouble relaxing enough to allow space for a partner's explorations, wanting them instead to stay nearby, just as anxious mothers tend to do. Such overly clingy partners may be fine for offering a secure base, but they cannot function as a safe haven. In contrast, avoidant people typically have no trouble letting their partner roam but are poor at offering a secure base of comfort—and virtually never come to their emotional rescue.

| **P O O R   L I A T** |

It could have been a scene straight out of the television show *Fear Factor*: Liat, a university student, had to endure a series of ordeals, each more trying than the one before. She was clearly horrified by her first task: looking at gory pictures of a hideously burned man and a grotesquely injured face.

Next, when she had to hold and stroke a rat, Liat was so dismayed that she almost dropped it. Then, instructed to plunge her arm into ice water up to the elbow and keep it there for thirty seconds, she found the pain too intense to keep it immersed for more than twenty.

Finally, when she next was supposed to reach into a glass terrarium and pet a live tarantula, it was just too much for her. Liat screamed, "I can't go on!"

Now here's the question: would you have volunteered to help Liat escape the ordeal by offering to take her place?

That very question was asked of fellow students who had volunteered for a study of how anxiety affects compassion, that noble extension of our instinct for caregiving. Their answers reveal that just as attachment styles can skew sexuality, they also lend their distinctive twist to empathy.

Mario Mikulincer, an Israeli colleague of Phillip Shaver in the research on attachment styles, argues that the innate altruistic impulse that follows from empathy with someone in need can become muddled, suppressed, or overridden when people feel the anxiety of insecure attachment. Through elaborate experiments, Mikulincer has shown that each of the three different attachment styles has a distinct impact on the ability to empathize.[4]

People who had various attachment styles were asked to watch poor Liat—who was, of course, an experimental confederate acting the part. The secure people were the most compassionate, both in feeling Liat's distress and in volunteering to take her place. Anxious people, however, were swallowed up by their own distressing reactions and could not bring themselves to come to her rescue. And avoidant people were neither upset nor prone to help.

The secure style seems optimal for altruism; such people readily attune to the distress of others and act to help them. Secure people are more likely than others to be actively caring in their relationships, whether as mothers helping their children, romantic partners offering emotional support to a partner feeling distress, caring for older relatives, or helping out a needy stranger.

But anxious people attune with an oversensitivity that can make them all the more upset at another person's suffering, swamped by contagion. While they feel the other's pain, those feelings can intensify into "empathy distress," a level of anxiety so strong that they become overwhelmed. Anxious people seem most vulnerable to compassion fatigue, burning out from their own anguish when faced with a relentless parade of others' suffering.

Avoidant people find compassion difficult, too. They protect themselves against painful emotions by suppressing them, and so in self-defense they close themselves off to emotional contagion from others who are suffering. Because they empathize poorly, they rarely help. The one exception seems to be when they might benefit personally in some way by helping; their occasions of compassion come with a "what's in it for me" flavoring.

Caregiving flows most fully when we are feeling secure, possessed of a stable foundation that allows us to feel empathy without being overwhelmed. Feeling cared for frees us to care for others—and when we don't feel cared for, we can't care nearly so well. That insight led Mikulincer to explore whether simply making people more secure might boost their capacity for caring.

Imagine you're reading in your local newspaper about the plight of a woman with three young children. She has no husband, no job, and no money. Every day she brings her hungry youngsters to eat at a soup kitchen; without that meager food, they would have none—they might suffer malnutrition or even die.

Would you be willing to donate some food for her once a month? Help her search the want ads for a job? Would you go so far as to accompany her to a job interview?

Those very questions were asked of volunteers in another study of compassion by Mikulincer. In these experiments, the volunteers first underwent an enhancement of their feelings of security; they received a short (one-fiftieth of a second), unconscious exposure to the names of people who made them feel secure (such as the person they like to talk upsetting things over with). They were also asked to bring these people to mind deliberately, by visualizing the faces of these caring figures in their lives.

Strikingly, anxious people overcame their empathy distress and their usual reluctance to help. Even this temporary boost allowed them to react like secure people, showing more compassion. A heightened sense of security seems to free up an abundant supply of attention and energy for the needs of others.

But avoidant people still failed to empathize and so suppressed their altruistic impulse—unless they stood to gain something from it. Their cynical attitude fits the theory that there is no such thing as true altruism, and that compassionate acts always contain within them at least a bit of self-interest, if not selfishness.[5] Mikulincer suggests that there *is* a grain of truth in that view—but mainly for people who are avoidant and so do not empathize well in the first place.[6]

Of the three attachment styles, the secure people were still the most willing among the volunteers to lend a hand. Their compassion appears to be directly proportional to the need they perceive: the greater the pain, the more they help.

THE LOW ROAD TO COMPASSION

Such empathy, Jaak Panksepp argues, has its roots in the low-road neural system for maternal nurturance, one we share with a wide range of other species. Empathy appears to be a primary response of this system. As every mother knows, her baby's cry has particular potency. Lab studies show that a mother's physiological arousal is distinctly stronger when she hears her own baby crying than when she hers another baby's wails.[7]

The baby's ability to elicit in his mother an emotion similar to what he's feeling offers the mother guidance on what the baby needs. This ability of an infant's cries to trigger on-target caregiving—a phenomenon seen not just in mammals but even in birds—suggests that it is a universal template in Nature, one with immense and rather obvious benefits for survival.

Empathy plays the pivotal role in caregiving, which after all centers on responding to the needs of others rather than our own. Compassion, a grand term, in its everyday guise can show as availability, sensitivity, or responsiveness—all signs of good parenting or friendship. And when it comes to a prospective mate, remember, both men and women rate kindness as the number-one trait they seek.

Freud noted a striking similarity in the physical intimacy between lovers and that between a mother and her baby. Lovers, like mothers and infants, spend much time gazing into each other's eyes, cuddling, nuzzling, suckling, and kissing, with ample skin-to-skin contact. And in both cases the contact offers a contented bliss.

Sex aside, the neurochemical key to the pleasures of such contact is oxytocin, the molecule of motherly love. Oxytocin, which the human body releases in women during childbirth and nursing as well as during orgasm, chemically triggers the flood of loving feelings that every mother feels toward her baby—and so the primal biochemistry of protection and caregiving.

As a mother nurses, oxytocin floods through her body, producing many effects. It induces a flow of milk; it also dilates the blood vessels in the skin around the mammary gland, thereby warming her baby. The mother's blood pressure falls as she feels more relaxed. Along with a sense of peacefulness, she feels more outgoing, wanting to engage with people—the more oxytocin she has, the more sociable she is.

Kerstin Uvnäs-Moberg, a Swedish neuroendocrinologist who has studied oxytocin extensively, contends that this chemical flood occurs whenever we engage in affectionate contact with someone we care for. The neural circuitry for oxytocin intersects with many low-road nodes of the social brain.[8]

The benefits of oxytocin seem to emerge in a variety of pleasant social interactions—especially caregiving in all its forms—where people exchange emotional energy; they can actually prime in each other the good feelings that this molecule bestows. Uvnäs-Moberg suggests that repeated exposures to the people with whom we feel the closest social bonds can condition the release of oxytocin, so that merely being in their presence, or even just thinking about them, may trigger in us a pleasant dose. Small wonder that cubicles in even the most soulless of offices are papered with photos of loved ones.

Oxytocin may be a neurochemical key to committed, loving relationships. In one study it was shown to bond members of one species of prairie vole in lifelong monogamous matches. Voles of another variety, who lack this oxytocin release, have sex promiscuously and never bond to a partner. In experiments where the hormone was blocked, monogamous voles that had already mated suddenly lost interest in each other. But when the hormone was released in the promiscuous voles that lacked it, they started bonding with each other.[9]

In humans, oxytocin may present a catch-22: the very chemistry of long-term love may sometimes suppress the chemistry of lust. The specifics are quite complex, but in one interaction vasopressin (oxytocin's close cousin) drives down levels of testosterone; in another testosterone suppresses oxytocin. Still, while the scientific specifics wait to be worked out, testosterone can sometimes enhance oxytocin, suggesting that at least hormonally passion need not fade with commitment.[10]

| SOCIAL ALLERGIES |

"Suddenly, all you're aware of is that there are too many wet towels on the floor, he's hogging the remote, and he's scratching his back with a fork. Finally, you come face to face with the immutable truth that it's virtually impossible to French-kiss a person who takes the new roll of toilet paper and leaves it resting on top of the empty cardboard roll."

That litany of complaints signals the blooming of a "social allergy," a strong aversion toward a romantic partner's habits that, like a physical allergen, at first contact causes no reaction—and would not in most other people—but becomes increasingly sensitized with each exposure.[11] Social allergies typically emerge when a dating couple spend more time together, getting to know each other "warts and all." The social allergy's irritating quality waxes as the inoculating power of romantic idealization wanes.

In research among American college students, most social allergies in women developed in reaction to their boyfriends' uncouth or thoughtless behavior, like that toilet-paper-roll habit. Men, on the other hand, became vexed when their girlfriends seemed self-absorbed or too bossy. Social allergies worsen with repeated exposure. A woman who shrugs off her partner's boorish behaviors at two months may find them barely tolerable after a year. These hypersensitivities have consequence only to the extent that they prime anger and distress: the more upset they make a partner, the more likely it is that that couple will break up.

Psychoanalysts remind us that our desire for the "perfect" person who will meet every one of our expectations and empathically sense and fulfill our every need is a primal fantasy impossible to achieve. When we learn to accept that no lover or spouse can ever satisfy all the unmet needs we bring from childhood, we can begin to perceive our partners more fully and realistically—rather than seeing them through the lens of our wishes and projections.

And neuroscientists add that attachment, caregiving, and sexual desire are but three of seven major neural systems that drive what we want and do. Exploration (which includes learning about the world) and social bonding are among the others.[12] Each of us ranks these basic neural drives in our own way—some people live to ramble, others to socialize. When it comes to love, though, attachment, caregiving, and sex are typically at the top of the list, in one order or another.

John Gottman, a pioneering researcher on emotions in marriages, proposes that the degree to which a partner meets the main needs of the other's dominant neural systems predicts whether their match will last.[13] Gottman, a psychologist at the University of Washington, has become the leading expert on what makes marriages succeed or fail, once coming up with a way to predict with more than 90 percent accuracy whether a couple would separate within the following three years.[14]

These days Gottman argues that when a primary need goes unmet—say, for sexual contact or for caring—we feel a steady state of dissatisfaction, one that can manifest as subtly as a vague frustration or as visibly as continual rancor. These needs, when frustrated, fester. The signals of such neural discontent are early warning signs of a union in jeopardy.

On the other hand, something rather remarkable tends to happen with couples who live together for decades, finding happiness with each other. Their continual rapport even seems to leave its mark on their faces, which come to resemble each other, apparently a result of the sculpting of facial muscles as they evoke the same emotions over the years.[15] Since each emotion tenses and relaxes a specific set of facial muscles, as partners smile or frown in unison they strengthen the parallel set of muscles. This gradually molds similar ridges, wrinkles, and lines, making their faces appear more alike.

That marvel was revealed in a study where people were shown two collections of photos of couples—the first from their wedding, the other taken twenty-five years later—and were asked which husbands and wives looked most similar to each other. The couples' faces had not only grown more alike, but the greater the facial similarity, the happier they reported being in their marriage.

In a sense, as time goes on the partners in a relationship "sculpt" each other in subtler ways, reinforcing desirable patterns in each other via countless small interactions. That sculpting, some research suggests, tends to push people toward their partner's ideal version of who they should be. This quiet push to get the love we want has been called the Michelangelo Phenomenon, where each partner shapes the other.[16]

The sheer amount of positive looping a couple does on any given day or over the years may be the best single barometer of the health of their marriage. Consider a study of dating couples on the verge of marriage, who agreed to undergo a fine-grained analysis of their interaction patterns during disagreements.[17] The couples returned to the lab for several follow-up sessions over the course of five years. Their interactions during that first session, before marriage, predicted surprisingly much about the course of their relationship over the years.

Understandably, negative looping boded poorly. The less satisfied couples tended to match their emotions the most closely during hostile arguments. The more negative the dating partners became during this early disagreement, the less stable their match turned out to be. Particularly damaging were expressions of disgust or contempt.[18] Contempt escalates negativity beyond mere criticism, often taking the form of an outright insult, delivered as though to someone on a lesser plane. With a partner's contempt comes the message that the other is unworthy of empathy, let alone love.

Such toxic loops become all the worse when spouses have accurate empathy. They know exactly the distress the other feels but don't care enough to help. As one seasoned divorce lawyer put it, "Indifference—not caring about, or even paying attention to, your mate—is one of the worst forms of cruelty in a marriage."

Also hurtful was a pattern where one disgruntlement triggered another, anger begetting hurt and sadness, with defiant challenges (*How can you say that!*) and partners interrupting each other before the other could finish speaking. Those patterns most strongly predicted the couple would break up, whether before or after marrying. Most broke up within a year and a half after their first session in the study.

As John Gottman told me, "In dating couples, the most important predictor of whether the relationship will last is how many good feelings the couple shares. In marriages, it's how well the couple can handle their conflicts. And in the later years of a long marriage, it's again how many good feelings the couple shares."

As husbands and wives in their sixties discuss something they enjoy, measures of their physiology show that they both become progressively more cheerful as the conversation continues. But for couples in their forties, their physiology rises to fewer peaks of resonance. That suggests why satisfied couples in their sixties are more openly affectionate with each other than are those in middle age.[19]

From his exhaustive studies of married couples, Gottman has derived a deceptively simple measure: the ratio of toxic to nourishing moments a couple has together has remarkable predictive power. A five-to-one ratio, far more positive moments than negative, indicates that a couple has a sound emotional bank account and a robust relationship that is almost certain to thrive long term.[20]

That ratio may predict more than just relationship longevity—it may also offer a reading of how physically *healthy* the partners will be. As we shall see, our relationships themselves form environments that can turn certain genes on or off. Suddenly our intimate relations have to be seen in an entirely new light: The invisible web of connectedness bestows surprising biological consequences on our closest human ties.

PART FIVE

HEALTHY CONNECTIONS

Stress Is Social

Just a week before their wedding, the Russian novelist Leo Tolstoy, then thirty-four, shared his personal diary with his fiancée Sonya, just seventeen. She was crushed to learn from its pages of Leo's profligate and conflicted sexual history, including a passionate affair with a local woman who had borne him an illegitimate child.[1]

Sonya then wrote in her own diary, "He loves to torment me and see me weep. . . . What is he doing to me? Little by little I shall withdraw completely from him and poison his life." This she resolved even as the preparations for their marriage were under way.

That inauspicious beginning was the emotional prelude to a forty-eight-year marriage. The Tolstoys' tumultuous and epic marital battle was punctuated by lengthy truces that saw Sonya give birth to thirteen children and dutifully decode and recopy from Leo's messy handwriting neat versions of twenty-one thousand manuscript pages for his novels, including *War and Peace* and *Anna Karenina*.

Yet despite her devoted service, during those years Leo wrote in his diary of Sonya, "Her unfairness and quiet egotism frighten and torment me." And Sonya countered in her diary, writing of Leo, "How can one love an insect that never stops stinging?"

By midlife, their marriage as recorded in their private journals seemed to have disintegrated into an unbearable hell for both of them, living as enemies in the same household. Toward the end of their lives—and shortly before Leo died while fleeing his troubled home in the middle of the night—Sonya wrote, "Every day there are fresh blows that scorch my heart." And these scorching blows, she added, "shorten my life."

Can Sonya have been right? Does such a stormy relationship shorten life? We certainly can't prove it from the case of the Tolstoys—Leo lived to be eighty-two, and Sonya lived for nine years after he died, to seventy-four.

How "soft" epigenetic factors like our relationships affect our health has been an elusive scientific question. Whether they do at all, and to what degree, can best be answered by looking at thousands of people over many years. Some influential studies seemed to suggest that the sheer number of other people in one's life predicts better health, but they miss the point: it is not the quantity but the *quality* that counts. Far more telling for our health than the absolute number of social ties we have may be the emotional tone of our relationships.

As the Tolstoys remind us, relationships can as readily be sources of angst as of joy. On the upside, the feeling that the people in one's life are emotionally supportive has a positive health impact. This link shows itself most powerfully in people whose condition is already fragile. For instance, in a study of elderly people hospitalized for congestive heart failure, those who had no one to rely on for emotional support were three times more likely to have another episode requiring a return to the hospital than were those with warm relationships.[2]

Love seemingly can make a medical difference. Among men getting angiography as part of treatment for coronary heart disease, those whose loved ones were reportedly least supportive had about 40 percent more blockage than those who reported having the warmest connections.[3] Conversely, data from a number of large epidemiological studies suggest that toxic relationships are as major a risk factor for disease and death as are smoking, high blood pressure or cholesterol, obesity, and physical inactivity.[4] Relationships cut two ways: they can either buffer us from illness or intensify the ravages of aging and disease.

To be sure, relationships alone tell only part of the story—other risk factors, from genetic susceptibility to smoking, all play their part. But the data put our relationships squarely among those risk factors. And now, with the social brain as the missing biological link, medical science has begun to detail the biological pathways through which others get under our skin, for better or worse.[5]

| A WAR OF ALL AGAINST ALL |

"Hobbes" was the name given to a macho male baboon by the researchers who observed him while he invaded a troop living in the jungles of Kenya. In the grim spirit of his namesake, the seventeenth-century philosopher Thomas Hobbes who wrote that beneath the veneer of civilization life is "nasty, brutish, and short," this baboon arrived primed to fight tooth and claw to reach the top of the group hierarchy.

The impact of Hobbes on the other males was measured by taking samples of cortisol from their blood, and it became clear that his raw aggression rippled through the endocrine systems of the entire group.

Under stress, the adrenal glands release cortisol, one of the hormones the body mobilizes in an emergency.[6] These hormones have widespread effects in the body, including many that are adaptive in the short term for healing bodily injuries.

Ordinarily we need a moderate level of cortisol, which acts as a biological "fuel" for our metabolism and helps regulate the immune system. But if our cortisol levels remain too high for prolonged periods, the body pays a price in ill health. The chronic secretion of cortisol (and related hormones) are at play in cardiovascular disease and impaired immune function, exacerbating diabetes and hypertension, and even destroying neurons in the hippocampus, harming memory.

Even as cortisol shuts down the hippocampus, it also stokes the amygdala, stimulating the growth of dendrites in that site for fear. In addition, heightened cortisol blunts the ability of the key areas in the prefrontal cortex to regulate the signals of fear coming from the amygdala.[7]

The combined neural impact of too much cortisol is threefold. The impaired hippocampus learns rather sloppily, overgeneralizing fearfulness to details of the moment that are irrelevant (such as a distinctive tone of voice). The amygdala circuitry goes on a rampage, and the prefrontal area fails to modulate signals from the overreacting amygdala. The result: the amygdala runs rampant, driving fear, while the hippocampus mistakenly perceives too many triggers for that fear.

In monkeys, the brain remains ever-vigilant for signs of a Hobbes-like stranger. In humans, that condition of vigilance and overreactivity has been called post-traumatic stress disorder.

In linking stress to health, the key biological systems are the sympathetic nervous system (SNS) and the hypothalamic-pituitary-adrenal (HPA) axis. When we are distressed, both the SNS and the HPA axis take up the challenge, secreting hormones that prepare us to handle an emergency or threat. But they do so by borrowing resources from the immune and endocrine systems, among others. That weakens these key systems for health, just for a moment or for years at a time.

The SNS and HPA circuits are turned on or off by our emotional states—distress for the worse, happiness for the better. Since other people affect our emotions with such power (through emotional contagion, for example), the causal linkage extends outside our body to our relationships.[8]

The physiological changes associated with the random ups and downs of relationships do not matter that much. But when those downs continue over many years, they create levels of biological stress (technically known as an "allostatic load") that can speed the onset of disease or worsen its symptoms.[9]

How a given relationship affects our health will depend on the sum total of how emotionally toxic or nourishing it has been over months and years. The more frail our condition is—after the onset of a serious disease, while we are recovering from a heart attack, in old age—the more powerful the health impact of our relationships.

The embattled, long-suffering, though long-lived Tolstoys seem a remarkable exception, like the odd centenarian who credits her longevity to eating lots of whipped cream and smoking a pack of cigarettes a day.

THE TOXICITY OF INSULT

Elysa Yanowitz stood by her principles though it cost her her job—and possibly a case of hypertension. One day a top executive from her cosmetics firm visited the perfume counter in a flagship San Francisco department store and ordered Yanowitz, the regional sales manager, to fire one of her best-performing salespeople.

The reason? He didn't think the saleswoman was attractive—or as he put it, "hot"—enough. Yanowitz, who felt the employee was not only a star at sales but perfectly presentable, found the executive's demand both groundless and disgusting. She refused to fire the woman.

Soon afterward Yanowitz's bosses seemed to sour on her. Though she had recently been selected as the company's sales manager of the year, now suddenly they told her she was making mistake after mistake. She feared they were building a case to force her out. Over these trying months Yanowitz began to suffer from high blood pressure. When she took a medical leave, the company replaced her.[10]

Yanowitz sued her former employer. However that case may be settled (as of this writing, it continues to wend its way through court), it raises the question of whether her hypertension might have been due in part to the way her own bosses treated her.[11]

Consider a British study of health care workers who had two supervisors on alternate days, one they dreaded and one they liked.[12] On the days the dreadful boss worked, their average blood pressure jumped 13 points for the systolic and 6 for diastolic (from 113/75 to 126/81). While the readings were still in a healthy range, that much of an elevation, if maintained over time, could have a clinically significant impact—that is, speed the onset of hypertension in someone otherwise susceptible.[13]

Studies in Sweden of workers at different levels and in the United Kingdom among civil servants show that people in the lower positions in an organization are four times more likely to develop cardiovascular disease than are those in the top rungs, who don't have to put up with the whims of bosses such as themselves.[14] Workers who feel unfairly criticized, or whose boss will not listen to their problems, have a rate of coronary heart disease 30 percent higher than those who feel treated fairly.[15]

In rigid hierarchies bosses tend to be authoritarian: they more freely express contempt for their subordinates, who in turn naturally feel a messy mix of hostility, fear, and insecurity.[16] Insults, which can be routine with such authoritarian managers, serve to reaffirm the boss's power while leaving their subordinates feeling helpless and vulnerable.[17] And because their salary and very job security depend on the boss, workers tend to obsess over their interactions, reading even mildly negative exchanges as ominous. Indeed, across the board, just about any conversation with someone of higher status at work elevates a person's blood pressure more than does a similar conversation with a coworker.[18]

Take how one handles an insult. In a relationship among peers, an affront can be challenged, an apology asked for. But when the insult comes from someone who holds all the power, subordinates (perhaps wisely) suppress their anger, responding with a resigned tolerance.

But that very passivity—with the insult going unchallenged—tacitly confers permission to a superior to continue in that vein.

People who respond to insults with silence experience significant hikes in blood pressure. As the demeaning messages continue over time, the person holding back feels increasingly powerless, anxious, and ultimately depressed—all of which, if prolonged over long periods, markedly increases the likelihood of cardiovascular disease.[19]

In one study a hundred men and women wore devices that took readings of their blood pressure whenever they interacted with someone.[20] When they were with family or enjoyable friends, their blood pressure fell; these interactions were pleasant and soothing. When they were with someone who was troublesome, there was a rise. But the biggest jump came while they were with people they felt ambivalent about: an overbearing parent, a volatile romantic partner, a competitive friend. A mercurial boss looms as the archetype, but this dynamic operates in all our relationships.

We try to steer clear of people we find unpleasant, but many unavoidable people in our lives fall into this "mixed" category: sometimes they make us feel good, and other times terrible. Ambivalent relationships put an emotional demand on us; each interaction is unpredictable, perhaps potentially explosive, and so requires a heightened vigilance and effort.

Medical science has pinpointed a biological mechanism that directly links a toxic relationship to heart disease. Volunteers for an experiment on stress had to defend themselves against a false accusation that they had shoplifted.[21] As they talked, their immune and cardiovascular systems mobilized in a potentially deadly combination. The immune system secreted T lymphocytes, while the walls of blood vessels emitted a substance that binds to those T cells, setting in motion the formation of artery-clogging plaque on the endothelium.[22]

Most surprising medically was that even relatively minor upsets seemed to trigger this mechanism. Presumably, this distress-to-endothelium chain reaction would put us at risk for heart disease if such stressful encounters become routine events in our daily lives.

THE CAUSAL CHAIN

It's all very well to find a general correlation between stressful relationships and poor health, and to identify a pathway or two in a possible causal chain. But despite the occasional studies suggesting biological mechanisms, skeptics often argue that very different factors may be at play. For instance, if a difficult relationship leads someone to drink or smoke too much or to sleep poorly, that might be a more immediate cause of ill health. So researchers have continued to look for a distinct biological link—one clearly separable from these other reasons.

Enter Sheldon Cohen, a psychologist at Carnegie Mellon University who has intentionally given colds to hundreds of people.[23] Not that Cohen has a malicious streak—it's all in the interest of science. Under meticulously controlled conditions, he systematically exposes volunteers to a rhinovirus that causes the common cold. About a third of people exposed to the virus develop the full panoply of symptoms, while the rest walk away with nary a sniffle. The controlled conditions allow him to determine why.

His methods are exacting. Cohen's experimental volunteers are quarantined for twenty-four hours before they are exposed, to be sure they have not picked up a cold elsewhere. For the next five days (and for $800) the volunteers are housed in a special unit with other volunteers, all of whom are kept at least three feet from one another, lest they reinfect someone.

During those five days their nasal secretions are tested for technical indicators of colds (like the total weight of their mucus) as well as the presence of the specific rhinovirus, and their blood samples are tested for antibodies. This way Cohen takes the measure of the cold with a precision that goes far beyond counting runny noses and sneezes.

We know that low levels of vitamin C, smoking, and sleeping poorly all increase the likelihood of infection. The question is, can a stressful relationship be added to that list? Cohen's answer: definitely.

Cohen assigns precise numerical values to the factors that make one person come down with a cold while another stays healthy. Those with an ongoing personal conflict were 2.5 times as likely as the others to get a cold, putting rocky relationships in the same causal range as vitamin C deficiency and poor sleep. (Smoking, the most damaging unhealthy habit, made people three times more likely to succumb.) Conflicts that lasted a month or longer boosted susceptibility, but an occasional argument presented no health hazard.[24]

While perpetual arguments are bad for our health, isolating ourselves is worse. Compared to those with a rich web of social connections, those with the fewest close relationships were 4.2 times more likely to come down with the cold, making loneliness riskier than smoking.

The more we socialize, the less susceptible to colds we become. This idea seems counterintuitive: don't we *increase* the likelihood of being exposed to a cold virus the more people we interact with? Sure. But vibrant social connections boost our good moods and limit our negative ones, suppressing cortisol and enhancing immune function under stress.[25] Relationships themselves seem to protect us from the risk of exposure to the very cold virus they pose.

THE PERCEPTION OF MALICE

Elysa Yanowitz is not alone in the indignities she suffered at work. A woman working at a pharmaceutical company sends me this e-mail: "I'm having personality clashes with my boss, who is not a very nice person. For the first time in my professional career, my confidence is shaken—and since she's friends with all of the upper hierarchy at my company, I feel I have no recourse. The whole thing is making me physically ill from the stress."

Is she merely imagining the link between her toxic boss and her physical illness? Perhaps.

On the other hand, her plight fits well with findings from an analysis of 208 studies involving 6,153 individuals who were subjected to stressors ranging from loud, obnoxious noises to confrontations with equally obnoxious people.[26] Of all the sorts of stress, the worst by far was when someone was the target of harsh criticism and was helpless to do anything about it—like both Yanowitz and the pharmaceutical employee who clashed with her boss.

Why this should be so has been revealed by Margaret Kemeny, an expert in behavioral medicine at the University of California Medical School in San Francisco, who analyzed hundreds of stress studies with her colleague Sally Dickerson. Threats or challenges, Kemeny told me, are most stressful "when you have an audience and feel you are being judged."

Stress reactions in all the studies were gauged by the rise in a person's level of cortisol.[27] The largest spikes in cortisol occurred when the source of stress was interpersonal—for example, when someone sat in judgment on a volunteer who had to subtract the number 17 from 1,242 aloud then continue to subtract 17 from the resulting number, as rapidly as possible. When a person performed such an onerous task while being judged on how they did, the effect on cortisol was about *three times* greater than when the stress was comparable but impersonal.[28]

Imagine, for example, that you're being interviewed for a job. As you talk about the talents and expertise that you believe qualify you, something unsettling happens. You see the interviewer responding to you with a stony, unsmiling expression, coolly making notes on a clipboard. Then, to make things worse, the interviewer makes critical remarks, belittling your skills.

That was the nerve-wracking predicament of volunteers for a devilish measure of social stress, all of whom were actually in the midst of applying for a job and had come for a practice interview. But the "practice sessions" were actually a stress test. Developed by researchers in Germany, this experimental ordeal has been used in labs around the world because it produces powerful data. Kemeny's lab routinely has used a variation of the test to assess the biological punch of social stress.

Dickerson and Kemeny argue that being evaluated threatens the "social self," the ways we see ourselves through others' eyes. This sense of our social value and status—and so our very self-worth—comes from the cumulative messages we get from others about how they perceive us. Such threats to our standing in the eyes of others are remarkably potent biologically, almost as powerful as those to our very survival. After all, the unconscious equation goes, if we are judged to be undesirable, we may not only be shamed, but suffer complete rejection.[29]

An interviewer's unnerving, hostile reaction reliably triggers the HPA axis to produce some of the highest levels of cortisol of any laboratory stress simulation ever tested. The social stress test hikes cortisol much more than does that classic lab ordeal, in which volunteers do increasingly difficult math problems under intense time pressure against annoying background noise, with a noxious buzzer signaling wrong answers—but without the presence of someone making nasty judgments.[30] Impersonal ordeals are soon forgotten, but judgmental scrutiny delivers a particularly strong—and lingering—dose of shame.[31]

Astonishingly, a symbolic judge existing only in the mind delivers just as large a dose of angst. A virtual audience can affect the HPA system as powerfully as a live one, Kemeny explains, because "the moment you think of something, you create an internal representation, which in turn acts on the brain" much as would the reality it represents.

Feeling helpless adds to the stress. In the cortisol studies analyzed by Dickerson and Kemeny, threats were perceived as all the worse when they were beyond the person's ability to do anything about them. When a threat persists no matter what efforts we might make, the cortisol rise magnifies. This parallels the predicament of someone, for example, who finds himself the target of vicious prejudice—or those two beleaguered women whose bosses turned against them. Relationships that are continually critical, rejecting, or harassing keep the HPA axis in constant overdrive.

When the source of stress seems impersonal, like an obnoxious auto alarm we are helpless to stop, our most basic need for acceptance and belonging goes unthreatened. Kemeny found that for such impersonal stress, the body got over its inevitable jump in cortisol within forty minutes or so. But if the cause was a negative social judgment, cortisol stayed high 50 percent longer, taking an hour or more to return to normal.

Brain imaging studies suggest which parts of the brain may react so strongly to such perception of malice. Recall from Chapter 5 the computer simulation in Jonathan Cohen's lab at Princeton, where volunteers in an MRI scanner played the Ultimatum Game. The game requires two partners to divide some money, with one making offers of a split that the other can accept or reject.

When a volunteer felt that the other person had made them an unfair offer, their brain showed activity in the anterior insula, which is known to activate during feelings of anger and disgust. Fittingly, they showed signs of bitterness and were more likely to reject not just this offer but the next one too, whatever it might be. Yet when they believed that the other "partner" in the game was just a computer program, their insula stayed quiet, no matter how seemingly one-sided the offer. The social brain makes a crucial distinction between accidental and intentional harm, and it reacts more strongly if it seems malevolent.

This finding may solve a puzzle for clinicians attempting to understand post-traumatic stress disorder (PTSD): why catastrophes of similar intensity more often lead to lasting suffering if the person feels their trauma was purposely inflicted by someone else rather than a random act of Nature. Hurricanes, earthquakes, and other natural catastrophes leave many fewer victims of PTSD than do malicious acts like rape and physical abuse. The aftereffects of trauma, like all stress, are worse the more personally targeted the victim feels.

THE CLASS OF '57

It was in 1957 that Elvis Presley broke into America's national consciousness by appearing on the Sunday night *Ed Sullivan Show,* then the most-watched hour on television. The American economy was in the midst of a lengthy postwar boom, Dwight D. Eisenhower was president, cars had grotesque tail fins, and teens socialized at heavily chaperoned school dances called "sock hops."

In that year researchers from the University of Wisconsin began to study about ten thousand graduating high school seniors, nearly a third of those in the entire state. These teens were later reinterviewed as they reached age forty, and again as they reached their mid-fifties. Then, as they approached sixty-five, a group of the grads were recruited for follow-up research by Richard Davidson at the University of Wisconsin and brought to the W. M. Keck Laboratory for Functional Brain Imaging and Behavior. Using measures far more sophisticated than anything available in 1957, Davidson undertook to correlate their social history, brain activity, and immune function.

The quality of the grads' relationships over the course of their lives had been discerned in the earlier interviews. Now it was compared to the wear and tear on their bodies. The grads were assessed on the chronic activity of systems that fluctuate as they handle stress, including blood pressure, cholesterol, and levels for cortisol and other stress hormones. The sum of these and similar measures predicts not just the likelihood of cardiovascular disease but also late-life declines in mental and physical functioning. A very high total score predicts an earlier death.[32] The researchers found that relationships mattered: there was a strong association between having a high-risk physical profile and an unfavorable cumulative emotional tone in the grads' most important life relationships.[33]

Take, for example, the anonymous Class of 1957 graduate I'll call Jane. Her relationship life had been tough, a litany of disappointments. Both Jane's parents were alcoholics, and she saw little of her father during most of her childhood. He molested her while she was in high school. As an adult, she was extremely fearful of people, alternately angry at and anxious with those closest to her. Though Jane married, she soon divorced, and her scant social life offered her little solace. In the medical survey for Davidson's study, she had nine out of twenty-two common medical symptoms.

On the other hand, Jill, one of Jane's high school classmates, was the picture of a full and rich relationship history. Although Jill's father had died when she was just nine, she felt her mother had been extremely caring. Jill was close to her husband and her four sons, and she felt her family life was extremely satisfying. So too was her active social life, filled as it was with many close friends and confidants. And in her sixties Jill reported having problems with only three of the twenty-two symptoms.

Again, correlation is not causation. To demonstrate a causal link between relationship quality and health includes identifying the specific biological mechanisms at work. Here the Class of 1957 provided some telling clues, based on Davidson's tests of brain activity.

Jill, the woman with the caring mother, satisfying relationships, and very few medical complaints in her sixties, was the member of the Class of '57 with the greatest activity in her left prefrontal cortex relative to the right. That brain activity pattern, Davidson has found, suggests that Jill's days were filled with mostly pleasant moods.

Jane, whose parents had been alcoholics and who was divorced with many medical problems in her sixties, had the opposite brain pattern. She had the highest activity in her right prefrontal area relative to the left of anyone studied in her class. That pattern suggests that Jane more often reacted to life with intense distress and recovered slowly from her emotional setbacks.

The left prefrontal area, as Davidson had found in earlier research, regulates a cascade of circuitry in lower brain areas that determine our recovery time from distress—that is, our resilience.[34] The more of this left prefrontal activity (relative to the right side), the better we are at developing cognitive strategies for emotional regulation and the faster our emotional recovery. That in turn determines how quickly cortisol returns to normal.

Resilient health depends in part on how well the high road has learned to manage the low.

Davidson's earlier study went one step further. His research group discovered that activity in the same left prefrontal area correlated highly with the ability of a person's immune system to respond to a flu shot. Those with the highest activation had immune systems that mobilized flu antibodies *three times more* than did others.[35] Davidson believes that these differences are clinically significant—in other words, that those with high left prefrontal activity are less likely to get the flu if exposed to the virus.

Davidson sees in such data a window on the anatomy of resilience. A soundly secure relationship history, he theorizes, gives people the inner resources to bounce back from emotional setbacks and losses—as was the case with Jill, the woman who lost her father at age nine but whose mother was so loving.

Those Wisconsin grads who endured relentless stress in childhood now as adults had poor stress recovery abilities, staying overwhelmed longer once they were upset. But those people who had been exposed to manageable levels of stress during childhood were most likely as adults to have the better prefrontal ratio. For this outcome, a caring adult who provides a secure base for emotional recovery seems essential. [36]

SOCIAL EPIGENETICS

Laura Hillenbrand, the author of the best-selling book *Seabiscuit,* has long suffered from chronic fatigue syndrome, a debilitating condition that can leave her feverish and exhausted, needing constant care for months at a time. While she was writing *Seabiscuit,* that care came from her devoted husband, Borden, who—even while struggling with his own work as a graduate student—somehow found the energy to be her nurse, helping her eat and drink, assisting her when she needed to walk, and reading to her.

But one night in her bedroom, Hillenbrand recalls, she "heard a soft, low sound." She looked down the stairway to see Borden "pacing the foyer and sobbing." She started to call out to him but stopped herself, realizing he wanted to be alone.

The next morning Borden was there to help her as usual, "cheerful and steady as ever." [37]

Borden did his best to keep his own anguish from upsetting his already-fragile wife. But like Borden, anyone who has to nurse a loved one day and night endures extraordinary, unabated stress. And that tension takes an inevitable toll on the health and well-being of even the most devoted caretaker.

The most powerful data on this point comes from a remarkable interdisciplinary research group at Ohio State University led by psychologist Janice Kiecolt-Glaser and her husband, immunologist Ronald Glaser.[38] In an elegant series of studies, they have shown that the effects of continual stress reach all the way down to the level of gene expression in the immune cells essential for fighting infections and healing wounds.

The Ohio State group studied ten women in their sixties, all of them caring for a husband with Alzheimer's disease.[39] The caregivers were under relentless strain, on duty twenty-four hours a day—and feeling terribly isolated and uncared for themselves. An earlier study of women under similar stress had discovered that they were virtually unable to benefit from flu shots; their immune system could not manufacture the antibodies that the shot ordinarily stimulates.[40] Now the researchers undertook more elaborate tests of immune function, revealing that the women in the Alzheimer's caregivers group had troubling readings on a wide range of indicators.

The genetic data, in particular, made headlines. A gene that regulates a range of crucial immune mechanisms was expressed 50 percent less in the caretakers than in other women their age. GHmRNA, the impaired gene, enhances the production of lymphocytes and also boosts the activity of natural killer cells and macrophages, which destroy invading bacteria.[41] That may also explain another earlier finding: stressed women took nine days longer to heal a small puncture wound than did women in a nonstressed comparison group.

A key factor in this impaired immunity may be ACTH, a precursor to cortisol and one of the hormones secreted when the HPA axis runs amok. ACTH blocks the production of the crucial immune agent interferon and diminishes the responsivity of lymphocytes, the white blood cells that mount the body's attack against invading bacteria. The bottom line: the continual stress of tireless caregiving in social isolation impairs the brain's control of the HPA axis, which in turn weakens the ability of immune system genes like GHmRNA to do their job fighting disease.

The toll of relentless stress also seems to strike the very DNA of the caretakers, speeding the rate at which cells age and adding years to their biological age. Other researchers doing genetic studies of DNA in mothers caring for a chronically ill child found that the longer they had been so burdened, the more they had aged at the cellular level.

The rate of aging was determined by measuring the length of the telomeres on the mothers' white blood cells. Telomeres are a piece of DNA at the end of a cell's chromosome that shrinks a bit each time the cell divides to duplicate itself. Cells reproduce repeatedly throughout their lifespan to repair tissue or, in the case of white blood cells, to fight disease. Somewhere after ten to fifty divisions (depending on the type of cell), the telomere becomes too short to replicate anymore, and the cell "retires"—a genetic measure of loss of vitality.

By this measure, the mothers caring for chronically ill children were, on average, ten years older biologically than others of their same chronological age. Among the exceptions were those women who, despite feeling overwhelmed in their lives, felt well supported by others. They had younger cells, even if they were caring for a disabled loved one.

Collective social intelligence can offer an alternative to the overwhelming toll of caregiving. Witness the scene in Sandwich, New Hampshire, where Philip Simmons sat in his wheelchair on a brilliant fall day, surrounded by friends and neighbors. At age thirty-five Simmons, a college English teacher with two small children, had been diagnosed with the degenerative neurological condition Lou Gehrig's disease and given two to five years to live. He had already outlived his prognosis, but now the paralysis was moving from his lower body to his arms, making him unable to perform even routine tasks. At this point he gave a friend a book called *Share the Care,* which describes how to create an ongoing support group for someone with a severe illness.

Thirty-five neighbors rallied to help Simmons and his family. Coordinating their schedule largely by phone and e-mail, they acted as cooks, drivers, babysitters, home aides—and, as on that fall day, yard workers—for the last several years of Simmons's life, until he died at age forty-five. This virtual extended family made an immense difference for Simmons and his wife, Kathryn Field. Not least, their help enabled Field to continue her work as a professional artist, easing the financial strain and giving the entire family, in her words, "a sense of being loved by our community."[42]

As for those who formed FOPAK (Friends of Phil and Kathryn), as they called themselves, most agreed that they were the ones receiving the gift.

Biological Allies

When my mother retired from teaching college, she found herself with a large, empty house and no one to fill it: her children had all ended up living in other cities, some quite distant, and my father had died years before. A former professor of sociology, she made what, in retrospect, seems a smart social move: my mother offered a free room to graduate students from her university, with a preference for those from East Asian cultures, where older people are appreciated and respected.

It's been more than thirty years since she retired, and this arrangement still continues. She has had a revolving series of housemates from places like Japan, Taiwan, and currently Beijing— with what seem to be great benefits for her well-being. When one couple had a baby while living with her, their daughter grew up treating my mother like her own grandmother. As a two-year-old, the toddler would go into my mother's bedroom every morning to see if she was up yet and routinely gave her hugs through the day.

That baby was born when my mother was almost ninety—and with that bundle of delight roaming the house, my mother actually seemed for a few years to get younger, both physically and mentally. We'll never know how much of my mother's longevity can be attributed to her living situation, but evidence suggests hers was a wise bit of social engineering.

The social networks of the elderly are pruned for them, as one old friend after another dies or moves away. But at the same time older people also tend to cut back their social networks selectively, preserving positive relationships.[1] That strategy makes good biological sense. As we grow old, our health inevitably becomes more fragile; as cells age and die, our immune system and other bulwarks for good health work less and less well. Dropping unrewarding social ties may be a preemptive move to manage our own emotional states for the better. Indeed, a landmark study of elderly Americans who were aging successfully found that the more emotionally supportive their relationships, the lower their indicators of biological stress like cortisol.[2]

Of course, our most meaningful relationships may not necessarily be the most pleasant and positive ones in our lives—a close relative can be someone who drives us crazy rather than delights us. Perhaps luckily, as older people prune away less significant social ties, many seem to develop a greater capacity for handling emotional complications, such as the mix of positive and negative feelings stirred up by a given relationship.[3]

One study found that when elderly people had an engaging, supportive social life, they displayed better cognitive abilities seven years later than did those who were more isolated.[4] Paradoxically, loneliness has little or nothing to do with how much time people actually spend by themselves, nor how many social contacts they have in a given day. Instead, it's the paucity of intimate, friendly contacts that leads to loneliness. What matters is the *quality* of our interactions: their warmth or emotional distance, their supportiveness or negativity. The sense of loneliness, rather than the sheer number of acquaintances and contacts a person actually has, correlates most directly with health: the lonelier a person feels, the poorer immune and cardiovascular function tends to be.[5]

There's another biological argument for becoming more intentional about our interpersonal world as we age. Neurogenesis, the brain's daily manufacture of new neurons, continues into old age, though at a slower rate than in earlier decades. And even that slowdown may not be inevitable, some neuroscientists suggest, but rather a side effect of monotony. Adding complexity to a person's social environment primes new learning, enhancing the rate at which the brain adds new cells. For this reason some neuroscientists are working with architects to design homes for the elderly where occupants have to interact more with others in the course of their daily routines—something my mother arranged for herself.[6]

| **THE MARITAL BATTLEGROUND** |

As I leave the grocery store in a small town, I overhear two elderly men sitting on a bench outside. One asks how a local couple is doing.

"You know how it is," comes the laconic reply. "They've only ever had one argument—and they're still having it."

Such emotional wear and tear in a relationship, as we've seen, takes its biological toll. Just why a marriage gone sour might sabotage health was found when newlyweds—all considering themselves "very happy" in their marriages—volunteered to be studied while they had a thirty-minute confrontation about a disagreement.[7] During the tiff, five of six adrenal hormones tested changed levels, including increases in ACTH that indicate a mobilized HPA axis. Blood pressure shot up, and indices of immune function were lowered for several hours.

Hours later there were long-term shifts for the worse in the immune system's ability to mount a defense against invaders. The more bitterly hostile their argument had been, the stronger the shifts. The endocrine system, the researchers conclude, "serves as one important gateway between personal relationships and health," triggering the release of stress hormones that can hamper both cardiovascular and immune function.[8] When a couple fights, their endocrine and immune systems suffer—and if the fights are sustained over years, the damage seems to be cumulative.

As part of the study of marital conflict, couples in their sixties (married an average forty-two years) were invited to the same laboratory for a closely monitored disagreement. Once again the argument spurred unhealthy declines in the endocrine and immune systems—the more rancor, the greater the drops. Since aging weakens the immune and cardiovascular systems, hostility between older partners can take a greater toll on health. Sure enough, the negative biological changes were even stronger in older couples than for the newlyweds during the marital battle—but only for the wives.[9]

This surprising effect held true for both newlywed and older married women. Understandably, the newlywed wives who showed the greatest decline in immune measures during and after the "fight" were the most dissatisfied with their marriages a year later.

For women, when husbands withdrew in anger during disagreements, stress hormones zoomed upward. On the other hand, wives whose husbands displayed kindness and empathy during the discussion reflected their relief in lower levels of the same hormones.

But for husbands, whether the talk was harsh or pleasant, their endocrine systems did not budge. The sole exception was at the extreme, among those who reported the most abrasive arguments at home. For these embattled couples, both husbands and wives had poorer immune responses from day to day than did more harmonious couples.

Data from multiple sources suggest that wives are more vulnerable to suffer the health costs of a rocky marriage than are their husbands. Yet women do not seem to be more biologically reactive than men in general. [10]

One answer may be that women put a greater emotional premium on their closest ties.[11] Many surveys of American women show that positive relationships are their major source of satisfaction and well-being throughout life. For American men, on the other hand, positive relationships rate lower in importance than a sense of personal growth or a feeling of independence.

In addition, women's instinct for caregiving means they take more personal responsibility for the fate of those they care about, making them more prone than men to getting distressed at loved ones' troubles.[12] Women are also more attuned to the ups and downs of their relationships and so are more susceptible to riding an emotional roller coaster.[13]

Another finding: wives spend far more time than their husbands ruminating about upsetting encounters, and they review them in their minds in more vivid detail. (They also remember the good times better and spend more time reminiscing about them.) Because bad memories can be intrusive, repeatedly popping into the mind unbidden, and because simply recalling a conflict can trigger the biological shifts that accompanied it, the tendency to mull over one's troubles takes a physical toll.[14]

For all these reasons, troubles in a close relationship drive adverse biological reactions in women more strongly than in men.[15] In the Wisconsin Study, for instance, women's cholesterol levels were directly linked to the amount of stress in their marriages—far more so than for men in the Class of '57.

In a study of patients with congestive heart failure, a stormy marriage was more likely to lead to an early death for women than for men.[16] Women are also more likely to have a heart attack when they experience emotional stress from a severe relationship crisis like a divorce or death, while for men the trigger is more likely to be physical exertion. And older women seem more vulnerable than men to life-threatening rises in stress hormones in response to a sudden emotional shock, like the unexpected death of a loved one—a condition doctors are calling the "broken heart syndrome."[17]

Women's greater biological reactivity to relationship ups and downs begins to answer that long-standing scientific puzzle, why men, but not women, seem to experience a health benefit from being married. That finding appears over and over in surveys of marriage and health—and yet is not necessarily true. What muddied the waters has been a simple failure of scientific imagination.

A different picture emerged when a thirteen-year study of close to five hundred married women in their fifties asked the simple question, "How *satisfied* are you in your marriage?" The results were crystal clear: the more pleased a woman was with her marriage, the better her health.[18] When a woman enjoyed the time she spent with her partner, felt they communicated well and agreed on matters like finances, enjoyed their sex life, and had similar interests and tastes, her medical data told the story. Levels of blood pressure, glucose, and bad cholesterol were lower for the satisfied women than for those unhappy in their marriages.

Those other surveys had lumped together data from miserable and happy wives. So while women appear to be more biologically vulnerable to the ups or downs in their marriage, the effects of that emotional roller coaster depend on the nature of the ride. When she has more downs than ups in her marriage, a woman's health suffers. But when her relationship gives her more ups, her health—like her husband's—benefits.

EMOTIONAL RESCUERS

Picture a woman in the maws of an MRI, lying on her back on a gurney that's been wheeled into a human-shaped cavity, one that leaves just inches to spare, in the midst of this vast piece of machinery. She's hearing the unsettling whine of huge electric magnets whirling around her and peering at a video monitor just inches above her face.

The screen flashes a sequence of colored geometric shapes—a green square, a red triangle—every twelve seconds. She's been told that when a certain shape and color come on the screen, she'll receive an electric shock—not very painful but unpleasant nonetheless.

At times she endures her apprehension alone. At other times a stranger holds her hand. And sometimes she feels the reassuring touch of her husband's hand.

That was the predicament of eight women who had volunteered for a study in Richard Davidson's laboratory, one designed to assess the extent to which the people we love can lend us biological assistance in moments of stress and anxiety. The results: when a woman held her husband's hand, she felt far less anxiety than when she faced the shock alone.[19]

Holding a stranger's hand helped a bit, though not nearly so much. Intriguingly, Davidson's group found that it was impossible to conduct the study so that the women were "blind" to whose hand they were holding: on a trial run, wives always guessed correctly whether the hand was their husband's or a stranger's.

When the wives faced the shock alone, fMRI analysis showed activity in regions of the brain that drive the HPA axis into its emergency response, pumping stress hormones through the body.[20] Had the threat been not just a mild shock but personal—say, a hostile job interviewer—these regions almost certainly would have been even more aroused.

Yet this volatile circuitry was pacified strikingly with the calming clasp of a husband's hand. The study fills in an important blank in our understanding of just how our relationships can matter biologically for better or for worse. We now have a snapshot of the brain undergoing emotional rescue.

Just as telling was another finding: the more highly satisfied a wife feels with her marriage, the greater the biological benefit from holding hands. This clinches the answer to that old scientific mystery of why some marriages appear to challenge women's health, while others protect it.

Skin-on-skin touch is particularly soothing because it primes oxytocin, as do warmth and vibration (which may explain much of the stress relief that comes from massage or a cozy cuddle). Oxytocin acts as a stress hormone "down-regulator," reducing the very HPA and SNS activity that, when sustained, puts our health at risk.[21]

When oxytocin releases, the body undergoes a host of healthy changes.[22] Blood pressure lowers as we slide into the relaxed mode of parasympathetic activity. That shifts metabolism from the ready-to-run large muscle boost of stress arousal to a restorative mode where energy goes into storing nutrients, growth, and healing. Cortisol levels plummet, signifying decreased HPA action. Our pain threshold rises, so that we are less sensitive to discomforts. Even wounds heal faster.

Oxytocin has a short half-life in the brain—it's gone in just a matter of minutes. But close, positive long-term relationships may offer us a relatively steady source of oxytocin release; every hug, friendly touch, and affectionate moment may prime this neurochemical balm a bit. When oxytocin releases again and again—as happens when we spend good time with people who love us—we seem to reap the long-term health benefits of human affection. The very substance that draws us closer to the people we love, then, converts those warm connections into biological well-being.[23]

Back to the Tolstoys. Despite all the rancor recorded in their journals, they managed to have thirteen children. That horde means they lived in a household that was bustling with abundant opportunities for affection. The couple did not have to rely only on each other; they were surrounded by emotional rescuers.

POSITIVE CONTAGION

Just forty-one, Anthony Radziwill lay dying in the intensive care unit of a New York hospital from fibrosarcoma, a deadly cancer. As his widow Carole tells it, Anthony was visited by his cousin John F. Kennedy, Jr., who was himself to die just months later when the plane he was piloting crashed off the island of Martha's Vineyard.

John, still in a tuxedo from the black-tie event he had just left, got the news as he entered the ICU that the doctors had given his cousin just hours to live.

So taking hold of his cousin's hand, John quietly sang "The Teddy Bears' Picnic," a song his own mother, Jackie Onassis, had sung to them both as a lullaby when they were small.

Anthony, near death, joined in softly.

John, as Radziwill recounts, "had taken him to the safest place he can find."[24]

That sweet touch surely eased Radziwill's final moments. And it bespeaks the sort of connection that intuitively seems the best way to help a loved one in such dire moments.

That intuition now has solid data to support it: physiologists have shown that as people become emotionally interdependent, they play an active role in the regulation of each other's very physiology. This biological entrainment means that the cues each partner receives from the other have special power to drive their own body, for better or for worse.

In a nourishing relationship, partners help each other manage their distressing feelings, just as nurturing parents do their children. When we are stressed or upset, our partners can help us rethink what's causing our distress, perhaps to respond better or simply to put things in perspective—in either case short-circuiting the negative neuroendocrine cascade.

Being separated from those we love for long periods deprives us of this intimate help; the longing for people we miss expresses in part a yearning for this biologically helpful connection. And some of the utter disorganization we feel after the death of a loved one no doubt reflects the absence of this virtual part of ourselves. That loss of a major biological ally may help explain the heightened risk of disease or death after a spouse passes away.

Again, an intriguing gender difference emerges. Under stress, a woman's brain secretes more oxytocin than a man's. This has a calming effect and moves women to seek out others—to take care of children, to talk to a friend. While women tend or befriend, as psychologist Shelley Taylor at UCLA discovered, their bodies release additional oxytocin, which calms them even more.[25] This tend-and-befriend impulse may be uniquely female. Androgens—male sex hormones—suppress the calming benefits of oxytocin. Estrogen, the female sex hormone, enhances it. This difference seems to lead women and men to very different reactions when they are facing a threat; women seek out companionship, while men go it alone. For instance, when women were told they would receive an electric shock, they chose to wait for it with other participants, while men preferred being by themselves. Men seem better able to calm their distress through sheer distraction; TV and a beer may suffice.

The more close friends women have, the less likely they are to develop physical impairments as they age, and the more likely they are to lead a joyful life in their later years. The impact appears to be so strong that friendlessness has been found to be as detrimental to a woman's health as smoking or obesity. Even after experiencing an enormous blow, like the death of a spouse, women with a close friend and confidante are more likely to escape any new physical impairments or loss of vitality.

In any close relationship, our own toolkit for managing our emotions—everything from seeking comfort to rethinking what's upsetting us—gets supplemented by the other person, who can offer advice or encouragement or help more directly via positive emotional contagion. The primal template for forming a tight biological link with those closest to us was set in early infancy, in the intimate physiology of our earliest interactions. These brain-to-brain mechanisms stay with us throughout life, connecting our biology with the people to whom we are most attached.

Psychology has an infelicitous term for this coalescing of two into one: a "mutually regulating psychobiological unit," a radical relaxing of the usual psychological and physiological line separating I and You, self and other.[26] This fluidity of boundaries between people who feel close allows a two-way coregulation, influencing each other's biology. In short, we help (or harm) each other not just emotionally but *at a biological level.* Your hostility bumps up my blood pressure; your nurturing love lowers it.[27]

If we have a life partner, a close friend, or a warm relative on whom we can rely as a secure base, we have a biological ally. Given the new medical understanding of just how much relationships matter for health, patients with severe or chronic disease may well benefit from tuning up their emotional connections. In addition to following the medical regimen, biological allies are good medicine.

| A HEALING PRESENCE |

When I was living in rural India many years ago, I was intrigued to learn that hospitals in my area typically provided no food for their patients. More surprising to me was the reason: whenever a patient was admitted, their family came along, camping out in their room, cooking their meals, and otherwise helping care for them.

How wonderful, I thought, to have the people who love a patient there with him day and night to ward off the emotional toll of his physical suffering. What a stark contrast with the social isolation so often found in medical care in the West.

A medical system that deploys social support and caring to help boost patients' quality of life may well enhance their very ability to heal. For example, a patient lying in her hospital bed, awaiting major surgery the next day, can't help but worry. In any situation, what one person feels strongly tends to pass to others, and the more stressed and vulnerable someone feels, the more sensitive they are, and the more likely to catch those feelings.[28] If the worried patient shares a room with another patient who also faces surgery, the two of them may well make each other more anxious and fearful. But if she shares a room with a patient who has just come out of surgery successfully—and so feels relatively relieved and calm—the emotional effect on her will be more soothing.[29]

When I asked Sheldon Cohen, who led the studies on rhinovirus infection, what he recommended for hospital patients, he suggested they deliberately seek out biological allies. For example, he told me that it can pay, he argues, to "graft new people on to your social network, especially people you can open up to." When a friend of mine got the diagnosis of a probably fatal cancer, he made a smart medical decision: he started seeing a psychotherapist he could talk with as he and his family went through the subsequent maelstrom of angst.

As Cohen told me, "The most striking finding on relationships and physical health is that socially integrated people—those who are married, have close family and friends, belong to social and religious groups, and participate widely in these networks—recover more quickly from disease and live longer. Roughly eighteen studies show a strong connection between social connectivity and mortality."

Devoting more time and energy to being with the people in our lives whom we find most nourishing, Cohen says, has health benefits.[30] He also urges patients, to the extent possible, to reduce the number of emotionally toxic interactions in their day, while increasing the nourishing ones.

Rather than having a stranger teach a heart attack victim how best to avoid a recurrence, Cohen suggests, hospitals should enlist the personal networks of patients on their behalf, educating those who care most about the patient to become allies in making the necessary lifestyle changes.

As important as social support is to the elderly and sick, other forces work against the fulfillment of their need for warm connection. Not least is the awkwardness and anxiety that friends and families often feel around a patient. Particularly when the patient has a condition that carries social stigma, or when a patient faces death, people who are ordinarily close can become too wary or anxious to offer help—or even to visit.

"Most of the people around me stepped backward," recalls Laura Hillenbrand, the author who was bedridden for months at a time with chronic fatigue syndrome. Friends would ask other friends how she was, but "after one or two get-well cards I stopped hearing from them." When she took the initiative to call old friends, the conversations were often awkward, and she ended up feeling foolish for calling.

And yet like anyone cut off by illness, Hillenbrand yearned for contact, for connection with those missing biological allies. As Sheldon Cohen says, the scientific findings "absolutely send a message to patients' family and friends not to ignore or isolate them—even if you don't know quite what to say, it's important just to go visit."

This advice suggests to all of us who care about someone suffering medically that, even if we feel at a loss for words, we can always offer the gift of a loving presence. Mere presence can matter surprisingly, even to patients in a vegetative state with severe brain damage who seem utterly unaware of what people say to them—who are in what medical jargon labels a "minimally conscious state." When someone emotionally close reminisces with such a patient about events from their past or touches them lightly, the patient activates the same brain circuitry in response as do people with intact brains.[31] Yet they appear totally out of touch, unable as they are to signal so much as a glance or word in response.

A friend tells me that by chance she read an article about people who had recovered from coma; they reported that they often could hear and understand what people said even as they lay there unable to move a muscle. She happened to read that article on a bus as she traveled to be with her mother, who was minimally conscious following resuscitation from congestive heart failure. This insight transformed her experience sitting at her mother's bedside as she drifted away.

Emotional closeness helps most when patients are medically fragile: when they have a chronic disease, or an impaired immune system, or when they are very old. While such caring is no panacea, emerging data suggests that it may sometimes make a clinically meaningful difference. In this sense, love is more than just a way to improve the emotional tone of a patient's life—it is a biologically active ingredient in medical care.

For that reason Mark Pettus, a physician, urges us to recognize the subtle messages that signal a patient's need for even a moment of caring connection, and to act on the "invitations to enter" that take the form of "a tear, a laugh, a look, or even silence."

Pettus's own young son was in the hospital for surgery, overwhelmed, scared, confused—and unable to understand what was happening because, developmentally slow, he had not yet learned to talk.[32] After surgery his young son lay in bed dwarfed by a web of tubes attached to him: an IV in his arm taped to a board; a tube through his nostril into his stomach; oxygen tubes in his nostrils; another sending anesthesia into his spinal canal; yet another running through his penis to his bladder.

Pettus and his wife felt heartbroken that their sweet child had to go through all this. Yet they could see in his eyes that they were able to help him through small gestures of human warmth: reassuring touches, heartfelt looks, simple presence.

As he says, "Love was our language."

A People Prescription

A medical resident in the spine clinic at one of the world's best hospitals was interviewing a woman in her fifties who was in great pain from severe disk degeneration in her neck. She'd had the problem for years, but she had never before consulted a physician. Instead, she had been going to a chiropractor whose manipulations brought her only temporary relief. The pain was gradually increasing, and she was afraid.

The woman and her daughter peppered the resident with their questions, doubts, and fears. For twenty minutes or so the resident tried to address their concerns and allay their fears, but he had not quite succeeded.

At that point the attending physician entered the room and briskly described the facet joint injections that she recommended to calm the inflammation, as well as the physical therapy that should follow to stretch and strengthen the neck muscles. The daughter could not understand how these treatments would help and started directing a stream of questions toward the physician, who by then had stood up and was backing toward the door.

Ignoring the physician's tacit cue that the conversation was ending, the daughter kept right on asking one question after another. After the attending physician left the room, the resident stayed with them another ten minutes, until the patient finally agreed to have the injection.

A short time later the attending physician took the resident aside and said, "That was nice of you, but you can't afford the luxury of that kind of prolonged conversation with a patient. We are scheduled for fifteen minutes per patient, and that includes dictation time. You'll be cured of this after you spend a few sleepless nights dictating your notes and have to come back early the next morning for a full day at the clinic."

"But I care about my connection with patients," the resident protested. "I want to establish rapport, really understand them—I'd spend a half hour with each one if I could."

At that the attending physician, a bit exasperated, closed a door so they could talk in private. "Look," she said, "there were eight other patients waiting—it was selfish of that woman to stay so long. You just can't spend more than ten minutes with each patient. That's all we have time for."

She then walked the resident through the mathematics at that hospital of time per patient, and the portion of each payment that finally reaches the doctor after "taxes" are taken—cuts deducted for malpractice insurance, for hospital overhead, and for other privileged parties. The results: if a doctor billed $300,000 each year to patients, he would be left with about $70,000 for his salary. The only way to make more money was to cram in more patients in less time.

The too-long waits and too-short doctors' visits that increasingly typify medicine please no one. It's not just the patients who suffer from the creeping takeover of medicine by the accountant's mentality. Increasingly, physicians complain that they just can't take the time they want with patients. This problem is not confined to the United States. As a European neurologist, who works for his country's national health plan, lamented, "They're applying the logic of machines to people. We report what procedures we do when, and they then compute how much time we should spend with each patient. But they don't include any time to talk to patients, to relate, to explain, to make them feel better. Lots of doctors are frustrated— they want to have time to treat the person, not just the disease."

The prescription for physician burnout is written during the notoriously grinding hours of medical school and residency. Combine that relentless workload with medical economics that demand more and more from physicians, and it's small wonder that a creeping desperation is growing. Surveys find signs of at least some degree of burnout in 80 to 90 percent of practicing physicians—a quiet epidemic.[1] The symptoms are clear: work-related emotional exhaustion, intense feelings of dissatisfaction, and a depersonalized I-It attitude.

| ORGANIZED LOVELESSNESS |

The patient in 4D had been admitted for multidrug resistant pneumonia. Given her advanced age and a host of other medical problems, the outlook was dire.

Over the weeks she and the night nurse had struck up something of a friendship. Other than that she had no visitors, not a soul listed to notify in case of death, and no known friends or relatives. As he dropped by on his night rounds, the nurse was her only visitor, and the visits were limited to the short conversations she could manage.

Now her vital signs were failing, and the nurse recognized that the patient in 4D was near death. So he tried to spend every spare minute on his shift in her room, just being present. He was there to hold her hand during her last moments of life.

How did his supervisor respond to this gesture of human kindness?

She reprimanded him for wasting time and made sure her complaint was registered in his personnel file.

"Our institutions are organized lovelessness," as Aldous Huxley put it so bluntly in *The Perennial Philosophy*. This maxim applies to any system that regards the people who inhabit it solely from an I-It stance. When people are treated as numbered units, interchangeable parts of no interest or value in themselves, empathy is sacrificed in the name of efficiency and cost-effectiveness.

Take a common predicament, the hospital inpatient who has been scheduled for an X-ray that day. He'll be told first thing in the morning, "You're going to radiology for an X-ray."

But he will not be told that the hospital makes more money (at least in the United States) from its outpatient X-rays than from those for inpatients, whose tests are paid for as part of a "bundled" payment from their insurance company. The hospital has to make do with whatever total amount is in that bundle—making that X-ray a potential money-loser.

And so inpatients are last in line, waiting—often anxiously—for a procedure they believe could come in five minutes, but that may not take place for five hours. Even worse, for some tests patients must fast starting at midnight the night before; if the test is delayed until the afternoon, the patient gets neither breakfast nor lunch.

"Revenue guides how services are handled," one hospital executive told me. "We don't consider how *we* would feel if it were us waiting. We don't pay enough attention to patients' expectations, let alone manage them as well as we could. Our operations and information flow are set up for the convenience of the medical staff, not the patients."

But our knowledge of the role of emotions in health suggests that ignoring patients as people, even in the interest of some vaunted efficiency, causes us to forfeit a potential biological ally: feeling human concern. I do not mean to argue for being "soft": a compassionate surgeon still must cut, and a compassionate nurse must still perform painful procedures. But the cut and the pain hurt less when an air of kindness and concern go along with them. Being noticed, felt, and cared for alleviates pain to a meaningful degree. Distress and rebuff amplify it.

If we are to shift to more humane organizations, change will be required at two levels: within the hearts and minds of those who provide the care, and in the ground rules—both explicit and hidden—of the institution. Signs of the desire for such a shift are abundant today.

RECOGNIZING THE HUMAN BEING

Imagine a doctor, a successful heart surgeon, who is emotionally detached from his patients. Not only is he lacking in compassion, but he is also quite dismissive, even disdainful of them and their feelings. A few days ago he operated on a man who had jumped out of a fifth-floor window in a suicide attempt and seriously injured himself. Now, in front of his students, all medical residents, the surgeon tells the patient that if he wanted to punish himself, he would have done better to take up golf. The students laugh—but the patient's face reveals his anguish and despair.

A few days later this same surgeon has become a patient. He feels a tickle in his throat and has been coughing up blood. The hospital's throat specialist examines him, and as the scene unfolds, the surgeon's face and actions reveal his fear, confusion, discomfort, and disorientation. The throat surgeon ends the examination by telling our hero that he has a growth on his vocal cords and will need a biopsy and other tests.

As she leaves to move on to her next patient, the throat surgeon mutters, "Busy day! Busy day!"

That tale was told by the late Peter Frost, a professor of management who undertook a campaign for medical compassion after his own experience in a cancer ward.[2] The key element lacking in this scenario, Frost pointed out, is the simple recognition of the human being, the person struggling for dignity, even for life.

That humanity too often gets lost in the impersonal machinery of modern medicine. Some argue that this mechanistic attitude leads to needless "iatrogenic suffering," the anguish added when medical personnel leave their hearts at home. Even with dying people, insensitive messages from doctors can sometimes engender more emotional suffering than the illness itself.[3]

This recognition has spurred a movement toward "patient-centered" or "relationship-centered" medicine, enlarging the focus of medical attention beyond mere diagnosis to include the person being treated and improving the quality of connection between physician and patient.

The movement to enlarge the place of communication and empathy in medicine highlights the difference between attitudes that are espoused and their actual practice. The first principle of the Code of Medical Ethics of the American Medical Association admonishes physicians to provide competent medical care *with compassion.* Most medical school curriculums include a module on doctor-patient relationships; practicing physicians and nurses are routinely offered brushup courses on interpersonal and communication skills. Yet only in the last few years did the U.S. licensing exam for medicine begin to include an assessment of a doctor's ability to establish rapport and communicate with patients.

Part of the impetus for this stricter new standard is defensive. A much-discussed study of how doctors talk to patients, featured in 1997 in the *Journal of the American Medical Association,* found that impaired communication—rather than the actual number of mishaps—largely predicted that a given physician would be sued for malpractice.[4]

By contrast, doctors whose patients felt more rapport sued them less. These doctors did simple things that helped: they told patients what to expect from their visit or treatment, engaged in small talk, touched them reassuringly, sat down with them, and laughed with them—humor builds rapport quickly and powerfully.[5] What's more, they made sure patients understood their comments, asked for their opinions, cleared up all their questions, and encouraged them to talk. In short, they showed an interest in the person, not just in the diagnosis.

Time is a key ingredient in such care: these office visits ran about three and a half minutes longer than those of doctors who were more likely to be sued. The shorter the visit, the more likely a malpractice claim. Establishing a good rapport takes a few minutes—a troubling observation given the increasing economic pressures on doctors to see more patients in less time.

Even so, the scientific case for rapport-building grows ever stronger. For instance, a review of studies found patients' satisfaction to be highest when they felt a doctor was empathic and gave useful information.[6] But patients' sense that a doctor's message was "informative" stemmed not just from *what* information was imparted but from *how*. A tone of voice that showed concern and emotional engagement made a doctor's words seem more helpful. A bonus: the more satisfied the patients, the better they could recall the physician's instructions and greater their compliance.[7]

Beyond the medical case for rapport, there is also a business one. At least in the United States, where the medical marketplace grows ever more competitive, "exit interviews" with patients who have decided to quit their health plan reveal that 25 percent leave because "I didn't like the way my physician communicated with me."[8]

Dr. Robin Youngson's transformation began the day his daughter was rushed to a hospital with a broken neck. For ninety days he and his wife agonized while their daughter, just five, lay tied down to a bed, able to see only the ceiling.

That tribulation inspired Dr. Youngson, an anesthesiologist in Auckland, New Zealand, to begin a campaign to alter his country's legal code of patients' rights. He wants to add the right to be treated with compassion to every patient's existing rights to dignity and respect.

"For much of my career as a doctor," he confesses, "I reduced the human being in front of me to a 'physiological preparation.' " But that I-It attitude, he now realizes, diminishes the full potential for a healing relationship. His daughter's hospitalization, he says, has "brought me back to my humanity."

To be sure, there are good-hearted people throughout any medical system. But the culture of medicine itself all too often stifles or destroys the expression of empathic concern, making caring into a victim not just of cost and time pressures but also of what Dr.

Youngson calls "dysfunctional styles of thinking and belief of physicians: linear, reductionistic, overly critical and pessimistic, intolerant of ambiguity. We think that 'clinical detachment' is the key to clear perception. Wrong."

In Dr. Youngson's diagnosis, his profession suffers from a learned disability: "We have utterly lost compassion." The main enemy, he says, is not so much the hearts of individual physicians and nurses—his own colleagues readily commit to kindness—but the inexorable press toward relying on medical technology. Add the relentless fragmentation of medical care, in which patients are shuttled from specialist to specialist, and the squeeze on nursing staff, in which one nurse covers ever more patients. Patients themselves often end up as the single person in charge of overseeing their medical care, whether they are equipped to do so or not.

The word "heal" comes from the Old English *hal*, "to make whole, or mend." Healing has a broader meaning than simply curing a disease; it implies helping a person regain a sense of wholeness and emotional wellness. Patients need healing along with their medical care—and compassion heals in ways that no medicine or technology can.

THE CAREGIVING FLOWCHART

Nancy Abernathy was teaching a seminar for first-year medical students on interpersonal and decision-making skills when the worst happened: her husband, just fifty, died of a heart attack while cross-country skiing in the woods behind their Vermont home. He died during her winter break.

Suddenly bereft, raising her two teenagers on her own, Abernathy struggled through the next semester, sharing with her students her own feelings of bereavement and loss—a reality they would face routinely in the families of their patients who died.

At one point Abernathy confided that she was dreading the next year, particularly the class that included showing photos of everyone's family. What pictures of her own family, she wondered, would she bring, and how much of her grief would she share? How could she avoid weeping as she told of her husband's death?

Even so, she signed up to teach the course the next year and bade her current students good-bye.

The next fall, on the day of that dreaded class, Abernathy arrived early, only to find that the room was already partly full. To her surprise, the seats were occupied by her students from the year before.

All second-year medical students now, they had come simply to lend their presence and offer their support.

"This is compassion," Abernathy testifies, "a simple human connection between the one who suffers and one who would heal."[9]

Just as they share a mission of caregiving, those who give the care need to look after one another. In any human service organization, staff-to-staff concern affects the quality of caring they can give.

Staff caregiving is an adult version of offering a secure base. It can be witnessed in the mundane mood-lifting interactions that go on in any workplace in the course of a day, from simply being available and lending a sympathetic ear, to stopping to listen to a complaint. Or it can take the form of giving respect or a word of admiration or a compliment, or by appreciating someone's work.

When people in the helping professions get little or no sense of having a secure base in those they work with or for, they become more susceptible to "compassion fatigue.[10] The hug, the listening ear, the sympathetic look all matter, but they are too easily lost amid the din of frenetic activity typical in any human services setting.

Careful observation can produce a map of the give-and-take of such caregiving. Indeed, a virtual flowchart for caregiving resulted from three years of observations by William Kahn, who cast an anthropological eye over the small daily exchanges among the staff of a social service agency.[11] The agency's mandate was to provide homeless children with an adult volunteer who would be companion, mentor, and role model. Like many nonprofits, the agency struggled with too few funds and too little staff.

Caring interactions are nothing special, Kahn discovered; rather, they are embedded in the daily life of any workplace. For instance, when a new social worker presented a difficult case at a weekly meeting, a more seasoned social worker listened attentively to his frustrations, asked probing questions, held back her most negative judgments, and said how impressed she was with the novice's sensitivity. That was a natural display of multiple modes of caregiving.

At another meeting, however, where the social workers' supervisor was supposed to discuss their most problematic cases, things went very differently. The supervisor blithely ignored the purpose of the meeting, instead launching into a monologue on administrative issues that were of more concern to her.

All the while she stared down at her notes, avoiding eye contact;

left little opportunity for questions, let alone comments; and made not a single inquiry about what the social workers thought. She expressed no empathy for the social workers' overwhelming caseloads, and when a question was asked about scheduling, she could not come up with the crucial information. Caregiving score: zero.

As for the flow of caregiving at this agency, let's start at the top. The executive director was fortunate in having a board of directors who enthusiastically supported him. His board president was a model secure base, listening sympathetically to the director's predicaments and frustrations, and offering help and reassurances that the board would not abandon him, while giving him the autonomy to do things his way.

But the executive director provided none of that caring to the overburdened social workers who did the main work of the agency. He never asked how they felt, encouraged them, or showed a wit of respect for their valiant efforts. His relationship with them was emotionally barren: he spoke to them only in the most abstract terms, oblivious to the frustration and outrage they expressed when given the rare chance. The result was only disconnection.

Still, the executive director did offer some caregiving down the ladder—to his fund-raiser, who reciprocated. The two formed a mutual support society, listening to each other's troubles, offering counsel and consolation. But neither of them gave a bit to anyone else at the agency.

Paradoxically, the social work supervisor, who reported to the executive director, gave far more support to her boss than he did to her. This kind of reverse caregiving is surprisingly common, with subordinates offering unreciprocated care to their superiors. The upward flow resembles the dynamic in dysfunctional families, where a parent abdicates responsibility and instead reverses roles, seeking care from the children.

The supervisor also reversed the flow with the social workers in her charge, giving them virtually no care but instead seeking it from them. For instance, in a meeting where one social worker asked the supervisor if she had as yet found out from another agency how they were to file forms reporting child abuse, the supervisor responded that she had tried but had had no luck. At that, another social worker offered to take over the task. The social workers took over many of their supervisor's other duties, like scheduling, and shielded her from the emotional force of their own distress.

The greatest volume of caregiving passed among the social workers themselves. Abandoned emotionally by their supervisor, faced with daunting pressures and fending off burnout, they tried to build an emotional cocoon around themselves. In meetings without their supervisor they would ask how each other was doing, listen and empathize, offer emotional and concrete support, and generally help each other out.

Many of the social workers told Kahn that when they felt cared about themselves, they were more willing and able to be active caregivers in their work. As one said, "When I'm feeling like I'm worthwhile around here, I throw myself into the supervision" of the children in their charge.

Even so, the social workers had a swelling emotional debit: they gave far more than they received. Their energy was being drained as they worked with their clients, despite their efforts to replenish one another. Month by month they would withdraw emotionally from their work, burn out, and eventually leave. Over two and a half years, fourteen people quit the six social work positions.

Lacking emotional refills, caregivers run on empty. To the degree that health care workers feel that others give them the emotional support they need, they will be better able to offer the same to their patients. But a burned-out social worker, doctor, or nurse has no emotional resources to draw on.

| HEALING HEALERS |

There's another pragmatic argument for enhancing the place of compassion in medicine: in terms of cost-effectiveness, that inarguable standard for so many organizational decisions, it helps retain valuable staff. The data here come from a study of the "emotional work" done by health care workers, mostly nurses.[12]

Those nurses whose work made them more upset lost track of their sense of mission and had poorer physical health—and most strongly wanted to leave their job. The researchers concluded that these problems stemmed from the nurses "catching" distress from the despair, anger, or anxiety of those they dealt with. This negativity threatened to spill over into the nurses' interactions with others, whether patients or coworkers.

But if a nurse had nourishing relationships with patients and frequently felt she improved their moods, she herself benefited emotionally. Things like simply speaking warmly and showing affection made nurses feel less psychological stress from their work, as did get-togethers for patients or staff. These more emotionally connected nurses had better physical health, as well as a sense of a meaningful mission. And they were far less likely to want to leave their jobs.

The more a nurse confronts or stirs up distress in patients, the more distress she catches; the more a nurse makes patients and their families feel good, the better *she* feels. In the course of a day's work, any nurse will surely do both, but the data suggest that the more times she primes good feelings, the better she herself will feel. And that ratio of positive-to-negative emotional interactions, to a great degree, is in the nurse's own hands.

One emotional task that often leads to catching distress is continually listening to someone's worries. This problem has been called "compassion fatigue," where a helper herself becomes overwhelmed by the anguish of those she tries to help. One solution for the helper is not to stop listening but rather to find emotional support. In a compassionate medical setting, people like nurses who operate at the front line of pain and despair need help to "metabolize" that inevitable suffering, rendering them more emotionally resilient. Institutions must make sure nurses and other staff have enough support themselves to be empathic without burning out.

Just as people whose work makes them vulnerable to repetitive stress injuries take stretch time-outs, those who do stressful emotional work can benefit from time-outs to calm down before reentering the fray. But such restorative breaks will never become routine unless the emotional work done by those in the medical professions become valued by administrators as an important, even crucial part of their task—one that needs to be done along with, rather than in spite of, other duties.

Typically the emotional component of health care jobs does not count as "real" work. But if the need for emotional care were routinely regarded as an essential part of the job, then health workers could do their jobs better. The immediate problem comes down to getting more of these qualities into medicine-as-practiced. Such emotional labor can be found nowhere in the job descriptions of health care workers.

Worse, medicine can be prone to the most common error in choosing leaders, what one wry observer noted as the tendency to promote people to their level of *in*competence. Someone is likely to become a department head or executive on the basis of their technical excellence as an individual performer, such as a brilliant surgeon—without regard for essential capacities like empathy.

"When people are promoted to management based on medical expertise, not people skills," notes Joan Strauss, senior project manager for service improvement at Massachusetts General, a famous Harvard Medical School hospital, "they sometimes need coaching. For instance, they may not know how to hold people accountable in a respectful and open way—without being a patsy on the one hand or Attila the Hun on the other."

Studies comparing superb leaders with mediocre ones have found that the competencies that distinguish the best from the worst in human services have little or nothing to do with medical knowledge or technical skill, and everything to do with social and emotional intelligence.[13] Of course, medical knowledge matters for health care leaders—but it's a given, a threshold competence that every health professional must have. What *distinguishes* leaders in medicine goes far beyond that knowledge, into interpersonal skills like empathy, conflict resolution, and people development. Compassionate medicine needs caring leaders, ones who themselves can give medical staff the sense of a safe emotional base to work from.

| HEALING RELATIONSHIPS |

Kenneth Schwartz, a successful Boston lawyer, was forty when he was diagnosed with lung cancer. The day before he was scheduled to have surgery, he came to his hospital's presurgery area and sat in a mobbed waiting area while harried nurses scurried about.

Finally his name was called, and he went to an office where a nurse conducted a presurgery interview. At first she seemed quite brusque—Schwartz felt like just another faceless patient. But when he told her he had lung cancer, her face softened. She took his hand and asked how he was doing.

Suddenly they left their nurse-patient roles, as Schwartz told her about his two-year-old son, Ben. She said her nephew was named Ben, too. By the end of their conversation, she was wiping tears from her eyes. Though she ordinarily did not go to the surgical floor in her job, she said she would come to visit him.

The next day, as he sat in a wheelchair waiting to be wheeled into the surgical suite, there she was. She took his hand and with teary eyes wished him luck.

That was but one of a series of compassionate encounters with medical staff, acts of kindness that, as Schwartz put it at the time, "made the unbearable bearable."[14]

Shortly before his death, just months later, Schwartz created a legacy that he hoped would make such moments of benevolence more likely to reach many more patients. He founded the Kenneth B. Schwartz Center at the Massachusetts General Hospital, to "support and advance compassionate health care" that offers hope to patients and support to caregivers, and that aids the process of healing.[15]

The Schwartz Center bestows an annual Compassionate Caregiver Award to honor medical staff who have shown extraordinary kindness in caring for patients and so can serve as role models. Another promising innovation from the center is a variation of the standard medical grand rounds, which typically update medical staff on new developments in their fields. Instead, the "Schwartz Center Rounds" give hospital staff a chance to come together to share their concerns and fears. The premise is that from gaining insight into their own responses and feelings, caregivers will be better able to make a personal connection with their patients.[16]

"When we had our first Schwartz Center Round," reports Dr. Beth Lown of Mount Auburn Hospital in Cambridge, Massachusetts, "we expected no more than sixty or seventy people, which is a good turnout. But to our surprise, around 160 medical staff showed up. These rounds really speak to a need for us to talk honestly with one another about what it's like to do our work."

As an officer of the American Academy on Physician and Patient, Dr. Lown has a unique perspective: "The motive to connect with people that draws so many into medicine gets slowly supplanted by the hospital culture—a biomedical orientation, technology-driven, and geared to getting patients in and out as quickly as possible. The question is not whether empathy can be taught, but what are we doing that drives it out of medical students?"

That medical certification exams now include an evaluation of interpersonal adeptness testifies to the new importance being placed on doctors cultivating skills like relationship- and rapport-building. One focus is the medical interview, which an average physician conducts up to two hundred thousand times over the course of a career.[17] This conversation is the best chance for a physician and patient to develop a good working alliance.

The ever-analytical medical mind has broken the patient interview into seven discrete parts, from opening the discussion through gathering and sharing information, to making plans for treatment.

The interview guidelines emphasize not the medical dimensions—that's taken for granted—but rather the human one.

Physicians are urged, for instance, to let a patient complete his first statement rather than commandeering the conversation from the first few seconds, and to elicit all of a patient's concerns and questions. They need to make a personal connection and understand how the patient perceives the illness and treatment. In other words, they need to deploy empathy and build rapport.

Such skills, Dr. Lown says, "can be taught and learned, but they must be practiced and cultivated like any other clinical skill." And doing so, she argues, not only makes physicians more efficient but means patients will adhere to treatment better and be more satisfied with their care.

Kenneth Schwartz, writing just a few months before he died, put it more directly: "Quiet acts of humanity have felt more healing than the high-dose radiation and chemotherapy that hold the hope of cure. While I do not believe that hope and comfort alone can overcome cancer, it certainly made a huge difference to me."

SOCIAL CONSEQUENCE

The Sweet Spot for Achievement

You are driving to work, planning an important meeting with a colleague, and intermittently reminding yourself that you must remember to turn left at the traffic light, not right as usual, so you can drop your suit at the cleaners.

Suddenly an ambulance screams up behind you, and you speed up to get out of the way. You feel your heart quicken.

You try to resume planning the morning's meeting, but your thoughts are disorganized now and you lose concentration, distracted. When you get to work, you berate yourself because you forgot to go to the cleaners.

This scenario comes not from some business primer but from the academic journal *Science,* as the beginning of an article called "The Biology of Being Frazzled."[1] The article summarizes the effects on thinking and performance caused by being mildly upset—frazzled from the hassles of daily life.

"Frazzle" is a neural state in which emotional upsurges hamper the workings of the executive center. While we are frazzled, we cannot concentrate or think clearly. That neural truth has direct implications for achieving the optimal emotional atmosphere both in the classroom and the office.

From the vantage point of the brain, doing well in school and at work involves one and the same state, the brain's sweet spot for performance. The biology of anxiety casts us out of that zone for excellence.

"Banish fear" was a slogan of the late quality-control guru W. Edwards

Deming. He saw that fear froze a workplace: workers were reluctant to speak up, to share new ideas, or to coordinate well, let alone to improve the quality of their output. The same slogan applies to the classroom—fear frazzles the mind, disrupting learning.

The basic neurobiology of frazzle reflects the body's default plan for emergency. When we are under stress, the HPA axis roars into action, preparing the body for crisis. Among other biological maneuvers, the amygdala commandeers the prefrontal cortex, the brain's executive center. This shift in control to the low road favors automatic habits, as the amygdala draws on knee-jerk responses to save us. The thinking brain gets sidelined for the duration; the high road moves too slowly.[2]

As our brain hands decision-making over to the low road, we lose our ability to think at our best. The more intense the pressure, the more our performance and thinking will suffer.[3] The ascendant amygdala handicaps our abilities for learning, for holding information in working memory, for reacting flexibly and creatively, for focusing attention at will, and for planning and organizing effectively. We plunge into what neuroscientists call "cognitive dysfunction."[4]

"The worst period I ever went through at work," a friend confides, "was when the company was restructuring and people were being 'disappeared' daily, followed by lying memos that they were leaving 'for personal reasons.' No one could focus while that fear was in the air. No real work got done."

Small wonder. The greater the anxiety we feel, the more impaired is the brain's cognitive efficiency. In this zone of mental misery, distracting thoughts hijack our attention and squeeze our cognitive resources. Because high anxiety shrinks the space available to our attention, it undermines our very capacity to take in new information, let alone generate fresh ideas. Near-panic is the enemy of learning and creativity.

The neural highway for dysphoria runs from the amygdala to the right side of the prefrontal cortex. As this circuitry activates, our thoughts fixate on what has triggered the distress. And as we become preoccupied by, say, worry or resentment, our mental agility sputters. Likewise, when we are sad activity levels in the prefrontal cortex drop and we generate fewer thoughts.[5] Extremes of anxiety and anger on the one hand, and sadness on the other, push brain activity beyond its zones for effectiveness.

Boredom fogs the brain with its own brand of inefficiency. As minds wander, they lose focus; motivation vanishes. In any meeting that has gone on too long (as most do), the vacant eyes of those trapped at the table will betray this inner absence. And we all remember days of ennui as students, absently staring out the window.

| AN OPTIMAL STATE |

A high school class is playing a game with crossword puzzles, working in pairs. Both partners have the same puzzle, but one's copy has words filled in where the other's has blanks. The challenge: help your partner guess the missing words by giving her clues. And since this is a Spanish class, those clues must be in Spanish, as are the words to be guessed.

The students get so swept up in the game that they are completely oblivious to the bell ringing at the end of class. No one gets up to leave—they all want to keep working on the puzzles. Not incidentally, the next day when they write essays in Spanish using the words they learned in the puzzles, the students show excellent comprehension of their new vocabulary. These students were having fun learning, yet they mastered their lessons well. Indeed, such moments of total absorption and pleasure may mark learning at its best.

Contrast that Spanish lesson with an English class. The topic that day was how to use commas. One student, bored and distracted, slipped her hand into her bag and discreetly pulled out a catalog for a clothing store. It was as though she had left one store in a mall for another.

Sam Intrator, an educator, spent a year observing high school classrooms like these.[b] Whenever he witnessed an absorbing moment like the one with the crossword puzzle in the Spanish class, he would canvass the students on what they had been thinking and feeling.

If most students reported a state of total involvement in what was being taught, he would rate the moment "inspired." The inspired moments of learning shared the same active ingredients: a potent combination of full attention, enthusiastic interest, and positive emotional intensity. The joy in learning comes during these moments.

Such joyous moments, says University of Southern California neuroscientist Antonio Damasio, signify "optimal physiological coordination and smooth running of the operations of life." Damasio, one of the world's leading neuroscientists, has long been a pioneer in linking findings in brain science to human experience. Damasio argues that more than merely letting us survive the daily grind, joyous states allow us to flourish, to live well, and to feel well-being.

Such upbeat states, he notes, allow a "greater ease in the capacity to act," a greater harmony in our functioning that enhances our power and freedom in whatever we do. The field of cognitive science, Damasio notes, in studying the neural networks that run mental operations, finds similar conditions and dubs them "maximal harmonious states."

When the mind runs with such internal harmony, ease, efficiency, rapidity, and power are at a maximum. We experience such moments with a quiet thrill. Imaging studies show that while people are in such exhilarating, upbeat states, the area of the brain that displays most activity is in the prefrontal cortex, the hub of the high road.

Heightened prefrontal activity enhances mental abilities like creative thinking, cognitive flexibility, and the processing of information.[7] Even physicians, those paragons of rationality, think more clearly when they are in good moods. Radiologists (who read X-rays to help other physicians make their diagnoses) work with greater speed and accuracy after getting a small mood-boosting gift—and their diagnostic notes include more helpful suggestions for further treatment, as well as more offers to do further consultation.[8]

AN UPSIDE-DOWN U

Plotting the relationship between mental adeptness (and performance generally) and the spectrum of moods creates what looks like an upside-down U with its legs spread out a bit. Joy, cognitive efficiency, and outstanding performance occur at the peak of the inverted U. Along the downside of one leg lies boredom, along the other anxiety. The more apathy or angst we feel, the worse we do, whether on a term paper or an office memo.[9]

We are lifted out of the daze of boredom as a challenge piques our interest, our motivation increases, and attention focuses. The height of cognitive performance occurs where motivation and focus peak, at the intersection of a task's difficulty and our ability to match its demand. At a tipping point just past this peak of cognitive efficiency, challenges begin to exceed ability, and so the downside of the inverted U begins.

We taste panic as we realize, say, we've procrastinated disastrously long on that paper or memo. From there our increasing anxiety erodes our cognitive efficiency.[10] As tasks multiply in difficulty and challenge melts into overwhelm, the low road becomes increasingly active. The high road frazzles as the challenges engulf our abilities, and the brain hands the reins to the low road. This neural shift of control from the high to the low road accounts for the shape of the upside-down U.[11]

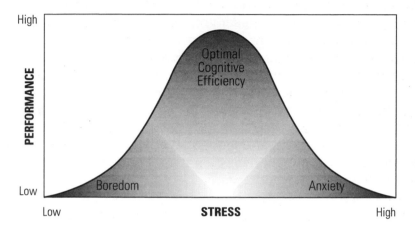

An upside-down U graphs the relationship between levels of stress and mental performance such as learning or decision-making. Stress varies with challenge; at the low end, too little breeds disinterest and boredom, while as challenge increases it boosts interest, attention, and motivation—which at their optimal level produce maximum cognitive efficiency and achievement. As challenges continue to rise beyond our skill to handle them, stress intensifies; at its extreme, our performance and learning collapse.

The inverted U reflects the impact of two different neural systems on learning and performance. Both build as enhanced attention and motivation increase the activity of the glucocorticoid system; healthy levels of cortisol energize us for engagement.[12] Positive moods elicit the mild-to-moderate range of cortisol associated with better learning.

But if stress continues to climb after that optimal point where people learn and perform at their best, a second neural system kicks in to secrete norepinephrine at the high levels found when we feel outright fear.[13] From this point—the start of that downward slope toward panic—the more stress escalates, the worse our mental efficiency and performance become.

During high anxiety the brain secretes high levels of cortisol plus norepinephrine that interfere with the smooth operation of neural mechanisms for learning and memory. When these stress hormones reach a critical level, they enhance amygdala function but debilitate the prefrontal areas, which lose their ability to contain amygdala-driven impulses.

As any student knows who has suddenly found himself studying harder as a test approaches, a modicum of pressure enhances motivation and focuses attention. Up to a point, selective attention increases as levels of pressure ratchet upward, like looming deadlines, a teacher watching, or a challenging assignment. Paying fuller attention means that working memory operates with more cognitive efficiency, culminating in maximum mental ease.

But at a tipping point just past the optimal state—where challenges begin to overmatch ability—increasing anxiety starts to erode cognitive efficiency. For example, in this zone of performance disaster, students with math anxiety have less attention available when they tackle a math problem. Their anxious worrying occupies the attentional space they need, impairing their ability to solve problems or grasp new concepts.[14]

All of this directly affects how well we do in the classroom—or on the job. While we are distressed, we don't think clearly, and we tend to lose interest in pursuing even goals that are important to us.[15] Psychologists who have studied the effects of mood on learning conclude that when students are neither attentive nor happy in class, they absorb only a fraction of the information being presented.[16]

The drawbacks apply as well to teachers and leaders. Foul feelings weaken empathy and concern. For example, managers in bad moods give more negative performance appraisals, focusing only on the downside, and are more disapproving in their opinions.[17] Surely the same holds for teachers.

We do best at moderate to challenging levels of stress, while the mind frazzles under extreme pressure.[18]

A NEURAL KEY TO LEARNING

It's a high school class in chemistry, and the tension in the room is palpable. Students are on edge because they know that at any moment their teacher may call on them at random, have them go to the board in front of the class, and then ask them to calculate the answer to a difficult chemical interaction on the spot. All but the brightest budding chemists fail at these questions. For the bright kids, it's a moment of pride; for the rest, shame.

The type of stress that most activates the stress hormones, and so shoots up cortisol levels, lurks in the classroom, in the form of social threats like fears of a teacher's judgment or of seeming "stupid" in the eyes of other students. Such social fears powerfully impair the brain's mechanisms for learning.[19]

People differ in their set points for where the U tips. Those students who can take the most stress without disabling their cognitive abilities will be unflappable at the blackboard, whether they get the question right or wrong. (As adults, they would likely thrive as Wall Street traders, who can make or lose a fortune in a wink of the market.) But those more susceptible to HPA arousal will freeze mentally even at low levels of distress—and if they are unprepared for the chemistry pop quiz or are slower learners, being called to the blackboard offers them only misery.

The hippocampus, near the amygdala in the midbrain, is our central organ for learning. This structure enables us to convert the contents of "working memory"—new information held briefly in the prefrontal cortex—into long-term form for storage. This neural act is the heart of learning. Once our mind connects this information with what we already know, we will be able to bring the new understanding to mind weeks or years later.

Whatever a student hears in class or reads in a book travels these pathways as he masters yet another iota of understanding. Indeed, everything that happens to us in life, all the details that we will remember, depend on the hippocampus to stay with us. The continual retention of memories demands a frenzy of neuronal activity. In fact, the vast majority of neurogenesis—the brain's production of new neurons and laying down of connections to others—takes place in the hippocampus.

The hippocampus is especially vulnerable to ongoing emotional distress, because of the damaging effects of cortisol. Under prolonged stress, cortisol attacks the neurons of the hippocampus, slowing the rate at which neurons are added or even reducing the total number, with a disastrous impact on learning. The actual killing off of hippocampal neurons occurs during sustained cortisol floods induced, for example, by severe depression or intense trauma. (However, with recovery, the hippocampus regains neurons and enlarges again.)[20] Even when the stress is less extreme, extended periods of high cortisol seem to hamper these same neurons.

Cortisol stimulates the amygdala while it impairs the hippocampus, forcing our attention onto the emotions we feel, while restricting our ability to take in new information. Instead we imprint what is upsetting us. After a day when a student gets panicked by a pop quiz, he'll remember the details of that panic far more than any of the material in the quiz.

In a simulation of the impact of cortisol on learning, college students volunteered to get injections that raised their cortisol levels, then to memorize a series of words and images. The result reflected the inverted U: in mild to moderate ranges, the cortisol helped the students remember what they had studied when tested on it two days later. But at extreme levels, the cortisol impaired their recall, apparently because it inhibited the crucial role of the hippocampus.[21]

This has profound implications for the kind of classroom atmosphere that fosters learning. The social environment, remember, affects the rate and fate of newly created brain cells. New cells take a month to mature and four more to fully link to other neurons; during this window the environment determines in part the final shape and function of the cell. The new cells that facilitate memory during the course of a semester will encode in their links what has been learned during that time—and the more conducive the atmosphere for learning, the better that encoding will be.

Distress kills learning. One classic finding dates back almost half a century to 1960, when Richard Alpert, then at Stanford, showed experimentally what every student already knew: high anxiety cripples test-taking ability.[22] A more recent study of college students taking math exams found that when they were told the test was a practice, they scored 10 percent better than when they thought they were part of a team that depended on their score to win a cash prize—under social stress their working memory was hampered. Intriguingly, the deficit in this most basic cognitive ability was greatest for the smartest students.[23]

A group of sixteen-year-olds scored in the top 5 percent on a national test of potential in math.[24] Some were doing extremely well in their math class, but others did poorly despite their aptitude for the subject. The crucial difference was that the high-achieving students experienced focused pleasure about 40 percent of the time they were immersed in their studies—more often than they felt anxious (about 30 percent). By contrast, while studying math the low achievers experienced such optimal states only 16 percent of the time and great anxiety 55 percent.

Given how emotions affect performance, the emotional task of teachers or leaders is one and the same: help people get and stay as close as possible to the top of the inverted U.

| P O W E R   A N D   E M O T I O N A L   F L O W |

Whenever a meeting threatened to lapse into malaise, the president of a company would suddenly launch into a critique of someone at the table who could take it (usually the marketing director, who was his best friend). Then he would swiftly move on, having riveted the attention of everyone in the room. That tactic invariably revived the group's failing focus with keen interest. He was herding those in attendance up the inverted U from boredom to engagement.

Displays of a leader's displeasure make use of emotional contagion. If artfully calibrated, even a burst of pique can stir followers enough to capture their attention and motivate them. Many effective leaders sense that—like compliments—well-titrated doses of irritation can energize. The measure of how well calibrated a message of displeasure might be is whether it moves people toward their performance peak or plummets them past the tipping point into the zone where distress corrodes performance.

Not all emotional partners are equal. A power dynamic operates in emotional contagion, determining which person's brain will more forcefully draw the other into its emotional orbit. Mirror neurons are leadership tools: Emotions flow with special strength from the more socially dominant person to the less.

One reason is that people in any group naturally pay more attention to and place more significance on what the most powerful person in that group says and does. That amplifies the force of whatever emotional message the leader may be sending, making her emotions particularly contagious. As I heard the head of a small organization say rather ruefully, "When my mind is full of anger, other people catch it like the flu."

A leader's emotional tone can have surprising power. When a manager delivered a piece of bad news (disappointment that an employee had failed to reach performance goals) with a warm demeanor, people nevertheless rated the interaction positively. When good news (pleasure that the goals had been met) was delivered with a sullen expression, the interaction paradoxically left people feeling bad.[25]

This emotional potency was tested when fifty-six heads of simulated work teams were themselves moved into a good or bad mood, and their subsequent emotional impact on the groups they led was assessed.[26] Team members with upbeat leaders reported that they were feeling in better moods. Perhaps more to the point, they coordinated their work better, getting more done with less effort. On the other hand, the teams with grumpy bosses were thrown out of synch, making them inefficient. Worse, their panicked efforts to please the leader led to bad decisions and poorly chosen strategies.

While a boss's artfully couched displeasure can be an effective goad, fuming is self-defeating as a leadership tactic. When leaders habitually use displays of bad moods to motivate, more work may seem to get done—but it will not necessarily be better work. And relentlessly foul moods corrode the emotional climate, sabotaging the brain's ability to work at its best.

In this sense, leadership boils down to a series of social exchanges in which the leader can drive the other person's emotions into a better or worse state. In high-quality exchanges, the subordinate feels the leader's attention and empathy, support, and positivity. In low-quality interactions, he feels isolated and threatened.

The passing of moods from leader to follower typifies any relationship where one person has power over another, such as teacher-student, doctor-patient, and parent-child. Despite the power differential in these relationships, they all have a benign potential: to promote the growth, education, or healing of the less powerful person.

Another powerful reason for leaders to be mindful of what they say to employees: people recall negative interactions with a boss with more intensity, in more detail, and more often than they do positive ones. The ease with which demotivation can be spread by a boss makes it all the more imperative for him to act in ways that make the emotions left behind uplifting ones.[27]

Callousness from a boss not only heightens the risk of losing good people, it torpedoes cognitive efficiency. A socially intelligent leader helps people contain and recover from their emotional distress. If only from a business perspective, a leader would do well to react with empathy rather than indifference—and to act on it.

BOSSES: THE GOOD, THE BAD, AND THE UGLY

Any collection of working people can readily recall two kinds of bosses they've known, one they loved to work for, and one they couldn't wait to escape. I've asked for such a list from dozens of groups, ranging from meetings of CEOs to conventions of school teachers, in cities as different as São Paulo, Brussels, and St. Louis. The lists that disparate groups generate, no matter where they are, are remarkably similar to this one:

Good Boss	Bad Boss
Great listener	Blank wall
Encourager	Doubter
Communicator	Secretive
Courageous	Intimidating
Sense of humor	Bad temper
Shows empathy	Self-centered
Decisive	Indecisive
Takes responsibility	Blames
Humble	Arrogant
Shares authority	Mistrusts

The best bosses are people who are trustworthy, empathic and connected, who make us feel calm, appreciated, and inspired. The worst—distant, difficult, and arrogant—make us feel uneasy at best and resentful at worst.

Those contrasting sets of attributes map well on the kind of parent who fosters security on the one hand, and anxiety on the other. In fact, the emotional dynamic at work in managing employees shares much with parenting. Our parents form our basic template for a secure base in childhood, but others continue to add to it as we go through life. In school, our teachers fill that position; at work, our boss.

"Secure bases are sources of protection, energy and comfort, allowing us to free our own energy," George Kohlrieser told me. Kohlrieser, a psychologist and professor of leadership at the International Institute for Management Development in Switzerland, observes that having a secure base at work is crucial for high performance.

Feeling secure, Kohlrieser argues, lets a person focus better on the work at hand, achieve goals, and see obstacles as challenges, not threats. Those who are anxious, in contrast, readily become preoccupied with the specter of failure, fearing that doing poorly will mean they will be rejected or abandoned (in this context, fired)—and so they play it safe.

People who feel that their boss provides a secure base, Kohlrieser finds, are more free to explore, be playful, take risks, innovate, and take on new challenges. Another business benefit: if leaders establish such trust and safety, then when they give tough feedback, the person receiving it not only stays more open but sees benefit in getting even hard-to-take information.

Like a parent, however, a leader should not protect employees from every tension or stress; resilience grows from a modicum of discomfort generated by necessary pressures at work. But since too much stress overwhelms, an astute leader acts as a secure base by lessening overwhelming pressures if possible—or at least not making them worse.

For instance, a midlevel executive tells me, "My boss is a superb buffer. Whatever financial performance pressures he gets from headquarters—and they are considerable—he does not pass them down to us. The head of a sister division in our corporation, though, does, subjecting all his employees to a personal profit-and-loss evaluation every quarter—even though the products they develop take two to three years to come to market."

On the other hand, if members of a work team are resilient, highly motivated, and good at what they do—in other words, if they have high tipping points on the inverted U—a leader can be challenging and demanding and still get good results. Yet disaster can result when such a high-pressure leader shifts to a less gung-ho culture. An investment banker tells me of a "hard driving, bottom line, 24/7" leader who yelled when displeased. When he merged his company with another, "the same style that worked for him before drove away all the managers in the acquired business, who saw him as intolerable. The company's stock price still had not risen two years after the merger."

No child can avoid emotional pain while growing up, and likewise emotional toxicity seems to be a normal by-product of organizational life—people are fired, unfair policies come from headquarters, frustrated employees turn in anger on others. The causes are legion: abusive bosses or unpleasant coworkers, frustrating procedures, chaotic change. Reactions range from anguish and rage, to lost confidence or hopelessness.

Perhaps luckily, we do not have to depend only on the boss. Colleagues, a work team, friends at work, and even the organization itself can create the sense of having a secure base. Everyone in a given workplace contributes to the emotional stew, the sum total of the moods that emerge as they interact through the workday. No matter what our designated role may be, how we do our work, interact, and make each other feel adds to the overall emotional tone.

Whether it's a supervisor or fellow worker who we can turn to when upset, their mere existence has a tonic benefit. For many working people, coworkers become something like a "family," a group in which members feel a strong emotional attachment for one another. This makes them especially loyal to each other as a team. The stronger the emotional bonds among workers, the more motivated, productive, and satisfied with their work they are.

Our sense of engagement and satisfaction at work results in large part from the hundreds and hundreds of daily interactions we have while there, whether with a supervisor, colleagues, or customers. The accumulation and frequency of positive versus negative moments largely determines our satisfaction and ability to perform; small exchanges—a compliment on work well done, a word of support after a setback—add up to how we feel on the job.[28]

Even having just one person who can be counted on at work can make a telling difference in how we feel. In surveys of more than five million people working in close to five hundred organizations, one of the best predictors of how happy someone felt on their job was agreement with the statement, "I have a best friend at work."[29]

The more such sources of emotional support we have in our worklife, the better off we are. A cohesive group with a secure—and security-promoting—leader creates an emotional surround that can be so contagious that even people who tend to be highly anxious find themselves relaxing.

As the head of a high-performing scientific team told me, "I never hire anyone for my lab without them working with us provisionally for a while. Then I ask the other people in the lab their opinions, and I defer to them. If the interpersonal chemistry is not good, I don't want to risk hiring someone—no matter how good they may be otherwise."

THE SOCIALLY INTELLIGENT LEADER

The human resources department of a large corporation arranged a daylong workshop by a famous expert in the company's area of specialty. A larger-than-expected crowd showed up, and at the last minute the event was switched to a larger room, one that could hold everyone but was poorly equipped.

As a result, the people in the back had trouble seeing or hearing the speaker. At the morning break, a woman sitting in the back marched up to the head of human resources shaking with rage and complaining that she could neither glimpse the screen on which the speaker's image was being projected, nor make out his words.

"I knew that all I could do was listen, empathize, acknowledge her problem, and tell her I'd do my best to fix things," the head of human resources told me. "At the break she saw me go to the audiovisual people and at least try to get the screen higher. I couldn't do much at all about the bad acoustics.

"I saw that woman again at the end of the day. She told me she couldn't really hear or see all that much better, but now she was relaxed about it. She really appreciated my hearing her out and trying to help."

When people in an organization feel angry and distressed, a leader, like that HR head, can at least listen with empathy, show concern, and make a goodwill effort to change things for the better. Whether or not that effort solves the problem, it does some good emotionally. By attending to someone's feelings, the leader helps metabolize them, so the person can move on rather then continuing to seethe.

The leader need not necessarily agree with the person's position or reaction. But simply acknowledging their point of view, then apologizing if necessary or otherwise seeking a remedy, defuses some of the toxicity, rendering destructive emotions less harmful. In a survey of employees at seven hundred companies, the majority said that a caring boss was more important to them than how much they earned.[30] This finding has business implications beyond just making people feel good. The same survey found that employees' liking for their boss was a prime driver of both productivity and the length of time they stayed at that job. Given the choice, people don't want to work for a toxic boss at nearly any wage—except to get enough "screw you" money to quit with security.

Socially intelligent leadership starts with being fully present and getting in synch. Once a leader is engaged, then the full panoply of social intelligence can come into play, from sensing how people feel and why, to interacting smoothly enough to move people into a positive state. There is no magic recipe for what to do in every situation, no five-steps-to-social-intelligence-at-work. But whatever we do as we interact, the single measure of its success will be where in the inverted U each person ends up.

Businesses are on the front lines of applying social intelligence. As people work longer and longer hours, businesses loom as their substitute family, village, and social network—yet most of us can be tossed out at the will of management. That inherent ambivalence means that in more and more organizations, hope and fear run rampant.

Excellence in people management cannot ignore these subterranean affective currents: they have real human consequences, and they matter for people's abilities to perform at their best. And because emotions are so contagious, every boss at every level needs to remember he or she can make matters either worse or better.

| A   SPECIAL   CONNECTION |

Maeva's school was in one of New York City's most impoverished neighborhoods. At thirteen she was only in sixth grade, two years behind her peers. She'd been held back twice.

And Maeva had a reputation as a troublemaker. Among the teachers at her middle school, she was notorious for storming out of class and refusing to return, instead spending most of the school day roaming the halls.

Before Pamela, Maeva's new English teacher, first met her charge, she was warned that Maeva was certain to be a behavior problem. So on the first day of class, after assigning her students to work on their own to pick out the main idea from a reading passage, Pamela went over to Maeva to help her out.

After just a minute or two Pamela realized what was bothering Maeva: her reading level was that of a kindergartner.

"So often behavior problems are because a student feels insecure about being unable to do the work," Pamela told me. "Maeva couldn't even sound out words. I was shocked she had gotten to sixth grade without learning how to read."

That day Pamela helped Maeva do the worksheet by reading it to her. Later that day Pamela sought out a special education teacher whose task included helping such students. The two teachers felt they had one last chance to keep Maeva from dropping out of school. The special ed teacher agreed to tutor Maeva daily in reading, starting from the very beginning level.

Even so, Maeva still proved a problem, as her other teachers had warned. She'd talk throughout class, be rude and pushy with other kids, and pick fights—anything to avoid reading. And if that wasn't enough, she'd exclaim, "I don't want to do this!" bolt out of class, and wander the school hallways.

Despite the resistance, Pamela doggedly gave Maeva extra help with her work in class. And when Maeva would blow up at another student, Pamela would take her into the privacy of the hallway and think through with her a better way to resolve things.

Mostly Pamela showed Maeva that she cared about her. "We'd joke around, spend extra time together. She'd come up to be with me in my classroom after she finished her lunch. I met with her mom."

Her mother was as surprised as Pamela had been to realize that Maeva could not read. But her mother had seven other children to handle; Maeva's problem had gone unnoticed amid the bustling crowd at home, just as it had gone uncorrected at school. Pamela got Maeva's mother to agree to help her daughter behave better and give her some extra attention and homework help at home.

Maeva's first-semester report card—when she had been with another English teacher—showed her failing most every class, as she had done for years. But after just four months with Pamela, there were marked changes for the better.

By the end of the semester she had stopped hiding her frustration by roaming the halls, now staying put in the classroom. Most important, her report card showed that Maeva had passed every class—most just barely, but with a surprisingly high grade in math. She had mastered the first two years of reading in just a few months.

Then came the moment in her reading circle when Maeva realized she was more adept than a few others, including one boy who had freshly arrived from West Africa. So she took it upon herself to help him unlock the secrets of reading.

That special connection between Pamela and Maeva represents a powerful tool in helping children learn. Mounting research shows that students who feel connected to school—to teachers, to other students, to the school itself—do better academically.[31] They also fare better in resisting the perils of modern adolescence: emotionally connected students have lower rates of violence, bullying, and vandalism; anxiety and depression, drug use, and suicide; truancy and dropping out.

"Feeling connected" here refers not to some vague niceness but to concrete emotional links between students and the people in their schools: other kids, teachers, staff. One powerful method to foster such links is to build just the sort of attuned relationship between student and adult that Pamela offered Maeva. Pamela became Maeva's secure base.

Consider what this could mean for the bottom 10 percent of students, those like Maeva most at-risk for failure. In a study of 910 first-graders from a national sample representative of the entire United States, trained observers evaluated their teachers, and assessed the effect of teaching style on how well the at-risk children learned.[32] The best results were found when teachers:

- Tuned in to the child and responded to his needs, moods, interests, and capabilities, letting them guide their interactions.

- Created an upbeat classroom climate with pleasant conversations, lots of laughter and excitement.

- Showed warmth and "positive regard" toward students.

- Had good classroom management, with clear but flexible expectations and routines, so that students followed rules largely on their own.

The worst outcomes resulted when teachers took an I-It stance and imposed their own agenda on students without tuning in, or were emotionally distant and uninvolved. Such teachers were angry at students more often and had to resort to punitive methods of restoring order.

Students who were already doing well continued to do so regardless of the setting. But at-risk students who had cold or controlling teachers floundered academically—even when their teachers followed pedagogic guidelines for good instruction. Yet the study found a stunning difference among the at-risk students: if they had a warm, responsive teacher, they flourished, learning as well as the other kids.

The power of an emotionally connected teacher does not end in first grade. Sixth-graders who had such a teacher earned better grades not only that year but the next as well.[33] Good teachers are like good parents. By offering a secure base, a teacher creates an environment that lets students' brains function at their best. That base becomes a safe haven, a zone of strength from which they can venture forth to explore, to master something new, to achieve.

That secure base can become internalized when students are taught to better manage their anxiety and so more keenly focus their attention; this enhances their ability to reach that optimal zone for learning. There are already dozens of programs in "social/emotional learning" that do just this. The best are designed to fit seamlessly into the standard school curriculum for children at every age, inculcating skills like self-awareness and managing distressing emotions, empathy and navigating relationships smoothly. A definitive meta-analysis of more than one hundred studies of these programs showed that students not only mastered abilities like calming down and getting along better, but, more to the point here, learned more effectively: their grades improved—and their scores on academic achievement tests were a hefty 12 percent higher than similar students who did not have the programs.[34]

Those programs work best if students feel teachers really care about them. But whether or not a school has such an offering, whenever teachers create an empathic and responsive environment, students not only improve in their grades and test scores—they become eager learners.[35] Even one supportive adult at school can make a difference to a student.[36]

Every Maeva needs a Pamela.

| 2 0 |

The Connectedness Corrective

Here's the list of life's scars that Martin, just fifteen, enumerated on a line drawing of his own body, starting from the bottom up:

His feet had been broken at ages eleven and twelve. Both hands were scarred from fighting and "stained" through their contact with drugs, stolen property, and "negative sexual relations." One arm had burns suffered while smoking marijuana; the other bore a knife wound.

Around Martin's head swarmed the sleeplessness he'd had since he was eleven; the emotional trauma he'd experienced since age two from ongoing physical abuse and sexual assaults (including from his own father at age seven); and brain injuries from a suicide attempt at eleven. And from age eight, he noted, his brain had been "fried" from abusing "pills, weed, meth, alcohol, shrooms, and opium."

Martin's appalling litany of wounds is typical of all too many teenagers currently serving sentences in juvenile jails. Youth prisons have become a seemingly inevitable stop for troubled lives, those for whom childhood abuse merges seamlessly with substance abuse and social predation.

While in many countries more humane social systems lead such teenagers to treatment instead of punishment, in the United States they too often get "care" in prison—exactly the wrong setting for healing. Most prisons for youth are a prescription for a life of crime, not a ticket out.

But Martin is one of the lucky ones: he lives in Missouri, a state that has led the way in treating young offenders rather than just punishing them. Missouri has come a long way; its main youth correctional facility was once described by a federal court as having a "quasi-penal-military" atmosphere, and it was condemned for frequently banishing unruly inmates to a dark solitary-confinement cell known as "the Hole." A former superintendent of that facility confessed, "I saw black eyes, battered faces, and broken noses among the boys. The usual corrective procedure among the guards was to knock a boy down with their fists, then kick him in the groin. Many of the men were sadists."[1]

That description from decades ago may still hold true in too many prisons. But now that Missouri has chosen to treat youthful offenders, Martin's facility offers a hopeful alternative. He lives in one of a network of small homes for troubled, law-breaking adolescents like himself. Established in 1983, some of the homes are in old school buildings or large houses; one is in an abandoned convent.

Each of them is home to no more than three dozen teens and a small staff of adults. These teens are not faceless cogs in some vast institution; everyone in each home knows the names of all the residents. They live as a "family," offering the teens continuing one-on-one relationships with caring adults.

There are no iron bars, no cells, few locked doors, and little security equipment of any kind, though video monitors keep track of what's going on. The atmosphere is more like that of a home than a jail. The teens are grouped into teams of ten or so, and members are responsible for seeing that they all follow the rules. The teams eat, sleep, study, and shower together—always with the supervision of two youth specialists.

If a resident does act up, there are no isolation cells, restraints, or handcuffs—the toolkit typical of most juvenile corrections facilities. Instead, the teams are taught how to safely restrain any member who threatens someone else's safety. They grab his arms and legs and wrestle their teammate to the ground. Then they simply hold him there until he calms down and regains composure. The program director reports there has never been a serious injury from such team restraint, and fights are nearly nonexistent.

Half a dozen times a day the members form into a circle to check in with each other to say how they feel. A team member may call for an extra circle to raise concerns or talk over a complaint—most often about issues of safety, courtesy, and respect. That way the focus can shift from a class, exercise, or cleanup to the compelling emotional undercurrents that, if ignored, can build into a blow-up. Each afternoon they meet for activities that are designed to enhance camaraderie and cooperation, to foster empathy and accurate perceptions of each other, and to build communication skills and trust.

All of that constructs a secure base and provides them with the social abilities they so desperately need. That aura of safety is crucial, particularly in getting the teens to open up about their troubled past. Trust is key: one by one they tell their life stories to the rest of their team, tales of domestic violence and sexual victimization, abuse and neglect. And they open up about their own wrongdoings and the crimes that sent them to the facility.

Treatment does not end the day the teens leave. Instead of simply being assigned to an overburdened parole officer—standard practice in most places—Missouri youngsters meet their postrelease coordinator when they arrive in the facility. By the time they are discharged, they have a long-standing relationship with the person who will guide them back into community life.

Aftercare is a core part of the Missouri formula. Each teen meets frequently with his coordinator and even more often with a "tracker"—typically someone from his hometown or a local college student—who monitors his day-to-day progress and helps him find a job.

Does all this elaborate treatment make much difference? Follow-up studies of teens who have been released from correctional facilities are rare. But a 1999 study found that the recidivism rate for the Missouri program was just 8 percent over the three years following a teenager's release—while in Maryland 30 percent of those released from juvenile correctional facilities were back in jail within three years. Another comparison looked at the rates at which released teens were returned to juvenile custody or adult prison or got probation during the first year after release. The rate in Missouri was just 9 percent, compared to 29 percent in Florida.[2]

And then there's the human cost of imprisoning youngsters in horrific jails. Over four recent years, 110 teenagers committed suicide in juvenile facilities nationwide. In the twenty years of the Missouri program, there have been no suicides.

THE KALAMAZOO MODEL

The small city of Kalamazoo, Michigan, was in turmoil; voters were riled up about a referendum to raise $140 million for a new youth prison. Everyone agreed that the old one was overcrowded and in-humane—that was no issue. The fight was over what should replace the antiquated building.

Some argued fiercely for just upgrading the building, using better barbed wire, cells, locks—and adding a bit more room. But their opponents rejoined that the community needed to find better ways to keep young people from committing crimes in the first place and from repeating if they did.

One of the local judges suggested that both sides talk things over at a one-day retreat at the nearby Fetzer Institute. Everyone involved in the debate came: church leaders, prisoner advocacy groups, the sheriff, judges, the superintendent of schools, mental health workers, and some of the most liberal Democrats and conservative Republicans.

That meeting in Kalamazoo is emblematic of a movement sweeping the country, as concerned citizens confront the failure of the prison system to protect them from criminals who simply repeat what they know best, crime. Groups everywhere are rethinking the very meaning of "corrections."

One dominant philosophy in penal circles is that convicts have committed acts that put them beyond the human pale and so must suffer for their crimes. To be sure, distinctions are made within the spectrum of crimes, and prisoners are sorted accordingly, into the levels of human ugliness they will endure day to day. For many, prison is a hellish realm, where convicts struggle in a tooth-and-nail battle; everyone fights to get respect, and toughness wins prestige. The prison yard becomes a jungle where the powerful prevail and fear rules. It's a psychopath's paradise, where coolheaded cruelty wins the day.

But the neural lessons learned from being trapped in an I-It universe are surely the worst. Survival there demands an amygdala that is set for paranoid hypervigilance, plus a protective emotional distance or outright distrust, and a readiness to fight. We could not design a better environment for fostering criminal instincts.

Are these the best "schools" for a society to be sending people to—most particularly those still in their teens and twenties, who have a full life ahead of them? If they live in such settings for months or years, small wonder so many go back to crime on their release and end up right back in those festering holes.

Instead of relying on approaches that simply breed more criminality, we could take advantage of what "correction" means from the viewpoint of social neuroplasticity, the shaping of brain circuitry through beneficial interactions. A great many of the people in prison are arguably there because of neural deficits in the social brain, like impaired empathy and impulse control.

One neural key to self-control is the array of neurons in the orbitofrontal cortex that can inhibit angry impulses from the amygdala. People with a deficit in the OFC are prone to brutality in moments when their violent urges swamp its ability to inhibit them. Our prisons are home to many such criminals. One neural pattern underlying this out-of-control violence appears to be an underactivation in the frontal lobes, often due to violent injuries in childhood.[3]

This deficit centers on the circuitry running from the OFC to the amygdala—the neural link that forms the brain's brake on destructive urges.[4] People with frontal lobe damage are poor at what psychologists call "cognitive control": they cannot voluntarily direct their thoughts, especially when swamped with powerful negative feelings.[5] This inability renders them helpless to resist the rush of destructive feelings: since their neural brakes are broken, their cruel impulses go unrestrained.

This crucial brain circuit continues to grow and be shaped into a person's mid-twenties.[6] From the neural perspective, during imprisonment society has a choice between strengthening the prisoners' circuitry for hostility, impulsivity, and violence, or strengthening their circuitry for self-control, thinking before acting, and the very ability to obey the law. Perhaps the greatest missed opportunity in the penal system has been the failure to treat younger prisoners who are still within the window where the social brain remains most plastic. The lessons they learn from day to day in the prison yard leave a profound and lasting imprint on their neural destiny, for better or worse.

At present, it is for the worst. The tragedy is double: not only do we waste that opportunity to help reshape the neural circuitry that can help these young lives get back on track, but we plunge them into a school for criminality. Nationwide, the cumulative lifetime recidivism for prisoners age twenty-five and under—those newest to a criminal career—inevitably runs the highest of any age group.

On any given day, the United States has more than two million people in prison, or 482 inmates per 100,000 residents—one of the highest rates of incarceration in the world, followed by Britain, China, France, and Japan.[7] The prison population today is seven times larger than it was three decades ago. The costs have risen even more, from around $9 billion in the 1980s to more than $60 billion by 2005; prison costs are the fastest-growing expenses for states, behind health care. The relentless increase in the number of inmates in American prisons has created a population explosion that has jails dangerously overcrowded and states and counties like Kalamazoo scrambling to find ways to pay for them.

More compelling than the economic costs are the human ones: once a person is caught up in the prison system, the odds that he will escape its gravitational pull are abysmally low. Two-thirds of those released from American prisons are arrested again within three years.[8]

Such were the raw realities contemplated by those concerned citizens of Kalamazoo. By the end of their day of retreat, they had found common cause: "to make Kalamazoo the safest, most just, community in the United States." Toward that end they scoured the country to find out what works: approaches that actually lowered the rate of return to prison, or had other concrete benefits, and the hard data to show it.

The result is a rarity, an evidence-based plan for turning lives around, in large part by restoring the connective tissue that links people in trouble to those who care what happens to them.[9] The Kalamazoo group's proposal spans efforts to prevent crimes in the first place, use prison time fruitfully, and reintegrate those released into a web of relationships that will help them stay out of jail.

The first guiding principle is that supportive connections prevent crime—and those connections must start in the neighborhoods where young people most at risk for crime live.

CONNECTED COMMUNITIES

In a down-and-out neighborhood on Boston's South Side, a vacant lot has been turned into a community garden, where neighbors gather each spring and summer to tend cabbage, kale, and tomatoes. On the fence a hand-painted sign reads: "Please respect our efforts."

This small message of hope calls for a willingness to help out a neighbor. Will a group of teens loitering on a corner be allowed to intimidate a smaller child walking by? Or will an adult tell them to disperse, perhaps even call their parents? Respect and caring make the difference, as they do between an abandoned, garbage-strewn lot frequented by drug dealers and a shared vegetable garden.[10]

In the mid-1990s a coalition of black ministers took to the stoops and corners in Boston's toughest neighborhoods to engage the kids hanging out on the streets and bring them into after-school programs led by local adults. The murder rate in Boston plunged from 151 in 1991 to just 35 ten years later—just as it did in other cities across the country.

During the 1990s a nationwide decline in crime rates was largely attributed to the economic boom. But apart from such broad forces, the question remains: can weaving people together, as those black ministers did, in itself help reduce crime on a given block? The answer to this street-level question has come from the largest analysis of community involvement and crime yet done, a ten-year study headed by psychiatrist Felton Earls of Harvard. It suggests that the answer is a strong yes.

With a research group, Earls made videotapes of 1,408 blocks of street life in 196 Chicago neighborhoods, including the poorest and most crime-ridden. They documented everything from church bake sales to drug deals. The tapes were compared with crime records for those same neighborhoods, as well as with interviews from 8,782 neighborhood residents.[11]

The Earls group found two primary influences on a neighborhood's crime rate. The first is the neighborhood's overall level of poverty: high poverty rates have long been known to hike crime (as does illiteracy, another hidden factor). The second is the degree of connection among the people in a community. The mix of poverty and disconnection, in tandem, exert a stronger influence over an area's crime rates than the standard factors usually cited, including race, ethnic background, or family structure.

Even in the poorest neighborhoods, Earls found, positive personal connections were associated not just with lower crime rates but also with less drug use among young people, fewer unwanted teen pregnancies, and a rise in children's academic performance. Many low-income African-American communities have strong mutual-help traditions, through churches and extended families. Earls sees extending this neighbor-helping-neighbor spirit as a fruitful crime-fighting strategy.[12]

If a local group cleans graffiti off the walls, future graffiti will likely be less than if the city's work crew comes in and cleans the walls. A neighborhood crime watch means the local kids have the security of knowing that caring eyes are on them. In the world's impoverished neighborhoods, that attitude counts most when it comes to neighbors acting to protect one another and most especially each other's children.

| N O   M O R E   S T I N K I N G   T H I N K I N G |

The son of an old friend—I'll call him Brad—became a binge drinker in his teen years, and when drunk he all too readily became combative and even violent. This behavior had led to a series of brushes with the law, until finally he was sentenced to prison for seriously hurting a classmate in a fight in his college dorm.

When I visit Brad in prison, he tells me, "No matter what the charge, basically all the guys are in here because of a bad temper." He was fortunate to have been assigned to a special pilot program for prisoners who show some promise for changing their ways. Those living in this six-cell special unit get a daily seminar on topics such as telling the difference between actions based on "creative thinking, stinking thinking, or no thinking."

In the rest of the prison, fights and posturing to intimidate are the order of the day. Brad's challenge, he knows, will be to learn to manage his anger in a social world where violence and toughness determine one's place in the hierarchy of the jailyard. That world, he tells me, is based on an us-versus-them paranoia, in which anyone in a uniform is "the enemy," as is anyone who works with them.

"All these guys are easily pissed off, irritated at the least little thing. And they settle any disagreement by fights. But in my program you don't have to live that way."

Still, Brad has had his hassles. "There was this one kid, about my age, who came into our program. He was continually taunting and ridiculing me, always ragging on me. He made me really mad—but I didn't let my anger take over. At first I would just walk away. But he would follow me wherever I went, always in my face. Then I told him he was just being stupid and that it didn't matter to me what he said. But he kept at it, relentlessly.

"Finally, I let myself feel my anger enough so I could yell at him. I stood my ground—I screamed in his face, telling him how stupid he was. Then we were just glaring at each other. It looked like we were going to get in a fight.

"The way you have a fight here is to go into a cell together and lock the door behind you. That way the guards don't see you. You fight until one guy gives up, and then you come out. So we went into my cell and locked the door. But I didn't want to fight. I just said to him, 'If you want to go ahead and take a punch at me, do it now. I've been hit lots of times—I can take it. But I'm not going to fight you.'

"He didn't punch me. We ended up talking for an hour or two. He told me what he was all about, and I told him what I was all about.

The next day he was transferred out of our unit. But when I see him in the yard now, he doesn't hassle me anymore."

Brad's program typifies those that the Kalamazoo task force identified as best for young offenders. Teens incarcerated for aggressive offenses who go through similar training programs—where they learn to stop and think before reacting, to consider solutions and the consequence of different responses, and to stay coolheaded—get in fewer fights and are less impulsive and inflexible.[13]

But unlike my young friend, most prisoners never get to correct the habits and circumstances that keep them trapped in the cycle of release, relapse, and prison again. Since only a minority of released prisoners avoid being sent back to prison, the term used for this system, "corrections," seems a tragic misnomer: nothing gets corrected.

Instead, for the most part prisons are colleges for crime, strengthening an inmate's predilection and skill sets for criminality. Younger prisoners make the very worst kind of connections in prison, typically becoming mentored by more seasoned inmates, so that on their release they are hardened, angry, and endowed with greater skills as criminals.[14]

The circuits of the social brain for empathy and for regulating emotional impulses—perhaps the two most glaring deficiencies among the prison population—are among the last parts of the human brain to gain anatomical maturity. A tally of prisoners in state and federal facilities shows that about one quarter are under the age of twenty-five—not too late to nudge these circuits into a more law-abiding pattern.[15] Careful evaluation of present-day prison rehabilitation programs has found that those targeting juvenile offenders are among the most successful in preventing a return to crime.[16]

Those programs might become more effective by borrowing methods from the many well-proven school-based courses in social and emotional learning.[17] These courses teach basic lessons like managing anger and conflicts, empathy, and self-management. In schools, these programs have reduced the number of fights by 69 percent, bullying by 75 percent, and harassment by 67 percent.[18] The question is how well these efforts could be adapted for use with a teenage or twenty-something prison population (or conceivably even older inmates).[19]

The prospect of reinventing prison to offer a remedial neural education is an intriguing point of leverage for society. To the extent that such programs for first-time offenders and young criminals spread, the number of prisoners nationwide will certainly fall as the years go on. Keeping the youngest criminals from embarking on a continued life of crime will do much to dry up the human rivers that now swell our prisons.

An exhaustive analysis of the 272,111 prisoners released from U.S. correctional facilities in 1994 found that over their criminal careers, they had been arrested for a total of nearly 4,877,000 crimes—an average of more than seventeen criminal charges each. And those were only the crimes they had been charged with.[20]

With the right corrective, that lifetime tally might well have ended right toward the beginning. But the odds now are that first-time offenders will go on to a career in crime, adding inexorably to their toll of lawbreaking as the years go on.

When I was young, we used to call juvenile prisons "reform schools." They actually could be such if they were designed as learning environments that enhance the skills people need to stay out of jail: not only literacy and job training (and placement), but self-awareness, self-control, and empathy. If they were, we could make prison a place where neural habits are literally re-formed—"reform" schools in the deepest sense.

As for Brad, when I checked two years later, he had gone back to college and was supporting himself with a bussing job in a fancy restaurant.

He had been living in a house with some of his old friends from high school. But as he told me, "They weren't at all serious about school—they were just into getting drunk and fighting. So I chose to move out." He moved in with his father and kept focused on his studies.

Although it meant losing some old friends, he says, "I have no regrets. I'm happy."

STRENGTHENING CONNECTIONS

Early one morning in June 2004 a fire ravaged the Mood's Covered Bridge, long a landmark in Bucks County, Pennsylvania. When the arsonists were arrested two months later, the community was shocked.

The six young men were well-known graduates of the local high school, all from "good" families. People were puzzled and outraged; the whole community felt victimized, robbed of a precious link to a more idyllic time.

At a meeting of townspeople with the six arsonists, one of the boys' fathers expressed his anger at strangers who had attacked him and his son in local media. But he also admitted, when asked how his son's crime had affected him, that he thought about it constantly, couldn't sleep, and felt his stomach was in knots. And then, overcome, he wept.

As they listened to the pain expressed by their family and their neighbors, the young men were distraught and contrite. They apologized, and said they wished they could undo what they had done.[21]

The meeting was an exercise in "restorative justice," which holds that in addition to punishment, criminals should face the emotional aftermath of what they have done and make amends where possible.[22] The Kalamazoo plan puts special emphasis on restorative justice among the active ingredients in effective crimefighting.

In such programs, mediators often arrange for some way the criminal can repair the specific damage done—whether by making payments, by hearing about the crime from the victim's point of view, or by apologizing with genuine remorse. In the words of the manager of one such program in a California prison, "The victim impact sessions are very emotional. For many men it's the first time they get the connection between their crime and the victim."

Emarco Washington was one of those California men. As a teenager, he had been addicted to crack, resorting to robbery and assault to support his habit. He was especially abusive to his mother when she would not give him money for drugs. By thirty, he had served time almost every year since he was a teen.[23]

After going through restorative justice programs—combined with training in violence reduction—in the San Francisco jail, Washington did something different on his release: he called his mother and apologized. "I told her I had been angry when she wouldn't give me money before, but the last thing I wanted to do was to hurt her. It was like a rain washing over me. That told me if I changed my behavior, my language, I could prove to myself and to others I wasn't a bad seed."

The emotional subtext of restorative justice urges offenders to change their perception of their victims from It to You—to awaken empathy. Many crimes by young people are committed while they are drunk or high; in a sense the victims don't exist for the perpetrators; nor do the youth have any sense of responsibility for hurting people. By forging an empathic link between the perpetrator and the victim, restorative justice adds to the circle of connection that can be so powerful in turning a young life around.

The Kalamazoo group identified another important turning point: that perilous moment when a young prisoner returns home. Without intervention, it's all too easy for young people to slip back into their old groups, their old habits—and more often than not, jail again.

Among the multitude of approaches that seek to keep ex-prisoners on the right track, one stands out as being particularly successful: multisystemic therapy.[24] The word "therapy" here may seem a misnomer; there are no fifty-minute sessions one on one in a therapist's office. Instead the intervention goes on smack in the midst of life: in the home, on the streets, at school—at whatever places and with whichever people the ex-inmate spends his time.

A counselor shadows a released offender, getting to know his private world. He searches that world for strengths, like a good kid who could be a friend, an uncle who could be a mentor, a church that could offer a virtual family. And then the counselor sees to it that his charge spends time with those nourishing people and stays away from the ones whose influence might well lead to more jail time.

No fancy therapeutics is involved here. The approach is pragmatic: ratchet up levels of discipline and affection at home, decrease time spent with trouble-prone peers, work harder at school or get a job, and take part in sports. Most important, cultivate a web of healthy connections that will surround the offender with people who care and who can model a more responsible way of living. It's all done with people: extended family, neighbors, and friends.[25]

Though it lasts just four months, multisystemic therapy seems to work. For young offenders who have gone through the program, recidivism rates tracked over three years after release drop by anywhere from 25 to 70 percent. More impressively, these results apply to the most intransigent, difficult prisoners, those whose crimes were violent and serious.

A government tally of prisoners' ages notes that the fastest-growing group in prison are those in middle age; virtually all of them have had years of crime behind them.[26] Most are at the inevitable endpoint of a life in crime that began with their first arrest, in their youth.

That first arrest is the golden opportunity for intervening, for changing the vector of their lives away from criminality. That moment is pivotal, shunting a young person either into the revolving door of jail or away from it.

If we adopt the programs that work, like reschooling the social brain, everyone will win. To be sure, a comprehensive plan like

Kalamazoo's has many more parts: the list of "what works" also includes literacy and a job that pays enough to live on, as well as taking responsibility for one's actions. But all the parts share one goal: to help offenders learn to be better people, not better criminals.

| **2 1** |

From Them to Us

It was during the last years of apartheid in South Africa, the system of complete segregation between the ruling Dutch-descended Afrikaaners and the "colored" groups. Thirty people had been meeting clandestinely for four days. Half were white business executives, half black community organizers. The group was being trained to conduct leadership seminars together, so they could help build governance skills within the black community.

On the last day of the program they sat riveted to a television set while President F. W. de Klerk gave a now-famous speech that heralded the coming end of apartheid. De Klerk legalized a long list of previously banned organizations and ordered the release of many political prisoners.

Anne Loersebe, one of the black community leaders there, was beaming: as each organization was named, she pictured the face of someone she knew who could now come out of hiding.

After the speech the group went through an ending ritual in which each person had a chance to offer parting words. Most simply said how meaningful the training had been, and how glad they were to have been there.

But the fifth person to speak, a tall, emotionally reserved Afrikaaner, stood and looked directly at Anne. "I want you to know," he told her, "that I was raised to think you were an animal." And with that, he broke into tears.[1]

Us-Them restates I-It in the plural: the underlying dynamics are one and the same. As Walter Kaufmann, the English translator of Martin Buber, put it, with the words "Us-Them," "the world is divided in two: the children of light and the children of darkness, the sheep and the goats, the elect and the damned."[2]

The relationship between one of Us and one of Them by definition lacks empathy, let alone attunement. Should one of Them presume to speak to one of Us, the voice would not be heard as fully or openly as would that of one of Us—if at all.

The gulf that divides Us from Them builds with the silencing of empathy. And across that gulf we are free to project onto Them whatever we like. As Kaufmann adds, "Righteousness, intelligence, integrity, humanity and victory are the prerogatives of Us, while wickedness, stupidity, hypocrisy, and ultimate defeat belong to Them."

When we relate to someone as one of Them, we close off our altruistic impulses. Take, for example, a series of experiments in which volunteers were asked if they would be willing to get an electrical shock in place of someone else. The catch: they could not see the potential victim but simply heard a description of him or her. The more unlike themselves the other person was described as being—the more one of Them—the more unwilling they were to come to their rescue.[3]

"Hatred," said Elie Wiesel, the Nobel Peace Prize winner and Holocaust survivor, "is a cancer that is passed from one person to another, one people to another."[4] Human history chronicles an endless stream of horrors perpetrated by one group that turns viciously against another—even when that other group has far more similarities to than differences from themselves. Northern Irish Protestants and Catholics, like Serbs and Croatians, have battled over the years, though genetically they are each other's closest biological brothers and sisters.

We confront the challenges of living in a global civilization with a brain that primally attaches us to our home tribe. As a psychiatrist who grew up amid the ethnic turmoil of Cyprus put it, groups that are so much alike move from Us to Them via the "narcissism of minor differences," seizing on small features that set the groups apart while ignoring their vast human similarities. Once the others are set at a psychological distance, they can become a target for hostility.

This process is a corruption of a normal cognitive function: categorization. The human mind depends on categories to give order and meaning to the world around us. By assuming that the next entity we encounter in a given category has the same main features as the last, we navigate our way through an ever-changing environment.

But once a negative bias begins, our lenses become clouded. We tend to seize on whatever seems to confirm the bias and ignore what does not. Prejudice, in this sense, is a hypothesis desperately trying to prove itself to us. And so when we encounter someone to whom the prejudice might apply, the bias skews our perception, making it impossible to test whether the stereotype actually fits. Openly hostile stereotypes about a group—to the extent they rest on untested assumptions—are mental categories gone awry.

A vague sense of anxiety, a tinge of fear, or mere uneasiness at not knowing the cultural signals of Them can be enough to start the skewing of a cognitive category. The mind builds its "evidence" against the other with each additional disquiet, each unflattering media depiction, each feeling of having been treated wrongly. As these incidents build, apprehension becomes antipathy, and antipathy morphs into antagonism.

Outright anger primes prejudice even in those whose biases are slight. Like a match on tinder, antagonism catalyzes the switch from Us *and* Them (the mere perception of difference) to Us *versus* Them, active hostility.

Anger and fear, both amygdala-driven, amplify the destructiveness of a budding bias. When flooded by these strong emotions, the prefrontal area becomes incapacitated, as the low road hijacks the high. This sabotages the ability to think clearly, thereby foiling a corrective answer to that essential question, does he really have all the bad traits I ascribe to Them? And if a damning view of Them has already been accepted, even in the absence of anger or fear that question is no longer asked.

IMPLICIT BIAS

Us-and-Them comes in many forms, from rabid hatred to unflattering stereotypes so subtle they elude even those who hold them. Such ultrasubtle prejudices hide in the low road, in the form of "implicit" biases, automatic and unconscious stereotypes. These quiet biases seem capable of driving responses—such as the decision of who to hire from a pool of equally qualified applicants—even when they do not fit our consciously held beliefs.[5]

People who show not the least outward sign of prejudice and who espouse positive views toward a group can still harbor hidden biases, as revealed by clever cognitive measures. For instance, the

Implicit Association Test offers you a word and asks you to match it to a category as quickly as you can.[6] Its scale for hidden attitudes about whether women are as qualified as men for careers in science asks you to match words like "physics" and "humanities" to either "women" or "men."

We can make such a match most quickly when an idea fits the way we already think about something. Someone who believed that men are better at science than are women would be quicker when matching "men" and science-related words. These differences are counted in mere tenths of seconds and are discernible only by computer analysis.

Such implicit biases, faint as they are, seem to skew judgments about people in a target group, as well as choices such as whether to work with someone, or judgments of a defendant's guilt.[7] When there are clear rules to follow, implicit biases have less effect—but the fuzzier the standards in a situation, the more powerful they become.

One cognitive scientist, a woman, was shocked to find that a test of implicitly held biases revealed that she unconsciously endorsed a stereotype against women scientists—like herself! So she changed the decor in her office, surrounding herself with photos of famous women scientists like Marie Curie.

Could that make a difference in her attitudes? It just might.

At one time psychologists saw unconscious mental categories like implicit attitudes as fixed; because their influence works automatically and unconsciously, the assumption was that their consequences were inevitable. After all, the amygdala plays the key role in implicit bias (as well as in blatant prejudice).[8] And low-road circuitry seemed difficult to sway.

But more recent research has shown that automatic stereotypes and prejudices are fluid—implicit biases do not reflect a person's "true" feelings but can shift.[9] At the neural level, this fluidity may reflect the fact that even the low road remains an eager learner throughout life.

Take a simple experiment in stereotype reduction.[10] People who held implicit biases against blacks were shown photos of widely admired blacks like Bill Cosby and Martin Luther King, Jr., and of disliked whites like the serial killer Jeffrey Dahmer. The exposure was minimal, just a fifteen-minute session with a carefully selected set of forty photos.

That brief tutorial for the amygdala resulted in a dramatic shift in how those people scored on the test of implicit attitudes: unconscious antiblack attitudes vanished. And the positive switch was still there when the volunteers were tested twenty-four hours later. Presumably, if such images of admired members of a target group were seen from time to time in "booster" sessions (or, say, as leading characters on a favorite TV show), the shift would persist. The amygdala learns continually and so need not stay stuck in a bias.

Many methods have been proven to reduce implicit bias, if only for the time being.[11] When people were told that an IQ test showed they had high intelligence, their negative implicit biases vanished— but when they were told the test showed they had low intelligence, the biases strengthened. Implicit bias against blacks diminished after people were given positive feedback by a black supervisor.

Social demands can do it: people who are put in a social setting where a prejudiced view is "out of step" register less implicit bias, too. Even the explicit resolve to ignore a person's membership in a target group can reduce hidden prejudice.[12]

This finding dovetails with some neural judo: when people think or talk about their tolerant attitudes, the prefrontal area activates and the amygdala, that seat of implicit prejudice, quiets.[13] As the high road engages in a positive way, the low road loses its power to stir bias. This neural dynamic may be at work in people who are going through programs that explicitly increase tolerance.

A very different, and rather novel, way to neutralize prejudice a bit was discovered in Israeli experiments where people's sense of security was activated via subtle methods, like bringing to mind loved ones. Feeling momentarily more secure shifted prejudiced participants to a positive stance toward groups like Arabs and ultra-Orthodox Jews, both of whom had been among their initial targets of bias. When told they could spend time with an Arab or an ultra-Orthodox Jew, they were far more willing than they had been just minutes before.

No one claims that such a fleeting sense of security can resolve long-standing historical and political conflict. Still, that demonstration adds to the case that even hidden prejudice can be lessened.[14]

CLOSING THE HOSTILE DIVIDE

Exactly what might repair Us-Them divides has been hotly debated for years among psychologists who study intergroup relations. But much of that debate has now been resolved by the work of Thomas Pettigrew, a social psychologist who has been studying prejudice ever since soon after the American civil rights movement destroyed legal barriers between races. Pettigrew, a native of Virginia, was one of the first psychologists to plumb the heart of racial hatred. He began as a student of Gordon Allport, a social psychologist who argued that friendly and sustained contacts erode prejudice.

Now, three decades later, Pettigrew has led the largest analysis of studies ever on what kinds of contact change hostile groups' views about each other. Pettigrew and his associates tracked down 515 studies dating from the 1940s to 2000 and combined them into a single massive statistical analysis, with responses from an astonishing 250,493 people from thirty-eight countries. The Us-Them divides in the studies ranged from black-white relations in the United States to a multitude of ethnic, racial, and religious animosities around the world, as well as biases against the elderly, disabled, and mentally ill.[15]

The strong conclusion: emotional involvements, like friendships and romances between individuals from either side of a hostile divide, make people far more accepting of each other's groups. For instance, having had a childhood playmate from another group typically inoculates people against prejudice later in life—as was found in one study of African-Americans who played with whites as children (though their schools were segregated at the time). The same effect operated under apartheid among those rural Afrikaaner housewives who had become friends with their African domestic workers.

Significantly, studies that track the time course of across-the-divide friendships show that the closeness itself leads to a reduction in prejudice. But mere casual contact on the street or at work does relatively little, if anything, to change hostile stereotypes.[16] Pettigrew argues that the essential requirement for overcoming prejudice is a strong emotional connection. Over time the warmth each person feels toward the other generalizes to all of Them. For instance, when people had good friends across tense ethnic divides in Europe—Germans with Turks, French with North Africans, British with West Indians—the friends had far less prejudice toward the other group as a whole.[17]

"You may still hold a general stereotype about them, but it's not connected to strong negative feelings anymore," Pettigrew told me.

The crucial role of contact—or its absence—in prejudice was shown in studies Pettigrew did in Germany with colleagues there. "East Germans are on average far more prejudiced against all groups, from Poles to Turks, than are people in West Germany,"

Pettigrew said. "For example, acts of violence against minorities are much more frequent in the former East Germany than West. When we studied those arrested for such violence, we found two things: they are intensely prejudiced, and they have had virtually no contact with the groups they hate so much.

"In East Germany, even when the Communist government took in large groups of Cubans or Africans, they were kept segregated," Pettigrew observed. "But in West Germany there have been decades of friendships across group lines. And we found the more contact Germans had with minorities, the more friendly they felt" toward the group as a whole.[18] When It becomes You, They turn into Us.

But what of implicit bias, the subtle stereotypes that slide under the radar of even those who profess to hold no bias? Don't they matter too? Pettigrew is skeptical.

"Groups often hold stereotypes about themselves that are widespread in their culture," he observed. "For instance, I'm a Scot; my parents were immigrants. Scots are stereotyped as skinflints. But we turn that around, saying we're just being thrifty. The stereotype remains, but the emotional valence has changed."

Tests for implicit bias look at a person's cognitive categories, which in themselves are but cool abstractions, devoid of feeling. What counts about a stereotype, Pettigrew argues, is the feeling tone that goes with it: simply holding a stereotype matters less than do the emotions attached.

Given the intensity, even violence, of some intergroup tensions, worrying about implicit bias may be a luxury reserved for places where prejudice has largely dwindled to subtleties rather than expressions of outright hatred. When groups are in open conflict, emotions are what count; when they are getting along, the mental residues of outright prejudice matter to the extent that they foster subtle acts of prejudice.

Pettigrew's research shows that holding negative feelings toward a group predicts hostile actions far more strongly than does holding an unflattering stereotype of Them.[19] Even after people from hostile groups form friendships, some of the original stereotypes remain. But their feelings warm up—and that makes the difference: "Now I like them, even if I still hold on to the general stereotype." Pettigrew speculates, "The implicit bias may stay, but if my emotions shift, my behavior will, too."

| **THE JIGSAW SOLUTION** |

To protect themselves from the intergroup frictions rampant in their large Manhattan high school, girls from Puerto Rico and the Dominican Republic united into a single clique. But within that tight-knit clan occasional bad feelings arose between Dominican and Puerto Rican factions.

One day a fight started between two girls, when a Puerto Rican put down a Dominican for being too proud for such a recent immigrant. The two became enemies, splitting the group's loyalties.

In high schools across America students increasingly find themselves in an ever-diversifying ethnic mix. In this new global microcosm the standard categories of discrimination—the ways Us and Them are defined—constantly reinvent themselves.[20] The old categories, like blacks and whites, have been replaced by much subtler strains. In that Manhattan school these divisions included not just blacks versus Latinos but, among the Asians, "ABCs" (American Born Chinese) and "FOBs" (Fresh Off the Boat). Given the projections for immigration into the United States over the next several decades, this multilayered ethnic mix, with its expanding varieties of in- and outgroups, will only thicken the varieties of Us and Them.

One sobering lesson in the costs of a socially splintered climate was the horrific shootings at Columbine High School on April 20, 1999, when two "outsider" kids sought revenge by killing several fellow students, a teacher, and themselves. That tragedy inspired social psychologist Elliot Aronson to examine the problem, which he saw as having roots in school atmospheres that are "competitive, cliquish and exclusionary."

In such a setting, Aronson saw, "teenagers agonize over the fact that there is a general atmosphere of taunting and rejection among their peers that makes the high school experience an unpleasant one. For many, it is worse than unpleasant—they describe it as a living hell, where they feel insecure, unpopular, put-down and picked on."[21]

Not only the United States, but countries from Norway to Japan have been grappling with the problem of how to stop children from bullying. Anywhere there are "in" students and outsiders whom other students shun and exclude, the problem of disconnection plagues the social world of the learner.

That fact may seem to some a trivial side effect of the normal social currents that make some students stars and place others off the map. But research with people who are made to feel left out or who are reminded that they belong to an "outsider" group shows that such rejection can plummet them into a state of distractedness, anxious preoccupation, lethargy, and a sense that their lives are meaningless.[22] Large doses of teen angst are brewed from this very fear of exclusion.

Remember that the pain of ostracism registers in the node of the social brain that also reacts to actual physical pain. Social rejection in students can torpedo academic performance.[23] Their capacity for working memory—the crucial cognitive ability for taking in new information—becomes impaired enough to account for an appreciable decline in mastery of subjects like math.[24] Beyond having difficulties in learning, such disengaged students tend to have higher rates of violence and disruptive behavior in class, show poor attendance, and drop out at higher rates.

The social universe of school is at the center of teenagers' lives. That fact presents a danger, as the data on alienation show, but also a promise: for school also offers every teenager a living laboratory for learning to connect positively with other people.

Aronson took up the challenge of helping students connect in healthy ways. From social psychology he knew one dynamic of moving from Them to Us: as people from hostile groups work together toward a common goal, they end up liking one another.

So Aronson advocated what he calls the "jigsaw classroom," where students labor in teams to master an assignment on which they will be tested. Just as in a jigsaw puzzle, each student in the group holds one piece essential for full understanding. In studying World War II, for example, each team member becomes a specialist on one area, like military campaigns in Italy. The specialist studies that one topic with students from other groups. They then go back to their home group and teach the others.

To master the subject, the whole group must listen intently to what each has to say. If the others heckle them or tune out because they don't like them, they risk doing poorly on the test that follows. Learning itself becomes a lab that encourages listening, respect, and cooperation.

Students in jigsaw learning groups quickly let go of their negative stereotypes. Likewise, studies in multicultural schools show that the more friendly contacts students have across group divides, the less their bias.[25]

Take Carlos, a fifth-grader who suddenly had to leave the school that most Mexican-American students like him attended and be bused across town to a school in a prosperous neighborhood. Kids in his new school were better informed in all the subjects than he was, and they ridiculed his accent. Carlos became an instant outsider, shy and insecure.

But in the jigsaw classroom, the same students who had made fun of him now had to depend on his piece of the learning puzzle for their own success. At first they put him down for his halting delivery, making him freeze—and they all did poorly. So they began to help and encourage him. The more they helped, the more relaxed—and articulate—Carlos became. His performance improved as his groupmates saw him in an increasingly favorable light.

Several years later, out of the blue, Aronson got a letter from Carlos as he was about to graduate from a university. Carlos recalled how he had been scared, had hated school, and had thought he was stupid—and how the other kids had been cruel and hostile. But once he took part in the jigsaw classroom, that had changed, and his tormentors had become his friends.[26]

"I began to love to learn," Carlos wrote. "And now I'm about to go to Harvard Law School."

FORGIVING AND FORGETTING

It was a cold December day, and the Very Reverend James Parks Morton, former dean of New York City's Episcopal Cathedral and now director of the Interfaith Center, had very bad news for his staff. Their largest donors had cut back funding, and the center could no longer pay its rent. It was about to become homeless.

Then just a few days before Christmas, an unlikely savior came. Sheikh Moussa Drammeh, an immigrant from Senegal, heard about their plight and offered the Interfaith Center room in a building where he was about to start a day care facility.

In this rescue by a Muslim of a center where Buddhists, Hindus, Christians, Jews, Muslims, and others could meet to work on common problems, Dean Morton saw a fitting parable, one that validated the very mission of his group. As Drammeh put it, "the more we know about each other and the more we are willing to sit down and drink and laugh together, the less we are inclined to shed blood."[27]

But what can be done to heal the hatred of peoples when they *have* shed blood? In the aftermath of intergroup violence, prejudice and animosity inevitably metastasize.

Once hostilities have ceased, over and above harmonious relations there are good personal reasons to speed the process. One is biological: holding on to hatred and grudges has grave physiological consequence. Studies of people posthostility reveal that every time they merely think of the group they hate, their own body responds with pent-up anger; it floods with stress hormones, raising their blood pressure and impairing their immune effectiveness. Presumably, the more often and intensely this sequence of muted rage repeats, the more risk of lasting biological consequence.

One antidote lies in forgiveness.[28] Forgiving someone we've held a grudge against reverses the biological reaction: it lowers our blood pressure, heart rate, and levels of stress hormones and it lessens our pain and depression.[29]

Forgiveness can have social consequences, like making friends with former enemies. But it need not take that form. Especially while wounds are still fresh, forgiveness does not require condoning some offensive act, forgetting what happened, or reconciling with the perpetrator. It means finding a way to free oneself from the claws of obsession about the hurt.

For a week psychologists coached seventeen men and women from Northern Ireland, both Catholic and Protestant, on forgiveness. Each of them had lost a family member to sectarian violence. During that week the bereaved aired their grievances and were helped to find new ways to think about the tragedy—most resolving not to dwell on their hurt but to honor the memory of their loved ones by dedicating themselves to a more hopeful future. Many intended to help others go through the same ritual of forgiveness. Afterward, the group not only felt less hurt emotionally but also reported a substantial drop in physical symptoms of trauma like poor appetite and sleeplessness.[30]

Forgive, perhaps, but don't forget—at least not entirely. There are larger lessons for humanity to learn from acts of oppression and brutality. They need to be held in mind as morality tales, reminders to the ages. As Rabbi Lawrence Kushner says of the Holocaust, "I want to remember its horror only to make sure that such a thing never happens to me or to anyone else ever again."[31]

As Kushner puts it, having learned the most horrible lesson about "what it means to be victimized by the full power of a technocratic state gone mad," the best response to that memory lies in helping other people who are in danger of genocide now.

That motive lies behind the production of *New Dawn*, a weekly radio soap opera that is popular in Rwanda, where from 1990 to 1994 rampaging Hutus slaughtered seven hundred thousand of their

Tutsi neighbors, along with moderate Hutus who might oppose the killings. The soap's plot, set in the present, follows the tensions simmering between two neighboring hardscrabble villages in dispute over fertile land that lies between them.

In a Romeo and Juliet twist, Batamuliza, a young woman, has a romantic interest in Shema, a young man in the other village. To thicken the plot, her older brother, Rutanagira, leads a faction in their village that tries to goad hatred toward the other village to foment an attack on them—and he's trying to force Batamuliza to marry one of his cronies. Batamuliza, though, belongs to a group with friends in both her own and the other village. These young people cook up ways to oppose the troublemakers, like tipping off the targets of the planned attack and speaking out against the instigators.

Just such active resistance to hatred was absent during the genocides of a decade ago. Cultivating the capacity to fight hatred is the subtext of *New Dawn,* a joint project of Dutch philanthropists and American psychologists.[32] "We're giving people an understanding of the influences that led to genocide, and what they can do to see it never repeats," said Ervin Staub, a psychologist at the University of Massachusetts at Amherst and one of the designers of the show.

Staub knows about the dynamics of genocide from personal experience as well as from his research. As a child, he was one of tens of thousands of Hungarian Jews saved from the Nazis by Swedish ambassador Raoul Wallenberg.

Staub's book *The Roots of Evil* summarizes the psychological forces that spawn such mass murder.[33] The groundwork gets laid during severe social upheavals, like economic crises and political chaos, in places that have a history of division between a dominant group and a less powerful one. The turmoil causes members of a majority group to find appealing the ideologies that scapegoat a weaker group, blaming them for the problem and envisioning a better future that They are preventing. The hatred spreads all the more readily when the majority group has itself been victimized in the past and still feels wounded or wronged. Already seeing the world as dangerous, when tensions rise they feel a need to resort to violence against Them to defend themselves, even when their "self-defense" amounts to genocide.

Several features make such violence more likely: when the targets are unable to speak up to defend themselves, and bystanders—those who could object, or people in nearby countries—say and do nothing. "If others are passive when you first harm the victims, the perpetrators interpret that silence as an endorsement," Staub says. "And once people start the violence, step by step they exclude their victim from the moral realm. Then there's nothing to hold them back."

Staub, working with psychologist Laurie Anne Pearlman, has been teaching these insights—and antidotes to hatred, like objecting openly—to Rwandan groups of politicians, journalists, and community leaders.[34] "We ask them to apply these insights to their own experience of what happened. It's very powerful. We're trying to promote community healing and build the tools to resist the forces of violence."

Their research shows that both Hutus and Tutsis who have gone through such training feel less traumatized by what happened to them and are more accepting of the other group. But it takes more than strong emotional connections and friendship to overcome the Us-Them divide. Forgiveness may not help when the groups continue to live next to each other, Staub finds, and when the perpetrators fail to acknowledge what they have done, show no regret, and express no empathy for survivors. The imbalance widens if the forgiveness is one-sided.

Staub distinguishes forgiveness from reconciliation, which is the honest review of oppression and efforts at making amends like those undertaken by the Truth and Reconciliation Commission in South Africa after the fall of apartheid. In his programs in Rwanda, reconciliation has meant that those on the side of the perpetrators admit what was done, and people on both sides come to see each other more realistically. That paves the way for both peoples to live together in a new way.

"Tutsis will tell you," Staub finds, " 'some Hutus tried to save our lives. I'm willing to work with them for the sake of our children. If they apologize, I can see myself forgive.' "

What Really Matters

I once met a man who had been invited to spend a week on a private yacht touring the Greek islands. It wasn't just any yacht but a "superyacht," a ministeamship so long it was listed in a special registry of the largest pleasure boats in the world. A copy of that registry sat on a table in its lounge: the thick, richly illustrated volume had a two-page spread devoted to the lavish details of each superyacht.

The dozen or so guests aboard were thrilled by the comforts and the sheer immensity of the sleek craft—until the day an even bigger yacht anchored nearby. Consulting the registry, they discovered that their new nautical neighbor was among the five largest yachts in the world and belonged to a Saudi prince. On top of that, it had an accompanying tender, a sister ship that carried its supplies, such as a huge water trampoline hanging from the bow. The tender itself was about the size of their own boat.

Can there be such a thing as yacht envy? Absolutely, according to Daniel Kahneman, a Princeton University psychologist. Such high-end envy results from what he dubs the "hedonic treadmill." Kahneman, who won a Nobel Prize in economics, uses the image of a treadmill to explain why enhanced life circumstances, like greater wealth, correlate poorly with life satisfaction.

In explaining why the wealthiest people are not the happiest, Kahneman argues that as we get more money, we adapt our expectations upward, and so we aspire to ever more lofty and expensive pleasures—a treadmill that never ends, even for billionaires. As he puts it, "The rich may experience more pleasure than the poor, but they also require more pleasure to be equally satisfied."[1]

But Kahneman's research also suggests one way to escape from the hedonic treadmill: a life rich in rewarding relationships. He and a research team surveyed more than one thousand American women, asking them to evaluate all their activities during a given day in terms of what they were doing, who they were with at the time, and how they felt. The most powerful influences on how happy the women felt were the people with whom they spent their time—not their income, not job pressures, and not their marital status.[2]

The two most pleasurable activities were, to no one's surprise, making love and socializing. Least enjoyable were the daily commute and work. And the rankings of which people primed happiness? Here is the list, from top to bottom:

Friends
Relatives
Spouse or partner
Children
Clients or customers
Coworkers
Boss
Being alone

Kahneman suggests, in effect, that we take stock of the people in our lives and the pleasure we get in being with them, then try to "optimize" our day by spending more time with them in satisfying ways (to the extent that schedules and money allow). But beyond such obvious logistical solutions, a richer possibility is to re-create our relationships to make them more mutually nourishing.

Surely much of what makes life worth living comes down to our feelings of well-being—our happiness and sense of fulfillment. And good-quality relationships are one of the strongest sources of such feelings. Emotional contagion means that a goodly number of our moods come to us via the interactions we have with other people. In a sense, resonant relationships are like emotional vitamins, sustaining us through tough times and nourishing us daily.

Among people around the world, nourishing relationships are the single most universally agreed-upon feature of the good life. While the specifics vary from culture to culture, all people everywhere deem warm connections with others to be the core feature of "optimal human existence."[3]

As we saw in Chapter 15, the marital researcher John Gottman has found that in a happy, stable marriage a couple experiences about five upbeat interactions for every negative one. Perhaps that same five-to-one ratio is an approximate golden mean for any ongoing connection in our lives. We could, in theory, do an inventory that evaluates the "nutritional" value of each of our relationships.

If, say, the ratio were reversed to five negative for every positive interaction, the relationship would be in urgent need of mending. A negative ratio, of course, does not necessarily mean we should end relationships just because they are sometimes (or even, too often) difficult. The point is to do what we can to alter the troubling behavior for the better, not banish the person. Armies of experts propose solutions here. Some work only if others are willing to try, too. If not, we can still boost our own resilience and social intelligence, so changing our part in the emotional tango.

Of course we also need to weigh how we affect the lives of those close to us. How we impact others speaks to how we fulfill our very responsibilities as caring spouses, relatives, friends, and members of our communities.

An I-You approach to others lets empathy proceed to its natural next step, concerned action. The social brain then acts as our built-in guidance system for charity, good works, and compassionate acts. Given the raw social and economic realities of our time, this caring sensibility in social intelligence may carry an ever greater premium.

SOCIAL ENGINEERING

Martin Buber believed that the growing preponderance of I-It relationships in modern societies threatens human well-being. He warned against the "thingification" of people—the depersonalization of relationships that corrodes our quality of life and the human spirit itself.[4]

One prophetic voice that anticipated Buber was George Herbert Mead, an early twentieth-century American philosopher. Mead originated the idea of the "social self," the sense of identity we form as we see ourselves in the mirror of our relationships. Mead proposed as a singular goal for social progress a "perfected social intelligence," with greatly heightened rapport and mutual understanding.[5]

Such utopian ideals for the human community may seem out of synch with the tragedies and frictions of the twenty-first century.

And the scientific sensibility in general—not just in psychology—has long been uncomfortable with the moral dimension, which many scientists would rather relegate to the humanities, to philosophy, or theology. But the exquisite social responsiveness of the brain demands that we realize that not just our own emotions but our very biology is being driven and molded, for better or for worse, by others—and in turn, that we take responsibility for how we affect the people in our lives.

Buber's message for us today warns against an outlook that is indifferent to how others suffer and that uses social skills for purely selfish ends. And it commends the stance that empathizes and cares, a nurturing outlook that takes responsibility for others as well as for oneself.

That dichotomy has implications for social neuroscience itself. As always, the identical scientific insights can find malign or benign applications. An Orwellian use of social neuroscience findings could be their misapplication in, say, advertising or propaganda; fMRI readings of a target group's response to a given message would be used to fine-tune and amplify the message's emotional impact. In such a scenario the science devolves into a tool that allows media manipulators to drive home exploitative messages ever more powerfully.

That's nothing new: unintended consequences of new inventions are an inevitable underside of technological progress. Each new generation of gadgetry floods society before we can fully know the difference it will make. The next new thing is always a social experiment in progress.

On the other hand, social neuroscientists are already planning far more benign applications. One of them would apply the discovery of a logarithm for empathy—that physiological match during moments of rapport—to train medical residents and psychotherapists to empathize better with patients. Another would use an ingenious fanny pack with physiology-monitoring wireless technology. Patients could wear it at home, twenty-four hours a day; it would automatically send a signal when it recognizes that the patient has begun falling, say, into an episode of depression—a virtual psychiatrist-on-call.[6]

Our emerging understanding of the social brain and the effects of our personal connections on our biology also point to a range of ways we might reengineer social institutions for the better. Given the nourishment offered by wholesome connection, the ways we treat the sick, the elderly, and the imprisoned must be reconsidered.

For the chronically ill or dying, for instance, we might do more than pool volunteers from a patient's family and social circle to help, but also find support for the helpers. For the elderly, who are now so often tucked away in bleak and solitary arrangements, we might instead offer "cohousing," residences where people of all ages live together and share many meals—so re-creating the extended family that harbored the aged through most of human history. And as we've seen, we can refocus our corrections system to affirm decent connections for prisoners rather than cutting them off from the very human ties that could help set them straight.

Then consider those who staff these institutions, from schools to hospitals to prisons. All these sectors are vulnerable to the accountant's delusion that social goals can be assessed by fiscal measures alone. That mentality ignores the emotional connections that drive our very ability to be—and work—at our best.

Leaders need to realize that they themselves set much of the emotional tone that flows through the halls of their organizations, and that this in turn has consequence for how well the collective objectives are met—whether the outcome is measured in achievement test scores, sales goals, or retention of nurses.

And for all of this, as Edward Thorndike proposed in 1920, we need to nurture social wisdom, the qualities that allow the people we connect with to flourish.

THE GROSS NATIONAL HAPPINESS

The small Himalayan kingdom of Bhutan takes seriously their country's "gross national happiness," which they deem as important as the gross domestic product, a standard economic indicator.[7] Public policy, the king declared, should be linked to people's sense of well-being, not just to economics. To be sure, the pillars of national happiness in Bhutan include financial self-reliance, a pristine environment, health care, education preserving local culture, and democracy. But economic growth in itself is just part of the equation.

The gross national happiness is not just for Bhutan: the notion of placing as much or more value on people's happiness and life satisfaction as on economic growth per se has been embraced by a small, but growing, international group of economists. They see as misguided the universal assumption in policy circles worldwide that the consumption of more goods means people feel better off. They are developing new ways to measure well-being in terms not just of income and employment but also of satisfaction with personal relationships and a sense of purpose in life.[8]

Daniel Kahneman noted the well-documented lack of correlation between economic advantages and happiness (apart from a large boost at the very bottom, when people go from being impoverished to being able to make a sparse living).[9] Recently the realization has dawned among economists that their hyperrational models ignore the low road—and emotions in general—and so fail to predict with full precision the choices people will make, let alone what makes them happy.[10]

The term "technological fix"—meaning tech-engineered interventions in human affairs—was coined by Alvin Weinberg, a longtime director of the Oak Ridge National Laboratory and founder of the Institute for Energy Analysis. Weinberg came of age in the science of the 1950s and 1960s, an era given to the utopian vision that coming technologies offered panaceas for a range of human and social ills.[11] One such proposal was a massive system of nuclear power plants that were supposed to lower energy costs radically—and if placed on an ocean shore, provide ample drinking water—so boosting the welfare of entire nations. (Lately a number of environmentalists have endorsed nuclear power as one solution to global warming.)

Now, as he has reached ninety, Weinberg's views have taken a philosophical and cautionary turn. "Technology makes it easier and easier to disconnect from other people, and from ourselves," Weinberg told me. "Civilization is in the midst of a vast singularity. What was once meaningful has been wiped away. Lives are lived sitting in front of a computer screen, getting personal connections at a distance. We live in a metaworld, with our focus fixed on the latest technology. But the issues that matter most are families, community, and social responsibility."

As a presidential science adviser in the 1960s, Weinberg wrote an influential paper on what he called "criteria for scientific choice." The paper introduced the notion that values could guide choices in science spending and were a valid question in the philosophy of science. Now, nearly a half-century later, he has been reflecting further on what's "useful," or worthwhile, in setting a nation's spending priorities. He tells me, "The conventional view holds that capitalism is the only efficient way to allocate resources. But it lacks compassion.

"I wonder whether the possibilities of our economic models are being exhausted—and whether the high level of global unemployment we're seeing is actually structural and very deep, not a passing phenomenon. Perhaps there will always be a sizable—and probably growing—number of people who just can't find good jobs. And then I wonder, how might we modify our system so that it's not just efficient but compassionate?"

Paul Farmer, the public health crusader legendary for his work in Haiti and Africa, also decries the "structural violence" done by an economic system that keeps so many of the world's poor too sick to escape their plight.[12] For Farmer, one solution lies in treating health care as a human right and making its delivery a prime concern rather than an afterthought. Along those lines, Weinberg proposes that "a compassionate capitalism would require us to change priorities, set aside a larger portion of a national budget to good works. Modifying the economic system so that it becomes adequately compassionate would also make it much more stable politically."

The economic theories that currently drive national policies, however, have few ways to take human suffering into account (although the economic costs of disasters like floods or famines are routinely estimated). One of the most graphic results has been policies that burden the poorest countries with such huge debts that they have too little left to pay for food or medical care for their children.

This economic attitude seems mindblind, lacking the ability to imagine the other's reality. Empathy is essential for a compassionate capitalism, one where human misery and its alleviation carry weight.

That argues for building a society's capacity for compassion. For example, economists might do well to study the wider benefits to society of socially intelligent parenting and of school curricula on social and emotional skills, both in the education system and in prisons.[13] Such societywide efforts to optimize the workings of the social brain might cascade into lifetime paybacks both for children and for the communities where they live out their years. These benefits would range, I suspect, from higher achievement in school to better performance at work, from happier and more socially able children to better community safety and lifetime health. And people who are more educated, safer, and healthier contribute the most to any economy.

Grand speculations aside, warmer social connections could have immediate payoffs for us all.

THE RAW BUZZ OF
FELLOW FEELING

The poet Walt Whitman, in his exuberant anthem "I Sing the Body Electric," put it lyrically:

> *I have perceiv'd that to be with those I like is enough,*
> *To stop in company with the rest at evening is enough,*
> *To be surrounded by beautiful, curious, breathing, laughing flesh is enough . . .*
>
> *I do not ask any more delight, I swim in it as in a sea.*
> *There is something in staying close to men and women and looking on them,*
> *and in the contact and odor of them, that pleases the soul well,*
>
> *All things please the soul, but these please the soul well.*

Vitality arises from sheer human contact, especially from loving connections. The people we care about most are an elixir of sorts, an ever-renewing source of energy. The neural exchange between a parent and child, a grandparent and a toddler, between lovers or a satisfied couple, or among good friends, has palpable virtues.

Now that neuroscience can put numbers to that raw buzz of fellow feeling, quantifying its benefits, we must pay attention to the biological impact of social life. The hidden links among our relationships, our brain function, and our very health and well-being are stunning in their implications.

We must reconsider the pat assumption that we are immune to toxic social encounters. Save for the passing stormy mood, we often suppose, our interactions matter little to us at any biological level. But this turns out to be a comforting illusion. Just as we catch a virus from someone else, we may also "catch" an emotional funk that makes us more vulnerable to that same virus or otherwise undermines our well-being.

From this perspective, strong distressing states like disgust, contempt, and explosive anger are the emotional equivalent of second-hand smoke that quietly damages the lungs of others who breathe it in. The interpersonal equivalent of health-boosting would be adding positive emotions to our surroundings.

In this sense, social responsibility begins here and now, when we act in ways that help create optimal states in others, from those we encounter casually to those we love and care about most dearly. In accord with Whitman, one scientist who studies the survival value of sociability says the practical lesson for us all comes down to "Nourish your social connections."[14]

Well and good for our personal lives. But all of us are buffeted by the vast social and political currents of our time. The last century highlighted what divides us, confronting us with the limits to our collective empathy and compassion.

Through most of human history, the bitter antagonisms that stoked hatred between groups were manageable in a strictly logistical sense: The limited means of destruction available kept the damage relatively small. In the twentieth century, however, technology and organizational efficiency made the destructive potential of such hatred immensely greater. As a poet of those times, W. H. Auden, so pungently prophesied, "We must love one another or die."

His stark outlook captures the urgency wrought by hatreds unleashed. But we need not be helpless. That sense of urgency can serve as a collective awakening, reminding us that the crucial challenge for this century will be to expand the circle of those we count among Us, and shrink the numbers we count as Them.

The new science of social intelligence offers us tools that can push those boundaries outward, step by step. For one, we need not accept the divisions that hatred breeds, but rather extend our empathy to understand one another despite our differences, and to bridge those divides. The social brain's wiring connects us all at our common human core.

The High and Low Roads: A Note

The low road operates on automatic, outside our awareness, and with great speed. The high road operates with voluntary control, requires effort and conscious intent, and moves more slowly. The high-low dichotomy as I use it here helps us identify a distinction that clearly matters for behavior, but it may also oversimplify the messily complicated and interwoven circuitry of the brain.[1]

The neural specifics of both systems have yet to be worked out and are still under debate. One helpful summary has been made by Matthew Lieberman of UCLA. Lieberman calls the automatic mode the "X-system" (it includes the amygdala among other neural areas) and the control mode the "C-system" (it includes the anterior cingulate cortex and areas of the prefrontal cortex, as well as others).[2]

These massive systems work in parallel, intermixing automatic and controlled functions in various ratios. As we read, for instance, we decide what to look at and we intentionally reflect on meaning—high-road abilities—while scads of automatic mechanisms perform the countless supporting functions of recognizing pattern, meaning, decoding syntax, and the like. There may, in actuality, be no purely "high-road" mental function, though there are certainly innumerable low-road ones. In point of fact, what I describe here as a dichotomy—high versus low—is in reality a spectrum.

The high- and low-road typology collapses the two dimensions of cognitive-affective and automatic-controlled into a single dimension: automatic-affective and controlled-cognitive. Cases such as intentionally generated emotions (rare, but seen in actors who can emote at will) are set aside for the purposes of this discussion.[3]

The low road's automatic processes appear to be the brain's default mode, whirring along day and night. The high road mainly kicks in when these automatic processes are interrupted—by an unexpected event, by a mistake, or when we intentionally grapple with our thoughts, such as in making a tough decision. In this view, much or most of our stream of thought runs on automatic, handling the routine—while saving what we must mull over, learn, or correct for the high road.

Nevertheless, if we so direct it, the high road can override the low, within limits. That very capacity gives us choice in life.

The Social Brain

In order for a new set of circuitry to arise in the brain, it has to have great value for those possessing it, heightening the chances that its possessor will live to pass that circuitry on through the generations. In the emergence of primates, living in groups was just such an adaptation. All primates live among others who can help meet the demands of life, thus multiplying the resources available to any single member of the group—and putting a premium on smooth social interactions. The social brain seems to be among Nature's adaptive mechanisms for meeting the challenge of survival as part of a group.

What do neuroscientists mean when they speak of a "social brain"? The idea that the brain consists of discrete areas, each in charge of a specific task in isolation, seems as antiquated as those nineteenth-century phrenology charts that "explained" the meaning of bumps in the skull. But in actuality the circuitry for a given mental task is not localized in one place but is distributed throughout the brain; the more complex the task, the wider its distribution.

The zones of the brain interconnect with dizzying complexity, and so phrases like "social brain" are fictions, albeit helpful ones. For convenience, scientists look at orchestrated systems of the brain that cooperate during a given function. So the centers for movement are conceptually grouped together in a shorthand term, the "motor brain"; for the activity of the senses, the "sensory brain." Some "brains" refer to more tightly knit anatomical zones, such as the "reptilian brain," those lower regions that manage automatic reflexes and the like, which are so ancient in evolution that we share them with reptiles. These heuristic labels are most useful when neuroscientists want to focus on higher-order levels of brain organization, the modules and networks of neurons that orchestrate during a specific function.

And so the "social brain"—those extensive neural modules that orchestrate our activities as we relate to other people—consists of circuitry that extends far and wide. There is no single site controlling social interaction anywhere within the brain. Rather, the social brain is a set of distinct but fluid and wide-ranging neural networks that synchronize around relating to others. It operates at the systems level, where far-flung neural networks are coordinated to serve a unifying purpose.

As yet neuroscience has no generally-agreed-upon specific map for the social brain, though converging studies are starting to zero in on areas most often active during social interactions. An early proposal identified structures in the prefrontal area, particularly the orbitofrontal and anterior cingulate cortices, in connection with areas in the subcortex, especially the amygdala.[1] More recent studies show that that proposal remains largely on target, while adding other details.[2]

Given the widely dispersed circuitry of the social brain, precisely which neural networks are involved depends to a great extent on what social activity we engage in. Thus during a simple conversation an array of sites keeps us in synch, while a different (though overlapping) system may activate while we ponder whether we like someone. Here's a quick survey of some findings to date on what circuitry activates during which activity.

Mirror neurons pepper the brain. Those in the prefrontal cortex or parietal areas (and likely elsewhere) handle shared representations—the mental images that spring to mind when we talk with someone about something we are both familiar with. Other mirror neurons involved in movement activate when we simply observe someone else's actions—including the intricate dance of gestures and body shifts that are part of any conversation. Cells in the right parietal operculum that encode kinesthetic and sensory feedback go to work as we orchestrate our own movements in response to our conversational partner.

When it comes to reading and responding to the emotional messages in another's tone of voice, mirror neurons prime circuitry that connects the insula and premotor cortex with the limbic system, particularly the amygdala. As the conversation continues, connections from the amygdala to the brain stem control our autonomic responses, heightening our heart rate should matters heat up.

Neurons in the fusiform area of the temporal lobe are dedicated to recognizing and reading emotions in faces as well as monitoring where a person's gaze has drifted. Somatosensory areas kick in as we sense the other person's state—and as we notice our own in response. And as we send our own emotional messages back, brain stem nuclei projections to our facial nerves create the appropriate frown, smile, or raised eyebrows.

While we attune to the other person, the brain undergoes two varieties of empathy: a fast low-road flow via connections between the sensory cortices, thalamus and amygdala, and on to our response; and a slower high-road flow that runs from the thalamus up to the neocortex and then down to the amygdala and on to our more thoughtful response. Emotional contagion runs through that first pathway, allowing our automatic neural mimicking of the feelings of the other person. But that second pathway, which loops up to the thinking brain, offers a more considered empathy, one that holds the possibility of shutting down our attunement if we choose to.

Here the connection from the limbic circuitry to the OFC and ACC comes into play. These areas are active in perceiving another person's emotion and in fine-tuning our own emotional reaction. The prefrontal cortex in general has the task of modulating our emotions in ways that are appropriate and effective; if what the other person says troubles us, the prefrontal area allows us to continue the conversation and remain focused despite our own upset.

If we have to think over what to make of the other person's emotional message, the dorsolateral and ventromedial prefrontal regions help us ponder what it all means and consider our alternatives. What response, for instance, will work both in the immediate situation and yet be in keeping with our long-term goals?

Beneath all this interpersonal dance, the cerebellum down at the base of the brain has been keeping our attention well targeted so that we can monitor the other person, picking up even subtle cues of fleeting facial expressions. Nonverbal, unconscious synchrony—say, the intricate choreography of a conversation—requires us to pick up an ongoing cascade of social cues. And that in turn depends on ancient structures in the brain stem, particularly the cerebellum and the basal ganglia. Their role in smooth interactions gives these lower-brain areas an ancillary role in the circuitry of the social brain.[3]

All these areas join in the orchestration of social interactions (even imagined ones), and damage to any of them impairs our ability to attune. The more complicated a social interaction, the more complex the interconnected networks of neurons activated. In short, numerous circuits and sites play their role in the social brain—a neural territory that we have barely begun to map in detail.

One way to begin to identify the core circuitry of the social brain might be to outline the minimal neural networks that are engaged during a given social act.[4] For instance, for the bare act of perceiving and imitating the emotions of another person, neuroscientists at UCLA have proposed the following sets of interlocking neural circuitry. The superior temporal cortex allows an initial visual perception of the other person, sending that description to neurons in those parietal areas that can match an observed act with the execution of that act. Then the matching neurons add more sensory and somatic information to the description. This more complex set of data goes to the inferior frontal cortex, which then encodes the goal of the action to be imitated. And then the sensory copies of the actions are sent back to the superior temporal cortex, which monitors the ensuing action.

When it comes to empathy, "hot" affective circuitry must tie in to these "cold" sensory and motor circuits—that is, the emotionally dry sensorimotor system must communicate with the affective center in the limbic system. The UCLA team proposes that the most likely candidate for this connector anatomically seems to be a region of the insula, which ties together limbic areas with parts of the frontal cortex.[5]

Scientists at the National Institute of Mental Health (NIMH) argue that in seeking to map the social brain, we are not talking about a single, unitary neural system but rather interlocking circuits that can work together for some tasks, and on their own for others.[6] For instance, for primal empathy—the direct person-to-person contagion of a feeling—neuroscientists nominate pathways connecting the sensory cortices with the thalamus and the amygdala, and from there to whatever circuits the appropriate response requires. But for cognitive empathy, as we sense the other person's thoughts, the circuits run from thalamus to *cortex* to amygdala, and then to the circuitry for the response.

Then when it comes to empathizing with specific emotions, the NIMH researchers suggest that further distinctions are possible. Some fMRI data suggest, for instance, that there are different pathways for reading another person's fear versus anger. Fearful expressions seem to light up the amygdala but rarely the orbitofrontal cortex, while angry ones activate the OFC and not the amygdala. That difference may relate to the differing function of each emotion: with fear, our attention goes to what has caused the fear, while with anger we focus on what to do to reverse that person's reaction. And when it comes to disgust, the amygdala stays out of the picture; the action instead involves structures in the basal ganglia and anterior insula.[7] All of these emotion-specific circuits activate both when we ourselves experience the given emotion, and when we witness someone else feeling it.

The NIMH scientists propose still other circuitry for one variety of cognitive empathy, not just getting an idea of what the other person's mindset might be but also deciding on what we should do in return. Here the key circuits seem to involve the medial frontal cortex, the superior temporal sulcus, and the temporal lobe.

The link between empathy and our sense of right and wrong has support at the neural level. Studies from patients who have had brain lesions that led them to abandon their previous moral standards, or to be confused when facing a question of right or wrong, suggest that these ethical acts require that the brain areas for evoking and interpreting visceral states be intact.[8] Those brain areas active during moral judgments—a string of circuitry running from parts of the brain stem (particularly the cerebellum) up to areas of the cortex—include the amygdala, thalamus, insula, and upper brain stem. All these areas are involved, too, in perceiving someone else's feelings, as well as our own. An interconnected circuit running between the frontal lobe and the anterior temporal lobe (including the amygdala and the insular cortex) has been proposed as crucial for empathy.

Brain function can be mapped by studying what other abilities are hampered in patients with other neural lesions. For instance, neurological patients with damage to various emotional circuits in the social brain were compared with patients whose lesions were in other areas of the brain.[9] While both groups were equally capable when it came to cognitive tasks, like answering questions on an IQ test, only the patients with compromised emotional areas had poor functioning in their relationships: they made bad interpersonal decisions, misjudged how other people felt, and were incapable of coping with life's social demands.

The patients with these social deficits all had lesions at points within a neural array called the "somatic marker" system by University of Southern California neurologist Antonio Damasio, in whose laboratory the study of the impaired patients was done. Linking areas in the ventromedial prefrontal, parietal, and cingulate areas, as well as the right amygdala and insula, somatic markers operate whenever we make a decision, particularly in our personal and social life.[10] The social abilities fostered by this key part of the social brain are essential for smooth relationships. For example, neurological patients with lesions in the somatic marker circuitry are poor at reading or sending emotional signals and so can readily make disastrous decisions in their relationships.

Damasio's somatic markers strongly overlap with the neural systems cited by Stephanie Preston and Frans de Waal in their perception-action model. Both models propose that when we perceive an emotion in someone else, mirror neurons activate the same neural pathways for that feeling in us, as well as circuitry for the related mental images and actions (or impulse to action). Separate fMRI studies suggest that the insula links the mirroring systems to the limbic area, generating the emotional component of the neural loop.[11]

The specifics of an interaction will, of course, determine which brain areas operate as we respond, as fMRI studies of differing social moments are revealing. For example, brain imaging while volunteers listened to stories about socially embarrassing situations (one told of someone spitting food into a plate at a formal dinner) revealed greater activity in the medial prefrontal cortex and the temporal areas (both activate when we empathize with the mental state of someone else) as well as in the lateral OFC and the medial prefrontal cortex.[12] These same areas become active when the story made the food-spitting involuntary (the person was choking). This neural network appears to handle the more general case of deciding whether a particular action will be socially appropriate, one of the endless small decisions we continually face in interpersonal life.

Clinical studies of neurological patients who fail to make that decision well—and so routinely commit faux pas or otherwise faulty interpersonal activities—show damage to the ventromedial region of the prefrontal cortex. Antoine Bechara, an associate of Damasio, observes that this region plays a crucial role in integrating brain systems for memory, emotion, and feeling; damage here compromises social decision-making. In the study of embarrassing moments, the most active systems suggested an alternative network in a dorsal region of the nearby medial prefrontal cortex—an area that includes the anterior cingulate.[13] This region, Damasio has found, forms a bottleneck interconnecting networks that handle motor planning, movement, emotion, attention, and working memory.

For the neuroscientist, these are all tantalizing clues, and far more needs to be known to untangle the web of the neurology of social life.

APPENDIX C

Rethinking Social Intelligence

The social brain became most highly developed in those species of mammals that live in groups, evolving as a mechanism for survival.[1] The brain systems that mark humans as different from other mammals grew in direct proportion to the size of the primal human bond.[2] Some scientists speculate social prowess—not cognitive superiority or physical advantage—may be what allowed Homo sapiens to eclipse other humanoids.[3]

Evolutionary psychologists argue that the social brain—and hence social intelligence—evolved to meet the challenge of navigating the social currents in a primate group: it equips one to determine who is the alpha male, who one can count on for defense, whom one must please and how (grooming is the usual answer here). In humans, our need to engage in social reasoning—particularly coordination and cooperation as well as competition—drove the evolution of our larger brain size and of intelligence generally.[4]

The major functions of the social brain—interaction synchrony, the types of empathy, social cognition, interaction skills, and concern for others—all suggest strands of social intelligence. The evolutionary perspective challenges us to think afresh about the place of social intelligence in the taxonomy of human abilities—and recognize that "intelligence" can include noncognitive abilities. (Howard Gardner notably made this case in his groundbreaking work on multiple intelligences.)

The new neuroscientific findings on social life have the potential to reinvigorate the social and behavioral sciences. The basic assumptions of economics, for example, have been challenged by the emerging "neuro-economics," which studies the brain during decision-making.[5] Its findings have shaken standard thinking in economics, particularly the notion that people make rational decisions about money that can be modeled by decision-tree–type analyses. Low-road systems, economists now realize, are far more powerful in such decision-making than the purely rational models can predict. Likewise, the field of intelligence theory and testing seems ripe for a rethinking of its basic assumptions.

In recent years social intelligence has been a scientific backwater, largely ignored by social psychologists and students of intelligence alike. One exception has been the boomlet in research on emotional intelligence sparked by the seminal work of John Mayer and Peter Salovey in 1990.[6]

As Mayer pointed out to me, Thorndike's original view saw a triad of mechanical, abstract, and social intelligence, but he subsequently failed to find a way to measure the social. In the 1990s, as the localization of emotions in the brain became better understood, Mayer noted, "Emotional intelligence could be groomed as the replacement member of the triumvirate where social intelligence failed."

The more recent emergence of social neuroscience means the time is ripe for a revival of social intelligence on a par with its sister, emotional intelligence. A rethinking of social intelligence should more fully reflect the operation of the social brain, so adding often-ignored capacities that nonetheless matter immensely for our relationships.

The model of social intelligence I offer in this book is merely suggestive, not definitive, of what that expanded concept might look like. Others may reshuffle its aspects differently or suggest their own; mine is but one of many ways to categorize. More robust and valid models of social intelligence will emerge gradually from cumulative research. My goal is simply to catalyze such fresh thinking.

How Social Intelligence Abilities Fit into the Emotional Intelligence Model

EMOTIONAL INTELLIGENCE	SOCIAL INTELLIGENCE
Self-awareness	**Social awareness** Primal empathy Empathic accuracy Listening Social Cognition
Self-management	**Social facility (or Relationship management)** Synchrony Self-presentation Influence Concern

Some psychologists may complain that the defining capacities of social intelligence I propose add to standard definitions of "intelligence" aptitudes from noncognitive domains. But that is precisely my point: when it comes to intelligence in social life, the brain itself mixes capacities. Noncognitive abilities like primal empathy, synchrony, and concern are immensely adaptive aspects of the human social repertoire for survival. And these capacities certainly allow us better to follow Thorndike's mandate to "act wisely" in our relationships.

The old concept of social intelligence as purely cognitive assumes, as many early intelligence theorists claimed, that social intelligence may be no different from general intelligence itself. Some cognitive scientists would no doubt argue that the two abilities are identical. After all, their discipline models mental life on the computer, and modules for processing information run along purely rational lines, following computational logic.

But an exclusive focus on mental abilities in social intelligence ignores the invaluable roles of both affect and the low road. I suggest a perspective shift, one that looks beyond mere knowing *about* social life to include the automatic abilities that matter so much as we engage, both high road and low. The various theories of social intelligence currently in vogue detail these intertwined capacities only spottily and to quirkily varying degrees.

Intelligence theorists' views on the social aptitudes for life can be better understood in light of their field's history. In 1920, when Edward Thorndike first proposed the concept of social intelligence, the newfangled concept of "IQ" was still shaping the thinking of an equally novel field, psychometrics, that aimed to find ways to measure human abilities. In those heady days psychology's recent successes in sorting out the millions of U.S. soldiers by IQ during the First World War, and so assigning them to tasks and posts they could handle effectively, aroused understandable excitement.

Early theorists of social intelligence sought to find an analog of IQ that applied to talent in social life. Guided by the nascent field of psychometrics, they looked for ways to assess differences in social aptitudes that would be the equivalent of, say, the differences in spatial and verbal reasoning measured by IQ.

Those early attempts fizzled, largely because they seemed to measure only people's intellectual grasp of social situations. For instance, one early test of social intelligence assessed cognitive abilities like identifying what social situation a given sentence would be most appropriate for. In the late 1950s David Wechsler, who developed one of the most widely used measures of IQ, basically dismissed the importance of social intelligence, seeing it merely as "general intelligence applied to social situations."[7] That judgment suffused psychology, and social intelligence dropped off the major maps of human intelligence.

One exception was the complex model of intelligence put forth by J. P. Guilford in the late 1960s; he enumerated 120 separate intellectual abilities, thirty of which had to do with social intelligence.[8] But despite extensive efforts, the Guilford approach was unable to yield meaningful predictions of how well people actually operated in the social world. More recent models relevant to social intelligence—Robert Sternberg's "practical intelligence" and Howard Gardner's "interpersonal intelligence"—have gained more traction.[9] But a cohesive theory of social intelligence that clearly distinguishes it from IQ and that has practical applications has eluded psychology.

The old view saw social intelligence as the application of general intelligence to social situations—a largely cognitive aptitude. This approach casts social intelligence merely as a fund of knowledge about the social world. But this approach makes this capacity no different from "g," general intelligence itself.

But what, then, distinguishes social intelligence from g? There is no good answer as yet to this challenge. One reason is that psychology as a profession is a scientific subculture, one into which people are socialized as they go through graduate school and other professional training. As a result psychologists tend to view the world largely through the mental lens of the field itself. This tendency, however, may be skewing psychology's ability to comprehend the true nature of social intelligence.

When ordinary people were asked to list what makes a person intelligent, social competence emerged as a prominant natural category. But when psychologists who were considered experts on intelligence were asked to come up with a similar list, their emphasis was on cognitive abilities like verbal and problem-solving skills.[10] Wechsler's dismissive view of social intelligence seems to live on in the implicit assumptions of his field.

Psychologists who sought to measure social intelligence have been stymied by startlingly high correlations between their results and the results of IQ tests, suggesting there may be no real difference between cognitive and social talent.[11] This was a major reason social intelligence research was largely abandoned. But that problem seems to result from the skewed definition of social intelligence as simply cognitive ability applied to the social arena.

That approach assesses interpersonal talent in terms of what people claim to know, asking whether people agree with assertions like "I can understand other people's behavior" and "I know how my actions make other people feel."

Those questions come from a recently developed social intelligence scale.[12] The psychologists who constructed the test asked fourteen other professors of psychology, a so-called "expert panel," to define social intelligence. The resulting definition was "the ability to understand other people and how they will react to different social situations"—in other words, pure social cognition.[13] Even so, the psychologists knew that definition would not suffice. So they made up some questions getting at how people actually get on socially, such as asking them if they agree with the assertion "It takes a long time before I get to know other people well."

But their test, like others, would do well to go further and assess the low-road abilities that matter so much for a rich life. Social neuroscience is detailing how multiple ways of knowing and doing spring into action as we engage with others. These ways include high-road abilities like social cognition, to be sure. But social intelligence also calls on low-road functions like synchrony and attunement, social intuition and empathic concern, and arguably, the impulse for compassion. Our ideas of what makes a person intelligent in social life would be more complete if they encompassed these abilities as well.

Such abilities are nonverbal, and they occur in the span of

microseconds, more quickly than the mind can formulate thoughts about them. Though low-road abilities may seem trivial to some, they shape the very platform for a smooth social life. Since low-road abilities are nonverbal, they elude what can be picked up in a paper-and-pencil test—and most current tests for social intelligence are such.[14] In effect, they quiz the high road about the low, a questionable tactic.

Colwyn Trevarthen, the developmental psychologist at the University of Edinburgh, argues compellingly that the widely accepted notions of social cognition create profound misunderstandings of human relations and the place of emotions in social life.[15] While cognitive science has served well in linguistics and artificial intelligence, it has limits when applied to human relationships. It neglects noncognitive capacities like primal empathy and synchrony that connect us to other people. The affective revolution (let alone the social one) in cognitive neuroscience has yet to reach intelligence theory.

A more robust measure of social intelligence would include not only high-road approaches (for which questionnaires are fine) but also low-road measures like the PONS or Ekman's test for reading microexpressions.[16] Or it could put test-takers in simulations of social situations (perhaps via virtual reality), or at least obtain other people's views of a test-taker's social abilities. Only then would we arrive at a more adequate profile of someone's social intelligence.[17]

In a little-remarked scientific embarrassment, IQ tests themselves have no underlying theoretical rationale supporting them. Rather, they were designed ad hoc, to predict success in the classroom. As John Kihlstrom and Nancy Cantor observe, the IQ test is almost entirely atheoretical; it was merely constructed to "model the sorts of things which children do in school."[18]

But schools themselves are a very recent artifact of civilization. The more powerful force in the brain's architecture is arguably the need to navigate the social world, not the need to get A's. Evolutionary theorists argue that social intelligence was the primordial talent of the human brain, reflected in our outsize cortex, and that what we now think of as "intelligence" piggybacked on neural systems used for getting along in a complex group. Those who would say that social intelligence amounts to little more than general intelligence applied to social situations might do better to reason the other way around: to consider that general intelligence is merely a derivative of social intelligence, albeit one our culture has come to value highly.

─── | A C K N O W L E D G M E N T S | ───

Many people have contributed to my thinking in preparing this book, though the conclusions drawn are my own. I owe a particular debt of gratitude to those topic experts who reviewed sections of my book, especially: Cary Cherniss of Rutgers University; Jonathan Cohen, Princeton University; John Crabbe, Oregon Health and Science Center and Portland VA Hospital; John Cacioppo, University of Chicago; Richard Davidson, University of Wisconsin; Owen Flanagan, Duke University; Denise Gottfredson, University of Maryland; Joseph LeDoux, New York University; Matthew Lieberman, UCLA; Kevin Ochsner, Columbia University; Phillip Shaver, University of California at Davis; Ariana Vora, Harvard Medical School; and Jeffrey Walker, JPMorgan Partners. If readers find factual errors in the text, please notify me through my website (www.Danielgoleman.info), and I will endeavor to correct them in future printings.

Among others who sparked my thinking, I thank:

Elliot Aronson, Stanford University; Neal Ashkanasy, University of Queensland, Brisbane, Australia; Warren Bennis, USC; Richard Boyatzis, Case Western Reserve University; Sheldon Cohen, Carnegie Mellon University; Jonathan Cott, New York City; Frans de Waal, Emory University; Georges Dreyfus, Williams College; Mark Epstein, New York City; Howard Gardner, Harvard University; Paul Ekman, University of California at San Francisco; John Gottman, University of Washington; Sam Harris, UCLA; Fred Gage, Salk Institute; Layne Habib, Shokan, N.Y.; Judith Hall, Northeastern University; Kathy Hall,

American International College; Judith Jordan, Wellesley College; John Kolodin, Hadley, Mass.; Jerome Kagan, Harvard University; Daniel Kahneman, Princeton University; Margaret Kemeny, University of California at San Francisco; John Kihlstrom, U.C. Berkeley; George Kohlrieser, International Institute for Management Development, Lausanne, Switzerland; Robert Levenson, University of California at Berkeley; Carey Lowell, New York City; Beth Lown, Harvard Medical School; Pema Latshang, New York City Department of Education; Annie Mckee, Teleos Leadership Institute; Carl Marci, Harvard Medical School; John Mayer, University of New Hampshire; Michael Meaney, McGill University; Mario Mikulincer, Bar-Ilian University, Ramat Gan, Israel; Mudita Nisker and Dan Clurman, Communication Options; Stephen Nowicki, Emory University; Stephanie Preston, University of Iowa Hospitals and Clinics; Hersh Shefrin, University of Santa Clara; Thomas Pettigrew, University of California at Santa Cruz; Stefan Rechstaffen, Omega Institute; Ronald Riggio, Claremont McKenna College; Robert Rosenthal, University of California at Riverside; Susan Rosenbloom, Drew University; John F. Sheridan, Ohio State University; Joan Strauss, Massachusetts General Hospital; Daniel Siegel, UCLA; David Spiegel, Stanford Medical School; Ervin Staub, University of Massachusetts; Daniel Stern, University of Geneva; Erica Vora, St. Cloud State University; David Sluyter, Fetzer Institute; Leonard Wolf, New York City; Alvin Weinberg, Institute for Energy Analysis (retired); Robin Youngson, Clinical Leaders Association of New Zealand.

Rachel Brod, my principal researcher, provided easy access to far-flung scientific sources. A huge thank-you goes to Rowan Foster, who's always ready for what's needed and who keeps everything running smoothly. Toni Burbank continues to be a superb editor and pleasure to work with. And as always, I feel endless gratitude to Tara Bennett-Goleman, remarkably insightful partner in writing and in life, and a guide to social intelligence.

---------------------------------| **N O T E S** |---------------------------------

Prologue: Unveiling a New Science

1. The soldiers at the mosque were reported on *All Things Considered,* National Public Radio, April 4, 2003.

2. On least force necessary, see, for example, law enforcement competence models in *MOSAIC Competencies: Professional & Administrative Occupations* (U.S. Office of Personnel Management, 1996); Elizabeth Brondolo et al., "Correlates of Risk for Conflict Among New York City Traffic Agents," in Gary VandenBos and Elizabeth Bulatao, eds., *Violence on the Job* (Washington, D.C.: American Psychological Association Press, 1996).

3. To see the way this expands our discourse, consider empathy versus rapport. Empathy is an individual ability, one that resides within the person. But rapport arises only *between* people, as a property that emerges from their interaction.

4. My intent here, as in *Emotional Intelligence,* is to offer what I see as a new paradigm for psychology and its inevitable partner, neuroscience. While the concept of emotional intelligence has met with pockets of resistance in psychology, the notion has also been embraced by many others—most particularly by a generation of graduate students who have made it the focus of their own research. Any science advances through the pursuit of provocative and fruitful ideas rather than the lockstep pursuit of safe but sterile topics. My hope is that the new understanding of relationships and the social brain presented here will stimulate a similar tide of research and exploration. This refocusing on what happens in interactions, as opposed to within the person, as the basic unit of study has been called for, but largely neglected, within psychology. See, for example, Frank Bernieri et al., "Synchrony, Pseudosynchrony, and Dissynchrony: Measuring the Entrainment Prosody in Mother-Infant Interactions," *Journal of Personality and Social Psychology* 2 (1988), pp. 243–53.

5. On tantrums, see Cynthia Garza, "Young Students Seen as Increasingly Hostile," *Fort Worth Star-Telegram,* August 15, 2004, p. 1A.

6. The American Academy of Pediatrics recommends that children under age two not watch TV at all and that older children watch no more than two hours a day.

The report on television and toddlers was presented by Laura Certain at the Pediatric Academic Societies annual meeting, Baltimore, April 30, 2003.

7. Robert Putnam, *Bowling Alone* (New York: Simon & Schuster, 2000).

8. Cited in "The Glue of Society," *Economist,* July 16, 2005, pp. 13–17.

9. On Hot & Crusty, see Warren St. John, "The World at Ear's Length," *New York Times,* February 15, 2004, sec. 9, p. 1.

10. The data on checking e-mail are cited in Anne Fisher, "Does Your Employer Help You Stay Healthy?" *Fortune,* July 12, 2005, p. 60.

11. Global average TV viewing was reported by Eurodata TV Worldwide, *One Television Year in the World: 2004 Issue* (Paris: Médiamétrie, 2004).

12. On Internet use, see Norman H. Nie, "What Do Americans Do on the Internet?" Stanford Institute for the Quantitative Study of Society, online at www.stanford. edu/group/siqss; rcportcd in John Markoff, "Internet Use Said to Cut into TV Viewing and Socializing," *New York Times,* December 30, 2004.

13. The earliest reference to the term "social neuroscience" I have found as yet is in a 1992 article by John Cacioppo and Gary Berntson. See "Social Psychological Contributions to the Decade of the Brain: Doctrine of Multilevel Analysis," *American Psychologist* 47 (1992), pp. 1019–28. The year 2001 saw the publication of an article hailing the emergence of this new discipline under an alternative term, "social cognitive neuroscience," by Matthew Lieberman (now at UCLA) and Kevin Ochsner (now at Columbia University). See Matthew Lieberman and Kevin Ochsner, "The Emergence of Social Cognitive Neuroscience," *American Psychologist* 56 (2001), pp. 717–34. Daniel Siegel coined the phrase "interpersonal neurobiology" to link the interpersonal and neurobiological dimensions of the human mind so that we can understand the development of mental well-being in a fuller way; this marks another root of social neuroscience. See Daniel Siegel, *The Developing Mind: How Relationships and the Brain Interact to Shape Who We Are* (New York: Guilford Press, 1999).

14. It has taken a decade for social neuroscience to reach critical mass as a field, but now there are dozens of scientific laboratories dedicated to this research. The first conference on Social Cognitive Neuroscience was held at UCLA, April 28–30, 2001, with thirty speakers and more than three hundred attendees from several countries. In 2004 Thomas Insel, director of the National Institute for Mental Health, declared that a decade of research had by then demonstrated that social neuroscience had come of age as a field. The search for the social brain, he predicted, would yield data valuable for the public good. See Thomas Insel and Russell Fernald, "How the Brain Processes Social Information: Searching for the Social Brain," *Annual Review of Neuroscience* 27 (2004), pp. 697–722. In 2007 Oxford University Press will launch a journal called *Social Neuroscience,* the field's first.

15. The phrase "social brain" has come into common usage in neuroscience within the last few years. For instance, an international science conference on "The Social Brain" was held in Goteborg, Sweden, March 25–27, 2003. The same year saw publication of the first scholarly collection on the subject, Martin Brüne et al., *The Social Brain: Evolution and Pathology* (Sussex, U.K.: John Wiley, 2003). The first international conference on the social brain was held in Germany, at the University of Bochum, in November 2000.

16. For the original definition of social intelligence, see Edward Thorndike, "Intelligence and Its Use," *Harper's Magazine* 140 (1920), pp. 227–35, at 228.

17. A caveat: Those readers seeking the standard review of the psychological concept "social intelligence" will not find it here; for that, I recommend the excellent summary by John Kihlstrom and Nancy Cantor. My intention here is to encourage a new generation of psychologists to expand beyond the limits of present concepts by integrating findings from social neuroscience, rather than adhere lockstep to the stan-

dard categories psychology has called "social intelligence." See John Kihlstrom and Nancy Cantor, "Social Intelligence," in Robert Sternberg, ed., *Handbook of Intelligence,* 2nd ed. (Cambridge, U.K.: Cambridge University Press, 2000), pp. 359–79.

18. Thorndike, "Intelligence," p. 228.

PART I

Chapter 1. The Emotional Economy

1. When I refer to the amygdala or any other specific neural structure, I usually mean not just that region but its connective circuitry to other neural areas as well. The exception occurs when I discuss some aspect of the structure itself.

2. Brooks Gump and James Kulik, "Stress, Affiliation, and Emotional Contagion," *Journal of Personality and Social Psychology* 72, no. 2 (1997), pp. 305–19.

3. This investigative function gets carried out through the amygdala's links to the cortex, which guides our attention to explore uncertainties. When the amygdala starts firing in reaction to a possible threat, it directs cortical centers to fixate our attention on the possible danger, and we feel distress, uneasiness, or even a bit frightened as it does so. So if someone has a high level of amygdala activation, their world is an ambiguous and perpetually threatening place. A devastating trauma, like being mugged, can ratchet up the amygdala's vigilance of the world, heightening levels of the neurotransmitters that keep us scanning for threats. Most of the symptoms of post-traumatic stress disorder, like overreaction to neutral events that are vaguely reminiscent of the original trauma, are signs of such an overreactive amygdala. See Dennis Charney et al., "Psychobiologic Mechanisms of Posttraumatic Stress Disorder," *Archives of General Psychiatry* 50 (1993), pp. 294–305.

4. See, for example, Beatrice de Gelder et al., "Fear Fosters Flight: A Mechanism for Fear Contagion When Perceiving Emotion Expressed by a Whole Body," *Proceedings of the National Academy of Sciences* 101, no. 47 (2004), pp. 16, 701–06.

5. At least that's one way we recognize emotion. The existence of other neural routes might mean, for instance, that we don't have to feel happy to recognize that someone else does.

6. Affective blindsight, in which a functionally blind person with certain brain lesions can register another person's emotions from facial expressions via the amygdala, has been found in other patients, too. See, e.g., J. S. Morris et al., "Differential Extrageniculostriate and Amygdala Responses to Presentation of Emotional Faces in a Cortically Blind Field," *Brain* 124, no. 6 (2001), pp. 1241–52.

7. The classic work on emotional contagion is Elaine Hatfield et al., *Emotional Contagion* (Cambridge, U.K.: Cambridge University Press, 1994).

8. The high road, however, can be used to intentionally generate an emotion; actors do so routinely. Another example is the systematic generation of compassion in religious practices; this purposeful generation of positive emotion uses the high road to drive the low.

9. Of course, cognition and emotion are usually not at odds. Most of the time the "high road" and the "low road" act synergistically, or at least weave closely parallel paths to the same place. Likewise, cognition and emotion typically work seamlessly together, to motivate and guide our behavior toward reaching our goals. But in some circumstances they diverge. These divergences produce the idiosyncrasies and seemingly irrational behaviors that have so puzzled behavioral scientists (including psychologists and economists). They also tell us much about the distinct characteristics of these two constituent systems in our brain—when two systems are working closely together, it is hard to tell what is contributing what; when they are in competition, it is easier to distinguish the contribution made by each.

10. The amygdala, in the midbrain below the cortex, handles automatic emotional processes; the prefrontal cortex, in its executive function, draws inputs from many other neural regions, integrates them, and makes plans accordingly. See Timothy Shallice and Paul Burgess, "The Domain of Supervisory Processes and Temporal Organization of Behaviour," *Philosophical Transactions of the Royal Society B: Biological Sciences* 351 (1996), pp. 1405–12.

11. The high road, however, is not immune to bias and perceptual skewing. On the high versus the low road, see Mark Williams et al., "Amygdala Responses to Fearful and Happy Facial Expressions Under Conditions of Binocular Suppression," *Journal of Neuroscience* 24, no. 12 (2004), pp. 2898–904.

12. For the two modes, see John Dewey, *Experience and Nature* (LaSalle, Ill., 1925), p. 256.

13. Roland Neumann and Fritz Strack, " 'Mood Contagion': The Automatic Transfer of Mood Between Persons," *Journal of Personality and Social Psychology* 79, no. 2 (2000), pp. 3022–514.

14. On facial mimicry of emotions, see Ulf Dimberg and Monika Thunberg, "Rapid Facial Reactions to Emotional Facial Expression," *Scandinavian Journal of Psychology* 39 (2000), pp. 39–46; Ulf Dimberg, "Facial EMG and Emotional Reactions," *Psychophysiology* 27 (1990), pp. 481–94.

15. See Ulf Dimberg, Monika Thunberg, and Kurt Elmehed, "Unconscious Facial Reactions to Emotional Facial Expressions," *Psychological Science* 11 (2000), pp. 86–89.

16. Edgar Allan Poe is quoted in Robert Levenson et al., "Voluntary Facial Action Generates Emotion-Specific Autonomic Nervous System Activity," *Psychophysiology* 27 (1990), pp. 363–84.

17. David Denby, "The Quick and the Dead," *New Yorker* 80 (March 29, 2004), pp. 103–05.

18. On the way movies play the brain, see Uri Hasson et al., "Intersubject Synchronization of Cortical Activity During Natural Vision," *Science* 303, no. 5664 (2004), pp. 1634–40.

19. On salience and attention, see, for example, Stephanie D. Preston and Frans B. M. de Waal, "Empathy: Its Ultimate and Proximate Bases," *Behavioral and Brain Sciences* 25 (2002), pp. 1–20.

20. Our brains are preprogrammed to pay maximal attention to such cues presumably because in the wild, moments of perceptual and emotional intensity may signal danger. In today's world, though, they may simply signal what's playing tonight.

21. Emily Butler et al., "The Social Consequences of Expressive Suppression," *Emotion* 3, no. 1 (2003), pp. 48–67.

22. That very attempt at suppression spurs repetitive thoughts about the matter; such thoughts intrude when we are trying to focus on something else or merely relax. Despite our desire to exert voluntary control and veto our natural impulses, we can't always do so 100 percent. If we intentionally suppress our heartfelt emotions— putting on a placid face when we actually feel troubled—our feelings leak nonetheless. Rapport grows stronger as we more openly show our feelings to others. By the same token, the more we try to suppress those feelings, and the stronger those hidden feelings are, the more we inadvertently heighten the tension in the air—a feeling familiar to anyone whose partner "hides" strongly felt emotions. On the costs of suppression see E. Kennedy-Moore and J. C. Watson, "How and When Does Emotional Expression Help?" *Review of General Psychology* 5 (2001), pp. 187–212.

23. The neural radar converged on the ventromedial area of the prefrontal cortex. See

Jean Decety and Thierry Chaminade, "Neural Correlates of Feeling Sympathy," *Neuropsychologia* 41 (2003), pp. 127–38.

24. On trustworthiness, see Ralph Adolphs et al., "The Human Amygdala in Social Judgment," *Nature* 393 (1998), pp. 410–74.

25. On wiring for trust, see J. S. Winston et al., "Automatic and Intentional Brain Responses During Evaluation of Trustworthiness of Faces," *Nature Neuroscience* 5, no. 3 (2002), pp. 277–83. In short, the amygdala scans everyone we meet, making an automatic judgment of trustworthiness. When it judges someone "untrustworthy," the right insula activates to transmit that to the viscera, and the face-responsive region of the fusiform gyrus lights up. The orbitofrontal cortex responds more strongly when the amygdala judges someone "trustworthy." The right superior temporal sulcus operates as an association cortex to process the verdict, which is then labeled by the emotional systems, including the amygdala and orbitofrontal cortex.

26. On gaze direction and lies, see Paul Ekman, *Telling Lies: Clues to Deceit in the Marketplace, Politics, and Marriage* (New York: W.W. Norton, 1985).

27. On clues to lying, see ibid.

28. On cognitive control and lying, see Sean Spence, "The Deceptive Brain," *Journal of the Royal Society of Medicine* 97 (2004), pp. 6–9. Lies demand extra cognitive and emotional effort from neural circuitry. This finding has spawned the notion that an fMRI could one day be used as a lie detector. But that day will come only after those using this imaging technology have solved knotty logistical challenges, such as the artifacts created in the signal by someone speaking.

29. On the way the partner with less power converges more, see Cameron Anderson, Dacher Keltner, and Oliver P. John, "Emotional Convergence Between People over Time," *Journal of Personality and Social Psychology* 84, no. 5 (2003), pp. 1054–68.

30. Frances La Barre, *On Moving and Being Moved: Nonverbal Behavior in Clinical Practice* (Hillsdale, N.J.: Analytic Press, 2001).

31. Though in the 1950s and 1960s there was a spate of psychophysiological studies of two people interacting, the methods of the time were not precise or powerful enough, and the line of research faded away, not to be revived until the 1990s.

32. On empathy and shared physiology, see Robert Levinson and Anna Ruef, "Empathy: A Physiological Substrate," *Journal of Personality and Social Psychology* 63 (1992), pp. 234–46.

Chapter 2. A Recipe for Rapport

1. On the study of psychotherapy, see Stuart Ablon and Carl Marci, "Psychotherapy Process: The Missing Link," *Psychological Bulletin* 130 (2004), pp. 664–68; Carl Marci et al., "Physiologic Evidence for the Interpersonal Role of Laughter During Psychotherapy," *Journal of Nervous and Mental Disease* 192 (2004), pp. 689–95.

2. For the ingredients of rapport, see Linda Tickle-Degnan and Robert Rosenthal, "The Nature of Rapport and Its Nonverbal Correlates," *Psychological Inquiry* 1, no. 4 (1990), pp. 285–93.

3. Frank J. Bernieri and John S. Gillis, "Judging Rapport," in Judith A. Hall and Frank J. Bernieri, *Interpersonal Sensitivity: Theory and Measurement* (Mahwah, N.J.: Erlbaum, 2001).

4. For rapport to bloom, full attention, positive feelings, and synchrony must arise in tandem. A boxing bout involves close physical coordination without positivity. Likewise, a marital tiff involves mutual attention and a bit of coordination devoid of affection. The combination of mutual attention and coordination devoid of positive feeling is typical of strangers walking toward each other on a crowded

sidewalk: they can brush past without colliding while taking no interest in each other.

5. On wincing and eye contact, see J. B. Bavelas et al., "I *Show* How You Feel: Motor Mimicry as a Communicative Act," *Journal of Social and Personality Psychology* 50 (1986), pp. 322–29. Likewise, to the degree that mutual focus becomes a joint absorption—as in an engrossing conversation—the entry of a third person will break the conversational spell.

6. On negative feedback with positive expression, see Michael J. Newcombe and Neal M. Ashkanasy, "The Code of Affect and Affective Congruence in Perceptions of Leaders: An Experimental Study," *Leadership Quarterly* 13 (2002), pp. 601–04.

7. Systematic studies of tipping find that the biggest tips for what customers perceive as better service come in the evening. In one study, the best-tipped waitress earned an average of 17 percent of the bill, while the lowest earned 12 percent. Averaged over a year, that would amount to a substantial difference in income. See Michael Lynn and Tony Simons, "Predictors of Male and Female Servers' Average Tip Earnings," *Journal of Applied Social Psychology* 30 (2000), pp. 241–52.

8. On matching and rapport, see Tanya Chartrand and John Bargh, "The Chameleon Effect: The Perception-Behavior Link and Social Behavior," *Journal of Personality and Social Psychology* 76 (1999), pp. 893–910.

9. On faking mimicry, the study was done by a student of Frank Bernieri and was reported in Mark Greer, "The Science of Savoir Faire," *Monitor on Psychology,* January 2005.

10. On moving in synch, see Frank Bernieri and Robert Rosenthal, "Interpersonal Coordination: Behavior Matching and Interactional Synchrony," in Robert Feldman and Bernard Rimé, *Fundamentals of Nonverbal Behavior* (New York: Cambridge University Press, 1991).

11. While strangers, even on a first meeting, can manage suitable nonverbal coordination, getting in synch heightens with familiarity. Old friends most readily fall into a smooth nonverbal duet, in part because they know each other well enough to adapt to personal quirks that might throw others off.

12. On breathing during conversation, see David McFarland, "Respiratory Markers of Conversational Interaction," *Journal of Speech, Language, and Hearing Research* 44 (2001), pp. 128–45.

13. On teacher-student rapport, see M. LaFrance, "Nonverbal Synchrony and Rapport: Analysis by Cross-lag Panel Technique," *Social Psychology Quarterly* 42 (1979), pp. 66–70; M. LaFrance and M. Broadbent, "Group Rapport: Posture Sharing as a Nonverbal Behavior," in Martha Davis, ed., *Interaction Rhythms* (New York: Human Sciences Press, 1982). The workings of this choreography can sometimes be counterintuitive; rapport actually feels stronger in a face-to-face interaction when the mimicking looks as it does in a mirror—that is, when person A lifts a right arm in response to person B lifting his left.

14. On the musicians' brains in synchrony: E. Roy John, personal communication.

15. On adaptive oscillators, see R. Port and T. Van Gelder, *Mind as Motion: Explorations in the Dynamics of Cognition* (Cambridge, Mass.: MIT Press, 1995).

16. On models for synchrony, see D. N. Lee, "Guiding Movements by Coupling Taus," *Ecological Psychology* 10 (1998), pp. 221–50.

17. For an overview of the research, see Bernieri and Rosenthal, "Interpersonal Coordination."

18. This movement-to-speech synchrony can be extraordinarily subtle. For example,

it is more likely to occur early in "phonemic clauses," the natural chunks of a sequence of syllables that are held together as a single unit of pitch, rhythm, and loudness. (A speaker's words fall into chains of such clauses, each ending with a barely perceptible slowing of speech before the next one begins.) See ibid.

19. On limb-to-limb synchrony, see Richard Schmidt, "Effects of Visual and Verbal Interaction on Unintended Interpersonal Coordination," *Journal of Experimental Psychology: Human Perception and Performance* 31 (2005), pp. 62–79.

20. Joseph Jaffe et al., "Rhythms of Dialogue in Infancy," *Monographs of the Society for Research in Child Development* 66, ser. no. 264 (2001). At around four months babies shift their interest from someone's actions that are perfectly timed to their own to actions that are coordinated but imperfectly timed with theirs—an indication that their inner oscillators are becoming able to better synchronize with the timing. See G. Gergely and J. S. Watson, "Early Socio-Emotional Development: Contingency Perception and the Social Feedback Model," in Philippe Rochat, ed., *Early Social Cognition* (Hillsdale, N.J.: Erlbaum, 1999).

21. On mother-infant interaction, see Beatrice Beebe and Frank M. Lachmann, "Representation and Internalization in Infancy: Three Principles of Salience," *Psychoanalytic Psychology* 11 (1994), pp. 127–66.

22. Colwyn Trevarthen, "The Self Born in Intersubjectivity: The Psychology of Infant Communicating," in Ulric Neisser, ed., *The Perceived Self: Ecological and Interpersonal Sources of Self-knowledge* (New York: Cambridge University Press, 1993), pp. 121–73.

Chapter 3. Neural WiFi

1. On fear, mimicry, and contagion, see Brooks Gump and James Kulik, "Stress, Affiliation, and Emotional Contagion," *Journal of Personality and Social Psychology* 72 (1997), pp. 305–19.

2. See, for example, Paul J. Whalen et al., "A Functional MRI Study of Human Amygdala Responses to Facial Expressions of Fear Versus Anger," *Emotion* 1 (2001), pp. 70–83; J. S. Morris et al., "Conscious and Unconscious Emotional Learning in the Human Amygdala," *Nature* 393 (1998), pp. 467–70.

3. The person who sees the face of someone in terror experiences the same inner arousal but less intensely. One main difference is in their level of autonomic nervous system reactivity, which is maximal in the terrorized person and far weaker in the one who sees that person. The more the witness's insula activates, the stronger their emotional response.

4. On mimicry, see J. A. Bargh, M. Chen, and L. Burrows, "Automaticity of Social Behavior: Direct Effects of Trait Construct and Stereotype Activation on Action," *Journal of Personality and Social Psychology* 71 (1996), pp. 230–44.

5. On speed of perception of fear, see Luiz Pessoa et al., "Visual Awareness and the Detection of Fearful Faces," *Emotion* 5 (2005), pp. 243–47.

6. For the discovery of mirror neurons, see G. di Pelligrino et al., "Understanding Motor Events: A Neurophysiological Study," *Experimental Brain Research* 91 (1992), pp. 176–80.

7. On the pinprick neuron, see W. D. Hutchinson et al., "Pain-related Neurons in the Human Cingulate Cortex," *Nature Neuroscience* 2 (1999), pp. 403–05. Other fMRI studies find that the identical brain areas activate when a person observes a finger movement and when they make that same movement; in one, activity was highest when the person made the movement in response to someone else doing so—that is, when mimicking the person: Marco Iacoboni et al., "Cortical Mechanisms of Human Imitation," *Science* 286 (1999), pp. 2526–28. On the other hand, some studies have found that observing a movement activated a different set of neural areas than did imagining making the movement; the interpretation

was that the areas involved in recognition of movements differ from those that contribute to the actual production of the movement—in this case, grasping an object. See S. T. Grafton et al., "Localization of Grasp Representations in Humans by PET: Observation Compared with Imagination," *Experimental Brain Research* 112 (1996), pp. 103–11.

8. On mirroring in humans, see, for example, L. Fadiga et al., "Motor Facilitation During Action Observation: A Magnetic Stimulation Study," *Journal of Neurophysiology* 73 (1995), pp. 2608–26.

9. That blocking is by inhibitory neurons in the prefrontal cortex. Patients with damage in this prefrontal circuitry are notoriously uninhibited, saying or doing whatever pops into their head. The prefrontal areas may have direct inhibitory connections, or posterior cortical regions that have local inhibitory connections may be activated.

10. To date, mirror neurons have been found in several areas of the human brain in addition to the premotor cortex, including the posterior parietal lobe, the superior temporal sulcus, and the insula.

11. On mirror neurons in humans, see Iacoboni et al., "Cortical Mechanisms."

12. See Kiyoshe Nakahara and Yasushi Miyashita, "Understanding Intentions: Through the Looking Glass," *Science* 308 (2005), pp. 644–45; Leonardo Fogassi, "Parietal Lobe: From Action Organization to Intention Understanding," *Science* 308 (2005), pp. 662–66.

13. See Stephanie D. Preston and Frans de Waal, "The Communication of Emotions and the Possibility of Empathy in Animals," in Stephen G. Post et al., eds., *Altruism and Altruistic Love: Science, Philosophy, and Religion in Dialogue* (New York: Oxford University Press, 2002).

14. If another person's actions hold high emotional interest for us, we automatically make a slight gesture or facial expression that reveals that we feel the same. This "preview" of a feeling or movement, some neuroscientists suggest, may have been essential for the development of language and communication among humans. One theory holds that in prehistory, the evolution of language stemmed from the activities of mirror neurons, initially for an idiom of gesture and then a vocal form. See Giacomo Rizzolatti and M. A. Arbib, "Language Within Our Grasp," *Trends in Neuroscience* 21 (1998), pp. 188–94.

15. Giacomo Rizzolatti is quoted in Sandra Blakelee, "Cells That Read Minds," *New York Times,* January 10, 2006, p. C3.

16. Daniel Stern, *The Present Moment in Psychotherapy and Everyday Life* (New York: W.W. Norton, 2004), p. 76.

17. Paul Ekman, *Telling Lies: Clues to Deceit in the Marketplace, Politics, and Marriage* (New York: W.W. Norton, 1985).

18. Robert Provine, *Laughter: A Scientific Investigation* (New York: Viking Press, 2000).

19. On the brain's preference for happy faces, see Jukka Leppanen and Jari Hietanen, "Affect and Face Perception," *Emotion* 3 (2003), pp. 315–26.

20. Barbara Fraley and Arthur Aron, "The Effect of a Shared Humorous Experience on Closeness in Initial Encounters," *Personal Relationships* 11 (2004), pp. 61–78.

21. The circuitry for laughing resides in the most primitive parts of the brain, the brain stem. See Stephen Sivvy and Jaak Panksepp, "Juvenile Play in the Rat," *Physiology and Behavior* 41 (1987), pp. 103–14.

22. On best friends, see Brenda Lundy et al., "Same-sex and Opposite-sex Best Friend Interactions Among High School Juniors and Seniors," *Adolescence* 33 (1998), pp. 279–88.

23. Darryl McDaniels is quoted in Josh Tyrangiel, "Why You Can't Ignore Kanye," *Time,* August 21, 2005.

24. Legend was quoted in "Bling Is Not Their Thing: Hip-hop Takes a Relentlessly Positive Turn," *Daily News of Los Angeles,* February 24, 2005.

25. On memes, see Susan Blakemore, *The Meme Machine* (Oxford, U.K.: Oxford University Press, 1999).

26. For a more thorough account of priming, see E. T. Higgins, "Knowledge Activation: Accessibility, Applicability, and Salience," *Social Psychology: Handbook of Basic Principles* (New York: Guilford Press, 1996).

27. On priming for politeness, see Bargh, Chen, and Burrows, "Automaticity of Social Behavior," p. 71.

28. On automatic trains of thought, see John A. Bargh, "The Automaticity of Everyday Life," in R. S. Wyer, ed., *Advances in Social Cognition* (Hillsdale, N.J.: Erlbaum, 1997), vol. 10.

29. On mind-reading accuracy, see Thomas Geoff and Garth Fletcher, "Mind-reading Accuracy in Intimate Relationships: Assessing the Roles of the Relationship, the Target, and the Judge," *Journal of Personality and Social Psychology* 85 (2003), pp. 1079–94.

30. On the confluence of two minds, see Colwyn Trevarthen, "The Self Born in Inter-subjectivity: The Psychology of Infant Communicating," in Ulric Neisser, ed., *The Perceived Self: Ecological and Interpersonal Sources of Self-knowledge* (New York: Cambridge University Press, 1993), pp. 121–73.

31. The emotional merge occurred whether or not the duo felt they had become close friends. Cameron Anderson, Dacher Keltner, and Oliver P. John, "Emotional Convergence Between People over Time," *Journal of Personality and Social Psychology* 84, no. 5 (2003), pp. 1054–68.

32. At the infamous Heysel disaster in 1985, British hooligans charged Belgian fans, causing a wall to collapse and thirty-nine deaths. In the intervening years there have been fatal or near-fatal soccer riots throughout Europe.

33. Elias Canetti, *Crowds and Power* (New York: Continuum, 1973).

34. The rapidity of group mood sweeps is noted in Robert Levenson and Anna Reuf, "Emotional Knowledge and Rapport," in William Ickes, ed., *Empathic Accuracy* (New York: Guilford Press, 1997), pp. 44–72.

35. On sharing emotions, see Elaine Hatfield et al., *Emotional Contagion* (Cambridge, U.K.: Cambridge University Press, 1994).

36. On emotional contagion in teams, see Sigal Barsade, "The Ripple Effect: Emotional Contagion and Its Influence on Group Behavior," *Administrative Science Quarterly* 47 (2002), pp. 644–75.

37. Looping in a group helps everyone stay on the same wavelength. In decision-making groups it fosters the kind of connection that can allow airing differences openly, without fear of blow-ups. Harmony in a group allows the widest range of views to be considered fully and the very best decisions to be made—provided people feel free to bring up dissenting views. During a heated argument it's hard for people to take in what another says, let alone attune.

Chapter 4. An Instinct for Altruism

1. On the Good Samaritan experiment, a classic in social psychology, see J. M. Darley and C. D. Batson, "From Jerusalem to Jericho," *Journal of Personality and Social Psychology* 27 (1973), pp. 100–08. I cited the study in my 1985 book, *Vital Lies, Simple Truths.*

2. As with the rushed students, social situations influence the degree of looping that seems appropriate and even whether looping occurs at all. We would, for instance, feel little need to rush to help someone moaning if we see ambulance attendants also approaching them. And since we loop most readily with people who seem similar to us, and progressively less so the more differences we perceive, we are more likely to offer help to a friend than to a stranger.

3. On the Good Samaritan and helping, see, for example C. Daniel Batson et al., "Five Studies Testing Two New Egoistic Alternatives to the Empathy-Altruism Hypothesis," *Journal of Personality and Social Psychology* 55 (1988), pp. 52–57.

4. English seems to be missing a word with the meaning of *kandou*, which Asian languages have named. In Sanskrit, for example, the word *mudita* means "taking pleasure in the goodness done by or received by someone else." But, English has readily adopted *Schadenfreude*, the exact opposite of *mudita*. See also Tania Singer et al., "Empathy for Pain Involves the Affective but Not Sensory Components of Pain," *Science* 303 (2004), pp. 1157–62.

5. See Jonathan D. Haidt and Corey L. M. Keyes, *Flourishing: Positive Psychology and the Life Well Lived* (Washington, D.C.: American Psychological Association Press, 2003).

6. On fish brains, see Joseph Sisneros et al., "Steroid-Dependent Auditory Plasticity Leads to Adaptive Coupling of Sender and Receiver," *Science* 305 (2004), pp. 404–07.

7. If the baby feels tired or upset, he does the opposite, moving in ways that close down his perceptual systems, as he curls himself up waiting to be held or caressed for calming. See Colwyn Trevarthen, "The Self Born in Intersubjectivity: The Psychology of Infant Communicating," in Ulric Neisser, ed., *The Perceived Self: Ecological and Interpersonal Sources of Self-knowledge* (New York: Cambridge University Press, 1993) pp. 121–73.

8. On empathy in evolution and across species, see Charles Darwin, *The Descent of Man* (1872; Princeton: Princeton University Press, 1998).

9. S. E. Shelton et al., "Aggression, Fear and Cortisol in Young Rhesus Monkeys," *Psychoneuroendocrinology* 22, supp. 2 (1997), p. S198.

10. On sociable baboons, see J. B. Silk et al., "Social Bonds of Female Baboons Enhance Infant Survival," *Science* 302 (2003), pp. 1231–34.

11. Earlier thinking on what allowed humans to develop such a large and intelligent brain had fixed on our ability to hold and make tools. In recent decades the utility for survival—and for raising children who survive into parenting age—that a sociable life offers has drawn more proponents.

12. Stephen Hill, "Storyteller, Recovering from Head-on Crash, Cites 'Miracle of Mother's Day,' " *Daily Hampshire Gazette*, May 11, 2005, p. B1.

13. The notion that empathy entails an emotional sharing has a long history in psychology. One of the earliest theorists, William McDougall, proposed in 1908 that during "sympathy" the first person's physical state is elicited in the second. Eighty years later Leslie Brothers suggested that understanding the emotion of another person required that we experience the same emotion to some degree. And in 1992 Robert Levenson and Anna Reuf, reporting a concordance of heart rate in partners having an emotional discussion, suggested this physiological similarity could be a basis for empathy.

14. The neuroscientist is Christian Keysers of the University of Groningen in the Netherlands, quoted in Greg Miller, "New Neurons Strive to Fit In," *Science* 311 (2005), pp. 938–40.

15. Constantin Stanislavski is quoted in Jonathan Cott, *On a Sea of Memory* (New York: Random House, 2005), p. 138.

16. Neural circuitry for our own and others' feelings is discussed in Kevin Ochsner et al., "Reflecting upon Feelings: An fMRI Study of Neural Systems Supporting the Attribution of Emotion to Self and Others," *Journal of Cognitive Neuroscience* 16 (2004), pp. 1746–72.

17. On circuitry active during observing or imitating an emotion, see Laurie Carr et al., "Neural Mechanisms of Empathy in Humans: A Relay from Neural Systems for Imitation to Limbic Areas," *Proceedings of the National Academy of Sciences* 100, no. 9 (2003), pp. 5497–502. The areas activated: premotor cortex, inferior frontal cortex and anterior insula, and right amygdala (which showed a significant increase from levels during observation alone to levels during imitation).

18. For *Einfühlung,* see Theodore Lipps cited in Vittorio Gallese, "The 'Shared Manifold' Hypothesis: From Mirror Neurons to Empathy," *Journal of Consciousness Studies* 8, no. 5–7 (2001), pp. 33–50.

19. On empathy and the brain, see Stephanie D. Preston and Frans B. M. de Waal, "Empathy: Its Ultimate and Proximate Bases," *Behavioral and Brain Sciences* 25 (2002), pp. 1–20.

20. This similarity, however, does not inevitably indicate empathy. It could be that at the current resolution of our measuring instruments, happiness from two different neural sources looks similar.

21. On brain circuitry in empathy, see Stephanie D. Preston et al., "Functional Neuroanatomy of Emotional Imagery: PET of Personal and Hypothetical Experiences," *Journal of Cognitive Neuroscience: April Supplement,* 126.

22. In technical terms, this neural shorthand is "computationally efficient," both in the processing of information and in the space needed to store it. Preston and de Waal, "Empathy."

23. On the felt sense, see Antonio Damasio, *The Feeling of What Happens* (New York: Harcourt, 2000).

24. On Hobbes, see J. Aubrey, *Brief Lives, Chiefly of Contemporaries, set down by John Aubrey, Between the years 1669 and 1696,* ed., A. Clark (London: Clarendon Press, 1898), vol. 1.

25. A softer version of "every man for himself" was put forth by the eighteenth-century British philosopher Adam Smith, who championed the creation of wealth in a laissez-faire economic system. Smith urged us to trust that individual self-interest would produce equitable markets, one of the economic assumptions underlying the free market system. Both Hobbes and Smith have frequently been cited in modern attempts to analyze the driving force of human behavior, particularly by those who favor pure self-interest—brutal in the case of Hobbes, rational in Smith.

26. Stephanie D. Preston and Frans de Waal, "The Communication of Emotions and the Possibility of Empathy in Animals," in S. Post et al., eds., *Altruism and Altruistic Love: Science, Philosophy, and Religion in Dialogue* (New York: Oxford University Press, 2002), argue that the selfish versus altruistic distinction is irrelevant from an evolutionary perspective, which can read a wide range of behaviors as technically "selfish."

27. Mencius quoted in Frans de Waal, *The Ape and the Sushi Master: Cultural Reflections by a Primatologist* (New York: Basic Books-Perseus, 2001), p. 256. Mencius proposes that if a child is about to fall into a well, anyone who sees has the impulse to help.

28. Jean Decety and Thierry Chaminade, "Neural Correlates of Feeling Sympathy," *Neuropsychologia* 41 (2003), pp. 127–38.

29. Ap Dijksterhuis and John A. Bargh, "The Perception-Behavior Expressway: Automatic Effects of Social Perception on Social Behavior," *Advances in Experimental Social Psychology* 33 (2001), pp. 1–40.

30. Charles Darwin, *The Expression of the Emotions in Man and Animals,* with commentary by Paul Ekman (1872; New York: Oxford University Press, 1998).

31. Beatrice de Gelder et al., "Fear Fosters Flight: A Mechanism for Fear Contagion When Perceiving Emotion Expressed by a Whole Body," *Proceedings of the National Academy of Sciences* 101 (2004), pp. 16701–06. The medial prefrontal-anterior cingulate circuit that responds to social stimuli like pictures of people in distress in turn recruits other brain systems according to the nature of the challenge.

32. On similarity see, for example, Dennis Krebs, "Empathy and Altruism: An Examination of the Concept and a Review of the Literature," *Psychological Bulletin* 73 (1970), pp. 258–302; C. D. Batson, *The Altruism Question: Toward a Scientific Answer* (Mahwah, N.J.: Erlbaum, 1991). Conventional experimental paradigms in social psychology may not present human need in an urgent enough manner to tap the empathy-action pathways. A checklist asking whether one would donate to a charity appeals to cognitive as well as emotional systems. But an equivalent of Mencius' test—seeing a baby about to fall in a well—should tap into a different neural circuit and so yield contrasting results.

33. Preston and de Waal, "Communication of Emotions," propose an emotional gradient in relating to someone else's distress. *Emotional contagion* elicits the same intense state in the observer as in the distressed person, softening the boundary between self and other. In *empathy* the observer takes on a similar—though weaker—emotional state but maintains a clear self-other boundary. In *cognitive empathy* the observer arrives at a shared state through thinking about the predicament of the one in distress at a distance. And *sympathy* is a sense of the other's distress, with little or no sharing of that state. The likelihood of helping increases with the strength of the emotional sharing.

34. On the case for kindness, see Jerome Kagan in Anne Harrington and Arthur Zajonc, eds., *The Dalai Lama at MIT* (Cambridge, Mass.: Harvard University Press, 2006).

35. One philosophical approach that offers a way to reconcile these positions: Owen Flanagan, "Ethical Expressions: Why Moralists Scowl, Frown, and Smile," in Jonathan Hodge and Gregory Radick, *The Cambridge Companion to Darwin* (New York: Cambridge University Press, 2003).

Chapter 5. The Neuroanatomy of a Kiss

1. The OFC has been called the "ultimate neural integrating convergence zone." Among the key brain areas with strong connections to the OFC are the dorsolateral prefrontal cortex, regulating attention; the sensory cortex, for perception; the somatosensory cortex and brain stem, for sensations within the body; the hypothalamus, the brain's neuroendocrine center that regulates hormones throughout the body; the autonomic nervous system, controlling bodily functions like heart rate and digestion; the medial temporal lobe, for memory; the association cortex, for abstract thought; and brain stem centers like the reticular formation, which regulates levels of arousal in the brain. For functions of the OFC and connecting brain structures, see, for example, Allan Schore, *Affect Regulation and the Origin of the Self: The Neurobiology of Emotional Development* (Hillsdale, N.J.: Erlbaum, 1994); Simon Baron-Cohen, *Mindblindness: An Essay on Autism and Theory of Mind* (Cambridge, Mass.: MIT Press, 1995); Antonio Damasio, *Descartes' Error: Emotion, Reason and the Human Brain* (New York: Grosset/Putnam, 1994).

2. The orbitofrontal region (Brodmann's areas 11, 12, 14, and 47) regulates a wide range of social behavior. It has rich connections to the amygdala, the anterior cingulate cortex, and the somatosensory areas. Another linked cortical area is the temporal lobe, crucial for identifying what an object is, or the significance

of things. All these areas play roles in coordinating smooth social interactions. The orbitofrontal lobe has an extensive network of projections throughout the emotional centers, allowing it to modulate emotional responses. One of the primary functions of these networks during a social interaction seems to be inhibiting emotional reactions, coordinating them with inputs about the social moment to make our responses well tuned. See, for example, Schore, *Affect Regulation.* See also Jennifer S. Beer et al., "The Regulatory Function of Self-conscious Emotion: Insights from Patients with Orbitofrontal Damage," *Journal of Personality and Social Psychology* 85 (2003), pp. 594–604; Jennifer S. Beer, "Orbitofrontal Cortex and Social Behavior: Integrating Self-monitoring and Emotion-Cognition Interactions," *Journal of Cognitive Neuroscience* 18 (2006), pp. 871–80.

3. The OFC connects directly to the autonomic system, making it a control center for bodily arousal and relaxation. Other cortical areas with autonomic projections include the anterior cingulate cortex and the medial prefrontal cortex.

4. During moments of motherly love the OFC essentially swamps other areas of the brain, presumably triggering a flood of warm thoughts. See Jack B. Nitschke et al., "Orbitofrontal Cortex Tracks Positive Mood in Mothers Viewing Pictures of Their Newborn Infants," *NeuroImage* 21 (2004), pp. 583–92.

5. On first impressions, see Michael Sunnafrank and Artemio Ramirez, Jr., "At First Sight: Persistent Relationship Effects of Get-Acquainted Conversations," *Journal of Social and Personal Relationships* 21, no. 3 (2004), pp. 361–79. Not surprisingly, the partner who is less drawn to the other has the most power in determining whether a friendship will blossom. If one person wants to connect while the other does not, the reluctant one has veto power. In other words, if you don't want to be my friend, I can't make you. Two factors that would intuitively seem to matter did not: initial attraction and a feeling of similarity.

6. The ACC is involved in a range of functions, notably guiding attention, sensing pain, noting errors, and regulating internal organs like breathing and heart rate. This part of the cortex has rich connections to emotional centers, such as the amygdala, lower in the brain; some neuroanatomical researchers speculate the ACC evolved as an interface connecting our thoughts with our feelings. This intertwining gives the ACC a key role in social awareness.

7. On spindle cells, see John M. Allman et al., "The Anterior Cingulate Cortex: The Evolution of an Interface Between Emotion and Cognition," *Annals of the New York Academy of Sciences* 935 (2001), pp. 107–17.

8. While most all the hundreds of types of neurons in the human brain are found in other mammals, spindle cells are a rare exception. We share them only with our closest cousins, the apes. Orangutans, a distant relative, have a few hundred; our closer genetic relatives the gorillas, chimps, and bonobos have far more. And we humans have the most, close to a hundred thousand of them.

9. See A. D. Craig, "Human Feelings: Why Are Some More Aware Than Others," *Trends in Cognitive Sciences* 8 (2004), pp. 239–41.

10. On ACC and social insight, see R. D. Lane et al., "Neural Correlates of Levels of Emotional Awareness: Evidence of an Interaction Between Emotion and Attention in the Anterior Cingulate Cortex," *Journal of Cognitive Neuroscience* 10 (1998), pp. 525–35. People who are so chronically depressed that medications do not help them typically have unusually little activity in the ACC.

11. On social emotions, see Andrea Bartels and Semir Zeki, "The Neural Basis of Romantic Love," *NeuroReport* 17 (2000), pp. 3829–34. Area F1 of the OFC and area Z4 of the ACC are rich in spindle cells.

12. On the ACC and OFC in social judgment, see Don M. Tucker et al., "Corticolimbic Mechanisms in Emotional Decisions," *Emotion* 3, no. 2 (2003), pp. 127–49.

13. Tanya Chartrand and John Bargh, "The Chameleon Effect: The Perception-Behavior Link and Social Interaction," *Journal of Personality and Social Psychology* 76 (1999), pp. 893–910.

14. The ACC may be only one region among many involved in a widely distributed liking-loathing neural system. Other candidates include the insula.

15. Henry James, *The Golden Bowl* (1904; New York: Penguin, 1987), pp. 147–49.

16. On the "people circuits," see J. P. Mitchell et al., "Distinct Neural Systems Subserve Person and Object Knowledge," *Proceedings of the National Academy of Sciences* 99, no. 23 (2002), pp. 15238–43. The neural circuits that activate during judgments about people: dorsal and ventral aspects of the medial prefrontal cortex, right intraparietal sulcus, right fusiform gyrus, left superior temporal and medial temporal cortex, left motor cortex, and regions of the occipital cortex. The three that are activated while the brain is at rest: dorsal and ventral aspects of the medial prefrontal cortex, and areas of the intraparietal sulcus.

17. Matthew Lieberman is director of the Social Cognitive Neuroscience Laboratory at UCLA. In 2001 he and Kevin Ochsner scored an unheard-of professional coup. An article they had written as lowly graduate students at Harvard was accepted in psychology's most prestigious journal, *The American Psychologist,* one where even famed professors can have a tough time getting published. Their article proclaimed the joining of social psychology, cognitive science, and brain studies, launching a major strand in social neuroscience. Lieberman will be the editor of that discipline's first scholarly journal, *Social, Cognitive, and Affective Neuroscience,* set to launch sometime in 2006.

18. On the default activity, see Marco Iacoboni et al., "Watching Social Interactions Produces Dorsomedial Prefrontal and Medial Parietal BOLD fMRI Signal Increases Compared to a Resting Baseline," *NeuroImage* 21 (2004), pp. 1167–73.

19. On emotions as the brain's value system, see, for example, Daniel J. Siegel, *The Developing Mind: How Relationships and the Brain Interact to Shape Who We Are* (New York: Guilford Press, 1999).

20. This binary decision yields a characteristic "yes" or "no" pattern of cell firing, the neural equivalent of a thumbs up or thumbs down. That neural firing signature lasts for just one-twentieth of a second, holding the decision in place for long enough to give other areas a chance to read it. It takes about ten times longer—around 500 milliseconds—for the yes/no pattern to eventually register distinctly in the OFC. This initial stage of the like/dislike decision takes roughly a half second.

21. If this is a bargaining session—that is, with opportunities for repeated interactions—then the rejection actually becomes rational (and common), as it establishes a bargaining position that pays off in later offers. The rejection is "irrational" only if it occurs in a "one-shot" confidential situation, where there is no opportunity to establish a bargaining position with the current partner.

22. The more prefrontal activity, the better the outcome of the Ultimatum Game; see Alan G. Sanfey et al., "The Neural Basis of Economic Decision-making in the Ultimatum Game," *Science* 300 (2003), pp. 1755–57.

23. The dorsolateral prefrontal area contains an inhibitory array that deploys when we consciously inhibit an impulse. Another route for inhibition travels via the medial area of the prefrontal cortex, which harbors excitatory neurons that activate inhibitory neurons within the amygdala. See Gregory J. Quirk and Donald R. Gehlert, "Inhibition of the Amygdala: Key to Pathological States?" *Annals of the*

New York Academy of Sciences 985 (2003), pp. 263–72. However, neuroscientists disagree about the specifics of pathways for inhibition.

24. On regret, see Natalie Camille et al., "The Involvement of the Orbitofrontal Cortex in the Experience of Regret," *Science* 304 (2004), pp. 1167–70.

25. The OFC is but one high-road mechanism for modulating the amygdala. The ventromedial area is another prefrontal region that does so. The influence runs both ways, with the amygdala affecting prefrontal function. Precisely what conditions determine whether the OFC and the amygdala inhibit each other or act synergistically have yet to be discovered.

26. This obliviousness is known as "social anosognia," the lack of insight into one's own inappropriateness. For OFC lesion and social gaffes, see Beer et al., "Orbitofrontal Cortex and Social Behavior."

27. The OFC seems important for regulating behavior implicitly, whereas the dorsolateral prefrontal cortex is important for doing so explicitly. If the latter remains intact, these patients *can* correct some of their behavior once they become explicitly aware of the fact that they behaved inappropriately. The trick for them is noticing they did something wrong in the first place.

28. On chat rooms, see Kate G. Niederhoffer and James W. Pennebaker, "Linguistic Style Matching in Social Interaction," *Journal of Language and Social Psychology* 21 (2002), pp. 337–60.

29. A sign of Internet disinhibition among girls in their early teens is "cyberbullying," excessively cruel harassment, teasing, and gossip that reduces the target to tears. See Kristin Palpini, "Computer Harassment: Meanness Bottled in a Message," *Daily Hampshire Gazette,* December 17, 2005, p. 1. A more ominous downside of cyberdisinhibition is the sleazy practice of adults who via the Internet lure teenagers to perform sex acts in front of webcams in their own homes, in return for payment. See Kurt Eichenwald, "Through His Webcam, a Boy Joins a Sordid Online World," *New York Times,* December 19, 2005, p. 1.

30. Kevin Ochsner et al., "Rethinking Feelings: An fMRI Study of the Cognitive Regulation of Emotion," *Journal of Cognitive Neuroscience* 14 (2002), pp. 1215–29. The thoughts of the woman are reconstructed from the description of the study.

31. Some MRI studies use special goggles to present the images instead.

32. The dorsolateral prefrontal cortex (PFC) appears to be involved when a person uses language and working memory to work out a new "solution" to an emotional problem, and does so via explicit, deliberative reasoning. By contrast, the OFC regulates emotion apparently via representations of social context, social rules, and so on, which are not explicitly verbalizable. Kevin Ochsner sees this process in terms of associative representations that link actions to affective values. The dorsolateral PFC can hold in mind descriptions of these associations and guide behavior on their basis. See Kevin Ochsner and James Gross, "The Cognitive Control of Emotion," *Trends in Neuroscience* 9 (2005), pp. 242–49.

33 On alternate routes, see Kevin Ochsner et al., "For Better or for Worse: Neural Systems Supporting the Cognitive Down- and Up-regulation of Negative Emotion," *NeuroImage* 23 (2004), pp. 483–99.

34. Kevin Ochsner, "How Thinking Controls Feeling: A Social Cognitive Neuroscience Approach," in P. Winkleman and E. Harmon-Jones, eds., *Social Neuroscience* (New York: Oxford University Press, 2006).

35. On naming an emotion, see A. R. Hariri et al., "Modulating Emotional Response: Effects of a Neocortical Network on the Limbic System," *NeuroReport* 8 (2000), pp. 11–43; Matthew D. Lieberman et al., "Putting Feelings into Words: Affect Labeling Disrupts Affect-related Amygdala Activity," UCLA, unpublished manuscript.

36. Though in the first moment of looping the brain matches our emotions with those we perceive, the high road then offers us a choice point, where we may follow with either of two types of responses. In one we continue to match how the other person feels—their joy gladdens us, their distress upsets us. In the other we feel, for example, envy at their joy or schadenfreude at their distress.

37. On stage fright, see David Guy, "Trying to Speak: A Personal History," *Tricycle* (Summer 2003).

38. On the amygdala and social phobia, see, for example, M. B. Stein et al., "Increased Amygdala Activation to Angry and Contemptuous Faces in Generalized Social Phobia," *Archives of General Psychiatry* 59 (2002), pp. 1027–34.

39. The lateral portion of the amygdala harbors a site where all sensory information first registers; the nearby central area holds the cells that acquire a fear, according to Joseph LeDoux.

40. For memory reconsolidation, see the work of Karim Nader at McGill University, cited by Joseph LeDoux, presentation at the meeting of the Consortium for Research on Emotional Intelligence in Organizations, Cambridge, Mass., December 14, 2004.

41. This strategy applies both to cognitive therapy and to pharmacological interventions like propranolol. When it comes to overcoming a traumatic fear, reconsolidating the memory with less fear would be neurally direct, according to LeDoux. The neurons that store the fearfulness of the memory are in a part of the amygdala that does not directly connect to the area of the prefrontal cortex that retrieves the conscious aspect of the memory, such as the details of what happened, where, and with whom. But intentional relaxation—as in extinction therapy—utilizes the part of the prefrontal area that links straight to the amygdala's fear center, offering a route to alter the fearful memory via reconsolidation. LeDoux proposes that each time we reexperience the original fear, we may have a two-hour window for reconsolidation of a fearful memory. Within that window, taking propranolol, which blocks the action of cells in the amygdala (or presumably undergoing deep relaxation as in extinction therapy), alters the reconsolidation so that the amygdala will not react with such fear the next time the traumatic memory is revisited.

42. An alternate theory holds that therapy strengthens prefrontal circuitry that projects to inhibitory circuitry in the amygdala: See Quirk and Gehlert, "Inhibition of Amygdala."

43. On anger reduction, see Elizabeth Brondolo et al., "Exposure-based Treatment for Anger Problems: Focus on the Feeling," *Cognitive and Behavioral Practice* 4 (1997), pp. 75–98. Increasingly, exposure to the stimulus is virtual, as in simulations of an airplane flight.

44. On therapy for social phobia, see David Barlow, *Anxiety and Its Disorders* (New York: Guilford Press, 1988).

45. LeDoux uses the terms "high" and "low road" here in a particular technical sense, to refer to sensory input pathways to the amygdala from the sensory thalamus and sensory cortex. The "low road" provides a quick and dirty sensory impression, while the high road provides more sensory information. The low road can't distinguish a snake from a stick, but the high road can. The low road hedges its sensory bets—better safe than sorry. In terms of automatic versus controlled processing—the sense in which I use the high-low road heuristic—LeDoux's high and low roads are both "low road," automatic and rapid.

46. The phrase "social brain" was used by noted neuroscientist Michael Gazzaniga in a different sense: not to refer to those parts of the brain active during social interactions, but as a metaphor for the very structure and function of the brain itself.

The brain operates like a small society, he argues, whose distinctly independent modules cooperate with one another to perform a given task—much as people agree to work together for a time on some project. However, in the sense I'm using the phrase here, the "social brain" is the module that orchestrates during person-to-person interactions.

47. Every area of the brain participates in a multitude of functions, so no area is exclusively "social," save perhaps specialized circuitry like mirror neurons. The fact that an area activates during a given social process does not mean it "causes" that process; involvement is not causation. For more caveats on relating neural activity to social process, see Daniel Willingham and Elizabeth Dunn, "What Neuroimaging and Brain Localization Can Do, Cannot Do, and Should Not Do for Social Psychology," *Journal of Personality and Social Psychology* 85 (2003), pp. 662–71.

48. On serotonin, see Michael Gershon, *The Second Brain* (New York: Harper, 1999); Michael Gershon, "Plasticity in Serotonin Control Mechanisms in the Gut," *Current Opinion in Pharmacology* 3 (1999), p. 600.

49. Precisely which networks are involved depends on the specific activity; all these circuits in aggregate make up the social brain. On the relationship pathway, see Stephanie D. Preston and Frans B. M. de Waal, "Empathy: Its Ultimate and Proximate Bases," *Behavioral and Brain Sciences* 25 (2005), pp. 1–20.

Chapter 6. What Is Social Intelligence?

1. The interaction was witnessed by Dee Speese-Linehan, director of the Social Development Department, New Haven Public Schools.

2. Edward L. Thorndike, "Intelligence and Its Use," *Harper's Monthly Magazine* 140 (1920), pp. 227–35. The abilities of social intelligence are embedded in my emotional intelligence model within the "social awareness" and "relationship management" domains.

3. That observation has now been borne out by hundreds of independent studies done within organizations to identify the competencies that set star performers, especially the most talented leaders, apart from the mediocre. See Lyle Spencer and Signe Spencer, *Competence at Work* (New York: John Wiley, 1993); Daniel Goleman, *Working with Emotional Intelligence* (New York: Bantam Books, 1998); Daniel Goleman, Richard Boyatzis, and Annie McKee, *Primal Leadership* (Boston: Harvard Business School Press, 2002).

4. David Wechsler, *The Measurement and Appraisal of Adult Intelligence,* 4th ed. (Baltimore: Williams and Wilkins, 1958), p. 75.

5. See Brian Parkinson, "Emotions Are Social," *British Journal of Psychology* 87 (1996), pp. 663–83; Catherine Norris et al., "The Interaction of Social and Emotional Processes in the Brain," *Journal of Cognitive Neuroscience* 16, no. 10 (2004), pp. 1819–29.

6. The prototype of emotional intelligence developed by John Mayer and Peter Salovey subsumes aspects of social intelligence. Reuven Bar-On has confronted this dilemma head on by renaming his model of emotional intelligence "emotional-social intelligence." See Reuven Bar-On, "The Bar-On Model of Emotional-Social Intelligence (ESI)," *Psicothema* 17 (2005). Appendix C explains how my own model incorporates social intelligence.

7. The need for this distinction between personal and social aptitudes was recognized by Howard Gardner in his groundbreaking *Frames of Mind: The Theory of Multiple Intelligences* (New York: Basic Books, 1983).

8. On primal empathy and mirror neurons, see Greg Miller, "New Neurons Strive to Fit In," *Science* 311 (2005), pp. 938–40.

9. Judith A. Hall, "The PONS Test and the Psychometric Approach to Measuring Interpersonal Sensitivity," in Judith A. Hall and Frank J. Bernieri, *Interpersonal Sensitivity: Theory and Measurement* (Mahwah, N.J.: Erlbaum, 2001). The PONS tests sensitivity to each channel of nonverbal cues for emotions and asks respondents to guess the social situation. So it may not represent a pure test of primal empathy (nor was it designed to be). Aspects of the PONS, however, do seem to pick up this dimension.

10. On the Reading the Mind in the Eyes test, see Simon Baron-Cohen, *The Essential Difference: Men, Women, and the Extreme Male Brain* (London: Allen Lane, 2003).

11. For an overview of theory, research, and practice on listening, see A. D. Wolvin and C. G. Coakley, eds., *Perspectives on Listening* (Norwood, N.J.: Ablex, 1993). Also B. R. Witkin, "Listening Theory and Research: The State of the Art," *Journal of the International Listening Association* 4 (1990), pp. 7–32.

12. This holds wherever someone's success depends on repeat customers or keeping a company's ongoing clients happy. On star sales people, see Spencer and Spencer, *Competence.*

13. C. Bechler and S. D. Johnson, "Leading and Listening: A Study of Member Perception," *Small Group Research* 26 (1995), pp. 77–85; S. D. Johnson and C. Bechler, "Examining the Relationship Between Listening Effectiveness and Leadership Emergence: Perceptions, Behaviors, and Recall," *Small Group Research* 29 (1998), pp. 452–71; S. C. Wilmington, "Oral Communication Skills Necessary for Successful Teaching," *Educational Research Quarterly* 16 (1992), pp. 5–17.

14. On outstanding helping professionals, see Spencer and Spencer, *Competence.*

15. See Edward Hollowell, "The Human Moment at Work," *Harvard Business Review* (January–February 1999), p. 59.

16. On physiological synchrony and listening, see Robert Levenson and Anna Reuf, "Emotional Knowledge and Rapport," in William Ickes, ed., *Empathic Accuracy* (New York: Guilford Press, 1997), pp. 44–72.

17. On empathic accuracy, see Ickes, *Empathic Accuracy,* p. 2.

18. Primal empathy seems to involve pathways connecting the sensory cortices with the thalamus and the amygdala, and from there to whatever circuits the appropriate response requires. But for cognitive empathy—like empathic accuracy or theory of mind—the likely circuitry travels from thalamus to *cortex* to amygdala, and then to the circuitry for the response. See James Blair and Karina Perschardt, "Empathy: A Unitary Circuit or a Set of Dissociable Neuro-cognitive Systems?" in Stephanie D. Preston and Frans B. M. de Waal, "Empathy: Its Ultimate and Proximate Bases," *Behavioral and Brain Sciences* 25 (2002), pp. 1–72.

19. People differ widely in how accurately they can notice, let alone read, these constant signals. But the wide spectrum of this ability in any given pool of people recommends just this accurate empathy as a way to evaluate individual differences, that stock in trade of psychometrics. See: William Ickes, "Measuring Empathic Accuracy," in Judith A. Hall and Frank J. Bernieri, *Interpersonal Sensitivity: Theory and Measurement* (Mahwah, N.J.: Erlbaum, 2001).

20. Victor Bissonette et al., "Empathic Accuracy and Marital Conflict Resolution," in Ickes, *Empathic Accuracy.*

21. Levenson and Reuf, "Emotional Knowledge."

22. I use the term "social cognition" here in a more limited sense than its more general meaning in social psychology. See, for example, Ziva Kunda, *Social Cognition* (Cambridge, Mass.: MIT Press, 1999).

23. People who are too agitated or confused to perceive or reflect well, or too impul-

sive in grasping a remedy or executing it, fare poorly. Hence the difficulties with social problem-solving among people with a range of psychiatric disorders. See Edward Chang et al., eds., *Social Problem Solving* (Washington, D.C.: American Psychological Association Press, 2004).

24. On the measure of social intelligence, see K. Jones and J. D. Day, "Discrimination of Two Aspects of Cognitive-Social Intelligence from Academic Intelligence," *Journal of Educational Psychology* 89 (1997), pp. 486–97.

25. The synergism of the elements of social awareness I propose here is, of course, a hypothesis awaiting rigorous testing.

26. While much of the research on interaction synchrony was done in the 1970s and 1980s, the area fell out of vogue and has been largely ignored by sociology and social psychology alike, despite more recent attempts to revive it. One of the early barriers to research—the immense effort required to score synchrony through human labor—may now yield to analysis by computer, though some researchers argue that human perception still outperforms a computer's abilities at pattern recognition. See Frank Bernieri et al., "Synchrony, Pseudosynchrony, and Dissynchrony: Measuring the Entrainment Prosody in Mother-Infant Interactions," *Journal of Personality and Social Psychology* 2 (1988), pp. 243–53. Still, correlation is not causation: the relationship may work in the other direction. For instance, a feeling of rapport may guide our bodies into harmony. For nonverbal facilitators of rapport, see the meta-analysis of eighteen studies in Linda Tickle-Degnan and Robert Rosenthal, "The Nature of Rapport and Its Nonverbal Correlates," *Psychological Inquiry* 1, no. 4 (1990), pp. 285–93.

27. Researchers at Emory University in Atlanta have designed a version of the PONS to diagnose this problem in youngsters. The test shows faces of children and adults expressing one of four major emotions: happiness, sadness, anger, and fear. It also has them hear a neutral sentence—like "I am going out of the room now but I'll be back later"—spoken in each of those four emotional tones. By age ten, most children can well identify these feelings when they hear the nuances of the sentence—but dyssemic kids can't. See Stephen Nowicki and Marshall P. Duke, "Nonverbal Receptivity: The Diagnostic Analysis of Nonverbal Accuracy (DANVA)," in Hall and Bernieri, *Interpersonal Sensitivity.*

28. Because these basic social aptitudes are so essential for forming satisfying relationships through life, there are now tutorial programs that help dyssemic children get up to speed. See Stephen Nowicki, *The Diagnostic Analysis of Nonverbal Accuracy-2: Remediation,* unpublished manuscript, Emory University; and Marshall P. Duke et al., *Teaching Your Child the Language of Social Success* (Atlanta: Peachtree Press, 1996). Another cause of being out of synch may be what some experts now call "sensory processing disorder." See Carol Stock Kranowitz, *The Out-of-Synch Child: Recognizing and Coping with Sensory Processing Disorder* (New York: Penguin, 2005).

29. For the children's checklist, see Nowicki and Duke, "Nonverbal Receptivity."

30. On adult dyssemia, see Stephen Nowicki and Marshall P. Duke, *Will I Ever Fit In?* (New York: Free Press, 2002).

31. On what accounts for dyssemia: Stephen Nowicki, personal communication.

32. On remedial programs for dyssemia, for adults, see Nowicki and Duke, *Will I Ever.* On programs for children, see Duke et al., *Teaching Your Child.* Nowicki, who first identified dyssemia and has designed remedial programs, tells me that regardless of the cause, everyone with these deficits can benefit from learning—though those who are neurologically or emotionally impaired will take longer.

33. In experiments that compare natural synchrony with intentional attempts to influence another person through, say, smiling or frowning, the artificial manipulation

fares poorly. See, for example, Brooks B. Gump and James A. Kulik, "Stress, Affiliation, and Emotional Contagion," *Journal of Personality and Social Psychology* 72 (1997), pp. 305–19.

34. Ronald E. Riggio, "Charisma," in Howard Friedman, ed., *Encyclopedia of Mental Health* (San Diego: Academic Press, 1998).

35. On the other hand, clever stage management can boost one's aura of power. As political handlers know, potent symbols and props, such as oceans of flags, an impressive stage, and the roars of a friendly crowd, can gin up the aura of charisma even for those who lack the necessary expressiveness or force of character.

36. On a crowd in synchrony, see Frank Bernieri quoted in Mark Greer, "The Science of Savoir Faire," *Monitor on Psychology* (January 2005).

37. On gender and emotion norms, see Ursula Hess et al., *Cognition and Emotion* 19 (2005), pp. 515–36.

38. Elizabeth Brondolo et al., "Correlates of Risk for Conflict Among New York City Traffic Agents," in Gary VandenBos and Elizabeth Brondolo, eds., *Violence on the Job* (Washington, D.C.: American Psychological Association Press, 1996).

39. Ronald Riggio and Howard Friedman, "Impression Formation: The Role of Expressive Behavior," *Journal of Personality and Social Psychology* 50 (1986), pp. 421–27.

40. Suppose one partner tactlessly expresses blunt, unpleasant truths to the other that cause pain or distress. In such a case greater empathic accuracy might raise doubts and create unpleasantness that could impair the relationship. In such cases Ickes proposes an alternative: "benevolent misconceptions." See Jeffrey Simpson et al., "When Accuracy Hurts, and When It Helps: A Test of the Empathic Accuracy Model in Marital Interactions," *Journal of Personality and Social Psychology* 85 (2003), pp. 881–93. On times when empathy does not help, see William Ickes and Jeffrey A. Simpson, "Managing Empathic Accuracy in Close Relationships," in Ickes, *Empathic Accuracy.*

41. A study comparing Chinese-Americans and Mexican-Americans found that while there was no difference in the actual emotions they experienced, the Mexican group was invariably more expressive than the Chinese. See Jose Soto et al., "Culture of Moderation and Expression," *Emotion* 5 (2005), pp. 154–65.

42. Reuven Bar-On's measure of emotional and social intelligence, in earlier versions, assessed empathy and social responsibility separately. But further testing revealed that the two are so closely associated that they seemed to be measuring the same qualities. The evolution of the Bar-On scale can be tracked by comparing the model set forth in Reuven Bar-On and James D. A. Parker, eds., *The Handbook of Emotional Intelligence* (San Francisco: Jossey-Bass, 2000), and the later revision described in Bar-On, "Bar-On Model."

43. A. R. Weisenfeld et al., "Individual Differences Among Adult Women in Sensitivity to Infants: Evidence in Support of an Empathy Concept," *Journal of Personality and Social Psychology* 46 (1984), pp. 118–24.

44. On donations, see Theo Schuyt et al., "Constructing a Philanthropy Scale: Social Responsibility and Philanthropy," paper presented at 33rd conference of the Association for Research on Nonprofit Organizations and Voluntary Action, Los Angeles, November 2004.

45. On empathic concern, see Paul D. Hastings et al., "The Development of Concern for Others in Children with Behavior Problems," *Developmental Psychology* 36 (2000), pp. 531–46.

46. On training in reading microexpressions, see MicroExpression Training Tool (METT), a CD available at www.PaulEkman.com. At present there have been no

published validation studies of the METT, though positive preliminary data is posted on the website. Further testing is needed to assess how long the gains from the training persist and how robust they are in real-life applications.

47. On the doctor and the tack, Joseph LeDoux was interviewed on www.Edge.com in February 1997.

48. LeDoux has made a critique of emotion researchers who ignore the low road. "It is widely recognized," he wrote, "that most cognitive processes occur unconsciously, with only the end products reaching awareness, and then only sometimes. Emotion researchers, though, did not make this conceptual leap," nor have those theorists of social intelligence who remain fixated on social cognition done so. For LeDoux's critique, see Joseph LeDoux, "Emotion Circuits in the Brain," *Annual Review of Neuroscience* 23 (2000), p. 156.

49. For example, see Karen Jones and Jeanne Day, "Cognitive Similarities Between Academically and Socially Gifted Students," *Roeper Review* 18 (1996), pp. 270–74; see also John Kihlstrom and Nancy Cantor, "Social Intelligence," in Robert Sternberg, ed., *Handbook of Intelligence,* 2nd ed. (Cambridge, U.K.: Cambridge University Press, 2000), pp. 359–79.

50. I find compelling the arguments of Colwyn Trevarthen, a developmental psychologist at the University of Edinburgh, who argues that the widely accepted notions of social cognition create profound misunderstandings of human relations and the place of emotions in social life. See Trevarthen, "The Self Born in Intersubjectivity: The Psychology of Infant Communicating," in Ulric Neisser, ed., *The Perceived Self: Ecological and Interpersonal Sources of Self-knowledge* (New York: Cambridge University Press, 1993), pp. 121–73.

51. Lawrence Kohlberg, foreword to John Gibbs and Keith Widaman, *Social Intelligence* (Englewood Cliffs, N.J.: Prentice-Hall, 1982).

PART II

Chapter 7. You and It

1. On agency and communion, see David Bakan, *The Duality of Human Existence* (Boston: Beacon Press, 1966). Since the 1950s theoretical models of interpersonal life have used agency and communion as the two main dimensions along which behavior arranges itself, beginning with Timothy Leary's influential "circumplex" model. See Timothy Leary, *Interpersonal Diagnosis of Personality* (New York: Roland, 1957). That tradition has had a revival of late: see Leonard M. Horowitz, *Interpersonal Foundations of Psychopathology* (Washington, D.C.: American Psychological Association Press, 2004).

2. On the question with "you," see Marcelle S. Fischler, "Vows: Allison Charney and Adam Epstein," *New York Times,* January 25, 2004, sec. 9, p. 11. Allison Charney Epstein, in an e-mail, told me she did not even have a chance to start the clock.

3. For a psychoanalytic account of intersubjectivity, see Daniel Stern, *The Present Moment in Psychotherapy and Everyday Life* (New York: W.W. Norton, 2004).

4. On I-You, see Martin Buber, *I and Thou,* trans. Walter Kaufmann 1937; (New York: Simon & Schuster, 1990). Buber's main focus in this aphoristic text was on a mode of relating that sacralizes everyday relationships, and on the human connection with a sacred dimension of being. Technically, *Du* should be translated as "Thou," the familiar form of "you." But because the usage "thou" has become archaic in English today—instead of connoting familiarity it suggests a ceremonial formality—I prefer the word "you" as the contemporary equivalent.

5. Buber observed that either party can begin that loop; it needn't come from both sides at first—though once one person attunes, the likelihood of two-way rapport increases. When people in a Swedish study described times they had been the

target of someone's empathy, they felt that the other person shared their feelings, understood them, and showed genuine concern. See Jakob Hakansson and Henry Montgomery, "Empathy as an Interpersonal Phenomenon," *Journal of Social and Personal Relationships* 20 (2003), pp. 267–84.

6. On *amae,* see Takeo Doi, *The Anatomy of Dependence* (New York: Kodansha International, 1973).

7. See, for example, Emmanuel Lévinas, "Martin Buber and the Theory of Knowledge," in Sean Hand, ed., *The Lévinas Reader* (Oxford, U.K.: Blackwell, 1989).

8. On mental similarities, see Roy F. Baumeister and M. R. Leary, "The Need to Belong: Desire for Interpersonal Attachments as a Fundamental Human Motivation," *Psychological Bulletin* 117 (1995), pp. 497–529.

9. Some theorists invoke this sense of oneness to explain how much people are likely to trouble themselves to help another—for instance, someone about to be evicted. Studies find that the choice to help is as strongly driven by the perceived closeness of the relationship as it is by the severity of the person's need. This sense of connectedness need not be limited to those we hold dear; simply *perceiving* closeness with someone has the same effect. See Robert Cialdini et al., "Reinterpreting the Empathy-Altruism Relationship: When One into One Equals Oneness," *Journal of Personality and Social Psychology* 73 (1997), pp. 481–94.

10. On high-intensity validation, see Lynn Fainsilber Katz and Erica Woodin, "Hostility, Hostile Detachment, and Conflict Engagement in Marriages: Effects on Child and Family Functioning," *Child Development* 73 (2002), pp. 636–52.

11. Buber, *I and Thou,* p. 11.

12. See Nicholas D. Kristof, "Leaving the Brothel Behind," *New York Times,* January 19, 2005, p. A19.

13. See Stephanie D. Preston and Frans de Waal, "The Communication of Emotions and the Possibility of Empathy in Animals," in S. Post et al., eds., *Altruism and Altruistic Love: Science, Philosophy, and Religion in Dialogue* (New York: Oxford University Press, 2002).

14. Jean-Paul Sartre, *Being and Nothingness,* trans. Hazel Barnes (New York: Philosophical Library, 1959), p. 59.

15. On rapport in helping relationships, see Linda Tickle-Degnan and Robert Rosenthal, "The Nature of Rapport and Its Nonverbal Coordinates," *Psychological Inquiry* 1, no. 4 (1990), pp. 285–93.

16. The story of Mary Duffy was told in Benedict Carey, "In the Hospital, a Degrading Shift from Person to Patient," *New York Times,* August 16, 2005, p. A1.

17. On social rejection and pain, see Naomi Eisenberger and Matthew Lieberman, "Why Rejection Hurts: A Common Neural Alarm System for Physical and Social Pain," *Science* 87 (2004), pp. 294–300.

18. On a neural alarm system, see Matthew Lieberman et al., "A Pain by Any Other Name (Rejection, Exclusion, Ostracism) Still Hurts the Same: The Role of Dorsal Anterior Cingulate Cortex in Social and Physical Pain," in J. Cacioppo et al., eds., *Social Neuroscience: People Thinking About People* (Cambridge, Mass.: MIT Press, 2005).

19. On laughter and tears, see Jaak Panksepp, "The Instinctual Basis of Human Affect," *Consciousness and Emotion* 4 (2003), pp. 197–206.

20. On number of contacts and loneliness, see, for example, Louise Hawkley et al., "Loneliness in Everyday Life: Cardiovascular Activity, Psychosocial Context, and Health Behaviors," *Journal of Personality and Social Psychology* 85 (2003), pp. 105–20.

21. On the psychoanalyst, see George Ganick Fishman, "Knowing Another from a Dynamic System Point of View: The Need for a Multimodal Concept of Empathy," *Psychoanalytic Quarterly* 66 (1999), pp. 1–25.

22. Hume's quotation has been slightly paraphrased. See David Hume, *A Treatise on Human Nature* (1888; London: Clarendon Press, 1990), p. 224; he is quoted in Stephanie D. Preston and Frans B. M. de Waal, "Empathy: Its Ultimate and Proximate Bases," *Behavioral and Brain Sciences* 25 (2002), p. 18.

Chapter 8. The Dark Triad

1. Delroy Paulhus and Kevin Williams, "The Dark Triad of Personality: Narcissism, Machiavellianism, and Psychopathy," *Journal of Research in Personality* 36, no. 6 (2002), pp. 556–63.

2. Harry Wallace and Roy Baumeister, "The Performance of Narcissists Rises and Falls with Perceived Opportunity for Glory," *Journal of Personality and Social Psychology* 82 (2002), pp. 819–34.

3. On narcissistic leaders, see Michael Maccoby, "Narcissistic Leaders," *Harvard Business Review* 78 (January–February 2000), pp. 68–77.

4. For the business school professor, see Howard S. Schwartz, *Narcissistic Process and Corporate Decay* (New York: New York University Press, 1990).

5. On the college men denied a sexual favor, see Brad J. Bushman et al., "Narcissism, Sexual Refusal, and Aggression: Testing a Narcissistic Reactance Model of Sexual Coercion," *Journal of Personality and Social Psychology* 84, no. 5 (2003), pp. 1027–40.

6. On narcissists, see Constantine Sedikides et al., "Are Normal Narcissists Psychologically Healthy? Self-esteem Matters," *Journal of Personality and Social Psychology* 87, no. 3 (2004), pp. 40–416, at 400.

7. On self-enhancement, see Delroy Paulhus et al., "Shedding Light on the Dark Triad of Personality: Narcissism, Machiavellianism, and Psychopathy," paper presented at the Society for Personality and Social Psychology conference, San Antonio, Tex., 2001.

8. Robert Raskin and Calvin Hall, "Narcissistic Personality Inventory," *Psychological Reports* 45 (1979), pp. 450–57.

9. On well-being in narcissists, see Sedikides et al., "Normal Narcissists."

10. Shinobu Kitayama and Hazel Markus, "The Pursuit of Happiness and the Realization of Sympathy," in Ed Diener and Eunbook Suh, eds., *Culture and Subjective Well-being* (Cambridge, Mass.: MIT Press, 2000).

11. To be sure, Machiavelli urged tyrants to act in ways that would make their citizens love them—if only just enough to ward off insurrections.

12. Paulhus et al., "Shedding Light."

13. The narcissist's lack of empathy is particularly striking when compared to people who assume that other people are basically trustworthy; such people attune to others' feelings with a high level of accuracy. Mark Davis and Linda Kraus, "Personality and Empathic Accuracy," in William Ickes, ed., *Empathic Accuracy* (New York: Guilford Press, 1997).

14. On emotional confusion, see Henry Krystal, *Integration and Self-Healing* (Hillsdale, N.J.: Analytic Press, 1988).

15. Even scientific studies of Machs carry a tone of moral disapproval. Behind the distaste lies an assumption that the Machiavellian person has *chosen* an evil path in life. But one recent look at the psychological mechanisms that propel opportunistic manipulation suggests that the Mach's deeds are not entirely volitional. This theory holds that Machs are simply doing their best to live well despite genuine

puzzlement about others' feelings. See Colin Wastell and Alexandra Booth, "Machiavellianism: An Alexithymic Perspective," *Journal of Social and Clinical Psychology* 22 (2003), pp. 730–44.

16. On the case of Peter, see Leo J. Potts et al., "Comprehensive Treatment of a Severely Antisocial Adolescent," in William H. Reid et al., eds., *Unmasking the Psychopath* (New York: W.W. Norton, 1986).

17. John McHoskey et al., "Machiavellianism and Psychopathy," *Journal of Clinical and Social Psychology* 74 (1998), pp. 192–210.

18. John Edens et al., "Further Validation of the Psychopathic Personality Inventory Among Offenders: Personality and Behavioral Correlates," *Journal of Personality Disorders* 15 (2001), pp. 403–15.

19. See, for example, Christopher Patrick, "Emotion in the Criminal Psychopath: Fear Imaging Processing," *Journal of Abnormal Psychology* 103 (1994), pp. 523–34; Adrian Raine and P. H. Venables, "Skin Conductance Responsivity in Psychopaths to Orienting, Defensive, and Consonant-Vowel Stimuli," *Journal of Psychophysiology* 2 (1988), pp. 221–25.

20. Paulhus, "Shedding Light."

21. On low anxiety in psychopaths, see Paulhus and Williams, "Dark Triad of Personality."

22. On brain imaging in psychopaths, see K. A. Kiehl et al., "Limbic Abnormalities in Affective Processing by Criminal Psychopaths as Revealed by fMRI," *Biological Psychiatry* 50 (2001), pp. 677–84; Adriane Raine et al., "Reduced Prefrontal Gray Matter Volume and Reduced Autonomic Activity in Antisocial Personality Disorder," *Archives of General Psychiatry* 57 (2000), pp. 119–27; Antonio Damasio, "A Neural Basis for Sociopathy," *Archives of General Psychiatry* 57 (2000), pp. 128–29.

23. On psychopaths' lack of emotional resonance, see Linda Mealey and Stuart Kinner, "The Perception-Action Model of Empathy and the Psychopathic 'Cold-heartedness,'" *Behavioral and Brain Sciences* 25 (2002), pp. 42–43.

24. On psychopaths' lack of impulse to help, see Linda Mealey, "The Sociobiology of Sociopathy," *Behavioral and Brain Sciences* 18 (1995), pp. 523–99.

25. On successful psychopaths, see Sharon Ishikawa et al., "Autonomic Stress Reactivity and Executive Functions in Successful and Unsuccessful Criminal Psychopaths from the Community," *Journal of Abnormal Psychology* 110 (2001), pp. 423–32.

26. On the sociopathic rapist, see Robert D. Hare, *Without Conscience: The Disturbing World of the Sociopaths Among Us* (New York: Pocket Books, 1993), p. 14.

27. On John Chaney, see Matt Vautour, "Temple Extends Chaney's Suspension," *Hampshire Daily Gazette,* February 26, 2005, p. D1.

28. On the supermarket display, see G. R. Semin and A. Manstead, "The Social Implications of Embarrassment Displays and Restitution Behavior," *European Journal of Social Psychology* 12 (1982), pp. 367–77.

29. On orbitofrontal patients, see Jennifer S. Beer et al., "The Regulatory Function of Self-conscious Emotion: Insights from Patients with Orbitofrontal Damage," *Journal of Personality and Social Psychology* 85 (2003), pp. 594–604.

30. On righteous anger, see D. J. de Quervain et al., "The Neural Basis of Altruistic Punishment," *Science* 305 (2004), pp. 1254–58.

Chapter 9. Mindblind

1. On Asperger's syndrome, see Simon Baron-Cohen, *The Essential Difference: Men, Women, and the Extreme Male Brain* (London: Allen Lane, 2003).

2. On testing a child's grasp of mindsight, see David Bjorklund and Jesse Bering, "Big Brains, Slow Development and Social Complexity: The Developmental and Evolutionary Origins of Social Cognition," in Martin Brüne et al., eds., *The Social Brain: Evolution and Pathology* (Sussex, U.K.: John Wiley, 2003). Daniel Siegel coined the term "mindsight" for the human capacity to sense the mind, in oneself and in others; See Daniel Siegel, *The Developing Mind: How Relationships and the Brain Interact to Shape Who We Are* (New York: Guilford Press, 1999).

3. When actual monkeys (chimps in this case) play a version of Mean Monkey, they fail to learn the lesson that others can have desires different from their own. In the chimp version, one chimp in a pair gets to choose which of two treats they can eat; the chosen treat, however, always goes to the other chimp, not to the one who selects it. With chimps—unlike four-year-old children—the lesson never gets learned. The reason seems to be that chimps are unable to restrain their desire for the more luscious treat, even merely to select the lesser one so that in the end they can get what they want.

4. On children's stages of empathy, see Phillipe Rochat, "Various Kinds of Empathy as Revealed by the Developing Child, not the Monkey's Brain," *Behavioral and Brain Science* 25 (2002), pp. 45–46.

5. On mirror neurons, see Marco Iacoboni, presentation at the annual meeting of the American Academy for the Advancement of Science, February 2005, reported in Greg Miller, "New Neurons Strive to Fit In," *Science* 311 (2005), pp. 938–40.

6. C. A. Sanderson, J. M. Darley, and C. S. Messinger, " 'I'm not as thin as you think I am' : The Development and Consequences of Feeling Discrepant from the Thinness Norm," *Personality and Social Psychology Bulletin* 27 (2001), pp. 172–83; Mark Cherrington, "The Sin in Thin," *Amherst* (Summer 2004), pp. 28–31.

7. See Temple Grandin and Catherine Johnson, *Animals in Translation: Using the Mysteries of Autism to Decode Animal Behavior* (New York: Scribner, 2005).

8. On all these assessments, those with autism or Asperger's score more poorly than do most men.

9. The differences in what Baron-Cohen calls the "male" and "female" brains emerge only at the far ends of a bell curve for the ratio of empathy and systematizing, among the 2 or 3 percent of men and women whose brains typify the utmost extremes. A further caveat: Baron-Cohen does not mean to attribute the "male" brain to all men, nor the prototypic "female" one to all women. Some men have a "female" brain, and some women a "male" one—about one in five people with autism are women. And while there are no quick-and-easy ways to estimate the number of men who have superb abilities at empathizing, there is every reason to expect there to be as large a pool of men with this attunement talent as there are women adept at systems thinking.

10. Layne Habib is with Circle of Friends, Shokan, N.Y.

11. The tale of Marie, which was used in a story comprehension test of theory of mind, comes from S. Channon and S. Crawford, "The Effects of Anterior Lesions on Performance of a Story Comprehension Test: Left Anterior Impairment on a Theory of Mind-type Task," *Neuropsychologia* 38 (2000), pp. 1006–17; quoted in R. G. Morris et al., "Social Cognition Following Prefrontal Cortical Lesions," in Brüne et al., *Social Brain,* p. 235.

12. For instance, what may seem obvious social facts baffle not just people with autism but those with any of a range of clinical disorders that damage key parts of the social circuitry, such as a common brain trauma from an auto accident. These brain deficits undermine a person's ability for accurate mindsight, and so they lack an accurate sense of what others think, feel, or intend. On brain trauma, see Skye McDonald and Sharon Flanagan, "Social Perception Deficits After Traumatic Brain

Injury," *Neuropsychology* 18 (2004), pp. 572–79. Related research reveals that the face area coordinates with a distributed network including the amygdala, the medial prefrontal cortices, and the superior temporal gyrus, which together interpret for us how to read and react during social interactions. This network performs the critical task of recognizing people and reading their emotions, as well as understanding relationships. Paradoxically, people with deficits in these neural circuits can sometimes have outstanding abilities in others. On neural networks for social interaction, see, for example, Robert Schultz et al., "fMRI Evidence for Differences in Social Affective Processing in Autism," presentation at the National Institute of Child Health and Development, October 29, 2003. Another brain basis of autism appears to be located in the fusiform, which MRI and other studies find is smaller in autistic than in nonautistic people. This deficit may lead to difficulties in learning the normal links between social perceptions and reactions—possibly at the most basic level, failing to attend to the appropriate stimuli. The lack of coordinating attention with another person leads autistic children to miss the most fundamental social and emotional cues, compromising their ability to share feelings—let alone empathize—with others. On failure to attend, see Preston and de Waal, "Empathy."

13. F. Gougoux, "A Functional Neuroimaging Study of Sound Localization: Visual Cortex Activity Predicts Performance in Early-Blind Individuals," *Public Library of Science: Biology* 3 (2005), p. e27 (e-published).

14. K. M. Dalton et al., "Gaze-fixation and the Neural Circuitry of Face Processing in Autism," *Nature Neuroscience* 8 (2005), pp. 519–26.

15. See Simon Baron-Cohen et al., "Social Intelligence in the Normal and Autistic Brain: An fMRI Study," *European Journal of Neuroscience* 11 (1999), pp. 1891–98. In addition, mirror neuron deficiencies are also part of the picture; see Lindsay M. Oberman et al., "EEG Evidence for Mirror Neuron Dysfunction in Autism Spectrum Disorders," *Cognitive Brain Research* 24 (2005), pp. 190–98.

PART III

Chapter 10. Genes Are Not Destiny

1. Even more heat was being generated in the 1970s by another theorist on the Harvard faculty, biologist Edwin O. Wilson, who had begun to articulate his theory of sociobiology, and by anthropologist Irven DeVore and his star student, Robert Trivers, who were just starting to develop their theory of evolutionary psychology—today, widely influential. At the time these schools of thought were vehemently opposed by a group led by paleontologist Stephen Jay Gould and geneticist Richard Lewontin, also Harvard faculty members.

2. John Crabbe et al., "Genetics of Mouse Behavior: Interactions with Laboratory Environment," *Science* 284 (1999), pp. 1670–72.

3. Some behavior geneticists objected to what they saw as an "emperor has no clothes" finding, largely because that was the angle played up in an accompanying commentary. But the more sober reading of the article was that a single test of the same behavior was no longer enough; the study raised the methodological bar for the field. Now, as Crabbe commented, "When someone knocks out a gene for anxiety, you see them using three tests to show the effect, where before they could get away with just one."

4. The methyl molecule consists of just four atoms—a carbon and three hydrogen; precisely how they attach to one gene determines what happens. In one formation, the methyl group inactivates the gene, coiling its DNA tighter so the gene cannot be expressed. In another configuration, the methyl group relaxes the DNA coils, enabling the gene to manufacture its particular RNA (and so its protein).

5. On genes and environment, see Robert Plomin and John Crabbe, "DNA," *Psychological Bulletin* 126 (2000), pp. 806–28.

6. Michael J. Meaney, "Nature, Nurture, and the Disunity of Knowledge," *Annals of the New York Academy of Sciences* 935 (2001), pp. 50–61.

7. On the plasticity of genetic mechanisms that regulate behavior, see Elizabeth Hammock and Larry Young, "Microsatellite Instability Generates Diversity in Brain and Sociobehavioral Traits," *Science* 308 (2005), pp. 1630–34.

8. On bad families of origin and kids adopted by good or bad homes, see R. J. Cadoret et al., "Genetic-Environmental Interaction in the Genesis of Aggressivity and Conduct Disorders," *Archives of General Psychiatry* 52 (1995), pp. 916–24.

9. Michael Meaney, "Maternal Care, Gene Expression, and the Transmission of Individual Differences in Stress Reactivity Across Generations," *Annual Review of Neuroscience* 24 (2001), pp. 1161–92.

10. On behavior genetics, see S. McGuire and J. Dunn, "Nonshared Environment in Middle Childhood," in J. C. DeFries et al., eds., *Nature and Nurture During Middle Childhood* (Oxford, U.K.: Blackwell, 1994).

11. On genetic closeness, see David Reiss et al., *The Relationship Code* (Cambridge, Mass.: Harvard University Press, 2000).

12. Every child's unique experience of the same family is called a "nonshared environment" in behavior genetics. See Judy Dunn and Robert Plomin, *Unshared Lives: Why Siblings Are So Different* (New York: Basic Books, 2000).

13. It gets more complicated by a genetic timetable. For example, the study discovered that about a third of the genes that influence antisocial behavior in the early teen years no longer do so by midadolescence; they are by then replaced by new social and genetic factors that were not operating earlier.

14. On the other hand, an outgoing baby who flirts and loves to cuddle gets more cuddling in return. As the child grows, she will continue to elicit warmth and engagement from others, reinforcing her own sociability. Either way, how parents treat the baby seems to intensify the genes involved, amplifying how the child acts one way or the other.

15. On neurogenesis: Fred Gage, Salk Institute, personal communication.

16. Fire together, wire together: For example, at the cellular level, the process of learning entails glutamate activating a receptor on one neuron while calcium channels open on another, which triggers the synthesis of proteins in the cell body that "glue together" their receptors. That connection results in a larger response from cell to cell. At the cellular level, learning means that the input from one cell now has a larger output. Joseph LeDoux, presentation at the meeting of the Consortium for Research on Emotional Intelligence in Organizations, Cambridge, Mass., December 12, 2004.

17. On experience and the development of neural systems, see B. J. Casey, "Imaging the Developing Brain: What Have We Learned About Cognitive Development?" *Trends in Cognitive Science* 9 (2005), pp. 104–10.

18. Such stress impairs neurogenesis, reduces hippocampal volume, produces alterations in HPA function, and results in emotional hyperreactivity. See C. L. Coe et al., "Prenatal Stress Diminishes Neurogenesis in the Dentate Gyrus of Juvenile Rhesus Monkeys," *Biological Psychiatry* 54 (2003), pp. 1025–34.

19. On neural defaults, see Gerald Edelman, *Neural Darwinism* (New York: Basic Books, 1987).

20. On spindle cells and stress while migrating to their proper place, see John Allman et al., "The Anterior Cingulate Cortex: The Evolution of an Interface Between

Emotion and Cognition," *Annals of the New York Academy of Science* 935 (2001), pp. 107–17.

21. Davidson adds that we still need to identify more precisely what circuits may be more malleable throughout the life span, and which circuits may be particularly plastic early in life but then become relatively fixed in adulthood.

22. Jerome Kagan and Nancy Snidman, *The Long Shadow of Temperament* (Cambridge, Mass.: Harvard University Press, 2004).

23. Carl Schwartz et al., "Inhibited and Uninhibited Infants 'Grown Up': Adult Amygdalar Response to Novel Versus Newly Familiar Faces," *Science* 399 (2003), pp. 1952–53.

24. On the once-fearful boy, see Kagan and Snidman, *Long Shadow,* pp. 28–29.

Chapter 11. A Secure Base

1. On the suicidal patient, see John Bowlby, *A Secure Base: Parent-Child Attachment and Healthy Human Development* (New York: Basic Books, 1988).

2. On secure children, see Mary Ainsworth et al., "Infant-Mother Attachment and Social Development: Socialization as a Product of Reciprocal Responsiveness to Signals," in M.P.M. Richards, ed., *The Integration of a Child into a Social World* (London: Cambridge University Press, 1974).

3. On protoconversation and thinking, see Trevarthen, "The Self Born in Inter-subjectivity: The Psychology of Infant Communicating," in Ulric Neisser, ed., *The Perceived Self: Ecological and Interpersonal Sources of Self-knowledge* (New York: Cambridge University Press, 1993), pp. 121–73.

4. On brain circuits for attachment, see Jaak Panksepp, *Affective Neuroscience: The Foundations of Human and Animal Emotions* (New York: Oxford University Press, 1998).

5. Attachment circuits include "the cingulate cortex, septal area, bed nucleus of the stria terminalis, and preoptic and medial areas of the hypothalamus, along with their respective mesencephalic projection areas," according to Panksepp, *Affective Neuroscience,* p. 249. Lesions in the bed nucleus of the stria terminalis, which has a profusion of oxytocin receptors, severely impair mothering.

6. On secure babies and their mothers, see Russell Isabella and Jay Belsky, "Interactional Synchrony and the Origins of Infant-Mother Attachments: A Replication Study," *Child Development* 62 (1991), pp. 373–94.

7. See, for example, M. J. Bakermans-Kranenburg et al., "The Importance of Shared Environment in Infant-Father Attachment: A Behavioral Genetic Study of the Attachment Q-Sort," *Journal of Family Psychology* 18 (2004), pp. 545–49; C. L. Bokhorst et al., "The Importance of Shared Environment in Mother-Infant Attachment Security: A Behavioral Genetic Study," *Child Development* 74 (2003), pp. 1769–82.

8. On attachment style, see Erik Hesse, "The Adult Attachment Interview: Historical and Current Perspectives," in Jude Cassidy and Phillip Shaver, eds., *Handbook of Attachment: Theory, Research and Clinical Applications* (New York: Guilford Press, 1999).

9. Synchrony between babies and their mothers was judged by their simultaneous movements, the similar tempos of their actions, and the coordination of their interactions. Frank Bernieri et al., "Synchrony, Pseudosynchrony, and Dissynchrony: Measuring the Entrainment Prosody in Mother-Infant Interactions," *Journal of Personality and Social Psychology* 2 (1988), pp. 243–53.

10. The lullaby in Italian: *"Batti, batti, le manine, / Che tra poco vie-ne papà. / Ti porta le cara-mel-line / Fabiana le man-ge-rà."*

11. On the depressed mother and baby, see Colwyn Trevarthen, "Development of Intersubjective Motor Control in Infants," in M. G. Wade and H.T.A. Whiting,

Motor Development in Children (Dordrecht, the Netherlands: Martinus Nijhoff, 1986), pp. 209–61.

12. On the depressed loop, see Edward Z. Tronick, "Emotions and Emotional Communication in Infants," *American Psychologist* 44 (1989), pp. 112–19.

13. Meaney argues that it makes more sense to identify not just the relevant genes but also the parenting styles (and any other such factors) that might alter levels of the expression of the genes for depression. In other words, what experiences might help inoculate that child against depression? Answers to that question could then guide essential interventions that might lower the risk the child will later become depressed herself. See Michael Meaney, "Maternal Care, Gene Expression."

14. On depressed mothers and infant cortisol, see Tiffany Field et al., "Maternal Depression Effects on Infants and Early Interventions," *Preventive Medicine* 27 (1998), pp. 200–03.

15. On preventing transmission of mood deficits, see A. Cumberland-Li et al., "The Relation of Parental Emotionality and Related Dispositional Traits to Parental Expression of Emotion and Children's Social Functioning," *Motivation and Emotion* 27, no. 1 (2003), pp. 27–56.

16. On children of depressed mothers, see Tronick, "Emotions and Emotional Communication."

17. On neglected children's emotion recognition, see Seth Pollak et al., "Recognizing Emotion in Faces: Developmental Effects of Child Abuse and Neglect," *Developmental Psychology* 36 (2000), pp. 679–88.

18. A poignant extreme can be seen in the thousands of infants placed in Romanian orphanages during the severe economic troubles in the 1980s. These infants spent up to twenty hours a day in their cribs, with no one to attend their needs. As eight-year-olds, a sample of those adopted by American families still showed troubling symptoms: they were ultrastoic, neither crying nor expressing pain; they were uninterested in playing; and they hoarded food. Many of their problems improved as they fit into their new families. Even so, brain scans showed that key areas of their social brains were underactive, including the orbitofrontal cortex. See Harry Chugani et al., "Local Brain Functional Activity Following Early Deprivation: A Study of Postinstitutionalized Romanian Orphans," *NeuroImage* 14 (2001), pp. 1290–1301.

19. On abused children and angry faces, see Seth Pollak et al., "P3b Reflects Maltreated Children's Reactions to Facial Displays of Emotion," *Psychophysiology* 38 (2001), pp. 267–74.

20. On scanning for anger, see Seth Pollak and Stephanie Tolley-Schell, "Selective Attention to Facial Emotion in Physically Abused Children," *Journal of Abnormal Psychology* 112 (2003), pp. 323–38.

21. On parents' shaping of the orbitofrontal cortex, see Allan Schore, *Affect Regulation and the Origin of the Self: The Neurobiology of Emotional Development* (Hillsdale, N.J.: Erlbaum, 1994).

22. On repairing childhood trauma, see Daniel J. Siegel, *The Developing Mind: How Relationships and the Brain Interact to Shape Who We Are* (New York: Guilford Press, 1999).

Chapter 12. The Set Point for Happiness

1. E. Z. Tronick and J. F. Cohn, "Infant-Mother Face-to-Face Interaction: Age and Gender Differences in Coordination and the Occurrence of Miscoordination," *Child Development* 60 (1989), pp. 85–92.

2. On hostile couples and preschoolers, see Lynn Fainsilber Katz and Erica Woodin,

"Hostility, Hostile Detachment, and Conflict Engagement in Marriages: Effect on Child and Family Functioning," *Child Development* 73 (2002), pp. 636–52.

3. On parents' and teachers' ratings of children, see John Gottman and Lynn Fainsilber Katz, "Parental Meta-emotion Philosophy and the Emotional Life of Families: The Theoretical Models and Preliminary Data," *Journal of Family Psychology* 10 (1996), pp. 243–68.

4. On positive affective core, see Robert Emde, "The Pre-presentational Self and Its Affective Core," *Psychoanalytic Study of the Child* 38 (1983), pp. 165–92.

5. On the three scenarios, see Daniel J. Siegel, *The Developing Mind: How Relationships and the Brain Interact to Shape Who We Are* (New York: Guilford Press, 1999).

6. On the orbitofrontal cortex, see Allan Schore, *Affect Regulation and the Origin of the Self: The Neurobiology of Emotional Development* (Hillsdale, N.J.: Erlbaum, 1994).

7. This attunement starts in the first year of life, when the sympathetic nervous system comes on line, branching beyond the brain out into the body to control physiological arousal such as heart rate. The sympathetic branch operates as an energizer for the body, generating upbeat emotions like excitement and interest, pleasure and joy—the exuberant happiness of infancy. When parents match this energy with their own—by, say, looping with a baby's joy—they teach their infant that joyousness and other positive states can be shared and that they can feel safe expressing them. In healthy families most communications between infant and parent during the first year of life are loops aligning positive feelings. In the second year of life the parasympathetic nervous system develops; this branch operates as a brake, modulating or inhibiting impulses—it calms us down and relaxes us. Note the felicitous timing: the parasympathetic branch matures just as babies become more mobile and independent—capable of climbing that table with a lamp. See ibid.

8. On parenting styles, see Siegel, *Developing Mind.*

9. Far more rare are parents who, in a rage, throw a lamp down. They respond to the child as an It, not a You. In such moments they have no empathy but are driven only by their worst impulses. Whenever such parents react to naughtiness with an utter failure to control their own emotional impulse, they fill their children with terror, who learn to fear for their own safety. Neurologically, Siegel proposes, the child endures a simultaneous, contradictory surge in the nervous system, as though accelerating and braking at the same time. The parent—often himself a victim of a troubled childhood—unwittingly offers a disorienting model and becomes an ongoing source of fear for the child rather than offering a secure base. The child suffers a "double insult," being engulfed by terror at the parent, and losing the one relationship that might have helped him emotionally survive by offering safety. As adults, such children often find their closest relationships stormy and chaotic; their history with partners typically is replete with intense emotions and confusing, disastrous endings.

10. Emily Fox Gordon, "In the Garden of Childish Delights," *Time,* January 17, 2005, p. A22.

11. Mary Ainsworth et al., *Patterns of Attachment* (Hillsdale, N.J.: Erlbaum, 1978).

12. On brain circuitry for play, see Jaak Panksepp, *Affective Neuroscience: The Foundations of Human and Animal Emotions* (New York: Oxford University Press, 1998).

13. Ibid.

14. On play and epigenetics, see Nakia Gordon et al., "Socially Induced Brain 'Fertilization': Play Promotes Brain-Derived Neurotrophic Factor Transcription in the

Amygdala and Dorsolateral Frontal Cortex in Juvenile Rats," *Neuroscience Letters* 341 (2003), p. 17.

15. Panksepp, *Affective Neuroscience.*

16. On tickling, see Jaak Panksepp et al., "Empathy and the Action-Perception Resonances of Basic Socio-emotional Systems of the Brain," *Behavioral and Brain Sciences* 25 (2002), pp. 43–44.

17. On ADHD and play, see Panksepp, *Affective Neuroscience.* The idea of a vigorous recess instead of medications, he notes, has never been rigorously tested and remains a speculation. However, since prolonged use of the medications commonly prescribed for ADHD may produce lasting changes in a child's catecholamine system, such nondrug interventions may be more desirable should they prove effective.

18. On charisma, see Panksepp, *Affective Neuroscience.*

19. On emotional set point, see R. J. Davidson and W. Irwin, "The Functional Neuroanatomy of Emotion and Affective Style," *Trends in Cognitive Neuroscience* 3 (1999), pp. 11–21.

20. As Davidson is the first to point out, such data are highly suggestive of a link between how we are parented and our lifelong happiness, but they by no means prove it. It may just be, for instance, that contented adults remember their good times from childhood more readily than the bad ones and so rate their parents as more caring than they actually were. It will take a longitudinal study of many children over decades to establish with greater scientific certainty the relationship between the kind of care we get as children and our brain's capacity for joy in adulthood.

21. Here parents must be sure not to deny or dismiss a child's fear or distress but rather to show empathy for it—and then be sure not to become trapped themselves within the child's bad mood but to confront the situation with a reassuring and optimistic sense that something can be done. By seizing moments of distress as an opportunity for empathy and intimacy, and for helping their child grow and learn, such parents become coaches in the art of managing life's ups and downs: evidence suggests that such parenting changes not only how a child behaves but her brain. One sign of this biological shift is that a child's physiology develops a greater ability to recover from the adverse arousal of stresses and strains. See Siegel, *Developing Mind.*

22. On preschoolers and HPA, see M. R. Gunnar et al., "Temperament, Social Competence, and Adrenocortical Activity in Preschoolers," *Developmental Psychobiology* 31 (1997), pp. 65–85.

23. For the child, the crucial lesson boils down to how to shift from distress to calm. Lacking the ability to shift readily out of distress, children can learn faulty ways to make themselves feel at least a bit better. Some overreact, suppressing distress in a tight overcontrol. Others simply become overwhelmed by anxiety. If such defensive strategies become habitual, they may rigidify, imprinting in the brain as lifelong mental maneuvers deployed to ward off dysphoria of all kinds.

24. On squirrel monkeys, see Karen Parker et al., "Prospective Investigation of Stress Inoculation in Young Monkeys," *Archives of General Psychiatry* 61 (2004), pp. 933–41.

PART IV

Chapter 13. Webs of Attachment

1. The three distinct types of love are crystal clear at the biochemical level. Appropriately, sex hormones—androgens and estrogens—largely fuel lust. Attraction,

that sine qua non of romantic attachment, seems driven by a mix of high levels of dopamine and norepinephrine (which increase pleasure and relaxation) and low levels of serotonin (which adds a pleasing mood). The chemistry that makes a re-lationship last fuels kindness and drives caregiving, which waxes and wanes with varying levels of oxytocin and vasopressin. See Helen Fisher, *Why We Love* (New York: Henry Holt, 2004).

2. John Bowlby, *Attachment and Loss*, vol. 1, *Attachment*, 2nd ed. (New York: Basic Books, 1982).

3. M. K. McClintock, "A Functional Approach to the Behavioral Endocrinology of Rodents," in D. Crews, ed., *Psychobiology of Reproductive Behavior* (Englewood Cliffs, N.J.: Prentice-Hall, 1987), pp. 176–203.

4. On the woman's gaze, see Sarah-Jayne Blakemore and Uta Firth, "How Does the Brain Deal with the Social World?" *NeuroReport* 15 (2004), pp. 119–28. On the four faces, see Knut Kampe et al., "Reward Value of Attractiveness and Gaze," *Nature* 413 (2001), p. 589.

5. The classic study of flirting was done by Irenäus Eibl-Eibesfeldt, who used a spe-cial camera to surreptitiously capture images of romantic couples in Samoa, Brazil, Paris, and New York. See I. Eibl-Eibesfeldt, *Human Ethology* (New York: Aline de Gruyter, 1989).

6. On the parallels between flirting in lovers and in babies, see Jaak Panksepp, *Affective Neuroscience: The Foundations of Human and Animal Emotions* (New York: Oxford University Press, 1998).

7. This consideration plays a larger role in how women weigh a potential partner than it does for men, which may be one reason men tend to fall in love more quickly than do women.

8. On love as an addiction, see Panksepp, *Affective Neuroscience*.

9. On drug addiction, see R. Z. Goldstein, "Drug Addiction and Its Underlying Neurobiological Basis: Neuroimaging Evidence for the Involvement of the Frontal Cortex," *American Journal of Psychiatry* 159 (2002), pp. 1642–52. This study shows that in addition to the subcortical circuitry long known to be at play in addiction, prefrontal areas provide the overly positive appraisal of the drug and disable the neuronal arrays for inhibition of impulse.

10. Brenda and Bob are used as an example in Eileen Kennedy-Moore and Jeanne C. Watson, *Expressing Emotion: Myths, Realities and Therapeutic Strategies* (New York: Guilford Press, 1999).

11. On attachment styles, see Jude Cassidy and Phillip Shaver, eds., *Handbook of Attachment Theory: Research and Clinical Applications* (New York: Guilford Press, 1999).

12. Judith Feeney, "Adult Romantic Attachment and Couple Relationships," in ibid. Feeney notes that there are differing typologies for attachment styles, including some with four types rather than three, and that these styles are not necessarily "frozen"—that one can adopt different styles with changing relationship experi-ences. There are no hard-and-fast boundaries among these types; people can blend them, or manifest one with some people and another with others.

13. On a secure partner, see Deborah Cohn et al., "Working Models of Childhood Attachments and Couple Relationships," *Journal of Family Issues* 13, no. 4 (1992), pp. 432–49.

14. On attachment style and brain mechanism, see Omri Gallath et al., "Attachment-style Differences and Ability to Suppress Negative Thoughts: Exploring the Neural Correlates," *NeuroImage* (in press).

15. The key neural circuitry for attachment styles seems to run between major high- and low-road landmarks of the social brain: the orbitofrontal area, the amygdala, the anterior temporal pole (ATP), the anterior cingulate, and the hippocampus. The amygdala activates the low road during feelings of fear, the ATP and cingulate during sadness. The high road opens when the orbitofrontal area engages, as when we try to think through our relationships and overcome any upsetting related emotions.

16. These structures are all activated on the brain's right side, which seems more involved in distressing emotions.

17. This retrieval of angst was signaled by heightened activity in their hippocampus, the site that goes to work retrieving memories in general.

18. The dorsal area of the cingulate monitors for situations that require greater control by the prefrontal cortex, such as distressing emotions. See Matthew M. Botvinick et al., "Conflict Monitoring and Anterior Cingulate Cortex: An Update," *Trends in Cognitive Sciences* 8, no. 12 (2004), pp. 539–46.

19. On the avoidant style, see Mario Mikulincer and Phillip Shaver, "The Attachment Behavioral System in Adulthood. Activation, Psychodynamics, and Interpersonal Processes," in Mark P. Zanna, ed., *Advances in Experimental Social Psychology* 35 (San Diego: Academic Press, 2003), pp. 53–152.

20. These brain activity patterns seem to explain discoveries made in earlier studies by Shaver's group. For instance, when people in long-term romantic relationships vividly imagined that their partner was leaving them for someone else, those who were anxiously attached were unable to shut off their worried train of thought, while those who were secure or avoidant could readily stop these upsetting ruminations. On shutting off worry, see R. C. Fraley and P. R. Shaver, "Adult Attachment and the Suppression of Unwanted Thoughts," *Journal of Personality and Social Psychology* 73 (1997), pp. 1080–91. But while vanquishing such worries comes easily to those who are secure, suppressing distressing feelings about relationships demands constant mental effort for avoidant types. See Mario Mikulincer et al., "Attachment-Related Strategies During Thought-Suppression: Ironic Rebounds and Vulnerable Self-representations," *Journal of Personality and Social Psychology* 87 (2004), pp. 940–56.

21. On avoidant types, see Feeney, "Adult Romantic Attachment," in Cassidy and Shaver, *Handbook.*

Chapter 14. Desire: His and Hers

1. On brain imaging while looking at a photo of the beloved, see H. A. Fisher et al., "Early Stage Intense Romantic Love Activates Cortical-basal Ganglia Reward/ Motivation, Emotion, and Attention Systems," poster presentation at the Annual Meeting of the Society for Neuroscience, New Orleans, November 11, 2003.

2. The two centers are the caudate nucleus and the septum.

3. On casual sex, see Helen Fisher, *Why We Love* (New York: Henry Holt, 2004), p. 117.

4. On attractive traits, see David Buss, "Sex Differences in Human Mate Preference: Evolutionary Hypotheses Tested in 37 Cultures," *Behavioral and Brain Sciences* 12 (1989), pp. 1–49.

5. On the sweat study, see Charles Wysocki, "Male Axillary Extracts Contain Pheromones that Affect Pulsatile Secretion of Luteinizing Hormone and Mood in Women Recipients," *Biology of Reproduction* 68 (2003), pp. 2107–13.

6. On the hip-to-waist-to-bust ratio, see Buss, "Sex Differences."

7. Devendra Singh, "Female Mate Value at a Glance: Relationship of Hip-to-Waist Ratio to Health, Fecundity, and Attractiveness," *Neuroendocrinology Letters,* suppl. 4 (2002), pp. 81–91.

8. The main areas activated during romantic love include the medial insula, the ACC, the caudate nucleus, and the putamen, all on both sides. These all light up during intense happiness. Just as important, portions of the cingulate gyrus and amygdala that activate during dysphoria were deactivated. See Andrea Bartels and Semir Zeki, "The Neural Basis of Romantic Love," *NeuroReport* 17 (2000), pp. 3829–34.

9. On sexual arousal and brain circuitry in men, see Serge Stoleru et al., "Neuroanatomical Correlates of Visually Evoked Sexual Arousal in Human Males," *Archives of Sexual Behavior* 28 (1999), pp. 1–21; S. L. Rauch et al., "Neural Activation During Sexual and Competitive Arousal in Healthy Men," *Psychiatry Research* 91 (1999), pp. 1–10.

10. The neural wiring for sex includes structures in the higher limbic brain like the septal area, bed nucleus of the stria terminalis, and preoptic areas, which connect through the anterior hypothalamus to the medial forebrain bundle of the lateral hypothalamus. See Jaak Panksepp, *Affective Neuroscience: The Foundations of Human and Animal Emotions* (New York: Oxford University Press, 1998).

11. The aggression circuitry concentrates in the temporal lobes, an area more active in males; the circuitry for tender nurturance, focused in the cingulate area, tends to be more active in women. Here, as everywhere in the brain, what happens depends on specifics: exactly how testosterone affects sexual desire in women differs with the dose; moderate levels increase libido, while very high levels suppress it. See R. C. Gur et al., "Sex Differences in Regional Cerebral Glucose Metabolism During a Resting State," *Science* 267 (1995), pp. 528–31.

12. Dopamine raises testosterone levels, and so the class of antidepressants that raise dopamine levels frequently increase libido as well. See J. P. Heaton, "Central Neuropharmacological Agents and Mechanisms in Erectile Dysfunction: The Role of Dopamine," *Neuroscience and Biobehavioral Reviews* 24 (2000), pp. 561–69.

13. Vasopressin can also impel aggression. Vasopressin and oxytocin act in the brains of both men and women, the one possibly energizing the more assertive side of mothering in women, and the other encouraging the gentler side of fatherhood in men.

14. This simplified account of the neurochemistry of love draws on Panksepp, *Affective Neuroscience.* Panksepp notes that a far wider array of brain chemicals are at play in sexuality, most of which are as yet little understood.

15. On afterplay, see C. S. Carter, "Oxytocin and Sexual Behavior," *Neuroscience and Behavioral Reviews* 16 (1992), pp. 131–44.

16. On the young lawyer and her fiancé, see Mark Epstein, *Open to Desire* (New York: Gotham, 2005).

17. Anne Rice talked about her sex fantasies in Katherine Ramsland, *Roquelaure Reader: A Companion to Anne Rice's Erotica* (New York: Plume, 1996).

18. On common fantasy themes, see Harold Leitenberg and Kris Henning, "Sex Fantasy," *Psychological Bulletin* 117 (1995), pp. 469–96.

19. Not all sex fantasies involve an elaborate scene; some are merely fleeting thoughts or images of a romantic or sexual activity. For a review of the current psychological consensus, see ibid.

20. On fantasizing, see Sigmund Freud, "Creative Writers and Daydreaming," in James Strachey, ed., *The Standard Edition of the Complete Psychological Works of Sigmund Freud,* vol. 9 (1908; London: Hogarth Press, 1962), p. 146.

21. On daydreams and lovemaking, see, for example, G. D. Wilson and R. J. Lang, "Sex Differences in Sexual Fantasy Patterns," *Personality and Individual Differences* 2 (1981), pp. 343–46.

22. But if the fantasy reality becomes imposed on the other, without their consent, then the I-You evaporates into I-It sexuality: *"it* arouses me" rather than *"you* arouse me."* The etiquette for navigating this borderline between consent and imposition has apparently been well defined in the subculture of bondage and discipline, where the very nature of the operative fantasies can all too easily stray into interpersonal disaster.

23. Michael J. Bader, *The Secret Logic of Sexual Fantasies* (New York: St. Martin's Press, 2002), p. 157.

24. On narcissists and sexual attitudes, see Brad J. Bushman et al., "Narcissism, Sexual Refusal, and Aggression: Testing a Narcissistic Reactance Model of Sexual Coercion," *Journal of Personality and Social Psychology* 48 (2003), pp. 1027–40.

25. On women forced into coercive sex, see Edward O. Laumann et al., *The Social Organization of Sexuality: Sexual Practices in the United States* (Chicago: University of Chicago Press, 1994).

26. E. J. Kanin, "Date Rapists: Differential Sexual Socialization and Relative Deprivation," *Archives of Sexual Behavior* 14 (1985), pp. 219–31.

27. On coerced sex as a turn-on or a turnoff, see Bethany Lohr et al., "Sexual Arousal to Erotic and Aggressive Stimuli in Sexually Coercive and Noncoercive Men," *Journal of Abnormal Psychology* 106 (1997), pp. 230–42.

28. K. E. Dean and N. M. Malamuth, "Characteristics of Men Who Aggress Sexually and of Men Who Imagine Aggressing," *Journal of Personality and Social Psychology* 72 (1997), pp. 449–55.

29. On testosterone, see Alan Booth and James Dabbs, Jr., "Testosterone and Men's Marriages," *Social Forces* 72, no. 2 (1993), pp. 463–78.

30. On arousal from depictions of rape, see G. Hall et al., "The Role of Sexual Arousal in Sexually Aggressive Behavior: a Meta-analysis," *Journal of Clinical and Consulting Psychology* 61 (1993), pp. 1091–95.

31. On convicted rapists' lack of empathy, see D. Scully, *Understanding Sexual Violence* (London: HarperCollinsAcademic, 1990).

32. On rapists and negative messages, see E. C. McDonell and R. M. McFall, "Construct Validity of Two Heterosocial Perception Skill Measures for Assessing Rape Proclivity," *Violence and Victims* 6 (1991), pp. 17–30.

33. Clinical evidence suggests that sex offenders masturbate regularly to fantasies of their preferred scenario. Some prisons for pedophiles, rapists, and exhibitionists try to lower the rate of repeat offenses after release by offering treatment programs. For many decades the treatment centered on trying to change the offender's fantasies, through such means as pairing the sex scenario during masturbation with a nauseating odor, or using hormone-blocking medications to extinguish the troubling desire. But today those approaches alone are seen as insufficient without one that also enhances the offender's empathy for their victims. So treatments can include having the offender meet real victims of crimes like their own to listen to the pain and suffering the victims felt. The treatments also address the perpetrator's distorted sense of how victims see them. Exhibitionists, for instance, are confronted with the fact that women they expose themselves to typically see them as pathetic rather than as awesome. Therapy also attacks the distorted thinking that lets a perpetrator rationalize the crime as harmless. On the other hand, trying to suppress the dangerous fantasies can have a paradoxical effect: they may increase instead of decreasing, the more we try to avoid them. So in the more effective programs offenders instead learn how to prevent a relapse by spotting the early stirrings of the dangerous fantasies and by nipping in the bud the habits that in the past had led them to act out those scenarios. See Leitenberg and Henning, "Sex Fantasy."

34. See, for example, Neil Malamuth, "Predictors of Naturalistic Sexual Aggression," *Journal of Personality and Social Psychology* 50 (1986), pp. 953–62.

35. On desire with empathy, see Judith Jordan, "Clarity in Connection: Empathic Knowing, Desire, and Sexuality," in *Women's Growth in Diversity* (New York: Guilford Press, 1997). On ego orgasm, see, for example, Masud Khan, "Ego-Orgasm in Bisexual Love," *International Review of Psycho-analysis* 1 (1974), pp. 143–49.

Chapter 15. The Biology of Compassion

1. The quote is slightly paraphrased from John Bowlby, *A Secure Base* (New York: Basic Books, 1988), p. 62.

2. On romantic partners, see Brooke Feeny, "A Secure Base: Responsive Support of Goal Strivings and Exploration in Adult Intimate Relationships," *Journal of Personality and Social Psychology* 87, no. 5 (2004), pp. 631–48.

3. On the other hand, someone who lacks confidence in his ability to deal with the world may actually find reassurance in a partner who takes control, welcoming the intrusiveness as comforting, relieved to have the chance to be dependent.

4. On attachment anxiety and caregiving, see Mario Mikulincer et al., "Attachment, Caregiving and Altruism: Boosting Attachment Security Increases Compassion and Helping," *Journal of Personality and Social Psychology* 89 (2005), pp. 817–39.

5. On selfish altruism, see R. B. Cialdini et al., "Empathy-based Helping: Is It Selflessly or Selfishly Motivated?" *Journal of Personality and Social Psychology* 52 (1987), pp. 749–58.

6. The secure types offered to help the woman even when her difficulties seemed more extreme: they were told that she was not only destitute but also severely depressed. Presumably she would still be down even if they helped her out, but they were nonetheless willing to lend a hand. This seems to refute theories that hold that people help others in order to feel the pleasure of making someone happy—interpreted by these theoreticians as a "selfish" motive for compassion.

7. Jack Nitschke et al., "Orbitofrontal Cortex Tracks Positive Mood in Mothers Viewing Pictures of Their Newborn Infants," *NeuroImage* 21 (2004), pp. 583–92.

8. Oxytocin is produced in nuclei of the hypothalamus, from where it flows to the pituitary and then is released into the bloodstream. In other pathways from the hypothalamus, oxytocin acts on many other areas, such as the amygdala, the raphe nuclei, and the locus coeruleus (among others), as well as the spinal fluid.

9. On voles and oxytocin, see C. Sue Carter, "Neuroendocrine Perspectives on Social Attachment and Love," *Psychoneuroimmunology* 23, no. 8 (1998), pp. 779–818.

10. On the complex connections between oxytocin and testosterone, see Helen Fisher, *Why We Love* (New York: Henry Holt, 2004).

11. On social allergies, see Michael R. Cunningham et al., "Social Allergies in Romantic Relationships: Behavioral Repetition, Emotional Sensitization, and Dissatisfaction in Dating Couples," *Personal Relationships* 12 (2005), pp. 273–95. The passage about the wet towels and toilet paper roll is quoted from the 2000 Rob Reiner film, *The Story of Us.*

12. On basic neural systems, see Jaak Panksepp, *Affective Neuroscience: The Foundations of Human and Animal Emotions* (New York: Oxford University Press, 1998).

13. On meeting emotional needs, see John Gottman, *The Relationship Cure* (New York: Three Rivers Press, 2002).

14. See John Gottman, *What Predicts Divorce: The Relationship Between Marital Processes and Marital Outcomes* (Hillsdale, N.J.: Erlbaum, 1993).

15. On facial similarity in couples, see R. B. Zajonc et al., "Convergence in the Physical Appearance of Spouses," *Motivation and Emotion* 11 (1987), pp. 335–46.

16. S. M. Drigotas et al., "Close Partner as Sculptor of the Ideal Self," *Journal of Personality and Social Psychology* 77 (1999), pp. 293–323.

17. Erik Filsinger and Stephen Thoma, "Behavioral Antecedents of Relationship Stability and Adjustment: A Five-Year Longitudinal Study," *Journal of Marriage and the Family* 50 (1988), pp. 785–95.

18. See, for example, Gottman, *What Predicts Divorce.*

19. On older couples and pleasures, see Robert W. Levenson et al., "The Influence of Age and Gender on Affect, Physiology, and Their Interrelations: A Study of Long-term Marriages," *Journal of Personality and Social Psychology* 67, no. 1 (1994), pp. 56–68.

20. On the five-to-one ratio, see Gottman, *Relationship Cure.*

PART V

Chapter 16. Stress Is Social

1. For the tale of the Tolstoy marriage, see William L. Shirer, *Love and Hatred: The Stormy Marriage of Leo and Sonya Tolstoy* (New York: Simon & Schuster, 1994).

2. On survival after congestive heart failure, see H. M. Krumholz et al., "The Prognostic Importance of Emotional Support for Elderly Patients Hospitalized with Heart Failure," *Circulation* 97 (1988), pp. 958–64.

3. Men who reported feeling loved most strongly had the very lowest levels of coronary artery disease. While having a loving mate offers protection, being trapped in a toxic relationship may be harmful to health. See T. E. Seeman and S. L. Syme, "Social Networks and Coronary Heart Disease: A Comparative Analysis of Network Structural and Support Characteristics," *Psychosomatic Medicine* 49 (1987), pp. 341–54.

4. On poor relationships as a health risk, see Janice Kiecolt-Glaser et al., "Marital Stress: Immunologic, Neuroendocrine, and Autonomic Correlates," *Annals of the New York Academy of Sciences* 840 (1999), pp. 656–63.

5. On relationships and disease, see Teresa Seeman, "How Do Others Get Under Our Skin: Social Relationships and Health," in Carol Ryff and Burton Singer, eds., *Emotion, Social Relationships, and Health* (New York: Oxford University Press, 2001).

6. Activation of the HPA axis starts when the hypothalamus releases corticotropin hormone (CRH), which in turn triggers the pituitary to release adrenocorticotropin hormone (ACTH), which then stimulates the adrenal cortex to release cortisol, which floods into the bloodstream and has widespread effects throughout the body. See Robert Sapolsky et al., "How Do Glucocorticoids Influence Stress Responses?" *Endocrine Reviews* 21 (2000), pp. 55–89. The Sapolsky laboratory was among the first to document that sustained stress can damage the hippocampus, a region of the brain central to learning and memory. Their work has pinpointed glucocorticoids, a class of steroid hormones secreted from the adrenal gland during stress, as critical to such neurotoxicity. Moreover, they were the first to demonstrate that glucocorticoids will impair the capacity of hippocampal neurons to survive a variety of neurological diseases, including stroke and seizure. A major focus of the laboratory is to examine the cellular and molecular events underlying hippocampal neuron death, and to identify the components of such death worsened by glucocorticoids.

7. The key areas are in the prelimbic cingulate.

8. Via the social brain, our interactions can matter biologically for our resilience in the face of threats to our health. But at this point researchers can only sketch the bare beginning of a map for the specific brain mechanisms involved. More specifically, social information is processed first by the sensory systems of the

neocortex; and it is then fed via the temporal lobe to the amygdala and hippocampus, which then send signals to the HPA axis and the noradrenergic and serotonergic systems. See Seeman, "How Do Others."

9. For better or worse, the steady accumulation of such emotions over years and years is what matters—not just a few intense but passing episodes—as was found when thousands of men and women were tracked for ten years in a study of stress and heart disease. If their stress soared only in the first year, or only in the tenth year, the likelihood that they would end up with cardiovascular problems was much lower because the stress was temporary, not chronic. But people who had high stress levels in both the first year *and* the last—suggesting that stress was more likely a constant feature of their emotional diet—were most at risk for getting heart disease. See James House et al., "Social Relationships and Health," *Science* 241 (1989), pp. 540–45.

10. On the case of Elysa Yanowitz, see Steven Greenhouse, "Refusal to Fire Unattractive Saleswoman Led to Dismissal, Suit Contends," *New York Times,* April 11, 2003, p. A14.

11. The causes of hypertension are, of course, complex. Medicine assumes that an underlying genetic predisposition is always at play, though life's stresses (as well as diet and exercise) also determine how rapidly or strongly that predisposition transforms into an actual malady. Naming a specific person as the "cause" of hypertension seems dubious.

12. Nadia Wager, George Feldman, and Trevor Hussey, "Impact of Supervisor Interactional Style on Employees' Blood Pressure," *Consciousness and Experiential Psychology* 6 (2001).

13. While the jury is still out on the case of Elysa Yanowitz's hypertension, medical data suggest that her disapproving bosses played at least some role in her rising blood pressure. Chronic jumps in blood pressure can raise the set point to which blood pressure returns after recovering from the rise, thus gradually leading to hypertension. In theory, epigenetics means that someone with a genetic vulnerability for hypertension could be rushed into the disease by distressing, ongoing circumstances like these. On the other hand, simple fluid hydraulics may accomplish the same thing. See, for example, B. D. Perry et al., "Persisting Psychophysiological Effects of Traumatic Stress: The Memory of States," *Violence Update* 1, no. 8 (1991), pp. 1–11. However, for a skeptical review see Samuel A. Mann, "Job Stress and Blood Pressure: A Critical Appraisal of Reported Studies," *Current Hypertension Reviews* 2 (2006), pp. 127–38.

14. S. P. Wamala et al., "Job Stress and the Occupational Gradient in Coronary Heart Disease Risk in Women," *Social Science and Medicine* 51 (2000), pp. 481–98; M. G. Marmot and M. J. Shipley, "Do Socio-economic Differences in Mortality Persist after Retirement? 25-Year Follow-up of Civil Servants in the First Whitehall Study," *British Medical Journal* 313 (1996), pp. 1177–80.

15. On fairness and bosses, see M. Kivimaki et al., "Justice at Work and Reduced Risk of Coronary Heart Disease Among Employees: The Whitehall II Study," *Archives of Internal Medicine* 165 (2005), pp. 2245–51.

16. Some have argued the higher rate of disease among those in lower rungs stems from their having less education, or lower salaries, or less control over how they do their job. Such factors certainly could play a role. But in extensive analyses, toxic interaction between bosses and employees has emerged as the critical variable. See: R. G. Wilkinson, *Unhealthy Societies: The Afflictions of Inequality* (London: Routledge, 1996).

17. Y. Gabriel, "An Introduction to the Social Psychology of Insults in Organizations," *Human Relations* 51 (1998), pp. 1329–54.

18. On status and blood pressure, see James Lynch, *The Broken Heart* (New York: Basic Books, 1979).

19. On heightened risk of cardiovascular disease, see, for example, S. P. Thomas, "Women's Anger: Relationship of Suppression to Blood Pressure," *Nursing Research* 46 (1997), pp. 324–30; T. M. Dembroski et al., "Components of Type A, Hostility, and Anger-in: Relationship to Angiographic Findings," *Psychosomatic Medicine* 47 (1985), pp. 219–33.

20. On blood pressure during interactions, see Julianne Holt-Lunstad et al., "Social Relationships and Ambulatory Blood Pressure: Structural and Qualitative Predictors of Cardiovascular Function During Everyday Social Interactions," *Health Psychology* 22, no. 4 (2003), pp. 388–97.

21. On false accusation and heart disease, see Jos A. Bosch et al., "Acute Stress Evokes Selective Motibliation of T Cells that Differ in Chemokine Receptor Expression: A Potential Pathway Linking Reactivity to Cardiovascular Disease," *Brain, Behavior and Immunity* 17 (2003), pp. 251–59.

22. This provoked the T cells to attack the endothelium, where deadly plaque formation begins. This recruitment of T cells, which inflame tissue as they fight off invading bacteria, fits the emerging understanding of the crucial role for such inflammation in atherosclerotic plaque buildup.

23. Cohen assessed the emotional quality of their social interactions in one of his groups of volunteers in the days before coming into the lab. Unpleasant interactions, especially prolonged conflicts (as with heightened levels of cortisol), predicted that a person would be more likely to come down with a severe cold. See Sheldon Cohen, "Social Relationships and Susceptibility to the Common Cold," in Ryff and Singer, *Emotion, Social Relationships*, pp. 221–44.

24. Sheldon Cohen et al., "Sociability and Susceptibility to the Common Cold," *Psychological Science* 14 (2003), pp. 389–95. The study measured social encounters in the weeks before exposure to the rhinovirus, rather than in the days during and after the exposure (since volunteers were in quarantine by then), and so it does not answer the question of whether pleasant or unpleasant encounters just before and on the day of exposure affect immune defenses. That study remains to be done.

25. Sociability—seeking out others in a friendly, genial way—was linked to better moods, better sleep efficiency, and lower levels of cortisol, which in turn predicted less risk of a cold. But, Dr. Cohen notes, searching for a more robust connection might show with greater precision how sociability might "get inside the body"—a question that remains a mystery in need of a more rigorous solution. See Sheldon Cohen, "Psychosocial Models of Social Support in the Etiology of Physical Disease," *Health Psychology* 7 (1988), pp. 269–97. Relationships with a spouse, grandchildren, neighbors, friends, fellow volunteers, or fellow religious congregants all predict that a person will be less susceptible to colds when exposed to rhinoviruses. See Sheldon Cohen, "Social Relationships and Health," *American Psychologist* (November 2004), pp. 676–84.

26. On meta-analysis, see Sally Dickerson and Margaret Kemeny, "Acute Stressors and Cortisol Responses: A Theoretical Integration and Synthesis of Laboratory Research," *Psychological Bulletin* 130 (2004), pp. 355–91.

27. Some of the studies also assayed levels of ACTH, another stress hormone activated by the HPA axis. The effects were much the same, although ACTH acts more quickly, peaking at around ten to twenty minutes after exposure to a stressor, while cortisol peaks later, around thirty to forty minutes after first exposure. There are two widely used scientific measures of cortisol: how much the body secretes and how long those levels take to fall back to normal. People differ greatly

in their recovery times; some bounce back quite quickly from a stressful moment, while others seem to remain stuck in the bad mood.

28. For some reason, we may not realize how greatly social stress actually affects our biology. Subjectively people rated the noise just as distressing as the subtraction task, despite the far greater cortisol hike from the subtraction.

29. Social stress tends to activate the following neural areas (all key in the social brain): right prefrontal cortex, amygdala, anterior cingulate, hippocampus, insula.

30. When they felt they were being evaluated during the math problems, their cortisol rise was, again, higher than when they were doing the math alone in a room. See Tara Gruenewald et al., "Acute Threat to the Social Self: Shame, Social Self-esteem, and Cortisol Activity," *Psychosomatic Medicine* 66 (2004), pp. 915–24.

31. When a critical observer made humiliating remarks, people continued to brood—and so maintain stress arousal—long afterward. But they did not obsess nearly so much if their ordeal was impersonal, like being shocked when a computer program detected they were too slow to push a button whenever they heard a tone. See Laura Glynn et al., "The Role of Rumination in Recovery from Reactivity: Cardiovascular Consequences of Emotional States," *Psychosomatic Medicine* 64 (2002), pp. 714–26.

32. On decline, see Teresa Seeman et al., "The Price of Adaptation: Allostatic Load and Its Health Consequences," *Archives of Internal Medicine* 157 (1997), pp. 2259–68; Teresa Seeman et al., "Exploring a New Concept of Cumulative Biologic Risk: Allostatic Load and Its Health Consequences," *Proceedings of the National Academy of Sciences* 98 (2001), pp. 4770–75.

33. On the cumulative emotional tone of relationships and health, see Ryff and Singer, *Emotion, Social Relationships.* The negative health impact of relationships was worse for men than for women, particularly because they tended to have higher readings for indicators of heart disease, while women adversely affected showed highly elevated readings of stress hormones.

34. The left dorsal-superior zone of the prefrontal cortex, to be precise.

35. On relationships and immune function, see Rosenkrantz et al., "Affective Style and In Vivo Immune Response: Neurobehavioral Mechanisms," *Proceedings of the National Academy of Sciences* 100 (2003), pp. 11, 148–52.

36. In his research on how mother lab rats treat their pups, Michael Meaney discovered that differences in parental care affect genes in the hippocampus that control HPA output via glucocorticoid, a precursor of cortisol. Glucocorticoids are steroids that regulate changes in blood glucose levels, heart rate, and neuron functioning. Genetic research on the complex ways that glucocorticoids themselves are regulated shows they are heavily influenced by social encounters, particularly stressful ones. The pups in Meaney's research whose moms licked and groomed them the most ended up with genes that expressed little of the stress hormone, while those pups who were neglected expressed a great deal. In well-nurtured pups the genes for regulating stress hormones were twice as active as those in neglected pups. The key zone of the left frontal area in the Wisconsin high schoolers appears identical to that found in Meaney's rodents as being altered by the amount of nurturance during puphood.

Meaney's research has identified precise mechanisms that tie nurturance to the body's response to stress. Under stress, the brain response begins with cells in the hypothalamus that secrete corticoid-releasing factor (CRF), which signals the brain to mobilize. CRF activates cells in the pituitary, which release ACTH into the blood, triggering the adrenals to secrete glucocorticoids. These hormones travel up to the brain, where they trigger cells in the hippocampus that monitor CRF levels; these cells in turn signal cells in the hypothalamus to lessen levels of CRF. This regulatory system for adjusting levels of CRF operates constantly. As Meaney notes, how those genes are modified during childhood has lifelong consequences: once their level of expression has been set, it persists in that pattern through life. Good parenting, Meaney finds, produces genes that make the hippocampus better at monitoring stress hormones, so that optimal levels are emitted when under stress—making a person more resilient. We humans share the identical stress hormone circuits with all mammals, including Meaney's lab rats. See Michael Meaney, "Maternal Care, Gene Expression, and the Transmission of Individual Differences in Stress Reactivity Across Generations," *Annual Review of Neuroscience* 24 (2001), pp. 1161–92.

37. On Borden, see Laura Hillenbrand, "A Sudden Illness—How My Life Changed," *The New Yorker,* July 7, 2003.

38. The group centers on Janice Kiecolt-Glaser, a psychologist, and her husband, Ronald Glaser, an immunologist, and has also included William B. Malarkey, a physician at Ohio State College of Medicine and John T. Cacioppo, a founder of social neuroscience, now at the University of Chicago. See, for example, John T. Cacioppo et al., "Autonomic, Endocrine, and Immune Response to Psychological Stress: The Reactivity Hypothesis," *Annals of the New York Academy of Sciences* 840 (1998), pp. 664–73.

39. On women caregivers, see William B. Malarkey et al., "Chronic Stress Down-Regulates Growth Hormone Gene Expression in Peripheral Blood Mononuclear Cells of Older Adults," *Endocrine* 5 (1996), pp. 33–39.

40. On an earlier study of Alzheimer's disease caregivers, see Janice Kiecolt-Glaser et al., "Slowing of Wound Healing by Psychological Stress," *Lancet* 346 (1995), pp. 1194–96

41. On cell aging, see Elissa Epel et al., "Accelerated Telomere Shortening in Response to Life Stress," *Proceedings of the National Academy of Science* 101 (2004), pp. 17,312–15.

42. Suki Casanave, "Embracing this Imperfect Life," *Hope* (March/April 2002), pp. 32–35.

Chapter 17. Biological Allies

1. On choosing pleasant relationships, see Robert W. Levenson et al., "The Influence of Age and Gender on Affect, Physiology, and Their Interrelations: A Study of Long-Term Marriages," *Journal of Personality and Social Psychology* 67, no. 1 (1994), pp. 56–68.

2. On emotional support and biological stress, see Teresa Seeman et al., "Social Ties and Support and Neuroendocrine Function," MacArthur Studies of Successful Aging, *Annals of Behavioral Medicine* 16 (1994), pp. 95–106. Earlier studies have found the same relationship, emotional support lowering risk, with a range of other biological measures, including lower heart rate and blood pressure, lower serum cholesterol, and lower norepinephrine: Teresa Seeman, "How Do Others Get Under Our Skin?" in Carol Ryff and Burton Singer, eds., *Emotion, Social Relationships, and Health* (New York: Oxford University Press, 2001).

3. On older people and emotional complexity, see L. L. Carstensen et al., "Emotional Experience in Everyday Life Across the Lifespan," *Journal of Personality and Social Psychology* 79 (2000), pp. 644–55.

4. On a supportive environment and cognitive ability in the elderly, see Teresa E. Seeman et al., "Social Relationships, Social Support, and Patterns of Cognitive Aging in Healthy, High-functioning Older Adults," *Health Psychology* 4 (2001), pp. 243–55.

5. On loneliness and health, see Sarah Pressman ct al., "Loneliness, Social Network Size, and Immune Response to Influenza Vaccination in College Freshmen," *Health Psychology* 24 (2005), pp. 297–306.

6. On social engineering in homes for the elderly speeding neurogenesis, see Fred Gage, "Neuroplasticity," paper presented at the twelfth meeting of the Mind and Life Institute, Dharamsala, India, October 18–22, 2004.

7. On newlyweds disagreeing, see Janice Kiecolt-Glaser et al., "Marital Stress: Immunologic, Neuroendocrine, and Autonomic Correlates," *Annals of the New York Academy of Sciences* 840 (1999), pp. 656–63.

8. Ibid., p. 657.

9. There was little relationship between the verbal struggle and endocrine measures in the older husbands.

10. Tor Wagner and Kevin Ochsner, "Sex Differences in the Emotional Brain," *Neuro-Report* 16 (2005), pp. 85–87.

11. On the importance of personal relationships, see Carol Ryff et al., "Elective Affinities and Uninvited Agonies: Mapping Emotion with Significant Others Onto Health," in Ryff and Singer, *Emotion, Social Relationships.* From middle age onward men place increasing importance on their relationships, but still to a lesser extent than women.

12. On women and caring, see R. C. Kessler et al., "The Costs of Caring: A Perspective on the Relationship Between Sex and Psychological Distress," in I. G. Sarason and B. R. Sarason, eds., *Social Support: Theory, Research and Applications* (Boston: Martinus Nijhoff, 1985), pp. 491–507.

13. On women being more sensitive, see M. Corriel and S. Cohen, "Concordance in the Face of a Stressful Event," *Journal of Personality and Social Psychology* 69 (1995), pp. 289–99.

14. On memories and biological shifts, see Kiecolt-Glaser et al., "Marital Stress."

15. Numerous studies find that women show stronger immune, endocrine, and cardiovascular reactions to marital arguments than do their husbands. See, for example, Janice Kiecolt-Glaser et al., "Marital Conflict in Older Adults: Endocrinological and Immunological Correlates," *Psychosomatic Medicine* 59 (1997), pp. 339–49; T. J. Mayne et al., "The Differential Effects of Acute Marital Distress on Emotional, Physiological and Immune Functions in Maritally Distressed Men and Women," *Psychology and Health* 12 (1997), pp. 277–88; T. W. Smith et al., "Agency, Communion, and Cardiovascular Reactivity During Marital Interaction," *Health Psychology* 17 (1998), pp. 537–45.

16. On women's deaths from heart disease, see James Coyne et al., "Prognostic Importance of Marital Quality for Survival of Congestive Heart Failure," *American Journal of Cardiology* 88 (2001), pp. 526–29.

17. On broken heart syndrome, see Ilan Wittstein et al., "Neurohumoral Features of Myocardial Stunning Due to Sudden Emotional Stress," *New England Journal of Medicine* 352 (2005), pp. 539–48.

18. On satisfaction and women's health, see Linda Gallo et al., "Marital Status and Quality in Middle-aged Women: Associations with Levels and Trajectories of Cardiovascular Risk Factors," *Health Psychology* 22, no. 5 (2003), pp. 453–63.

19. On holding hands, see J. A. Coan et al., "Spouse, But Not Stranger, Hand Holding Attenuates Activation in Neural Systems Underlying Response to Threat," *Psychophysiology* 42 (2005), p. S44; J. A. Coan et al., "Lending a Hand: Social Regulation of the Neural Response to Threat," *Psychological Science* (2006), in press.

20. The circuitry encompasses the insula, hypothalamus, right prefrontal cortex, and anterior cingulate.

21. On neuroendocrinology and oxytocin, see C. Sue Carter, "Neuroendocrine Perspectives on Social Attachment and Love," *Psychoneuroimmunology* 23 (1998), pp. 779–818. The data for the health benefits of oxytocin are strong, but in map-

ping biological impacts of relationships, researchers will undoubtedly find that other neuroendocrine pathways are also involved in the mix.

22. On the health benefits, see Kerstin Uvnäs-Moberg, "Oxytocin Linked Antistress Effects: The Relaxation and Growth Responses," *Acta Physiologica Scandanavica* 161 (1997), pp. 38–42. While oxytocin has a short half-life—a matter of minutes—it seems to trigger a cascade of secondary mechanisms that have broad health advantages.

23. On blood pressure and oxytocin, see ibid.

24. Carole Radziwill, *What Remains: A Memoir of Fate, Friendship, and Love* (New York: Scribner's, 2005).

25. On women and stress, see Shelley E. Taylor et al., "Female Responses to Stress: Tend-and-Befriend, not Fight-or-Flight," *Psychological Review* 107 (2000), pp. 411–29. See also Shelley E. Taylor, *The Tending Instinct* (New York: Times Books, 2002).

26. On relationships as emotional regulators, see Lisa Diamond and Lisa Aspinwall, "Emotion Regulation Across the Life Span: An Integrative Perspective Emphasizing Self-regulation, Positive Affect, and Dyadic Processes," *Motivation and Emotion* 27, no. 2 (2003), pp. 125–56.

27. Some argue that our overall pattern of cardiovascular and neuroendocrine activity varies to a significant degree as a function of the emotional status of our most major relationships. See, for example, John Cacioppo, "Social Neuroscience: Autonomic, Neuroendocrine, and Immune Responses to Stress," *Psychophysiology* 31 (1994), pp. 113–28.

28. On stress and contagion, see Brooks Gump and James Kulik, "Stress, Affiliation, and Emotional Contagion," *Journal of Personality and Social Psychology* 72, no. 2 (1997), pp. 305–19.

29. On patients and surgery, see James Kulik et al., "Stress and Affiliation: Hospital Roommate Effects on Preoperative Anxiety and Social Interaction," *Health Psychology* 12 (1993), pp. 118–24.

30. In this sense, the network of people who deeply care about a patient's well-being is an underutilized health resource.

31. On brain activity in minimally conscious patients, see N. D. Schiff et al., "fMRI Reveals Large-scale Network Activation in Minimally Conscious Patients," *Neurology* 64 (2005), pp. 514–23.

32. Mark Pettus, *The Savvy Patient* (Richmond, Va.: Capital Books, 2004).

Chapter 18. A People Prescription

1. On rates of burnout, see Sameer Chopra et al., "Physician Burnout," *Student JAMA* 291 (2004), p. 633.

2. On the heart surgeon turned patient, see Peter Frost, "Why Compassion Counts!" *Journal of Management Inquiry* 8 (1999), pp. 127–33. The saga of the heart surgeon as told by Frost is loosely based on the story of Fitzhugh Mullan, a physician who wrote about his own shift from doctor-in-charge to helpless patient suffering from cancer in *Vital Signs: A Young Doctor's Struggle with Cancer* (New York: Farrar, Straus and Giroux, 1982). I, in turn, have slightly modified and shortened Frost's version.

3. David Kuhl, *What Dying People Want* (Garden City, N.Y.: Doubleday, 2002).

4. On rapport and lawsuits, see W. Levinson et al., "Physician-Patient Communication: The Relationship with Malpractice Claims Among Primary Care Physicians and Surgeons," *Journal of the American Medical Association* 277 (1997), pp. 553–59.

5. Fabio Sala et al., "Satisfaction and the Use of Humor by Physicians and Patients," *Psychology and Health* 17 (2002), pp. 269–80.

6. On patient satisfaction, see Debra Roter, "Patient-centered Communication," *British Medical Journal* 328 (2004), pp. 303–04.

7. Doctors, it turns out, are not the best judges of how well their patients understand them. When patients being treated for myocardial infarction or pneumonia were surveyed about their posthospital treatment plans, just 57 percent said they comprehended the plans. But when the very physicians who made up those plans and had explained them to their patients were asked the same question, they said 89 percent understood. That gap showed up again when just 58 percent of patients knew when they could resume their normal activities, while their physicians assured the researchers that 95 percent knew. See Carolyn Rogers, "Communications 101," *American Academy of Orthopedic Surgeons' Bulletin* 147 (1999), p. 5.

8. On exit interviews, see ibid.

9. On the second-year medical students, see Nancy Abernathy, "Empathy in Action," *Medical Encounter* (Winter 2005), p. 6.

10. On security and compassion, see Omri Gillath et al., "An Attachment-Theoretical Approach to Compassion and Altruism," in P. Gilbert, ed., *Compassion: Conceptualizations, Research, and Use in Psychotherapy* (London: Routledge and Kegan Paul, 2004).

11. For the flowchart for caregiving, see William Kahn, "Caring for the Caregivers: Patterns of Organizational Caregiving," *Administrative Science Quarterly* 38 (1993), pp. 539–63.

12. Lyndall Strazdins, "Emotional Work and Emotional Contagion," in Neal Ashkanasy et al., eds., *Managing Emotions in the Workplace* (Armonk, N.Y.: M.E. Sharpe, 2002).

13. For a detailed study of leadership excellence in the medical sector and service professions generally, see Lyle Spencer and Signe Spencer, *Competence at Work: Models for Superior Performance* (New York: John Wiley, 1993).

14. On making the unbearable bearable, see Kenneth B. Schwartz, "A Patient's Story," *Boston Globe Magazine,* July 16, 1995.

15. The Kenneth B. Schwartz Center has a website at www.theschwartzcenter.org.

16. These rounds might be on any topic pertinent to the personal aspects of patient care, ranging from handling a difficult or hostile patient or family, to coping with the emotional price of caring for seriously ill patients. They are regularly scheduled at Mass General (as Harvard Medical School's most renowned hospital is known) and have been adopted by more than seventy other hospitals. The Schwartz Center offers help to other hospitals interested in starting such rounds.

17. Mack Lipkin et al., *The Medical Interview* (New York: Springer-Verlag, 1995).

PART VI

Chapter 19. The Sweet Spot for Achievement

1. Amy Arnsten, "The Biology of Being Frazzled," *Science* 280 (1998), pp. 1711–13.

2. That suggests the wisdom of Nature's design in extreme situations—at least for people who have well-honed expertise to rely on. The problem arises when that same response gets triggered when there is no threat to life—just the symbolic perils of modern life. For the most part in those situations we need to call on the brain's executive center, not our primal habits. To work at our best we need the low road to support the high—not to command it.

3. On stress intensity and impairment, see J. T. Noteboom et al., "Activation of the

Arousal Response and Impairment of Performance Increase with Anxiety and Stressor Intensity," *Journal of Applied Physiology* 91 (2001), pp. 2039–101.

4. Though that dysfunction holds for the brain's temporarily crippled executive centers, the brain still makes a hedged bet that can work well. Consider studies of people under extreme stress in settings like firehouses, combat units, and basketball teams. Under dire pressure, the most seasoned leaders did best by relying on habits and expertise formed over years. A fire captain, for instance, could direct his firemen amid the chaotic uncertainty and terror of a blaze by trusting intuitions forged in a long history of similar situations. While old-timers instinctively know what to do in such high-intensity moments, for a novice the best theory can fail. See Fred Fiedler, "The Curious Role of Cognitive Resources in Leadership," in Ronald E. Riggio et al., eds., *Multiple Intelligences and Leadership* (Mahwah, N.J.: Erlbaum, 2002).

5. On brain correlates of sadness and joy, see Antonio R. Damasio et al., "Subcortical and Cortical Brain Activity During the Feeling of Self-generated Emotions," *Nature Neuroscience* 3 (2002), pp. 1049–56.

6. Sam Intrator, *How Teaching Can Inspire Real Learning in the Classroom* (New Haven, Conn.: Yale University Press, 2003).

7. Positive moods, for example, can make people more realistic; when people who are feeling good have an important goal that they want to achieve, they will seek out potentially useful information even when it might be negative and upsetting. See, for example, L. G. Aspinwall, "Rethinking the Role of Positive Affect in Self-regulation," *Motivation and Emotion* 22 (1998), pp. 1–32. On the other hand, an elevated mood is not necessarily best for every task: being too giddy bodes poorly for detail work like checking a contract. Indeed, negative moods can sometimes make our perceptions more realistic rather than overly rosy. At the right time, it pays to get serious. For a further review, see Neal M. Ashkanasy, "Emotions in Organizations: A Multi-level Perspective," in Neal Ashkanasy et al., eds., *Emotions in the Workplace: Research, Theory, and Practice* (Westport, Conn.: Quorum Books, 2000).

8. On radiologists' diagnoses, see C. A. Estrada et al., "Positive Affect Facilitates Integration of Information and Decreases Anchoring in Reasoning Among Physicians," *Organizational Behavior and Human Decision Processes* 72 (1997), pp. 117–35.

9. The more difficulty we have performing a given task, the more diffuse and unfocused the pattern of active sites will be in our brain. A diffusely activated brain occurs, for instance, when we are bored and daydreaming, or when we are highly anxious. The brain activation pattern during peak cognitive efficiency looks highly specific to the task at hand. Brain imaging taken while the person is performing a task well shows that the brain has mobilized the sites most pertinent to that activity, and not others that are irrelevant (and so represent an extraneous action or distraction). Cognitive efficiency demands that the specific tools of the brain contribute to the task at hand in a well-orchestrated manner.

10. Anxiety erodes cognitive efficiency. For example, students with math anxiety have less capacity in their working memory when they tackle a math problem. Their anxiety occupies the attentional space they need for math, impairing their ability to solve math problems or grasp new concepts. See Mark Ashcroft and Elizabeth Kirk, "The Relationship Among Working Memory, Math Anxiety, and Performance," *Journal of Experimental Psychology* 130, no. 2 (2001), pp. 224–27.

11. That argument, in terms of the "X-system" and the "C-system" (roughly the low and high roads, respectively), is made by Matthew Lieberman et al., "A Pain by Any Other Name (Rejection, Exclusion, Ostracism) Still Hurts the Same: The Role

of Dorsal Anterior Cingulate Cortex in Social and Physical Pain," in J. Cacioppo et al., eds., *Social Neuroscience: People Thinking About Thinking People* (Cambridge, Mass.: MIT Press, 2005).

12. On cortisol and the inverted U, see Heather C. Abercrombie et al., "Cortisol Variation in Humans Affects Memory for Emotionally Laden and Neutral Information," *Behavioral Neuroscience* 117 (2003), pp. 505–16.

13. Moderate stress enhances focused attention. See Eran Chajut and Daniel Algom, "Selective Attention Improves Under Stress: Implications for Theories of Social Cognition," *Journal of Personality and Social Psychology* 85 (2003), pp. 231–48.

14. On anxiety and working memory, see Mark Ashcroft and Elizabeth Kirk, "The Relationship Among Working Memory, Math Anxiety, and Performance," *Journal of Experimental Psychology* 130 (2001), pp. 224–27.

15. See, for example, Mario Mikulincer et al., "Attachment, Caregiving and Altruism: Boosting Attachment Security Increases Compassion and Helping," *Journal of Personality and Social Psychology* 89 (2005), pp. 817–39.

16. Mihalyi Csikszentmilhalyi and Reed Larson, *Being Adolescent: Conflict and Growth in the Teenage Years* (New York: Basic Books, 1984).

17. On managers in bad moods, see J. M. George and A. P. Brief, "Motivational Agendas in the Workplace," *Research in Organizational Behaviour* 18 (1996), pp. 75–109.

18. In describing the relationship between mood and performance in terms of the inverted U, I am oversimplifying a bit. Every major emotion has its distinctive influence on how we think. Our moods sway our judgments; when we are in a sour mood, we more readily dislike what we see; in contrast, we are more forgiving or appreciative while we are upbeat. See Neal M. Ashkanasy, "Emotions in Organizations: A Multilevel Perspective," in Neal Ashkanasy et al., eds., *Emotions in the Workplace: Research, Theory, and Practice* (Westport, Conn.: Quorum Books, 2000). While good moods have great benefits, negative emotions can be useful in specific situations. "Bad" moods can enhance certain kinds of performance, such as attending to detail in a search for errors or making finer distinctions among choices. This mood-task fit has been mapped in more detail in the work of John Mayer at the University of New Hampshire. For a review of how moods affect performance, see David Caruso et al., *The Emotionally Intelligent Manager* (San Francisco: Jossey Bass, 2004). Neuroscientists have started to map the specific ways different emotional states might boost various intellectual abilities. In the mild mood range at least, moods can facilitate specific tasks—and on a limited range of specific tasks, negative moods help at times and positive moods sometimes hurt. For instance, anxiety (at least at the levels instilled by watching a clip of a horror film) seems to augment tasks largely processed by the right prefrontal cortex, such as face recognition. Enjoyment (induced by watching a comedy) enhances left-hemisphere tasks such as verbal performance. See Jeremy R. Gray et al., "Integration of Emotion and Cognition in the Lateral Prefrontal Cortex," *Proceedings of the National Academy of Sciences* 199 (2002), pp. 4115–20.

19. On social stress and working memory impairment, see Bernet Elizuya and Karin Rochlofs, "Cortisol-Induced Impairments of Working Memory Requires Acute Sympathetic Activation," *Behavioral Neuroscience* 119 (2005), pp. 98–103.

20. Destroying the hippocampus ends the ability to learn; neurological patients with damage there live every moment as though the last has not occurred. Some conditions—notably trauma and chronic depression—shrink the hippocampus by killing off cells. As patients recover from these disorders, their hippocampus gradually grows back.

21. On cortisol and the inverted U, see Abercrombie et al., "Cortisol Variation in Humans."

22. R. Alpert and R. N. Haber, "Anxiety in Academic Achievement Situations," *Journal of Abnormal and Social Psychology* 61 (1960), pp. 207–15.

23. Sian Beilock and Thomas Carr, "When High-powered People Fail: Working Memory and 'Choking Under Pressure' in Math," *Psychological Science* 16 (2005), pp. 101–05.

24. Jeanne Nakamura, "Optimal Experience and the Uses of Talent," in Mihalyi and Isabella Csikzentmihalyi, eds., *Optimal Experience: Psychological Studies of Flow in Consciousness* (New York: Cambridge University Press, 1988).

25. Oddly, the combination of good news delivered with a gloomy expression was perceived even more negatively than bad news delivered with a tone of gloom. On the effects of a positive facial expression in managers, see Michael T. Newcombe and Neal M. Ashkanasy, "The Code of Affect and Affective Congruence in Perceptions of Leaders: An Experimental Study," *Leadership Quarterly* 13 (2002), pp. 601–04.

26. Thomas Sy et al., "The Contagious Leader: Impact of the Leader's Mood on the Mood of Group Members, Group Affective Tone, and Group Processes," *Journal of Applied Psychology* 90 (2005), pp. 295–305.

27. M. T. Dasborough, "Cognitive Asymmetry in Employee Emotional Reactions to Leadership Behaviors," *Leadership Quarterly*, 17 (2006), pp. 163–178

28. Neal Ashkanasy et al., "Managing Emotions in a Changing Workplace," in Ashkanasy et al., *Emotions in the Workplace.*

29. James Harter, Gallup Organization, unpublished report, December 2004.

30. The poll is cited in Amy Zipkin, "The Wisdom of Thoughtfulness," *New York Times,* May 31, 2000, p. C5.

31. Students tend to feel more a part of things at school the more their teachers are supportive and caring, and the more good friends and favorite extracurricular involvements they have there. See the special edition of the *Journal of School Health* 74, no. 7, September 2004.

32. For the study of teaching style and student achievement, see Bridget Hamre and Robert Pianta, *Child Development* 76 (2005), pp. 949–67.

33. K. Wentzel, "Are Effective Teachers Like Good Parents? Teaching Styles and Student Adjustment in Early Adolescence," *Child Development* 73 (2002), pp. 287–301.

34. Joseph Durlak and Roger Weisberg, "A Major Meta-Analysis of Positive Youth Development Programs," presentation at the annual meeting of the American Psychological Association, Washington, D.C., August 2005.

35. On the educational benefits of a caring environment, see, for example, K. F. Osterman, "Students' Needs for Belonging in the School Community," *Review of Educational Research* 70 (2000), pp. 323–67.

36. See, for example, the special issue of the *Journal of School Health* (September 2004) on school connectedness.

Chapter 20. The Connectedness Corrective

1. Former superintendent John Tindall, as quoted in 1949 by the *St. Louis Dispatch* in a report by the Annie E. Casey Foundation, *Small Is Beautiful* (Missouri Division of Youth Services, 2003). My account of the Missouri system is based on that report.

2. On recidivism rates, see ibid. However, comparisons across states should be viewed with caution; they may not reflect identical measures. A better comparison would include all states, tracking in the identical way those released. Such data do not yet exist.

3. On prefrontal damage, see Adriane Raine et al., "Brain Abnormalities in Murderers Indicated by Positron Emission Tomography," *Biological Psychiatry* 42 (1997), pp. 495–508.

4. Adriane Raine et al., "Reduced Prefrontal Gray Matter Volume and Reduced Autonomic Activity in Antisocial Personality Disorder," *Archives of General Psychiatry* 57 (2000), pp. 119–27. Many violent people have atrophy in the amygdala; see R. J. Davidson, K. M. Putnam, and C. L. Larson, "Dysfunction in the Neural Circuitry of Emotion Regulation—A Possible Prelude to Violence," *Science* 289 (2000), pp. 591–94.

5. On prefrontal lobe and cognitive control, see E. K. Miller and J. D. Cohen, "An Integrative Theory of Prefrontal Cortex Function," *Annual Review of Neuroscience* 24 (2001), pp. 167–202.

6. This neurological timeline was the basis for a 2005 Supreme Court decision against allowing the execution of juveniles, because young brains have not matured to the point that their decision-making and impulse-control abilities are at levels of adults.

7. Nationally, the annual cost of this vast prison system surpassed $60 billion in 2002. On the prison population, see Bureau of Justice Statistics, U.S. Department of Justice, November 2005.

8. On costs and recidivism rates, see Patrick Langer and David Levin, "Recidivism of Prisoners Released in 1994," report from the Bureau of Justice Statistics, NCJ 193427, (June 2002).

9. Kalamazoo County Coalition on Criminal Justice, "A Plan for Integrating Prevention, Intervention, Corrections, and Reintegration Programs in the Kalamazoo County Criminal Justice System," September 15, 2004.

10. On connectedness and crime, see Dr. Felton Earls, interview by Dan Hurley, "On Crime as Science (A Neighbor at a Time)," *New York Times,* January 6, 2004, p. C1.

11. On analysis of neighborhoods, see Robert J. Sampson et al., "Neighborhoods and Violent Crime: A Multi-level study of Collective Efficacy," *Science* 277 (1997), pp. 918–24.

12. The creation of greater cohesiveness is a social experiment waiting to be done well.

13. Nancy Guerra and Ronald Slaby, "Cognitive Mediators of Aggression in Adolescent Offenders: 2. Intervention," *Developmental Psychology* 26 (1990), pp. 269–77.

14. On younger inmates, see "Childhood on Trial: The Failure of Trying and Sentencing Youth in Adult Criminal Court," Coalition for Juvenile Justice, 2005 Annual Report.

15. These circuits remain somewhat malleable throughout life; if a person of any age has the motivation to learn, they still can do so with some success, given the proper model of learning. But after this window has closed in the twenties, it takes far more effort and time to shape them—and so requires that the person be more highly motivated and be given more personalized help. For the apt model of learning, see Part Two in Daniel Goleman et al., *Primal Leadership* (Boston: Harvard Business School Press, 2002). See also "Best Practices" at www.eiconsortium.org.

16. On rehab in prison, see James McGuire, ed., *What Works: Reducing Reoffending* (New York: John Wiley, 1995); James McGuire, *Offender Rehabilitation and Treatment* (New York: John Wiley, 2002).

17. On programs in social and emotional learning, see www.casel.org.

18. On lower rates, see Wendy Garrard, "Does Conflict Resolution Education Reduce Antisocial Behavior in Schools? The Evidence Says Yes," presented at the annual meeting of the Ohio Commission on Dispute Resolution and Conflict Management, Columbus, Ohio, November 2005.

19. The National Emotional Literacy Project for Youth-at-Risk is one pilot program that adapts social-emotional abilities to young prison populations (www.lionheart.org). Another pilot program teaches social intelligence skills to youth offenders in Connecticut prisons—for example, they learn better social problem-solving skills and ways to disengage from anger. See Zak Stambor, "Can Teaching Troubled Teens Social Problem-solving Keep Them Out of Trouble?" *Monitor on Psychology* (December 2005), pp. 90–91.

20. On highest recidivism among youngest prisoners, and those with the longer records, see Bureau of Justice Statistics, 2005.

21. On the Bucks County meeting, see Laura Mirsky, "Directing *Burning Bridges*, a Documentary About a Restorative Conference," at www.realjustice.org.

22. On restorative justice, see Gerry Johnstone, *Restorative Justice* (London: Willan Publishers, 2001).

23. See Kathleen Kenna, "Justice for All," *Greater Good* (Spring/Summer 2005).

24. On recidivism in multisystemic therapy, see C. M. Boruin et al., "Multisystemic Treatment of Serious Juvenile Offenders: Long-term Prevention of Criminality and Violence," *Journal of Consulting and Clinical Psychology* 63 (1995), pp. 569–78.

25. Ibid.

26. On age of prisoners, see Paige Harrison and Alan J. Beck, "Prisoners in 2003," *Bulletin,* Bureau of Justice Statistics, Washington, D.C., November 2004.

Chapter 21. From Them to Us

1. The Afrikaaner and Anne were witnessed by Peter Senge and recounted in Peter Senge et al., *Presence: Human Purpose and the Field of the Future* (Cambridge, Mass.: Society for Organizational Learning, 2004).

2. On Us-Them, see Walter Kaufmann, prologue to Martin Buber, *I and Thou* (1937; New York: Simon & Schuster, 1990), p. 13.

3. On similarity and shocks, see, for example, Dennis Krebs, "Empathy and Altruism; An Examination of the Concept and a Review of the Literature," *Psychological Bulletin* 73 (1970), pp. 258–302; C. Daniel Batson, *The Altruism Question: Toward a Scientific Answer* (Hillsdale, N.J.: Erlbaum, 1991).

4. Elie Wiesel made these remarks at the sixtieth anniversary of the liberation of Auschwitz. See *Jerusalem Post,* January 25, 2005.

5. For instance, data from the Implicit Association Test suggest that in the United States most whites and about half of blacks are quicker to associate positive terms like "joy" with whites and negative ones like "bomb" with blacks. Even people who espouse antiracist views are often chagrined to find that they, too, are quicker to be positive about whites and negative about blacks.

6. On the Implicit Association Test, see Anthony Greenwald et al., "Measuring Individual Differences in Implicit Cognition: The Implicit Association Test," *Journal of Personality and Social Psychology* 74 (1998), pp. 1464–80.

7. T. Andrew Poehlman et al., "Understanding and Using the Implicit Association Test: III. Meta-analysis of Predictive Validity," unpublished manuscript.

8. Brain imaging reveals that the stronger a person holds such subtle prejudice, the more active the amygdala while looking at the photo of someone in the target group, be it whites, women scientists, or the elderly. See Alan Hart et al.,

"Differential Response in the Human Amygdala to Racial Out-group Versus In-group Face Stimuli," *NeuroReport* 11 (2000), pp. 2351–55; Elizabeth Phelps and Mahzarin R. Banaji, "Performance on Indirect Measures of Race Evaluation Predicts Amygdala Activation," *Journal of Cognitive Neuroscience* 12 (2000), pp. 729–38. And when images of faces from a Them group are shown quickly (or masked) so that the conscious mind has no idea what it has seen, the amygdala reacts more strongly to these barely glimpsed images than to ones that are consciously seen. See also William A. Cunningham et al., "Separable Neural Components in the Processing of Black and White Faces," *Psychological Science* 15 (2004), pp. 806–13.

9. Irene V. Blair, "The Malleability of Automatic Stereotypes and Prejudice," *Personality and Psychology Review* 202 (2002), pp. 242–61.

10. On stereotype reduction, see Nilanjana Dasgupta and Anthony Greenwald, "On the Malleability of Automatic Attitudes: Combating Automatic Prejudice with Images of Admired and Disliked Individuals," *Journal of Personality and Social Psychology* 81 (2001), pp. 800–14.

11. On methods to reduce implicit bias, see Blair, "The Malleability."

12. Intriguingly, people who hold an ongoing resolve to suppress negative stereo-types are able to do so as long as they are aware of the moment they see a person in the target group. But when the exposure to that person is subliminal (a blink, just 33 milliseconds), the implicit bias remains. See Blair, "The Malleability."

13. On prefrontal and amygdala activity, see Matthew Lieberman et al., "A Pain by Any Other Name (Rejection, Exclusion, Ostracism) Still Hurts the Same: The Role of Dorsal Anterior Cingulate Cortex in Social and Physical Pain," in J. Cacioppo et al., eds., *Social Neuroscience: People Thinking About Thinking People* (Cambridge, Mass.: MIT Press, 2005).

14. This study also suggests why demagogues have always stirred fear and anger into the mix with hostility toward Them. A group's sense of security poses a threat to one thing: prejudice.

15. On intergroup studies, see Thomas Pettigrew and Linda Tropp, "A Meta-analytic Test of Intergroup Contact Theory," *Journal of Personality and Social Psychology* (2006, in press).

16. Casual contact counts less than relationships that people feel are important. See Rolf van Dick et al., "Role of Perceived Importance in Intergroup Conflict," *Journal of Personality and Social Psychology* 87, no. 2 (2004), pp. 211–27.

17. On ethnic divides in Europe, see Thomas Pettigrew, "Generalized Intergroup Contact Effects on Prejudice," *Personality and Social Psychology Bulletin* 23 (1997), pp. 173–85.

18. On Germans and prejudice, see Ulrich Wagner et al., "Ethnic Prejudice in East and West Germany: The Explanatory Power of Intergroup Contact," *Group Processes and Intergroup Relations* 6 (2003), pp. 22–36.

19. On affect versus cognitive categories, see Pettigrew and Tropp, "Meta-analytic Test."

20. On categories breaking down, see Susan Rakosi Rosenbloom and Niobe Way, "Experiences of Discrimination Among African American, Asian American and Latino Adolescents in an Urban High School," *Youth & Society* 35, (2004), pp. 420–51.

21. Elliot Aronson, *Nobody Left to Hate* (New York: W. H. Freeman, 2000), p. 15.

22. On the toll of not belonging, see Mean Twenge et al., "Social Exclusion and the Deconstructed State: Time Perception, Meaninglessness, Lethargy, Lack of Emotion,

and Self-awareness," *Journal of Personality and Social Psychology* 85 (2003), pp. 409–23.

23. National Center for Chronic Disease Prevention and Health Promotion, Division of Adolescent and School Health, *School Connectedness: What We Know That Makes a Difference in Students' Lives* (Atlanta, Ga., 2004).

24. On the decrement in working memory, see Toni Schmader and Michael Johns, "Converging Evidence that Stereotype Threat Reduces Working Memory Capacity," *Journal of Personality and Social Psychology* 85 (2003), pp. 440–52.

25. Samuel Gaertner et al., "The Contact Hypothesis," in Judith Nye and Aaron Brower, *What's Social about Social Cognition?* (Thousand Oaks, Calif.: Sage, 1996).

26. On the letter, see Aronson, *Nobody Left,* p. 151.

27. On the gift, see Joseph Berger, "A Muslim Santa's Gift to an Interfaith Group: Free Rent," *New York Times,* December 24, 2004, p. B3.

28. Forgiveness, of course, comes more readily when the offender offers an authentic apology. As one Israeli proposed, a leader on either side of the Israeli rift with the Palestinians could make a ritual apology like, "You have been through so much because of us. We are sorry. We are sorry because we didn't mean to hurt you, we only wanted to build a nation." That might help the peace process. See Lucy Benjamin, "Impasse: Israel and Palestine," Conference at Columbia University, New York, November 20, 2004.

29. On the physiology of forgiveness, see Fred Luskin, *Forgive for Good* (San Francisco: HarperSanFrancisco, 2001).

30. On forgiveness in Northern Ireland, see ibid.

31. Rabbi Lawrence Kushner was interviewed in Jonathan Cott, *On a Sea of Memory* (New York: Random House, 2005), p. 153.

32. The producer of *New Dawn* is George Weiss, La Benevulencija Productions, Amsterdam. The Rwanda Project has its website at www.Heal-reconcile-Rwanda.org.

33. Ervin Staub, *The Roots of Evil* (New York: Cambridge University Press, 1992).

34. Ervin Staub and Laurie Anne Pearlman, "Advancing Healing and Reconciliation in Rwanda and Other Post-conflict Settings," in L. Barbanel and R. Sternberg, eds., *Psychological Interventions in Times of Crisis* (New York: Springer-Verlag, 2006).

Epilogue: What Really Matters

1. On the hedonic treadmill, see Daniel Kahneman et al., "A Survey Method for Characterizing Daily Life Experience: The Day Reconstruction Method," *Science* 306 (2004), pp. 1776–80, at 1779.

2. The other strong factors in creating unhappiness were being depressed and not sleeping well, both of which can sometimes be indirect measures of relationships.

3. On vibrant relationships, see Ryff and Singer, "The Contours of Positive Human Health," *Psychological Inquiry* 9 (1988), pp. 1–28.

4. On thingification, see James Gustafson, "G. H. Mead and Martin Buber on the Interpersonal Self," in Ulric Neisser, ed., *The Perceived Self* (New York: Cambridge University Press, 1993).

5. On perfected social intelligence, see George Herbert Mead, *Mind, Self, and Society* (Chicago: University of Chicago Press, 1934), p. 310.

6. Carl Marci of Massachusetts General Hospital has proposed teaching empathy via the physiological logarithm and (working with colleagues at MIT's Media Lab) has already designed a prototype for a patient-monitoring fanny pack.

7. While Bhutan's king declared this national priority decades ago, only in 2004 did the idea gain enough traction to inspire an international conference, held in Thimbu, the nation's capital. Proceedings of an earlier seminar were published in 1999 by the Centre for Bhutan Studies as *Gross National Happiness: A Set of Discussion Papers* (Thimbu, Bhutan).

8. One proposal for a measure of national well-being would include life-satisfaction factors like trustworthy and engaging relationships, as a more comprehensive assessment of the consequences of public policy. For the index of social good, see www.neweconomics.org.

9. David Myers, *The Pursuit of Happiness* (New York: William Morrow, 1992).

10. Colin Camerer et al., "Neuroeconomics: How Neuroscience Can Inform Economics," *Journal of Economic Literature* 43 (2005), pp. 9–64.

11. Alvin Weinberg was for several decades director of one of America's largest national nuclear science laboratories at Oak Ridge, Tennessee, and was also a science policy adviser to two presidents. The lab he directed led the "swords into plowshares" movement, seeking to find peaceful applications of nuclear and related technologies—pioneering in nuclear medicine, alternative energy sources, global climate studies, genetics and biomedical assays, among other areas. See Alvin Weinberg, *Reflections on Big Science* (Cambridge, Mass.: MIT Press, 1967).

12. On structural violence, see Paul Farmer, *Pathologies of Power* (Berkeley: University of California Press, 2003).

13. For information on parent education programs, see, for example, www.families_first.org. For social and emotional learning, including data on the effectiveness of such programs, and their benefits for academic achievement, see www.casel.org.

14. Susan Alberts, a Duke University biologist, is quoted in "Social Baboons Make Better Mums," *New Scientist* (November 2003).

Appendix A. The High and Low Roads: A Note

1. For a fuller discussion of these systems, see Colin Camerer, "Neuroeconomics: How Neuroscience Can Inform Economics," *Journal of Economic Literature* 43 (2005), pp. 9–64.

2. Lieberman proposes as candidates for the neural wiring of the X-system, the amygdala, basal ganglia, lateral temporal cortex, ventromedial prefrontal cortex, and dorsal anterior cingulate cortex. He proposes that the control mode involves the anterior cingulate cortex, lateral prefrontal cortex, posterior parietal cortex, and hippocampus, among others. See: Matthew D. Lieberman, "The X- and C-systems: The Neural Basis of Automatic and Controlled Social Cognitions," in E. Harmon-Jones and P. Winkielman, *Social Neuroscience* (New York: Guilford Press, 2006). Daniel Siegel suggests a different "high-low road" dichotomy, using the "high" to signify an intact and well-functioning social and emotional apparatus, and "low" an impaired mode. See Daniel Siegel, *The Developing Mind: How Relationships and the Brain Interact to Shape Who We Are* (New York: Guilford Press, 1999).

3. Some cognitive theorists would argue that many emotional reactions involve a mix of cognition and affect, both to some degree automatic and controlled—another way in which this dichotomy oversimplifies complexities.

Appendix B. The Social Brain

1. Leslie Brothers, "The Social Brain: A Project for Integrating Primate Behavior and Neurophysiology in a New Domain," *Concepts in Neuroscience* 1 (1990), pp. 27–51.

2. For instance, another tentative mapping of the social brain has been offered by

Preston and de Waal in their review of the neuroanatomy of empathy. See Stephanie D. Preston and Frans B. M. de Waal, "Empathy: Its Ultimate and Proximate Bases," *Behavioral and Brain Sciences* 25 (2002), pp. 1–20.

3. Ibid.

4. On minimal circuitry, see Marco Iacoboni and Gian Luigi Lenzi, "Mirror Neurons, the Insula, and Empathy," *Behavioral and Brain Sciences* 25 (2002), pp. 39–40.

5. On emotional resonance, see Marco Iacoboni, "Understanding Intentions Through Imitation," in Scott Johnson, ed., *Taking Action: Cognitive Neuroscience Perspectives on Intentional Acts* (Cambridge, Mass.: MIT Press, 2003), pp. 107–38.

6. On interlocking and independent circuits, see James R. Blair and Karina S. Perschardt, "Empathy: A Unitary Circuit or a Set of Dissociable Neuro-Cognitive Systems?" *Behavioral and Brain Sciences* 25 (2002), pp. 27–28.

7. On disgust, see Anthony Atkinson, "Emotion-specific Clues to the Neural Substrate of Empathy," *Behavioral and Brain Sciences* 25 (2002), pp. 22–23.

8. On moral judgment and empathy, see Paul J. Eslinger et al., "Emotional and Cognitive Processing in Empathy and Moral Behavior," *Behavioral and Brain Sciences* 25 (2002), pp. 34–35; Iacoboni and Lenzi, "Mirror Neurons."

9. On the emotional brain and relationships, see Reuven Bar-On et al., "Exploring the Neurological Substrates of Emotional and Social Intelligence," *Brain* 126 (2003), pp. 1790–1800.

10. On somatic markers, see Antonio Damasio, *Looking for Spinoza: Joy, Sorrow, and the Feeling Brain* (New York: Harcourt, 2003).

11. On the role of the insula, see Iacoboni and Lenzi, "Mirror Neurons."

12. On embarrassing moments, see S. Berthoz et al., "An fMRI Study of Intentional and Unintentional Embarrassing Violations of Social Norms," *Brain* 125 (2002), pp. 1696–1708.

13. On the neurology of social decision-making, see Antoine Bechara, "The Neurology of Social Cognition," *Brain* 125 (2002), pp. 1673–75.

Appendix C. Rethinking Social Intelligence

1. Stephanie D. Preston and Frans B. M. de Waal, "Empathy: Its Ultimate and Proximate Bases," *Behavioral and Brain Sciences* 25 (2002), pp. 1–20.

2. The more members of a primate band in a species, the larger the neocortex relative to the rest of the brain. See T. Sawaguchi and H. Kudo, "Neocortical Development and Social Structures in Primates," *Primates* 31 (1990), pp. 283–89.

3. Sarah-Jayne Blakemore and Uta Firth, "How Does the Brain Deal with the Social World?" *NeuroReport* 15 (2004), pp. 119–28.

4. On the social origins of intelligence, see Denise Cummins, *Human Reasoning: An Evolutionary Perspective* (Cambridge, Mass.: Bradford/MIT Press, 1997).

5. On neuro-economics, see Colin Camerer et al., "Neuroeconomics: How Neuroscience Can Inform Economics," *Journal of Economic Literature* 43 (2005), pp. 9–64.

6. Mayer, a psychologist at the University of New Hampshire, with his colleagues set the standard for theory and research in this area. As Peter Salovey and Mayer (and others, including myself) define emotional intelligence, the concept overlaps social intelligence. For example, see John Mayer and Peter Salovey, "Social Intelligence," in Christopher Peterson and Martin E. P. Seligman, eds., *Character Strengths and Virtues: A Handbook and Classification* (New York: Oxford University Press, 2004).

7. David Wechsler, *The Measurement and Appraisal of Adult Intelligence,* 4th ed. (Baltimore: Williams and Wilkins, 1958), p. 75.

8. J. P. Guilford, *The Nature of Intelligence* (New York: McGraw-Hill, 1967).

9. See, for example, Robert Hogan, "Development of an Empathy Scale," *Journal of Consulting and Clinical Psychology* 33 (1969), pp. 307–16; Robert Sternberg, *Beyond IQ: A Triarchic Theory of Human Intelligence* (New York: Cambridge University Press, 1985); Howard Gardner, *Multiple Intelligences: The Theory in Practice* (New York: Basic Books, 1993).

10. On what makes a person intelligent, see Robert Sternberg et al., "People's Conceptions of Intelligence," *Journal of Personality and Social Psychology* 41 (1981), pp. 37–55.

11. On the high correlations with IQ, see, for example, Ronald Riggio et al., "Social and Academic Intelligence: Conceptually Distinct but Overlapping Domains," *Personality and Individual Differences* 12 (1991), pp. 695–702.

12. David H. Silvera et al., "The Tromso Social Intelligence Scale," *Scandinavian Journal of Psychology* 42 (2001), pp. 313–19.

13. In another study, when psychologists, all experts on intelligence, were asked to come up with a similar list, they ignored practical social skills in favor of more abstract cognitive abilities like verbal and more abstract social problem-solving skills. See Sternberg et al., "People's Conceptions."

14. Psychometricians have until recently found paper-and-pencil tests most convenient, and so aspects of intelligence that can be assessed in that format have prevailed. This may be one hidden factor in the dominance of cognitive abilities as the current gold standard in assessing social intelligence. The low road will, no doubt, come more readily within the purview of social intelligence measures with the unstoppable forward march of digital media.

15. Colwyn Trevarthen, "The Self Born in Intersubjectivity: The Psychology of Infant Communicating," in Ulric Neisser, *The Perceived Self: Ecological and Interpersonal Sources of Self-knowledge* (New York: Cambridge University Press, 1993), pp. 121–73.

16. The PONS is one such widely used nonverbal measure. Paul Ekman's Web-based measure of the ability to detect microemotions already is a novel means for assessing someone's ability to empathize at a noncognitive level, a prerequisite for emotional attunement. Some tests for emotional intelligence (which overlaps with social intelligence), such as the MSCEIT, already use some noncognitive measures; see, for example, John Mayer et al., "Emotional Intelligence: Theory, Findings, and Implications," *Psychological Inquiry* 60 (2004), pp. 197–215. Ekman's Web-based assessment of microemotions is at www.paulekman.com. Encouragingly, Ekman's assessment also reveals the social brain to be an eager learner for reading microemotions, suggesting that some key abilities of social intelligence can be strengthened through coaching via electronic media.

17. The model of social intelligence I propose here is a heuristic, intended to prime new thinking about social intelligence. I assume it will be challenged and revised, hopefully on the basis of data generated from fresh theories. To abilities familiar from existing social intelligence models, this list adds four that, so far as I know, are found on no inventory as yet: primal empathy, attunement, synchrony, and concern. These will be controversial for some in the intelligence-measuring field. My view is that social intelligence should reflect the interpersonal aptitudes of the social brain—and neural logic does not necessarily track the conventional wisdom. Even so, there are already a number of tests and scales assessing various aspects of these "soft" skills. None, as yet, encom-

passes them all. The best measure would cover the spectrum of social intelligence, and identify interpersonal stars while spotting social deficits. See John Kihlstrom and Nancy Cantor, "Social Intelligence," in Robert Sternberg (ed.), *Handbook of Intelligence,* 2nd ed. (Cambridge, U.K.: Cambridge University Press, 2000), pp. 359–79.

18. Kihlstrom and Cantor, ibid.

INDEX

orbitofrontal cortex and, 63–65,
68–69
reactions to, 68–69
speed of (spindle cells), 65–67,
68–69
vs. judgments about things, 68
juvenile correctional facilities,
285–287

Kagan, Jerome, 62, 147–148, 160–161
Kahn, William, 257–259
Kahneman, Daniel, 311–312, 316
Kalamazoo model, 287–288, 290, 295,
296, 297
Kaufmann, Walter, 299
Kemeny, Margaret, 230–232
Kennedy, John F., Jr., 244
Kiecolt-Glaser, Janice, 235–236
Kihlstrom, John, 334
Kinsey, Alfred, 205–206
kissing, 63–64
Kohlberg, Lawrence, 101
Kohlrieser, George, 277
Kristof, Nicholas, 110–111
Kushner, Lawrence, 308

leaders, 88
characteristics of, 88, 93, 276–279
concern and, 97
emotional contagion and, 275–276
empathy from, 279–281
expression of anger by, 93, 94
Machiavellian, 125
in medicine, 260–261
narcissistic, 119–120
as secure base, 277–278, 279–280
social intelligence, 83
learning, 42, 269–274, 281–284
LeDoux, Joseph, 78–80, 100
left prefrontal area, 234–235
Legend (John Stevens), 45, 46
Lévinas, Emmanuel, 109
Lieberman, Matthew, 67–68, 321
like/dislike. *See* judgments about
people
Lipps, Theodore, 58
listening, 87–88
lobotomies, 70–71
Loersebe, Anne, 298
loneliness, 238–239
looping
couples, 204–205, 219
emotional contagion, 39–40

empathy and, 115
Internet and, 74
I-You relationships and, 110
parent-child, 164–165, 166, 177
psychotherapy and, 172
love and affection, 189–190, 224. *See
also* attachment; caregiving;
marriage; sex and desire
Lown, Beth, 262, 263
low road. *See* high road/low road
lying, 23–24

Maccoby, Michael, 119, 120
Machiavelli, Niccolò, 125
Machiavellians (Machs), 124–127, 128,
130–132
malice, 230–232
Marci, Carl, 28
marriage. *See also* attachment;
caregiving; sex and desire
courtship, 190–193
disagreements (conflict), 174–175,
219, 240–242
emotions and, 25–26, 218–220
empathic accuracy and, 89
health and, 240–242
indifference in, 219
similarity of facial expressions, 218
stress and, 223–224
Massachusetts General Hospital, 262
Mayer, John, 330
McDaniels, Darryl, 45
Mead, George Herbert, 313
Meaney, Michael, 153–154, 157–158,
168
Mean Monkey hand puppet, 136
medicine, 250–263
compassion and healing, 255–256,
261–262
I-It interactions, 250–253
improving patient/physician
interactions, 253–256, 262–263,
380
leadership in, 260–261
malpractice suits, predicting,
254–255
stress and, 259–260
memes, 46
memories, 78–79, 273
men
emotional expression, 94
empathy quotient, 139
extreme male brain, 138–140